Handsome Brute

Handsome Brute

The True Story of a Ladykiller

SEAN O'CONNOR

**SIMON &
SCHUSTER**

London · New York · Sydney · Toronto · New Delhi

A CBS COMPANY

First published in Great Britain by Simon & Schuster UK Ltd, 2013
This paperback edition published by Simon & Schuster UK Ltd, 2014
A CBS COMPANY

Copyright © 2013 by Sean O'Connor

The right of Sean O'Connor to be identified as the author of this work
has been asserted by him in accordance with sections 77 and 78 of the Copyright,
Designs and Patents Act, 1988.

1 3 5 7 9 10 8 6 4 2

Simon & Schuster UK Ltd
1st Floor
222 Gray's Inn Road
London WC1X 8HB

www.simonandschuster.co.uk

Simon & Schuster Australia,
Sydney

Simon & Schuster India,
New Delhi

A CIP catalogue record for this book is available from the British Library

The author and publishers have made all reasonable efforts to contact copyright
holders for permission, and apologise for any omissions or errors in the form
of credit given. Corrections may be made to future printings.

ISBN: 978-1-47110-134-2
ISBN: 978-1-47110-135-9 (ebook)

Typeset by Hewer Text UK Limited, Edinburgh
Printed in the UK by CPI (UK) Ltd, Croydon CR0 4YY

This is an astonishing case, is it not? The probability is, of course, that Heath knows no more about the state of his mind than any of us do about our own minds. It is something that is part of his nature; it is natural; to him it would not appear extraordinary.

J. D. Casswell KC

Is there any cause in nature that makes these hard hearts?
Shakespeare, *King Lear* (III, vi)

For Jo O'Keefe
1969–2010

CONTENTS

PART THREE: Group Captain Rupert Robert Brook

PART FOUR: The Twisting of Another Rope

FOREWORD

So much for Raffles. Now for a header into the cesspool.
George Orwell, 'Raffles and Miss Blandish', 1944

Heath's story is not a pretty one . . . it will be remembered as
a sort of sadistic bloodbath not untypical of an age of crime
where sadism and bloodbaths are, if anything, coming to be
the rule rather than exceptions.
Nigel Morland, *Hangman's Clutch*, 1954

With the passing of the Second World War generation
into history, the story of Neville George Clevely
Heath, once regarded as 'the most dangerous criminal modern
Britain has known'[1] and 'the most atrocious murderer in
modern times',[2] has dwindled in our collective memory in
the sixty-eight years between 1946 and today.

Heath's reputation – once a byword for sadistic perversion
and psychopathic violence – has not held the popular imagination as Christie's or the Moors Murderers' have. This is
despite the fact that the case caused a media furore at the
time, providing gruesome (and titillating) copy in newspapers
dominated by the grey realities of austerity Britain: the
national debt, the initiation of bread rationing and the pain-
fully slow process of demobilization. The case was a gift for
the tabloids with its sensational ingredients of aberrant sex
and violent death, set in a world undergoing a process of
radical change. The blond, handsome Heath, still tanned
from his time abroad, was a great distraction for a nation in
flux, exhausted by six years of wartime privation and looking
towards an uncertain future. All the elements of the case
came together to make a classic English narrative: a charming
but vicious protagonist ridden with class anxiety, an ambitious detective, a national manhunt for a killer on the loose.

From a twenty-first-century perspective, the background
to the murders – the pubs, bars and nightclubs of west
London and the genteel hotels of south-coast seaside resorts
– conjure a lost, very English world. It's the socially and
sexually anxious environment of Agatha Christie and
Terence Rattigan, filtered through the prism of Patrick
Hamilton's drink-sodden novel, *Hangover Square*. But
despite the classic and comfortable mid-twentieth-century
English setting, the savagery of the crimes and Heath's at
once charming, yet pathological, personality anticipate an
American style of slaughter much more akin to Bret Easton
Ellis's *American Psycho* or Jim Thompson's *The Killer Inside
Me*. And despite the period details – the Royal Air Force
slang, the pipe clenched in the teeth and the old school tie
– Heath's laconic attitude both to his crimes and to the
prospect of his own extinction is redolent of the casual
cruelty of contemporary murderers like John Maden, who

killed his niece Tia Rigg in Manchester in 2010, 'because I felt like it'. When he was finally arrested, Heath responded in a similarly offhand manner: 'Oh, all right.'[3]

Such was the appetite for news of the case at the time, that in the summer of 1946 when newspapers were generally restricted to four skimpy pages because of newsprint rationing, the Heath case received enormous coverage. In reporting the trial, journalists took licence to report – in surprising detail – the most graphic revelations of the murders as well as the more salacious details of Heath's sex life. The trial offered an opportunity to examine the darker avenues of sexuality in modern Britain – and this was all available over the breakfast table with the post and the toast. Heath's friends even negotiated a newspaper deal for him in order to give his exclusive side of the story.

Curiously, given the nature of his crimes, the audience for Heath's story was primarily female. Some women, it was reported, queued for fourteen hours outside the Old Bailey in the hope of getting just a glimpse of this most notorious of ladykillers. 'Rarely', noted the *People,* 'have women been so strangely fascinated by a murder trial.'[4]

For a society struggling to negotiate its place in the new world order, Heath's story articulated an alarming new post-war anxiety. With millions of soldiers, sailors and airmen returning to Britain – many of them trained killers – the Heath trial exposed the tension created by re-integrating servicemen *en masse* into the hugely changed communities and families they had left years earlier. Newspapers of the time are filled with tragic stories of servicemen returning home and killing their estranged wives, unable to settle into the brave new, post-war world. Commenting on the case of one former soldier who had done just that, which resulted in the conviction being commuted to manslaughter, Mr Justice Charles warned that 'the law of the jungle'[5] was creeping into

English courtrooms. The *News Chronicle* worried that 'it would seem from some recent murder trials that the unfaithful wife of a serviceman is an outlaw with no benefit of law whatsoever. She may be murdered with impunity.'[6]

Heath's career encapsulated the civilian population's particularly ambivalent attitude towards pilots from Bomber Command. Taking their lead from Winston Churchill, the public had lauded 'the Few', the brave boys in Spitfires who defended the nation from invasion in 1940, dog-fighting the Luftwaffe across the skies above the South Downs. But Bomber Command had flown into Europe causing devastation on an unprecedented scale, wiping out civilian and military targets alike with a seeming disregard for human life. They were at once glamorous but deadly – the creators of those iconic symbols of wartime destruction, Berlin, Hamburg and Dresden.[7] In his study of the RAF during World War II, *The Flyer*, Martin Francis observes 'a broader ambivalence among the public and the men of the RAF themselves, as to whether they were chivalric knights of the air or merciless agents of violent destruction'.[8] Neville Heath – the charmer turned killer – absolutely embodies this disorientating anxiety, and this may well be a key to the extraordinary interest the public took in the case; for Heath's story dramatized one of the unspoken fears of the age.

As early as 1947, only a year after the murders, a serial killer with remarkable similarities to Heath appears in Ken Annakin's ostensibly upbeat film, *Holiday Camp*.[9] Dennis Price plays Squadron Leader Hardwick, a suave ex-RAF pilot, charming lonely women with tales of his wartime exploits, whilst hiding his true nature as the 'mannequin murderer'. The references to Heath would have been very clear to cinema-goers at the time. The film attempts to examine the new democracy ushered in by the Welfare State. All strata of society get to take a holiday – even if that only means a chilly week at Butlins in Bognor. But despite the optimism for the new Albion inherent in the film, it's clear that the murderous Squadron Leader Hardwick – and Heath himself – articulated the unease in British society at welcoming home a whole generation of men, many of whom had killed during the war. Having fuelled and channelled these violent instincts on behalf of the state, where were they to be directed now? And, indeed, could they be channelled at all? Or were these dark instincts to become a reality of the post-war world?[10]

The fascination with Heath continued after his trial and began to fill more than just newspaper copy. Two sensational monographs about the case were published with indelicate haste after Heath's trial, both by journalists who claimed to have known Heath personally. Gerald Byrne's *Borstal Boy: The Uncensored Life of Neville Heath* was published in 1946, printed to economy standards and bearing a suitably sombre black and white cover. Full of salacious (and often unsubstantiated) detail, it is a paperback shocker masquerading as a morality tale, 'of a man . . . who stopped at nothing to satisfy his own craving for position, money and power'.[11]

Sydney Brock's *The Life and Death of Neville Heath* followed swiftly in 1947. Though the text attempts a serious examination of Heath's life and crimes from a first-hand point of view, it has a Mills & Boon-style subtitle: *The Man No Woman Could Resist*. The cover of this railway bookstore paperback depicts a sexy young woman in a saucy short skirt – a whip to her side, hanging sinisterly in mid-air. The cover promises a 'Sensational-Sadistic-Romantic-True Story'.[12] This uncomfortable tone – exploiting the case as soft pornography – came to dominate non-fiction writing about Heath. James Hodge, who published the much-admired *Notable British Trials* series, had hesitated about covering the Heath trial at all, precisely because the facts of the case could too easily result in something of dubious value, bordering on exploitative porn.

Eventually Macdonald Critchley successfully edited the case in 1951, winning resounding praise from Hodge:

> Heath could very well have deteriorated into a wretched book in less capable hands and that is why I did not want to include it in our series before, in view of the less savoury angle some might have taken.[13]

Heath's story continued to fascinate the public and resonated throughout popular culture in the years following the trial. In 1949, the writer, Elizabeth Taylor, reinvented Heath's story as a dark romance in her novel, *A Wreath of Roses*.[14] Shortly afterwards, Patrick Hamilton wrote a trilogy of novels focusing on an amoral con man, Ralph Gorse, in his *Gorse Trilogy* (1951–55). Even if Gorse's career as a petty criminal doesn't actually lead to murder (though there's a clear sense that he's capable of it), it's apparent that in his depiction of this satanic womanizer, Hamilton had drawn heavily on details from Heath's biography, including incidences of cruelty in childhood and the manipulation of women as an art form, both with a strong undercurrent of sadomasochism.[15] All these facts were readily available in the popular press at the time of Heath's arrest and trial.

In 1954, the criminologist and novelist Nigel Morland remarked on the dramatic qualities inherent in the Heath case, 'in that it unfolds almost like a film story, with backgrounds slightly out of focus'.[16] It's no surprise then that Alfred Hitchcock, renowned especially in his later works for his explorations of sex and psychopathy – particularly after the success of *Psycho* in 1960 – was drawn to Heath's personality and spent several years developing a film inspired by the events of the case. The script, originally written by Benn Levy, was called *Frenzy* (latterly *Kaleidoscope*).[17] By 1967 Hitchcock was already making camera tests for the film and had shot an hour of silent footage. This was to be Hitchcock as he'd never been seen before – informed by the European New Wave with a particular emphasis on realism, graphic sex and violence.[18] But this new Hitch proved too radical for the studio executives at MCA. They rejected the script and the Heath project was shelved. Howard Fast, who also worked on the script, claimed that the studio told Hitchcock that they'd never allow him to shoot it as 'his pictures were known for elegant villains and here was an impossibly ugly one'.[19] The title was eventually recycled for Hitchcock's more accessible 1971 British come-back featuring Barry Foster as Rusk, the 'necktie murderer'.[20] But the essence of the film *Frenzy* – a charming but ultimately terrifying sex killer – shares much in common with the character of Heath, Rusk's fetish for neckties echoing Heath's widely reported fetish for handkerchiefs.

Though the facts of the case created an international media sensation, reported in newspapers and magazines across the globe, the trial was very English in tone; low-key and devoid of histrionics. The dramatic focus of the three-day hearing was a debate about Heath's sanity. This was assessed by a statute over 100 years old – the M'Naghten Rules of 1843 – which posed the question: 'Did the Defendant know what he was doing – and, if so, did he know what he was doing was wrong?' This made no concessions for the developments in psychology and psychiatry since the turn of the twentieth century. The plea of diminished responsibility was not to reach the British statute books for another decade with the passing of the Homicide Act in 1957. This was to state that:

Where a person kills or is party to a killing of another, he shall not be convicted of murder if he was suffering from such abnormality of mind . . . as substantially impaired his mental responsibility for his acts and omissions in doing or being a party to the killing.[21]

No such plea was available to Heath's defence in 1946.

Key witnesses, who may have been able to offer crucial evidence in relation to Heath's past behaviour, his service career and his psychological state in the months leading up to the murders, were never called to the trial. With the lack of such evidence the issue of Heath's sanity (or insanity) was never fully debated. Beyond the categorization of Heath as a malevolent killer and sexual sadist, there was little curiosity, from either the prosecution or the defence, in examining Heath's character or background. Heath didn't deny committing the murders once he'd been arrested – consequently, there was no attempt at the trial to try and explain them. What provoked Heath to do what he did remains a mystery. Though he later gave a version of events to the press, this may have been motivated by his wish to leave money to his family and pay off his debts, rather than any desire to leave behind his version of the 'Truth'. And, with regard to *any* story Heath told, it's important to bear in mind that he was a sophisticated and practised liar, having talked his way into and out of dramatic situations since his schooldays.

In his essay, *Decline of the English Murder*, published in the same year as the trial, George Orwell observed a sea change in the culture of murder in Britain and firmly pointed to the Second World War as the tipping point.[22] He lamented the passing of the 'Elizabethan age' of English murder which, he suggested, spanned from 1850 to 1925 and included classic cases like Crippen, Seddon, Mrs Maybrick, Thompson and Bywaters – all domestic crimes motivated by money, sex or respectability. He contrasted these with the 'Cleft Chin Murder' of 1944, committed by Elizabeth Marina Jones and Karl Hulten, a meaningless killing set against 'the anonymous life of dance-halls and the false values of the American film'. In effect, he suggested that the average reader of the *News of the World* or the *Sunday Pictorial*[23] enjoyed the brutality of this new American style of murder because, as a culture, Britain had been brutalized by the effects of the war.

Orwell had first outlined this theory in 'Raffles and Miss Blandish', comparing the author E. W. Hornung's popular character, Raffles – the gentleman thief – with James Hadley Chase's hard-boiled American tale *No Orchids for Miss Blandish*, a novel of murder, torture, sadistic violence and rape. Significantly this became one of the most popular novels of the war years and Orwell was clear in what he felt lay at the heart of its huge success – it articulated the sublimated anxieties of the age:

> In his imagined world of gangsters Chase is presenting, as it were, a distilled version of the modern political scene, in which such things as mass bombing of civilians, the use of hostages, torture to obtain confessions, secret prisons, execution without trial, floggings with rubber truncheons, drownings in cess-pools, systematic falsification of records and statistics, treachery, bribery, and quislingism are normal and morally neutral, even admirable when they are done in a large and bold way. *The average man is not directly interested in politics, and when he reads, he wants the current struggles of the world to be translated into a simple story about individuals* [my italics].[24]

This may well be another reason why Heath's story touched such a popular nerve at the time, articulating as it did a brutal and violent strain in modern culture, unnervingly close to the surface, through the story of a once-heroic individual turned bad.

For the first time, this book examines evidence and witness statements that have been held in previously restricted files from the Home Office and the Metropolitan Police. Some evidence relating to third parties remains restricted in the National Archives until 2045 as do the scene of crime and post-mortem photographs, which were described at the time as 'grotesque'. The post-mortem reports themselves are sufficiently graphic to make it clear the appalling nature of these images.

My intention is to examine the tragic events of 1946 in the fuller context of what we now know about the period and the case, as well as examining issues unexplored at the time concerning Heath's life leading up to the killings, which might have some bearing on his subsequent actions. What was the combination of circumstances that brought the crisis in Heath's life to a head that summer? And how far is Heath's case emblematic or indeed symptomatic of the age in which he lived? For in a country battered and exhausted by six years of war, a culture in a moment of change, and the sense of a new morality around the corner, Heath was regarded as 'the incarnation of war-time and post-war vices'.[25]

Throughout 1946, the major international news stories were the increasing violence in Palestine and the trials of the Nazi war criminals at Nuremberg. With the revelation of the horrors of the death camps, there's a sense that mankind was capable of a depth of cruelty, a lack of humanity barely imaginable in the relative innocence of the pre-war period. Certainly with Gordon Cummins, the 'blackout ripper', who mutilated the sexual organs of his victims with a can-opener, followed soon after by Heath, then the acid-bath murderer Haigh and the necrophiliac Christie, there does seem a real sense of extremity – a ferocity and violence extremely rare in British crime since the Whitechapel murders at the end of the nineteenth century.

Early in the investigation, Detective Superintendent Lovell of the Dorset Constabulary first articulated the intriguing power of Heath's complex nature: 'Certainly his personality is an extremely puzzling one, and capable of more than one single interpretation.'[26] Heath's solicitor, Isaac Near, later commented that 'whatever the facts of the case, Heath had certainly a remarkable personality – a personality that made one like him'.[27] As well as a startling lack of remorse, the persona Heath reveals in his letters from prison show real tenderness and self-awareness. He was capable of inspiring genuine affection in many of the people he knew, yet it's impossible not to be repelled by the atrocities he committed. What continues to fascinate is his elusive, contradictory character. How do we reconcile the suburban confidence trickster, the charismatic and articulate ladies' man with the savage and pitiless murderer who had the capacity not just to kill, but to violate the bodies of his victims with such ferocity that war-hardened police officers vomited on seeing them?

At times it's uncomfortable to examine the records of this case and find the lives of both killer and his victims described in such forensic detail, a knowledge denied to even their closest friends and family; not just a list of dates and places, but the most intimate details of their lives – the money they had (or more often didn't have), the dates of their menstrual cycle, their sexual predilections, their innermost secrets. But it's this sometimes invasive detail that diminishes the passage of time and brings home the fact that they may not be 'fools in old-style hats and coats' at all; that perhaps we share more with the wartime generation than we thought, and their ambitions and anxieties – despite the years between us – remain constant and universal, urgent and real.

William Bixley served for fifty years in Court No. 1 as supervising officer at the Old Bailey. He had held a uniquely privileged position, attendant at the most distressing and dramatic of trials. Yet, in his memoir of 1957, Bixley reflected that, of all the trials he had witnessed throughout his half-century of service, Heath's case was 'the most upsetting'.

The reason for the feeling of revulsion and dread which, I think, permeated the minds of everyone in that Court was

that Heath seemed ostensibly so normal, and one had deep
forebodings that only by a hair's breadth did other seemingly
decent and pleasant young men escape from the awful sexual
sadism which, at times, makes man lower than any animal
that walks or crawls on the face of the earth.[28]

It's that hair's breadth that separates us from Heath that
continues to chill us, too. How could this 'seemingly decent
and pleasant' young man also be capable of some of the most
brutal acts in British criminal history?

CHARACTERS

21 MERTON HALL ROAD, WIMBLEDON

Neville George Clevely Heath, 29   *ex-RAF pilot*
William Heath, 56   *his father*
Bessie Heath, 55   *his mother*
Michael (Mick) Heath, 17   *his brother*

'STRATHMORE', WARREN ROAD, WORTHING

Yvonne Marie Symonds, 21   *ex-WRNS*
Major John Charters Symonds, 55 *her father*
Gertrude Symonds   *her mother*

24 OAKHOLME ROAD, SHEFFIELD

Margery Aimee Brownell
Gardner, 32   *artist*
Peter Gardner, 32   *her husband*
Melody Gardner, 2   *her daughter*
Elizabeth Wheat, 67   *her mother*
Gilbert Wheat, 30   *her brother, a schoolteacher*
Ralph Macro Wilson, 43   *family solicitor*

19 WOODHALL DRIVE, PINNER

Doreen Margaret Marshall, 21   *ex-WRNS*
Charles Marshall, 59   *her father*
Grace Marshall, 53   *her mother*
Joan Grace Cruickshanks, 25   *her married sister*

LONDON

Strand Palace Hotel
Leonard William Luff, 58   *assistant manager*
Thomas Paul, 59   *head porter*
Pauline Miriam Brees, 21   *model*

Pembridge Court Hotel
Elizabeth Wyatt, 65   *manageress*
Alice Wyatt, 40   *her daughter-in-law*
Rhoda Spooner, 26   *waitress*
Barbara Osborne, 32   *chambermaid*

Panama Club
Solomon Josephs, 56   *receptionist*
Harold Harter, 40   *taxi driver*

Associates of Neville Heath
Leslie Terry, 43   *restaurant owner*
Harry Ashbrook, 38   *journalist*
Ralph Fisher   *commercial pilot*
Zita Williams, 23   *shorthand typist*
Jill Harris, 20   *shorthand typist*
William Spurrett
Fielding-Johnson, 54   *squadron leader, RAF*

Associates of Margery Gardner
Peter Tilley Bailey, 29   *gentleman thief*
Trevethan Frampton, 26   *student*
Iris Humphrey, 29   *civil servant*
John Le Mee Power, 33   *building firm accountant*
Joyce Frost, 33   *friend of Margery Gardner*

Metropolitan Police
Reginald Spooner, 43   *divisional detective inspector*

Shelley Symes, 41   *detective inspector*
Thomas Barratt, 48   *superintendent, Scotland Yard*

JOHANNESBURG

Elizabeth Armstrong, 26   *Armstrong's wife*
Robert Michael Armstrong, 2   *their son*
Moira Lister, 23   *actress*

BOURNEMOUTH

Tollard Royal Hotel
Ivor Relf, 35   *manager*
Arthur White, 38   *head night porter*
Frederick Charles Wilkinson, 33   *night porter*
Alice Hemmingway, 47   *chambermaid*
Peter Rylatt, 31   *demobbed lawyer*
Gladys Davy Phillips, 62   *married woman*
Winifred Parfitt, 40   *married woman*
Heinz Abisch, 30   *designer, wire company*
Peggy Waring, 37   *student*

Bournemouth Police
George Gates, 45   *detective inspector*
George Suter, 40   *detective constable*
Leslie Johnson, 38   *detective sergeant*
Francis Bishop, 46   *detective sergeant, Dorset*

THE OLD BAILEY

Isaac Elliston Near, 45	*Heath's solicitor*
Mr Justice Morris, 50	*judge*
Anthony Hawke, 51	*counsel for the Crown*
J. D. Casswell, KC, 60	*counsel for the defence*
Dr Keith Simpson, 39	*pathologist*
Dr Crichton McGaffey, 43	*pathologist*
Dr Hugh Grierson, 60	*psychiatrist*
Dr William Hubert, 42	*psychiatrist*
Dr Hubert Young, 57	*psychiatrist*

PROLOGUE
Mrs Brees

In the early hours of Saturday morning on 23 February 1946, a guest on the fourth floor of the Strand Palace Hotel was disturbed by violent noises from the room directly above. Something fell on the floor, a woman screamed for help. The guest reported the commotion to the head porter, Thomas Paul. Paul was accustomed to the realities of hotel life during wartime and was used to turning a blind eye to the excesses of alcohol and sex, so he discreetly went up to the fifth floor to see if there was a problem. When he got to Room 506, he listened at the locked door and heard a woman screaming from inside.

'Stop! Stop! For God's sake, stop!'

Concerned by the severity of her cries, Paul ran down the stairs to get his colleague, Leonard William Luff, the assistant manager.[1]

The Strand Palace was (and remains) a large building on the north side of the Strand, parallel to the Thames. Its exterior was built in the grand Empire style in 1909, but the hotel had been expanded and refurbished during the 1920s and by the Second World War boasted 980 bedrooms. The famous foyer of the hotel was remodelled in 1930. Claridges, the Savoy and the newly constructed Dorchester all had sumptuous Art Deco foyers, but Oliver P. Bernard's designs for the Strand Palace had made his creation one of the most celebrated hotel interiors in London.[2] The foyer combined traditional and contemporary marbles and made innovative use of glass and lighting. The walls were clad in pink marble and the floor with limestone. The balustrades, columns and door surrounds were made of mirror, chromed steel and translucent moulded glass. The foyer became regarded as an iconic Art Deco masterpiece and, indeed, is now preserved at the Victoria and Albert Museum after its removal from the hotel in 1969. Back in 1946, the hotel seemed to represent the epitome of pre-war elegance, bringing a touch of Hollywood glamour to war-torn London.[3]

Conveniently located amongst the pubs, bars, nightclubs and restaurants of London's West End, the Strand Palace had been popular with American forces during the war and had only recently been decommissioned as an official rest and recuperation residence for US servicemen. Now, with thousands of American troops awaiting shipment back home and huge numbers of British officers and service personnel newly repatriated to the UK, London was teeming with servicemen and the hotel was fully booked.

Ten months earlier, on VE Day, nearly 5 million Britons had been in uniform across the globe. The process of repatriation and demobilization was to take months, and in some cases, even years.[4] The large West End hotels provided discreet but accessible havens of transition between the past dangers and thrills of service life and the post-war world of spouses, families and responsibility. For many, such hotels represented the last opportunity for illicit liaisons, as well as offering the possibility of sensual indulgence amongst the legion of prostitutes in central London – a profession that had boomed during the war years.

The occupant of Room 506 at the Strand Palace was known to be Captain James Robert Cadogan Armstrong of the South African Air Force. Armstrong had checked into the Strand Palace on the previous Saturday, 16 February. On his uniform he wore the ribbons of the Africa Star and the DFC (Distinguished Flying Cross). He seemed to be a regular hero.

In response to the woman's screams, Thomas Paul and Leonard Luff headed upstairs to deal with the matter. When Luff opened the door with his pass-key, the two men were met by a shocking sight; a young woman lay face down on the bed, stripped naked and rendered helpless, with her hands tied behind her back. Standing over her, also naked, was Armstrong – tall, tanned, blue-eyed and handsome.[5] The woman twisted her face to the intruders, exclaiming, 'Thank God you came in.'

Armstrong turned to Paul and Luff in a fury.[6]

'What the hell are you doing, breaking in here?'

Mr Luff explained who they were, but Armstrong made no answer. Luff asked what had been going on, but the girl asked to be untied first. Luff told Armstrong to do so and the girl was freed. He then adopted a nonchalant attitude and tried to bluster the matter out, demanding what right the staff had to enter his room, but when Luff mentioned that he would call the police, Armstrong became more reasonable.

Luff asked the woman, Pauline Brees, if she knew the man and she said she did. She claimed that he had knocked her out and then undressed her. She turned to Armstrong and asked if he had raped her. This question he avoided at first, but finally denied. Asked by Luff if they should call the police, Pauline insisted that they shouldn't. She just wanted to leave the hotel and didn't want any publicity.

Despite Pauline's story, Luff didn't believe her. There were no marks of violence on her, her clothing was on a chair by the bed – undamaged – and there were no signs of a struggle having taken place. Luff thought that Pauline 'looked to me like a prostitute'.[7] He told Pauline and Armstrong to collect their things and leave. They got dressed and Armstrong took Pauline home in a taxi to her lodgings. He then checked out of the hotel himself that Sunday morning. Though the incident had raised alarm, it was regarded as embarrassing rather than serious.

Pauline, who had been widowed just six months earlier, had been introduced to Armstrong about a week before by a mutual friend at Oddenino's – a restaurant in Regent Street much frequented by RAF officers. When they met, Armstrong was wearing the khaki uniform of a lieutenant colonel in the South African Air Force. On the following Wednesday (20 February), Armstrong telephoned Pauline at her home in Maida Vale and invited her to lunch the next day. So, on Thursday, they lunched together at the Berkeley Restaurant in Knightsbridge. Afterwards they parted company in good spirits.[8]

On Friday, Pauline and Armstrong met again by appointment at Oddenino's and from there went to the Berkeley again for a drink. This initiated something of an all-day pub-crawl that took them from the Falstaff in Fleet Street where they had lunch and then to Shepherd's pub in Shepherd Market followed by the Brevet Club in Mayfair, which were both popular drinking venues with the Royal Air Force. They left the Brevet Club at about 10 p.m. as the club had run out of beer. This was a common occurrence throughout London at the time as publicans dealt with reduced supplies of beer as well as the increased demand for it since the outbreak of war.

Armstrong suggested that they go back to his room for a nightcap. Pauline agreed to accompany him to the Strand Palace where she knew he was staying but told him that she had to be home by 11.30 p.m. as she had an awkward land-lady. The pair went up to the fifth floor to a double room overlooking the Strand and opposite the Art Deco entrance to the Savoy Hotel and the Savoy Theatre.[9]

In Room 506, Pauline sat on the bed while Armstrong poured himself a drink. Pauline refused to join him as she didn't like whisky. He went over to the bed and kissed her. As he became more persistent, Pauline told him that she had to be going.

'Oh no, you're not,' said Armstrong. 'You're staying the night with me.'[10]

At this point, events took a darker turn. Pauline got up, telling him not to be ridiculous as she headed for the door. But he had locked it. Grabbing her, he seized her arm and twisted it behind her back. Though she realized that she was in some danger, she claimed she didn't scream because she didn't want to embarrass him by getting him turned out of the hotel.

'Why are you doing this?' she asked him.

'I hate women,' said Armstrong.

He pulled off her coat and ordered her to strip. When she refused, they started to struggle. At 5 feet 11 inches, power-fully built and an accomplished rugby player, Armstrong threw her against the wall with such force that she lost consciousness. When she came to, Pauline realized that she had been stripped naked. Half conscious, she rushed for the door, but Armstrong grabbed her again.

'Oh, no you don't,' he said. 'We'll soon fix this.'

He took a handkerchief and tied her hands behind her

back, pushing her on to the bed. He then took off his own clothes. At this point, Pauline claimed that she didn't scream because she was 'only half conscious and paralysed with fright'. Armstrong then tried to turn her over, so that her face was in the pillow. But Pauline couldn't breathe and struggled to free herself again. He now threatened her.

'I'll make you do exactly what I want you to do.'

Forcing himself on to her prostrate body, he attempted to rape her 'in an un-natural way' but she struggled so intensely that they fell off the bed. He then put his hands around her throat. Now terrified for her life, Pauline screamed.

'Stop! Stop! For God's sake. Stop!'

Armstrong punched Pauline in the face with his fist, rendering her unconscious again. The next thing she was aware of was the arrival in the room of the assistant manager and the head porter. 'I was lying on the bed but I don't know how I got there,' she said later. Mr Luff told Armstrong and Pauline to get out, but he was, she remembered, 'quite nice to [her]'.

Some months later, it was established that James Robert Cadogan Armstrong was actually Neville George Clevely Heath, by then standing trial for murder. Reginald Spooner of the Metropolitan Police questioned Pauline Brees and was clear in his interpretation of the incident at the Strand Palace Hotel; she did not want to prosecute Heath because she admitted she had gone knowingly with him to the bedroom to be stripped and beaten.

The matter was forgotten, at least for several months. It seemed to be an illicit liaison, a sexual adventure that had got out of hand – typical in this period of transition. Many people were tasting their last moments of freedom before settling down to post-war life. Maybe too much alcohol was consumed in the various pubs, clubs and restaurants that the couple had visited; both Heath and Pauline had drunk consistently throughout their time together. Perhaps both parties misinterpreted the desires of the other? Or Pauline hadn't quite anticipated the intensity of 'Armstrong's' intentions? But this incident – referred to only obliquely as 'that incident at the London hotel' or 'a certain case not mentioned here'[11] – was to take on a much darker significance at Heath's trial. Had Pauline Brees chosen to prosecute Heath at the time, or had the hotel staff alerted the police to his behaviour, the whole series of tragic events that followed over the next six months might well have been prevented.

As it stood, by the end of the year, three young people would be dead, their families devastated and the nation appalled by the events of the summer of 1946.

PART ONE

London

CHAPTER ONE

Summer 1946

This is your victory! It is the victory of the cause of freedom in every land. In all our long history we have never seen a greater day than this. Everyone, man or woman, has done their best. Everyone has tried. Neither the long years, nor the dangers, nor the fierce attacks of the enemy have in any way weakened the independent resolve of the British nation. God bless you all.

Winston Churchill, VE Day, 8 May 1945

As the number of turkeys available this Christmas will not be sufficient to meet the demand, the Food Minister asks turkey retailers to spread the limited supplies among the largest number of families by cutting birds into two parts for sale. Half a turkey, he believes, will supply a good meal for most families.

The Times, 15 December 1945

The summer of 1946 was one of extremes.
A national sigh of relief had punctuated the end of the war and a concerted effort was made to move on from the conflict and look towards the future. After the popular rejection of Churchill's Conservative party in the 1945 election, Attlee's reforming Labour government had put social welfare at the heart of their agenda. These new social policies – particularly those regarding health, housing, education and pensions – seemed to embody the hopes for a new era for Britain, with Attlee declaring, 'We are on the eve of a great advance in the human race.'[1] But not everybody was so optimistic. The ultra-conservative Noël Coward observed, 'I always felt that England would be bloody uncomfortable during the immediate post-war period, and now it is almost a certainty that it will be so.'[2]

Balancing the government's progressive new initiatives, from the beginning of 1946 there was a reassuring effort to re-establish the pre-war patterns of British life. The Grand National and the Derby ran for the first time since 1940 and both the Cup Final and the Boat Race reappeared in the sports calendar. Even tennis was played at Wimbledon, despite bomb damage to Centre Court. In February, it was announced that London would host the Olympic Games in 1948.

The focus for June was the Victory Day (or 'V' Day) Celebration held in London over the Whit weekend, which was to formally mark the end of the Second World War. This was an opportunity to salute the people who had helped win the war and to showcase victorious Britain to the world – and the great survivor, London. The occasion was also to mark the first major outing for television broadcasting – a service still in its infancy when it had been curtailed by the outbreak of hostilities. 'Remember me?' asked announcer Jasmine Bligh as she introduced the same Mickey Mouse cartoon that had been playing when television stopped in September 1939. The message was clear; normal service had been resumed.[3]

On Saturday 8 June the Victory parade left Regent's Park heading towards Tower Hill, culminating in a royal salute on the Mall. As many as 10 million Londoners – as well as visitors from out of town – came to celebrate. Some had taken up their positions in the Mall on Thursday and Friday to secure the best view, bringing with them 'food, blankets and radios'. Many arrived on one of the seventy-five special 'Victory Express' trains that brought in sightseers from all over the country.[4] Typically, despite the weather reports optimistically forecasting 'ideal weather – plenty of sunshine, but not too hot',[5] after a promisingly sunny morning heavy rain fell throughout the rest of the day, drowning the city. But despite the weather, the crowd that braved it was determined to celebrate.

The parade was more than four miles long and consisted of over 500 vehicles from the navy, the RAF, British Civilian Services and the army. This was followed by a marching column of 20,000 troops and eighteen marching bands, which went from Marble Arch to Whitehall then along the Mall and up to Hyde Park Corner. The marching column was headed by the flags of the Allies, each with a guard of honour (apart, controversially, from Poland). Next came units representing the services of the British Empire and these were followed by units from all the British services. It took forty-five minutes for the whole marching column to pass any given point. The pageant, a spectacle 'never surpassed in Britain' marched in front of the royal family who stood for an hour and forty-eight minutes – much of it in the pouring rain – on the saluting base in the Mall, honouring the procession. Finally, 'under a weeping sky' came 'the most enthralling spectacle of all', as 307 RAF and Royal Navy planes roared over Trafalgar Square. This was followed by dancing, community singing, orchestral concerts and Punch and Judy shows in the various parks of central London as well as a free performance of *As You Like It* at the Regent's Park Open-Air Theatre. As one newspaper reporter observed, 'this beats everything – the coronation, the Jubilee and any of the cup finals'. At sunset, after years of blackout, the iconic buildings of London were lit by floodlights for the first time – the Houses of Parliament, Buckingham Palace, the National Gallery, St James's Palace, the Tower of London, Westminster Abbey, Horse Guards' Parade, Nelson's Column, the War Office and, most poignantly of all, St Paul's Cathedral – still standing indomitably, but surrounded by the devastation wreaked by the Blitz of 1940–41. Despite the sense of celebration, it was clear that recent wounds were barely healed.

The royal family appeared on the balcony at Buckingham Palace before travelling to Chelsea where the King and Queen embarked on the royal barge, accompanied by the young princesses, Elizabeth and Margaret Rose. The barge proceeded down the Thames to Westminster, with crowds packed on both banks of the river, as well as on the six bridges left open to the public that day. Ticker tape was dropped from Westminster Bridge as the King disembarked at the Houses of Parliament.

> Perhaps the most impressive moment in a day of memories came when, after the King had landed, the packed crowds thronging the bridges, streets, windows and roofs high above the river joined in singing 'God Save The King' to music relayed over 500 speakers.

The festivities continued at 11 p.m. with a firework display over central London, concentrated on the Thames. Fireworks and coloured water displays were accompanied by cascades of fire from temporary bridges across the river and bonfires burned along the Mall. The *News of the World* noted that 'in visual effect it was the Blitz all over again and floodlit buildings gave the impression of the aftermath of an enemy incendiary raid'.[6] Traffic came to a standstill and motorists and pedestrians 'talked to each other freely as they waited to move on'. After a year of peace, the whole event was a reminder of the spirit and camaraderie that had helped the nation through six arduous years of war. A second RAF fly-past at 11.15 p.m. helped reinforce this feeling. Responding to the still enormous crowds outside Buckingham Palace, the royal family made a final appearance on the balcony at 12.25 a.m. before retiring to bed, though parties continued across the city well into the night.

The colour newsreel that recorded the celebrations for posterity ended with images of the fireworks on the Thames – the 'most brilliant firework display in London's history', accompanied by strains of 'Land of Hope and Glory'. Stanley Maxted, the distinguished Canadian war correspondent, brought his feelings about the day to a suitably patriotic close, echoing one of Churchill's best-remembered wartime speeches:

And this ends a great day, a day belonging to the little man of the free peoples. Tomorrow, with this day's glory in his heart, he – and the woman beside him – will return to the business of carving out the future of the nation. While behind him in his memory will rest this Victory Day to which he passed through his finest hour.[7]

Despite some grumbling ('We haven't got much to celebrate about'; 'People have had enough of it'),[8] 'V' Day was a great success, but it was a momentary highlight of celebration in what was to be a year of great anxiety and privation for the majority of the population. Britain was exhausted, bankrupt and bereft of basic commodities, not the least of these being food. The housing shortage had reached crisis point. During the war years, 116,000 houses had been destroyed across Greater London. Another 1,300,000 were in need of repair. Bombed-out families had nowhere to live and returning servicemen were exacerbating the problem. Building materials were scarce and many skilled tradesmen were yet to be demobilized. Desperate families became illegal squatters in empty houses and offices in Mayfair and Piccadilly, many of them garnering popular support from the general public. Just a few days after 'V' Day, on 19 June, Tom Williams, the Minister for Agriculture, observed that Britain faced 'a grim and melancholy situation' that was 'worse than the hardest days of the war'.[9]

In 1939, 70 per cent of Britain's food had been imported – including 50 per cent of meat and 70 per cent of cereals and fats. One of the main strategies of the Axis powers during the war had been to attack imports to Britain, thereby undermining British industry and potentially starving the nation into submission. The government had responded with an immediate programme of rationing in order to equitably feed and clothe the population.[10] Rationing had quickly become a way of life and continued to dominate conversation and headlines throughout the war and well into the next decade, only to fully cease in 1954; the whole period of rationing in Britain lasting fifteen years. Petrol rationing had begun immediately the war broke out and this had been swiftly followed by the rationing of foodstuffs. Bacon, butter and sugar were rationed first, soon followed by meat, tea, jam, biscuits, cereals, cheese, eggs, lard, milk and tinned fruit. Some imported fruits all but vanished – 80 per cent had been imported in 1939 – hence the iconic disappearance of bananas. By 1946 many basic foods and clothing had been rationed for years. Restrictions continued to affect almost every consumer product from basics like sheets and blankets to luxury items like nail varnish and nylons. Books continued to be printed to 'Wartime Economy Standard', with thin paper, narrow margins and cheap bindings. Newspapers were also still restricted, often to four pages – effectively just a single folded sheet. If the general populace had hoped that the end of the war was to bring an end to the misery of rationing, they were bitterly disappointed.

Clothing was rationed on a 'points' system. Initially the allowance had been for approximately one new outfit per year but as the war had progressed, points were reduced to such an extent that the purchase of a coat constituted almost an entire year's ration. By 1946 pre-war wardrobes had been 'cannibalized to destruction' as everybody attempted to 'make do and mend'. All demobilized servicemen, though, were fitted out with a 'demob suit': a complete civilian outfit from cufflinks to shoes. But 'it was strange to walk around a lot of young men your age wearing virtually the same suit', observed one young recently demobbed soldier. The demob suit was simply 'one uniform in exchange for another'.[11] To make matters worse, the quality of these suits was very poor, held in low esteem by the men who had to wear them; variously dismissed as 'foul', 'gaudy' and 'like walking around in a pair of pyjamas'.[12]

The food crisis was not only affecting Britain – it was global. As well as attempting to feed the nation fairly, the government, rather altruistically, was also trying to stave off famine abroad following poor harvests in Europe and Asia. In the summer of 1946, a 15 per cent cut in malting barley for brewers was made. The British public was told that it was being processed into animal feed, but in reality, the bulk of the barley was being sent abroad, 'particularly', noted an indignant *Daily Express*, 'to Germany'. This resulted in a 50 per cent cut in supplies of beer in many pubs and clubs. The situation was exacerbated by a change in British drinking habits. By June 1946, the average man (and now woman) was drinking 25 per cent more beer than they had done before the war started. Beer was cheaper than spirits, which were extremely expensive now that the duty on them was so high. Added to this, men who had generally favoured spirits before the war had changed their drinking habits after spending years in the army, where beer had been the most popular, accessible and affordable tipple for the majority of conscripts. Women were also drinking more beer as drinks like sherry had become expensive or unobtainable during the war years. Harvey's famous Bristol Cream Sherry was still unobtainable in 1946.

Consequently many venues regularly ran out of supplies of beer and had to close intermittently. Pubs in some areas were only able to open for three 'priority' hours a day: lunchtime, after work and for one hour in the evening. A chalked-up sign saying 'Sorry, Closed: No Beer' became a common sight in London to such an extent that the *Daily Express* suggested that beer should come under state control, much as the nationalized Coal Board was to supervise the provision of coal.

But the most emotive issue was the peacetime rationing of bread, which had never been restricted during the war. This was to prove very hard for the general populace, but particularly to housewives, who were already making do with the 'National Loaf' – the smallest and darkest that had been produced since the First World War ('We have stood everything else, but this is the last straw,' one housewife complained to her local newspaper). The issue was fiercely debated in parliament, with Winston Churchill commenting that the prospect of bread rationing was 'one of the gravest announcements I have ever heard in time of peace'. If Britain couldn't supply herself with her own daily bread, what hope was there for her future? When bread was finally rationed to an average 9 oz a day on 21 July 1946, it was front-page news both in

Britain and America. In practice, however, the bread ration proved to be adequate for most families' needs, but as David Kynaston notes in *Austerity Britain*, 'the very fact of peacetime bread rationing would remain a symbolic sore as long as it remained in force'.[13]

As well as adding more stress to the life of the average housewife, scarcity had also given birth to a new sort of crime wave, and it was around this time that the black-market 'spiv' began to emerge as a recognizable type – the opportunistic patter, the wide lapels, the gaudy tie, the pencil moustache. Many perfectly respectable citizens both condemned *and* used the black market. Some organized gangs stole basics – hundreds of thousands of poultry and millions of eggs were illegally traded. Others specialized in the luxury market for cars, furs and jewellery. These crimes were severely dealt with by the courts. One licensee, Gertrude Bryan of Epsom, was fined £1,236 (the cost of a semi-detached house at the time) for charges of receiving clothing coupons and stealing corned beef. Her accomplice, Frederick Gilbert, was sentenced to nine months in prison. The magistrate gave real weight to their sentences:

> When the whole of Europe is tightening its belt we have before us these offences connected with the abuse of rationing. It might be that people would go short because of these cases. The whole fair distribution of food might break down if these offences became widespread.[14]

Throughout the summer, the economist John Maynard Keynes attempted to negotiate a grant or financial gift from the United States that might help alleviate Britain's perilous situation (he referred to it later as a 'financial Dunkirk'). But despite his high hopes, all he could arrange was a reluctant loan. The Americans were very loathe to make the loan and the British equally loathe to need it so desperately. Ultimately, the Anglo-American loan of £1.1 billion was finally negotiated on 15 July 1946. It was only paid off sixty years later, in 2006.

Buffeted between severity and celebration, Britain in 1946 was suffused with a mixture of relief and uncertainty, hope and exhaustion. Even the weather, as if to reflect the confusions of the period, was unseasonably changeable. At the end of May, after a transatlantic depression lost its way, Britain was drenched by twenty-eight days of rain while Iceland basked in a typical British summer. The weather that followed in June was a mixture of sunshine and showers, so that nobody was sure whether to prepare themselves with headscarves or sunglasses. An artist and occasional film extra, Margery Gardner, unsure what to expect from day to day, carried both in her handbag: a pair of white sunglasses and a headscarf given to her by a boyfriend who had been in the RAF.

On Midsummer Day, Monday 24 June, the temperature reached 75 degrees in London – the highest of that summer – but was followed by violent thunderstorms. Houses were flooded, crops damaged and roads turned into rivers. In some areas, fields were white with hailstones as big as marbles. It was 'the worst June weather for nearly forty years'.[15]

The summer of 1946 was one of extremes.

CHAPTER TWO

Miss Symonds

15–23 JUNE 1946

Tall and slim, 21-year-old Yvonne Symonds was an attractive brunette, with blue eyes, olive skin and a 'Grecian nose'.[1] She had been demobbed from the WRNS in January 1946 and had since been living with her parents at their family home in a respectable suburb of Worthing, a seaside resort on the south coast.

Yvonne was one of many young women who had joined the services since 1941, when on 18 December the National Service Act had introduced the conscription of women. Every 'mobile' woman in the country between the ages of eighteen and fifty had been conscripted on behalf of the war effort – some to factory work, others to one of the three female services: the ATS (Auxiliary Territorial Service), the WAAF (Women's Auxiliary Air Force) and the WRNS

(Women's Royal Naval Service). As it became clear that the idea of merely volunteering for war work or to join the services would soon be abandoned, many women had joined up quickly before decisions were made for them. At the time, few women had any idea what the different services had to offer and for many the decision was made lightly – some going on instinct while others went for the uniform that appealed the most. Christian Oldham, the convent-educated daughter of an admiral, joined the WRNS in 1940 and was very taken with the 'flattering double-breasted jacket, svelte skirt and pert tricorne hat' that made up a Wren officer's uniform.[2] In 1942, Queen Elizabeth gave the royal blessing to the distinctive Wren hats. She had tried one in front of one of the mirrors at Buckingham Palace and declared that 'the children loved it!'[3] Certainly the WRNS was thought to be the most fashionable of the services,[4] the uniform having been designed by the couturier Molyneux, who had created Gertrude Lawrence's costumes for the original production of *Private Lives* in 1930 and the wedding dress of Princess Marina of Greece in 1934. In 1939 there had been only 3,000 serving WRNS personnel; by 1944 the number had reached a peak of 74,620.[5]

In the early part of the war, Wrens had only been allocated to five categories covering office or domestic work, but by the time Yvonne had joined the service, women were working in twenty-five categories covering a broad range of roles from mechanics to boat crew, from signallers to 'torpedomen'.[6] She had joined the WRNS at the age of eighteen in 1943 and had been stationed at various stone frigates – land-based naval depots – including HMS *Shrapnel*, which was actually the Great Western Hotel in Southampton, and HMS *Grasshopper*, which was the naval name for Weymouth Harbour where combined operations were focused on Operation Neptune, the D-Day landings. Yvonne had also

worked in Portsmouth on HMS *Marshal Soult*, a disarmed
World War One warship that was used as a depot ship to
supply clothing and food stores to the ships that were to take
part in the invasion of Normandy.

On Saturday 15 June, Yvonne attended a WRNS reunion
dinner dance at a pub in Chelsea. She'd arranged to stay
overnight at the Overseas Club just behind the Ritz in St
James's so she wouldn't have to travel back to Worthing late
on the Saturday night. Whilst at the reunion, Yvonne was
struck by a tall, tanned, handsome man – blond, well-built,
with eyes a peculiar shining blue. From his uniform she
could see that he was a decorated officer in the South African
Air Force. He had a plain gold ring on the little finger of his
left hand and also wore a gold watch with a leather strap. He
was extremely attractive, good company and full of stories
about his wartime exploits. There was the occasion when he
flew a plane under a bridge – much to the chagrin of his
commanding officer – and the time he baled out of a burning bomber over Holland – hence the caterpillar badge that
he wore proudly on his lapel. These were worn exclusively
by members of the Caterpillar Club – flyers who had baled
out of their aircraft and survived. Referring to the silk from
which parachutes were made, the club's motto was 'Life
depends on a silken thread': fragile, precious and fraught
with danger. Handsome, heroic and charming, the airman
fascinated Yvonne. He introduced himself as Lieutenant
Colonel 'Jimmy' Heath.[7]

Yvonne was not alone in succumbing to the glamour and
romance of air force flyers like Heath. Many observers of the
period noted the particular effect that airmen's uniforms had
on women. Joan Wyndham, who left a bohemian background in Chelsea to join the WAAF, recalls a dance she
attended shortly after joining the service. Hopeful of romance
with a glamorous young airman, she was distressed to find no

pilots present and that she would have to make do with 'pint-sized Romeos' and other 'wingless wonders'. An airman's wings were a badge of heroism and the uniform had a particular sexual allure ('I can't describe the effect wings have on a WAAF!').[8] In *The Naked Civil Servant*, Quentin Crisp makes a keen distinction between the sort of servicemen his gay friends fancied (young, lower-ranking sailors) and those his female friends were attracted to: '[Women] prefer airmen, by which they always mean the higher ranks.'[9] Romantic novels of the period were keen to exploit the iconography of these new 'Knights of the Air' in titles such as *Flying Wild*, *A Flying Visit*, *Winged Love*, *Air Force Girl* and *Wellington Wendy*.[10] One airman, William Simpson, summed up the appeal of his uniform to women; in a nutshell, it was 'redolent of glamour and courage'.[11]

Having charmed Yvonne with his wartime tales, Heath suggested that she join him at the Panama Club in South Kensington, where he was a member. They'd be able to have an after-hours drink. For a guileless young woman like Yvonne, this must have seemed to be the epitome of metropolitan sophistication. The Panama Club was only a short taxi ride away from Chelsea, situated near the Natural History Museum and just round the corner from South Kensington underground station. The club had been set up here at 23–24 Cromwell Place in August 1945 after its former premises had been destroyed by enemy action. Open from 3 p.m. to midnight, the club provided drinks, food and entertainment for members only. After drinking in public houses, many non-members tried to get into the club when the pubs closed, so the staff, led by receptionist Solomon Joseph, supervised admission to the club very strictly. He had been in trouble with the law before for licensing and betting offences and was determined not to have any more brushes with the police.[12]

At the reception area of the club, Heath signed himself in

with Yvonne as his guest on the yellow visitors' form. Solomon Joseph unbolted the door and ushered them into the club. For Yvonne this was an adventure into a glamorous night-time society, escorted by the most dashing of men – a world away from the cosseted life she lived with her parents in Worthing. Heath led her through the reception area and up the short flight of stairs to the first floor where there was a small bar. They carried on up to the club room on the second floor.

The club room at the Panama was partitioned into two sections – the area to the right was a dining room about 16 feet wide and 37 feet long with a dozen tables lining the longer walls, with sofas behind them and some small chairs. At the far end of the room was an area for the band, which played every night from 8 p.m. The dance floor dominated the centre of the room and was in full swing when Heath and Yvonne arrived.[13] The Perry Como hits 'Surrender' and 'Prisoner of Love', The Ink Spots' 'To Each His Own' and Margaret Whiting's version of the old Al Bowlly classic 'Guilty' were all popular tunes with dance bands that summer.

The left-hand section of the second floor was a lounge and bar where members had drinks served to them by two waitresses, Joyce and Phyllis, who had worked there since the club had moved premises. It was in the club room while the band played dance music that Heath first suggested that Yvonne should sleep with him that night. Yvonne, despite her time in the WRNS, was a polite and well-brought-up young woman. She was also a virgin. She refused. After their evening together, Heath hailed a taxi and dropped Yvonne off at the Overseas Club in Park Place. He took her rejection of his advances with good grace. So she had no concerns about arranging to meet him again the next day. He seemed the perfect gentleman.

On Sunday morning, Heath rang Yvonne at the Overseas Club and suggested that they spend the day together. Yvonne met Heath at the club dressed in a blue and white print dress with a full-length light summer coat.[14] They took a taxi to Knightsbridge to one of Heath's regular haunts, the Nag's Head, a mews pub in Kinnerton Street, where they stayed until about 2.30 p.m. From there they went for tea to an hotel, most probably the Normandie, another favourite haunt of Heath's, which overlooked Knightsbridge Green. At tea, he again pressurized Yvonne to sleep with him, 'over-persuading' her. As was clear from many of his relations with women, Heath was deeply charismatic, very convincing and had a winning way with words. He was confident in his looks and took great care with his appearance. He was very aware of the seductive power of both his uniform and his tales of wartime heroism, and extremely confident in his physical allure. After the trial, an officer friend of Heath's who had known him a number of years stated that 'women were fascinated by him. Such was his magnetism that it was invariably embarrassing to be in his company when the girls were about'.[15]

Yvonne, trusting, inexperienced and swept along with the force of this apparently whirlwind romance, was conflicted. She was hugely attracted to this handsome, charming man. He told her that he loved her; why didn't they get married? If they were 'unofficially engaged', surely that would make it acceptable for them to sleep with each other? With wartime brief encounters still very recent history, there was nothing unusual in the swift trajectory of this courtship. The war had encouraged young people particularly to live for the moment and, as Virginia Nicholson observes in *Millions Like Us*, her study of women's lives in the 1940s, 'sex was a way to challenge extinction'.[16] This sense of impetuous desire with little-known bedfellows continued into the early post-war period and Heath was expert at exploiting it.

There's a sense too that he was well aware that women's attitude to sex had evolved since the 1930s. Since the outbreak of war, more women were having sex before marriage – or with men other than their husbands – more women were using contraceptives and more were contracting sexually transmitted diseases. The diarist Joan Wyndham confessed to the intimacy of her journal that she was aware at the time she was writing that pre-war mores were breaking down: 'Inside me I could feel every moral code I had ever believed in since childhood begin to crumble away.'[17]

For Yvonne, the speed and illicit nature of her romance with Heath intensified the experience, like one of the films she'd seen at the pictures. And here she was, living it herself – two young people desperately in love, wanting to be together. Now that marriage had been proposed, the engagement felt tangible; Yvonne agreed to sleep with him.

The couple took a taxi to Victoria to pick up Heath's luggage and then on to the Overseas Club to pick up Yvonne's small, cream overnight bag. Around 7 p.m., Heath telephoned ahead to an hotel he knew in Notting Hill to tell the manageress that they were coming. He told her that he was calling from a telephone box at Euston. Half an hour later, they arrived at the Pembridge Court Hotel, just off Notting Hill Gate.[18]

The Pembridge Court was a private hotel known for its 'good class clientele'. Elizabeth Wyatt ran the business with her husband Henry and her daughter-in-law, Alice. It was a typical mid-nineteenth-century double-fronted, stuccoed building with a pillared front porch entrance. It stood (as it still does) on Pembridge Gardens, nestled just off the south-west corner of Pembridge Square. It consisted of a ground, first and second floors with a basement beneath. On the first floor were three bedrooms, numbers 1, 3 and 4, as well as two private rooms. On the second floor were bedrooms 5 to

10 and a bathroom. On the intermediate landing between the two floors were a communal bathroom and lavatory.

Yvonne followed Heath through the outside gate and up the five stone steps to the entrance hall. He signed the register as Lieutenant Colonel and Mrs N. G. C. Heath of Black Hill Cottages, Romsey. Mrs Wyatt asked Heath how long they would want the room for? He said that he would like to book it for three or four nights, possibly five. He told her that he had stayed at the hotel a couple of years earlier when he was in the South African Air Force. Mrs Wyatt felt sure that she recognized him and that he had been a guest at the hotel on a couple of previous occasions.

Lieutenant Colonel Heath was offered Room 4 on the first floor. He was given a key to the room and another to open the front door, which was locked at 10 p.m. every night. Mrs Wyatt accompanied the couple up the stairs to show them their room. This was situated at the back of the building, at the top of the flight of stairs. The room was typical of the price range and period – 19 feet by 15 feet with a window overlooking the back garden. Opening the door, the wardrobe was against the left-hand wall. Behind the door, to the right, were twin beds, a couple of feet apart. On the wall opposite the foot of the beds was a fireplace with a gas fire and a small gas ring. The gas fire was to prove crucial later on. As there was no open fire in the grate, there was no necessity for a poker. Mrs Wyatt later confirmed that there had never been a poker in the room.

Between the fireplace and the foot of the beds were two armchairs, positioned side-on to the fireplace, facing into the centre of the room. To the left of the chimneybreast was a chest of drawers and to the right a dressing table at an angle. Another table sat beneath the window in the right-hand wall. To the right of the window, in the corner, was a washbasin. After explaining about breakfast and guiding them through the facilities, Mrs Wyatt left Heath and his 'wife' to settle in.

That night, in Room 4 of the Pembridge Court Hotel, Yvonne surrendered her virginity to Heath. They had intercourse twice, which brought about some bloodstaining on the sheets of the bed nearest the door. Throughout their night together, according to her testimony, Heath was very gentle with Yvonne and treated her with nothing but kindness and sensitivity.

The next morning, Monday 17 June, Mrs Wyatt sent Rhoda Spooner, the hotel waitress, up to Room 4 with tea and toast. Rhoda didn't usually serve meals in any of the guest rooms, but Mrs Wyatt had made an exception for the charming lieutenant colonel and his pretty young wife. When Rhoda entered the room with the tea, Heath and Yvonne were both in the bed nearest to the door. Rhoda went to open the curtains and left the tea tray. She noticed Heath's large brown suitcase on the table near the window and a flying helmet with large goggles hanging on one of the chairs. At about 11 a.m. that morning, there was a knock on the door from Barbara Osborne, the chambermaid.[19] Barbara generally cleaned and changed the beds between guest occupancies. By now, Yvonne was standing by the chest of drawers in her sky-blue dressing gown. Heath was sitting up in the bed nearest the window, wearing his red dressing gown.

'Will you be long?' asked Barbara, 'I'm keen to get on with my work.'

'I was just going to get up and come back later,' said Heath.

He suggested to Yvonne that she should stay with him at the hotel for another day or two, but she'd promised her parents that she would return to Worthing that day. They had sex again that afternoon, then Heath saw her off on the 9.28 p.m. train from Victoria to Worthing. He promised to phone her and that he would come and see her later in the

week. Yvonne gave Heath her address in Warren Road and
her telephone number, Swandean 906.

Yvonne arrived home that evening after 11 p.m., full of
her romantic weekend with her handsome pilot. She was
engaged to Jimmy and couldn't wait for her parents to meet
him. He had said that he was coming down to Worthing that
week anyway to attend the opening of the Shoreham Airport
that was re-opening the following weekend. As he had promised, Heath telephoned Yvonne on the Tuesday, the
Wednesday and then again on Thursday 20 June, like any
ordinary, infatuated boyfriend who couldn't keep himself
from chatting to his fiancée every day. Such excitement had
rarely intruded into Yvonne's life before whilst growing up
in one of the most archetypal of English seaside resorts.

In an age before foreign travel, Worthing was a hugely
popular – if polite – holiday destination with none of the
excesses and vulgarity of Blackpool, Margate or the 'some-
what overgrown' Brighton.[20] The town styled itself very
much as a middle-class resort. Only eighty-six minutes from
Victoria by the electric train, it was also popular with businessmen who worked in the City of London and commuted
home at night. Increasingly Worthing had promoted itself as
a winter resort and it appealed – as it still does today – to an
older clientele of the well-heeled retired. The *Ward Lock
Guide* of the time observed that:

> [. . .] perhaps the best evidence of a genial all-the-year climate
> is the large number of residences built in recent years at West
> Worthing and elsewhere in the borough by Anglo-Indians
> and others to whom sunshine is almost a necessity.[21]

In 1941 the threatened German invasion ('Operation Sealion')
had seen a dramatic transformation along the beaches of the
south coast from Lyme Regis in the west to Ramsgate in the

east. Barbed wire and landmines took the place of buckets and spades as coastal defence had become a priority – especially during 1940 42 when the invasion of Britain seemed imminent. Consequently Worthing's famous pier, one of the principle attractions of the resort that had stood since 1862, was partially demolished and closed in 1940. Six years on, it remained a prominent and silent scar at the centre of the town.

At Whitsuntide of 1946, the weekend of 'V' Day, the local council had hoped that they could draw holidaymakers back to the resort, but a planned Victory parade through the town had been aborted due to lack of interest. As a focus to reinvigorate the tourist trade, the council had organized the reopening of the pavilion and bandstand on the parade. The opening was hugely anticipated as a matter of local pride. But despite their best-laid plans, the opening was, literally, a wash-out, cursed like the rest of that summer by bad weather. The *Worthing Herald* reported that 'June 1946 was the DULLEST for twenty-three years; the COLDEST for eighteen years; the WETTEST for thirteen years'.[22]

Inside from the pelting rain, Worthing's repertory company offered a weekly changing programme at the Connaught Theatre. That week the Overture Repertory Players presented *Fear Walks Behind* by Sydney Horler and Norman Lee. The town's four cinemas were packed. With such terrible weather and television still a novelty, 1946 was the peak of cinema attendance in Britain with some 1.6 billion attendances – 3 million cinema-goers a day. The cinema offerings at Worthing that summer were a mixture of long-forgotten titles and the occasional classic, the majority from Hollywood. The Rivoli played *She Wouldn't Say Yes* and *Cornered*. At the Odeon, Alan Ladd and Veronica Lake starred in *The Blue Dahlia*. Lana Turner smouldered in a risque two-piece swimsuit in the screen version of James M. Cain's amoral murder story, *The Postman Always Rings Twice* and Ingrid Bergman suffered beautifully in *Spellbound*, the poster asking boldly, 'Will he kiss me or kill me?'[23]

On Friday 21 June, Yvonne was surprised but delighted when Jimmy telephoned her at about midday, telling her that he was actually in Worthing and couldn't wait to see her. Yvonne quickly changed into her most flattering green dress and met Heath in the centre of town. When they met, he told her that he was planning to stay for about ten days so that he could see more of her and meet her parents. He was smartly dressed, out of uniform this time in a grey pin-striped suit, collar and tie, but no hat. He'd left his luggage at the railway station until he'd decided on a place to stay. But finding an hotel at the start of the most anticipated holiday season since the beginning of the war would be no easy feat.

That weekend, Worthing was to be overrun with holiday-makers, many taking their first holiday since 1939. Two thirds of the population were to take a holiday that summer and the south-coast seaside resorts braced themselves for the enormous demand. Trains, stations, hotels and boarding houses were packed with thousands of people. Mile-long queues formed at daybreak at London stations when the railways handled the biggest crowds they had seen for years. Some luggage-laden travellers waited throughout the night to catch early trains. At Paddington a 'crocodile' of people wound its way into the side streets as there was no more standing space in the station itself. Everybody, it seems, was in holiday mood and aiming for the seaside.

Yvonne and Heath had lunch and with her local knowledge she advised him about places to stay. In Heath's *Daily Telegraph* for that day there was a prominent advertisement for the Ocean Hotel, right on the seafront.

WORTHING OCEAN HOTEL
'A Sun Trap on the Sea Front'
Unrivalled Position
45 Bedrooms ~ World–famous Cuisine
Completely Redecorated ~ Central Heating
Dancing to Bob Crowder and his band.[24]

That afternoon, Heath and Yvonne called at the hotel on Marine Parade, opposite the beach. At the reception, the couple met George Girdwood, the hotel manager. Heath said that he was looking for accommodation for himself for the next ten days.[25] The hotel being full at the time, Girdwood suggested that Heath could be accommodated for a couple of days in the hotel annexe, round the corner at 11 West Buildings, after which they could accommodate him in the main hotel. Heath readily agreed to this. He said his name was Lieutenant Colonel Heath and signed the register accordingly. He gave his address – this time – as South Africa House in Trafalgar Square and his nationality as South African, but Yvonne didn't seem to notice. She and her new fiancé then left together to pick up his luggage from Worthing Railway Station. They returned to the hotel shortly afterwards with one of Heath's large brown suitcases. He went alone to the annexe to his room, but then returned to have tea with Yvonne in the hotel lounge.

At this point, Heath asked Yvonne what time the evening papers came from London. She told him that they were already out, so he bought two. Throughout tea he glanced through the pages of the newspapers and was reading them intently. Yvonne remarked to him about this, but he didn't reply. After he had finished with the papers, Yvonne flicked through them herself, but saw nothing to interest her. She thought that Heath was rather quiet and that something might be worrying him. Was it something she'd done? Or said? Perhaps he was cooling towards her? Now that she had allowed him to sleep with her, perhaps he had lost interest? But Yvonne kept her insecurities to herself. Whatever Heath's feelings, he too was unwilling to give voice to them. He said he would be all right tomorrow, and that he had been 'up all Thursday night'. He then jokingly mentioned some shirts that needed washing. Yvonne, eager to please her new lover, was only too happy to say that she'd wash them through for him at home and would collect them from him later. After tea, they went out together, but returned to the hotel for dinner at about 7 p.m. They were not seen together again that night, but they could easily have gone back directly to the hotel annexe without being seen. They certainly had sex again at the hotel and this may well be the occasion on which it occurred.

The next day was Saturday 22 June. Before she left her parents' house, Yvonne washed the shirts that she had taken from Heath the night before. As she was washing them, she noticed that one of the shirts had a number of small brown stains on the tail, but she wasn't quite sure what they were. Once washed, she put them out to dry, intending to iron them the next day. She then headed into Worthing to meet her fiancé.

At about 12.15 p.m., Heath and Yvonne went to the Ship Hotel in South Street, which was a quirky character pub modelled on an old galleon.[26] Again, Heath was wearing his 'civvies'. He was delighted to bump into an old friend, Angus Bruce, and introduced him to Yvonne. Bruce was drinking there with his friend, Dick Hollis, and the foursome had a drink together. Bruce asked what his friend was doing in Worthing?[27] Heath told him that he was staying ten days at the Ocean Hotel. He'd been demobbed and was about to start a business buying planes in England to sell abroad.

Bruce had known Heath for about two years. He had been

manager of the South Western Hotel in Wimbledon where Heath had been a regular. They'd once had a night out on the town drinking at Oddenino's and the Haymarket Club in Shaftesbury Avenue. But at that time, which wasn't too long ago, Heath had been known as 'Captain Armstrong' of the South African Air Force. Heath explained that he had been demobbed with the rank of lieutenant colonel and had received a letter of pardon from the King for a previous indiscretion in the RAF. He was no longer known as 'Armstrong' but as 'Heath'. This must have elicited some curiosity from Yvonne, who was witness to the conversation, but, as Jimmy had explained, he'd had a letter of pardon and besides, it was all in the past now.

Before they left the Ship, to celebrate their engagement, Bruce invited Heath and Yvonne to be his guests that evening to a dinner dance that was being held at the Blue Peter Club. The club was owned by his drinking companion Dick Hollis, who was Bruce's boss, as he was now working there as catering manager. The club was in Angmering-on-Sea near Littlehampton, just a short drive from Worthing. The young couple said they'd be delighted.

Yvonne and Heath went back to eat at the Ocean Hotel. Over lunch, he wondered if Yvonne had heard anything about an incident that had taken place in the hotel they had stayed in the previous Sunday? Yvonne had heard nothing about it, but was curious to hear more. Heath went on. A woman, he said, had been killed – murdered – there during the week. But before Yvonne could ask any more, Heath reminded her that they had an appointment to get to. They were to meet her parents at Worthing Golf Club, just near the Symonds' family home. He said that he would tell her all about the murder later on.

Arriving at the golf club, 'Jimmy' Heath was introduced to his future parents-in-law, John and Gertrude.[28] John Charters

Symonds (always known as Jack) was a civil engineer and had been a major in the RASC during the First World War. Either during or just after the end of the war, he had met and married Gertrude Werther in Belgium before bringing her back with him to England.[29] Yvonne, their only child, had been born in 1925.

Heath explained that he was South African, though educated in England. Whilst at Cambridge, he had joined the University Flying Club, from which he obtained a commission in the South African Air Force. He told Major Symonds about his wartime experiences with the SAAF where he had seen active service in North Africa and El Alamein. He also claimed to be related to Lady Heath, the Irish aviatrix, who had been one of the most famous women in the world during the 1920s. Flying, Heath explained, was something of a family obsession – both his parents also being flyers themselves. His present job was buying and selling aircraft and he proposed to continue in this line for the next five years after which his father wanted him to give up flying and return to South Africa to join the family stockbroking business. The meeting went very well, with Heath expounding on life in South Africa and his time during the war. Finally, Major Symonds delightedly accepted Heath's suit for his daughter's hand in marriage.

Now properly engaged, the young couple left the golf club at about 1.30 p.m. to spend the afternoon together. Yvonne returned to her parents' house at 6 p.m. to change for dinner. At 7 p.m., Heath arrived to take them to the dinner dance at Angmering. While Yvonne finished dressing, Major Symonds chatted with Heath downstairs. A military man himself, he noted that Heath was in British khaki battledress with a lieutenant colonel's insignia with two rows of decorations, led by the DFC and Bar. He also wore pilot's wings and had red ribbons on his epaulettes, denoting the SAAF.

Yvonne was finally ready, a taxi was ordered and the smart young couple were driven off to Angmering. To Jack and Gertrude Symonds, Yvonne's fiancé seemed the ideal son-in-law – an educated gentleman; charming, well connected and a war hero to boot.

The Blue Peter Club was situated right on the pebble beach at Angmering, twenty minutes' drive from Worthing.[30] Heath and Yvonne arrived at about 8.15 p.m. The day had gone well and Yvonne's parents had been impressed with her new beau. But one thing had been troubling Yvonne ever since Jimmy had mentioned it – the story of the murder at the Pembridge Court Hotel. At dinner, she took the opportunity to remind him that he was going to tell her about it. As the band played on in the background, Jimmy seemed only too keen to tell her everything, in all its shocking, graphic detail.

'Jimmy, you were going to tell me about the murder? At the hotel?' said Yvonne.[31]

'Yes. So I was. Well, after you left for Worthing on Monday, I stayed on at the Pembridge Court. On Thursday, I was at an hotel with a journalist friend and we got into conversation with a couple near us, so we all had a drink together. The girl was pretty well known as a prostitute. The man said he wanted to spend the night with her, but had nowhere to take her. So I said, why don't you use my room?'

For the young girl from Worthing, this tale of Heath offering up his hotel room (indeed *their* hotel room where they had spent such a romantic weekend) for an acquaintance to spend the night with a prostitute must have seemed distasteful enough – certainly outside Yvonne's experience. But having only recently lost her virginity to her fiancé, maybe this was another rite of passage, a swift education in the ways of the adult world where things were different and which she felt too inexperienced to question.

'What about the landlady?' she asked.

'I told her that if anyone called for me, they could contact me in Hendon where I was going to stay the night. So I gave my room key to the man – in front of my reporter chum.'

'I see,' said Yvonne.

'The next day,' Heath continued, 'on Friday morning, I was at Hendon and had a telephone call from an Inspector Barratt of the Metropolitan Police.[32] He said he wanted to talk to me as soon as possible, so he'd send a car to bring me back to the hotel. He was keen to establish that I hadn't slept in my hotel room, as a murder had been committed there. And he wanted me to identify the body. Obviously this was the woman I'd met in company with my friend the night before. So Barratt took me to Room 4 at the Pembridge Court.'

'And?'

'I saw the body of the woman. It was a gruesome sight. She'd been tied by her legs and thighs. Her body was very bruised. I've never seen so much blood in my life.'

'What had happened to her?'

'Inspector Barratt said that a poker had been stuck up her. That it was the poker that killed her. I'm not so sure. I think it's more likely that she'd been suffocated. He asked me to stay in town so that I could assist in trying to identify the man I gave the key to.'

'Who would do such a terrible thing?'

'It can only have been done by a sexual maniac.'

'Yes.'

'And, of course, you know it wasn't me.'

Here was Yvonne's fiancé, sitting before her and telling her the truth. Of course it couldn't have been him.

'No.'

'I've treated you kindly whenever we've been alone together, haven't I?'

Whatever she felt about this extraordinary tale, Yvonne said nothing. Jimmy bumped into some RAF friends and as the evening wore on, it receded in her mind. She and Heath met Angus Bruce again, as he was working that night at the club. Heath wondered if they might pop in once more in the morning and Bruce said he'd be delighted to see them. The couple stayed at the club until midnight and Yvonne clearly felt safe enough with Heath to share a taxi with him to her parents' house in Warren Road, where he dropped her off before going on to his hotel. It was the end of an eventful engagement day that Yvonne would never forget.

Back at home, Yvonne began to puzzle over the shocking story that Jimmy had told her. The more she turned it over in her mind, the more questions it raised. Jimmy had said at some point that he knew the woman had no money, but didn't say how he knew this. He didn't once mention the name of the mysterious man he had lent his key to and that the police were now looking for, nor the name of the woman who had been killed. And who was the journalist who had witnessed the transaction? Crucially, why had Jimmy come to Worthing? Hadn't the police specifically asked him to stay in London?

The next morning – Sunday – Yvonne woke early and started ironing the shirts that Jimmy had asked her to launder, ready to return to him later in the day. Then, a weekly ritual: the Sunday newspapers arrived before breakfast. Glancing at the headlines, Yvonne's parents were stunned; her fiancé was front-page news.

6ft MAN SOUGHT IN HOTEL CRIME

Scotland Yard detectives seeking a clue to the murder of Mrs. Margery Gardner, 33-year-old film extra, in an hotel in

Pembridge Gardens, Notting Hill issued a description yesterday of a man they wish to interview. They appealed to
anyone who sees a man answering this description to go at
once to a police station. The man is described as Neville
George Clevely Heath, aged 29.

He is 5 feet 11½ inches tall of medium build, fresh
complexion, fair hair and eyebrows, blue eyes, broad nose,
firm chin, square face with good teeth and he is probably
wearing a double-breasted light grey suit with a thin stripe
and a cream-coloured shirt with collar attached or a check
sports jacket, flannel trousers, dark brown trilby and dark
brown suede shoes. He walks with a military gait and is
known to frequent good-class hotels and guest-houses.

Mrs. Gardner's unclothed, bruised body was found in a
first floor bedroom of the hotel on Friday afternoon with her
legs and ankles bound. She is believed to have been
suffocated.[33]

Major and Mrs Symonds were stunned. But when they
showed her the paper, Yvonne did not seem at all surprised.
She told her parents all about the conversation she had had
with her fiancé the night before, outlining the details of the
murder in Notting Hill. Yvonne's father told her that she
should telephone Jimmy at once. At 9.30 a.m., Yvonne
phoned the Ocean Hotel, but was told by the receptionist
that Jimmy couldn't reply as he was sleeping in the annexe.
Yvonne left her parents' telephone number — even though
she knew he had it — and a message for him to call her
urgently on Swandean 906.[34]

Twenty minutes later, Heath telephoned her. Yvonne
explained that she and her parents had read the newspapers
and that they were very worried. 'Yes,' said Heath with
extraordinary understatement, 'I thought they would be.'[35]
He told her not to worry. He had a car and was going to

drive up to Scotland Yard right away. He would return to Worthing that evening and would ring her later on. Yvonne felt calmer. He was going to sort everything out. It must be some sort of mistake.

All Sunday evening Yvonne waited for a call from Jimmy. But he didn't ring her that evening. She hoped he might ring the next morning; he did not. She was never to speak to him again. The next time she would see him, she would be in the witness box and he would be in the dock in a police court. The story of her whirlwind romance and the intimate details of the loss of her virginity were to be crucial evidence in one of the most sensational murder trials of the century.

That Sunday night, Yvonne was left with her thoughts, stunned by the speed with which her romantic dream had mutated into a nightmare; her heroic pilot seemingly a devil; the fiancé she had fallen for, a sadistic killer. She was learning that the cinema-style romance she had imagined she was living was actually a very different sort of film. Like the picture where Ingrid Bergman seems to be losing her mind or the one where she falls in love with a man she suspects is a murderer ('Will he kiss me or kill me?').

Heath did not drive up to London that Sunday. He left Worthing in a hurry on Monday morning, leaving many of his possessions behind at the Ocean Hotel: his brown suede shoes, copies of the magazines *Flight*, *Aeroplane* and *Men Only*. Amongst the possessions he left were five newspapers: the *Daily Telegraph*, *Daily Mail*, *Daily Herald*, *Daily Mirror* and *Daily Express*. All were dated Saturday 22 June.[36] Clearly, Heath had a very specific interest in the news of that particular day. Each newspaper contained an account of the murder of Margery Gardner and the news that the police were attempting to trace a man 'Wanted for Interview': Neville George Clevely Heath.

After the trial, Yvonne Symonds was thought to be the luckiest girl in England because of her narrow escape. Though Heath may have taken her virginity, he had not taken her life. Margery Gardner had not been so fortunate.

CHAPTER THREE
Mrs Gardner

Mrs. Elizabeth Wheat   24 Bramham Gardens
24 Oakholme Road   S.W.5
Sheffield

16th June 1946

My Darling Mum,
Please excuse this paper, but I seem to have mislaid mine – and am
too late to get any more. Very many thanks for the £3, it has been
terribly axceptable as all this trouble has come back again – and I
have to see Dr Kelly again on Monday.

  I get so tired, so quickly that I still have to lie down every
afternoon – but perhaps its just because I'm expecting the 'curse'
this week-end, according to my reckoning – since it started on the
21st. 'Iris Products' have closed temporarily, [because] Charles

has to be away so much but hope to re-open again − however I couldn't go back to their work at present, as I think I tried to explain before, they have no work there which doesn't require standing. I still have hopes of the toys, but have at the moment lost my only contact with the men as the boyfriend[1] has gone away, but in any case don't worry as I shall contact him and write again next week.

The grey suit has cleaned OK except that the skirt is lighter than the coat, it isn't too good. Please send the black and blue dress as soon as possible.

Now must go to catch the post, all my love,

Margy

P.S. I would like very much to go home for a bit, but feel that it would be a mistake, as my nerves have gone to hell.

24 Bramham Gardens
S.W.5

20th June 1946

My Darling Mum,
Many thanks for your letter and enclosure − I'm always kept on tenterhooks until the last minute, in case it doesn't arrive and today was a bit of a close shave. I have just 'phoned Dr Kelly again and hope to see her at the end of the week to get some more of a tonic she gave me which seems to have done me a lot of good.

The boy friend came back on Sunday and is seeing the man about the toys at the end of the week. Unfortunately I can't be there myself. No you don't have to be trained to make these toys apparently − all I would have to do would be to sew the skin together, which sounds very simple. As regards Iris Products there was nothing creative about the work there and even the nursery

[lamp] *shades, which I had looked forward to designing, were done by stencil, which is purely mechanical.*

I may have to go into the hospital again, but I sincerely hope not, because it wouldn't really be much of a rest, as I should be worrying the whole time. If only I had a tiny private income, no matter how small, with which I could buy myself a few necessary clothes and therefore gain confidence in myself, one of the first steps to a good job. Both our minds, I feel sure, would be easier, but as it is we have to make do with things that are really completely worn out, and which even the second hand dress shops wont take. Please send me the blue and black dress before you go away.

The weather here has been appalling, rained day after day but even the plastic macs are £5 upwards and cost 9 coupons.

Will you let me know if this letter is entirely readable or no, but the pen seems to be getting very bad,

All my love,

Margery[2]

Margery Gardner's letter of 20 June was the last communication her mother would have from her daughter. Within twenty-four hours, she would be dead, her body beaten and savaged. She was thirty two years old.

Married, but estranged from her husband, Margery lived an insecure existence, moving between various bedsits and furnished flats in the Chelsea and Earls Court areas of west London. A middle-class woman by birth, from a distinguished Sheffield family, her life had been destabilized as much by her own ambitions as by the seductive but disorientating opportunities of the war years.

The journey of her life was a movement away from suburban security towards the attractions and dangers of a metropolitan, bohemian world in the midst of war. Though a trained and talented artist, by 1946 she had no regular income and lack of funds was the constant, exhausting issue in her life. She earned a little money from a series of unskilled jobs – turning her hand to anything including the odd session as a film extra. Though she sold some of her artwork to friends and was privately commissioned to paint murals, this never amounted to enough to make ends meet. Her husband provided no maintenance for her or their baby daughter, leaving it to Margery's mother and brother to help her out. This hand-to-mouth existence made Margery very dependent on the goodwill of her friends and the various men she had relationships with. Happy for them to stand her drinks and buy her dinners, she was sometimes similarly happy to sleep with them. She was promiscuous, certainly, but not (as was claimed by Heath after her death) a prostitute. Indeed, Detective Inspector Spooner observed that she was a woman of 'good breeding and education as well as good looks'.[3] A memorable figure on the drinking scene in Chelsea, she was popular and well liked, often seen in the neighbourhood wearing her signature coat – made of ocelot or 'leopardette' – a highly patterned leopardskin fur.

Margery lived a 'bohemian kind of life'[4] amongst a milieu of outsiders: artists, homosexuals (she was friends with Quentin Crisp) and petty criminals. When the war against Fascism had come to an end, the war against crime in London began. In 1946, the Metropolitan Police had 7 million people within its jurisdiction. Thousands of police officers had joined the armed forces; hundreds had been killed or wounded and recruitment had been stopped during hostilities. The Met was 4,000 men below strength – just as a new wave of crime exploded.

Against the depleted ranks of the police force was ranged a new type of criminal – cunning, ruthless and well informed. Many had served in the armed forces, some with distinction, and many more were deserters. They were younger, fitter, harder, more resourceful and more energetic than their pre-war equivalent. Crucially they also operated in a world with a new, post-war morality. Many commodities were scarce or rationed. Cigarettes and liquor carried heavy duties which had increased their prices to four times their pre-war costs. Years of hardship and scarcity had bred a public hungry for the comforting extras of life. Even the most honest citizen couldn't resist the temptation to buy 'something on the side'. The black market was booming and the new style of post-war crook took advantage of it. Housebreaking, robbery, shoplifting, even kidnapping became more common as the police struggled to control increasingly powerful criminal gangs.

In September 1945, Margery was questioned by the police herself. She was riding as one of five passengers in a car driven by a friend she'd known for about two years, Peter Tilley Bailey.[5] Tilley Bailey was a small-time gentleman crook with several convictions for stealing cars and burglary. He had been drinking and had stolen the car, driving eastwards at fifty miles an hour along Knightsbridge on the wrong side of the road, ignoring the traffic lights. The stolen vehicle was recognized by a police patrol car, which soon gave chase. One of the police officers jumped on the running board of the stolen car, but missed his footing and fell off. A member of the public driving a high-powered vehicle then joined in the car chase, ramming Bailey's car but failing to stop him. Tilley Bailey accelerated, but the police car continued to pursue him, following him twice around Hyde Park at great speed. Bailey then abandoned the car at Hyde Park Corner and tried to run away. Shortly afterwards, when he was caught by the police, he said, 'Well, I gave you a good run for it.'[6] Tilley Bailey was arrested and charged at West London Magistrates' Court for dangerous driving and carrying housebreaking implements (these were actually rubber gloves). In his defence, he said that he had been drinking and that it was only a prank. The magistrate, Sir Gervais Rentoul, took a very dim view of the case.

> I cannot conceive anything much worse than the lives and limbs of citizens being at the mercy of a drunken fellow driving round the West End at fifty miles an hour chased by the police.[7]

Tilley Bailey was jailed for six months and disqualified from driving for five years.[8] Margery, claiming she had no idea that the car was stolen, was released without charge. This fringe of small-scale criminality amongst Mayfair crooks and Chelsea opportunists was the world that Margery Gardner inhabited.

Like many of her generation, Margery's short life was bookended by cataclysmic world conflict. She had been born Margery Aimee Brownell Wheat on 21 May 1914, just a month before the assassination of Archduke Ferdinand and his wife plunged the world into the Great War. She was the eldest daughter of John and Elizabeth Wheat, a respectable couple from Sheffield. Her parents had married in 1912 when John Bristowe Wheat had reached the age of fifty-three, claiming that he could not afford to marry until his own father retired from the family business, a venerable firm of solicitors that had been in the family since 1763. His wife, Elizabeth Brownell, was twenty years his junior and also from an old Sheffield family. The couple rented 24 Oakholme Road in Sheffield shortly after their marriage and the family would remain there for the next forty-seven years.

The house remains – now a hall of residence for Sheffield University. It is a spacious semi-detached property built of

local yellow sandstone and sits on a quiet road of similar properties in a leafy suburb of the city near the botanical gardens.
With large rooms, but a small garden, it was a comfortable and
manageable home for the Wheats to bring up their family.
After Margery was born, a boy, Robin, followed in 1915,
then Gilbert in 1916. Two hand-tinted studio photographs
survive of Betty Wheat and her three children, showing a
close and happy family. However, soon after the photograph
was taken, the family was shaken by the loss of young Robin
who died from a constricted bowel before he had reached his
fourth birthday.

Margery attended a local kindergarten in Sheffield, before
going to live with an aunt in Chippenham where she shared
a governess with her cousin.[9] At the age of fifteen, she was
sent to a private school, the Manor House, in Brondesbury,
north-west London, where she stayed until she was eighteen.
Here her interests developed in the arts, which were to
continue throughout her life – singing, acting and painting.
She spent most of her time drawing and was particularly
skilled at drawing horses, but always in motion: battles, bull-
fights and scenes from the Wild West. From an early age,
Margery was impelled by a sense of adventure.

Her drawing abilities led to a Bronze Medal awarded by
the Royal Drawing Society and her headmistress thought the
young Margery precociously talented, 'more than half a
genius'.[10] It was no surprise to her family that, having left
school, Margery wanted to continue her art studies in
London. Her father, however, wouldn't allow her to do so
until she had reached the age of twenty-one, so she returned
to the north and attended the Sheffield School of Art. It was
while studying here that Margery began the first of her ill-
starred relationships with men. According to Mrs Wheat,
Margery fell in love with a man named Moseley whom she
had met in London. But Margery's mother very much

disapproved of the relationship – not thinking it 'a suitable association' – and, in order to affect an end to it, she encouraged Margery to return to London to continue her studies at the Chelsea School of Art.

Mrs Wheat had her way and succeeded in splitting up Moseley and her daughter. But her plans to protect Margery were to have unforeseen and far-reaching consequences. This was 1935 and the 21-year-old Margery Wheat was now a rebellious young woman curious about the world around her. Dark-haired, fashion-conscious and extremely good-looking, she was also as headstrong and single-minded as the horses that she loved to draw. London offered glamour, excitement and freedom, in contrast to the safe but parochial life of her family. Both temperamentally and generationally, Margery was alien to her parents, her father being seventy-five when she was only twenty, very much an eminent Victorian in contrast to his daughter, who was yearning for the new, the extraordinary, the modern.[11]

The temptations and freedoms of metropolitan life enthralled Margery and the idea of London as somewhere to finish her education or pursue a career took second place to her pursuit of adventure. She was distracted from her studies at Chelsea and started socializing with what her mother considered 'undesirable company'. Soon, Mrs Wheat suspected that her daughter's interest in the study of art was little more than a pretext for living an increasingly bohemian life in London. In 1936, she still held sufficient sway with Margery to prevent her making a trip to France with her Chelsea friends, but her influence on her daughter's life was already beginning to wane as Margery established her life – and her independence – in London.

In March 1936, Margery was living in an hotel for single middle-class ladies in South Kensington and was embracing life at the heart of the Chelsea art scene during one of its most colourful periods. Tutors at Chelsea at the time included Henry Moore, William Roberts and Ceri Richards. But it was the social life surrounding the world of Chelsea artists and students that Margery was most enamoured with. Her brother Gilbert later commented:

> [It was] the night life of the capital, and the unusual and unconventional ways of the Chelsea art world that appealed to her. More and more she became involved in a world as far removed from the home she had left as it is possible to imagine.[12]

Margery's letters home during this period are a detailed catalogue of gallery visits, exhibition openings, parties, romances, 'very jolly evenings at the flicks'[13] with drinks and debate at Chelsea's famous Blue Cockatoo restaurant. At one of the parties she attended in 1936, Margery met 22-year-old Peter Gardner. He was the son of a brigadier in the regular army and had been born in Cairo in 1914. Peter's mother had died of malaria when he was only fourteen and from then on he proved a troublesome son. He had been expelled from school and though he trained as an officer at Sandhurst, he had been dismissed before completing the course in 1933. He was estranged from his father, who had married again since the death of his wife and started a new family. In October 1936, Margery's father died at the age of seventy-eight. Soon after, she and Peter Gardner became lovers.

With the political crisis in Europe looming, Margery married Peter at Chelsea Old Church on Cheyne Walk in the spring of 1939. In their wedding photograph, Margery and Peter make a stylish couple and according to Margery's mother, 'she seemed very much in love with him'. But for Margery the reality of married life with Peter was to prove frustrating. With him seemingly unable to hold down a regular job ('he tried several jobs but could never keep a position very long'),[14] the couple moved from rented flat to rented bedsit at various addresses in Chelsea; they never had a secure home of their own. When war was finally declared in September, Gardner took a position with the Air Ministry. Towards the end of 1940, he was called up for service with the RAF as Aircraftsman 1st Class, but never advanced any further, despite his officer-class background and credentials.

Margery accompanied her husband, living with him near each of the RAF camps where he was stationed. When he was based in Blackpool, eager to work, she took an apprentice position at a hairdressing and beauty salon where she had to pay £1 a week 'for the privilege of learning the trade'.[15] It was a far cry from her romantic dream of bohemian, metropolitan life.

In Sheffield too, Mrs Wheat was also facing a difficult war. With Margery now married and Gilbert away fighting in France, she was left alone to face the bombings that targeted the steelworks for which Sheffield was world-famous as well as the armaments factories that had been set up to bolster the war effort. On the 12 and 15 December 1940, Sheffield suffered the hardest night of the Blitz. Opposite Paradise Square, the home of the Wheat family business, the cathedral was damaged and Marples Hotel took a direct hit. Six hundred and eighty people were killed and 1,500 injured. Forty thousand people were made homeless.[16]

Margery and Peter's itinerant married life was soon to feel both internal and external pressure. In the summer of 1941 Margery gave birth prematurely to a stillborn child. But there was little time to mourn. For its size, Chelsea was one of the most heavily blitzed boroughs in London, due to its position on the river, situated close to two power stations and near the centre of government. The worst night of bombing was 16 April 1941 when 450 German bombers attacked south and central London for eight hours. The loss of life and property was considerable. Though the population of Chelsea had dwindled from 58,000 in 1939 to only 16,000 people, 1,000 civilians were killed in the attack, with twice as many seriously injured. Nowhere seemed safe – even the Royal Hospital Infirmary was hit, as were eighteen hospitals and thirteen churches. Chelsea Old Church where Peter and Margery had been married only three years earlier suffered a direct hit, leaving the church a devastated wreck.[17] With the familiar landmarks of London and Chelsea obliterated overnight and the knowledge that home in Sheffield was just as vulnerable to attack, Margery must have been under constant strain. Nothing was secure, nothing was certain and the world around her was in chaos. At the same time, her marriage began to fracture, with Peter revealing himself to be a troubled and needy man – alcoholic and highly strung.

Whilst based with the RAF in Grantham, Peter was hospitalized with a nervous condition. But he still managed to leave hospital every afternoon to go on illicit pub-crawls. Having little money, he began stealing cash from pubs in order to fund his drinking. On 13 October 1941 he stole £10 13s. 11d. from the Red Lion Hotel in Grantham and was duly arrested and charged. When he appeared before Grantham Quarter Sessions on 15 January 1942, he pleaded guilty to a string of offences. The recorder at Grantham thought the case 'a very painful one':

> I have a duty to the public to perform. If you go to prison you will be looked after by the doctor and, if necessary, be treated for your mental weakness, and perhaps your moral weakness, but your long list of serious offences are such that I cannot overlook them. You have been cunning enough at any rate to go on what you call 'pub-crawls' and steal money and commit other larcenies. You have mentality enough for that.[18]

He went on to say that he felt that Gardner was a danger to himself and others and was amazed that a man with his mental-health issues should have been allowed to join the RAF. He was sentenced to two years' hard labour, 'such as [he] could perform'.[19] Hearing the sentence, Margery left the court in tears. She returned home to stay with her mother in Sheffield, where she worked for a time in a factory making parts for aeroplanes. But relations between Margery and her family were strained at this point with regard to Peter; she was still keen to support her husband but her brother Gilbert was very critical of him. After only six months, she decided that she would return to London, find herself a job and fix up a home for Peter on his release from prison. She would need to help him find a job as well, as he had also been discharged from the RAF after his conviction.

But the return to London was not the success that either Margery – or her mother – had hoped for. As she had promised, Margery provided a home for Peter when he was discharged from prison, but after staying with him for several months, she returned to Sheffield again – and this time her feelings towards him seem to have changed. According to her mother, she claimed that he was 'mad and that he had maltreated her and had behaved dreadfully'.[20] Despite this, she returned to him a couple of weeks later. The relationship was by now dysfunctional, with both parties changeable, inconsistent and unreliable.

Margery found herself pregnant again in 1943 and perhaps she felt that this might be the opportunity for a fresh start. She gave birth at St Mary Abbot's hospital in Kensington. The baby, a girl named Melody Ann, was born prematurely on Wednesday 24 May 1944 weighing only 3 lb 2 oz. Since the war had started, St Mary Abbot's was one of the very few London hospitals that would still take maternity cases and it may be Melody's premature arrival that prevented Margery from travelling to Sheffield to have her baby there. Margery proudly sent a postcard to her brother Gilbert in Burma telling him that Melody was adored by the nursing staff and prospering on oxygen and brandy.[21]

Margery was still recuperating at the hospital when, on the morning of 6 June, the Allies began the invasion of Normandy by land, sea and air led by Eisenhower and Montgomery – the greatest combined operation in history.[22] By the end of the day, 150,000 Allied troops had landed in northern France and began their march into occupied Europe. For Londoners like Margery following the Allied advance on the wireless, this was a huge relief. However, exactly a week later, the Germans retaliated and once again Hitler targeted London. He was convinced that the 'secret weapon' he'd been developing would bring the country to its knees. On 13 June the first pilotless planes were sighted in Kent – the deadly V1s.[23]

These weapons caused indiscriminate destruction as they terrorized the city. They gripped the population in constant fear and anxiety as they fell relentlessly at all hours of the day and night. As they left no craters when they fell, their blast power was much greater than conventional bombs. Within three days of the arrival of the first V1, 137,000 buildings were damaged or destroyed, 499 people were killed and 2,000 injured.[24] The flying bombs were soon popularly christened 'doodlebugs' or 'buzz bombs'.

As the doodling or buzzing grew louder, those below waited tensely in case the engine cut out. When the V1 ran out of fuel it crashed to earth with a deep-throated roar followed by a blinding flash and a tall, sooty plume of smoke. If the noise seemed to stop directly above them, people flung themselves on the floor, under the table or into doorways.[25]

The artist, Frances Faviell, visited St Mary Abbot's hospital at this time and observed several heavily pregnant and terrified women begging the nurses to be put under their beds for safety. Faviell asked the nurses how the patients coped with the growing intensity of the doodlebugs. 'They're not too bad . . . sometimes we get one who panics – that's dangerous – they all panic then.'[26]

At 4.05 a.m. on 17 June, the hospital was devastated when a V1 scored a direct hit. The bomb struck the nurses' home and the children's ward. One of the nurses, asleep in the nurses' home, had been wakened by the sound of the approaching rocket. 'It looked like a ball of fire in the sky,' she recalled. 'In a matter of seconds, there was a terrific explosion and the whole place seemed to blow up.'[27]

Nurses, patients and children were trapped under the debris of the building. Five nurses, six children and seven adult patients were killed. Thirty-three casualties were taken to St George's Hospital and the remaining patients, including Margery and her daughter, were evacuated. With London once again a target for destruction from increasingly sophisticated German weapons and the Gardners' marriage under immense strain, Melody was sent to be cared for at the Wellgarth Nursery, a nurses' training college which had evacuated from Hampstead to Bourton House in Shrivenham near Swindon. The fees were paid by Margery's mother from her limited widow's income. Children as young as ten days old up to the age of five were looked after at the nursery which tutored trainee nurses in the care of infants. Melody was one of forty children who lived there. The matron, Miss Talbot, fondly remembered their times at Bourton House, with bicycle rides over the hills, village socials and Christmas Days together with the children. The nursery relocated back to Hampstead in January of 1946, Melody returning with them.

In her correspondence Margery makes frequent reference

to the state of her health and the weekly medication that she was taking. It's possibly due to this that she was not called up by one of the women's services for war work. Her constant worries were about money and work. The only options that seemed open to her were unskilled jobs 'drudging' as a waitress or a cinema usherette, which would only bring in £2 a week. This she wasn't prepared to do. Writing to her mother, she despaired: 'I could do it for someone I loved, I suppose, in order to keep a home together, but I just haven't the heart to do it for myself.'[28]

She had been working as an artists' model but for a two-hour session she'd only earned 7s., so she resolved to join the Film Guild to see if she could get work as a film extra. However, she feared it would be 'a dog's life' of getting up early, with long hours and lots of hanging around doing nothing. The greatest frustration for Margery was that she couldn't find a way of making her art work pay a sufficient income, but with the city in the midst of war, art was not a priority for many. At this point in her life, Margery seemed paralysed by a sense of helplessness and possibly depression, when even the benefit of her former pleasures seemed to elude her. As she wrote in a letter to her mother on 27 July 1945, 'I feel altogether too worried and unhappy to want to draw.'

It was presumably due to this malaise, her deteriorating marriage, her worries about money and her ill-health that she decided against looking after her daughter herself, though she visited Melody frequently and exchanged regular letters with Miss Talbot at the Wellgarth Nursery.

Despite the birth of their daughter, as the war came to an end, the relationship between Margery and Peter seems to have deteriorated. Though Mrs Wheat thought that her daughter and son-in-law had stopped living together by the November of 1945, she suspected that they continued a casual sexual relationship. Peter claimed that he and Margery had got on very well together for four years, but that the relationship then began to fall apart. In his statement after Margery's death, he said that she was drinking heavily and spending too much time in pubs and clubs. Though it is certainly true that Margery lived at the heart of the Chelsea drinking scene, many witnesses challenged this, several saying that they had never seen Margery drunk.

The Gardners' unstable relationship was typical of many of the fractured marriages that floundered in this period. As the war had progressed and ended, the number of divorces had reached record numbers. In 1944 divorces had risen sharply to 12,314 (almost twice the number in 1939) and by 1947 they would reach a peak of 60,190.[29] The war had confronted ordinary men and women with the realities of conflict and the fragility of mortality – and in this war, death, destruction, injury and loss were not the sole preserve of foreign battle-fields, but experienced as never before, close-up, first-hand in the streets of Chelsea and the suburbs of Sheffield. Such experiences led many couples to reassess their relationships in an attempt to redefine their post-war lives.

By VE Day on 8 May 1945, Margery and her family had come through the conflict alive, if not intact, and she now faced a precarious future with no income and a marital relationship that was at best draining and at worst, violent. With the war over, Margery attempted to at least resolve this latter issue by getting a divorce. She arranged to meet the family solicitor, Ralph Macro Wilson, who was also godfather to her daughter. He had known Margery for ten years, having started to look after the family's interests when her father had died. On 2 July, he travelled down from Sheffield to discuss the state of her marriage. Margery met him at Waterloo Station where they discussed the options for divorcing or arranging a legal separation from Peter on grounds of 'venereal disease, desertion and ill treatment'.[30] However, no action was subsequently taken and Margery and Peter remained legally married.

In the last year of her life, relations between Margery and Peter were unresolved, though he had left her in order to live with a woman called 'Tiddles'. In a letter to her mother on the 27 July 1945, Margery was exhausted by emotional and financial problems, but her prevailing worry was now her husband.

The biggest burden of all is Peter and I'll try to make you understand just how I feel about him and what a spot he has put me in. I met him the other day – he saw me coming along the road, dodged into a doorway and then popped out so that I almost ran into his arms almost at once he started begging me to come back to him and told me a lot of lies about his home life with 'T[iddles]' etc. I knew he was lying but he persisted and finally flew into a rage when he tried to find out if I'd seen anything of Tony or anyone else and when I said I wanted a separation he dashed off, having first tried to get back the 10/- he'd just given me. He told me that he wasn't making any money at Car Driving – he's not working at Max's – so couldn't give me any. In reality, he's keeping Tiddles and the child (by her former husband) in a ghastly place miles from here, as she told me the next day. She was nearly crying as she told me what a hell he's making of her life – apparently he talks of me and Melody every night and is terrified of a divorce. The awful thing is that she tells me that she 'would crawl on her knees for him' which is just what he's making her do – they both get dead drunk every night and from what she told me it's pretty plain that Peter is rapidly getting worse – and I feel that I can only thank God for sparing me (if he has) from some awful end.

Now what can I do? I can't go and tell the police – they've got enough on him as it is and his one great boast is that I never will – if I do he'll go inside for failing to pay for my maintenance and

*what would happen to that little bunch of misery and her child? By
this he means the woman he is living with now. At the same time
it's not fair that he should be supporting her instead of me — his
lawful wife. Now, can you understand why I seem to be doing
nothing? I just can't bring myself to administer the death blow —
which is what it would amount to. Everyone else says I must do so
and have no pity for him and only feel very sorry for me — but I
understand Peter better than anyone — and I know he's not responsible for what he does. However, as I realize it can't go on like this
— I'm being pressed on all sides — I will see my lawyer friend, with
Michael and discuss with him the possibility of writing to P[eter]
and telling him what I intend to do.*

*I must stop now — I shall be very grateful for what you can spare,
tho' everyone's been very sweet in helping me out — but I will pay
you back over and over some day, I hope.*

All my love,

Margy[31]

In August 1945, Margery met a man named Daniel Hamilton
Shields at one of her local pubs, the Lord Nelson in the King's
Road. At the time Shields was serving as a private in the 13th
Holding Battalion based in Herne Bay. They were immediately attracted to each other. Margery told Shields about her
unstable married life and that her husband had been in prison.
As she was apparently penniless at the time he met her, Shields
suggested that Margery should come and live with him in
Herne Bay. He had a friend there called Ruth Wright who
could offer her a room for a while at her home in Tankerton,
near Whitstable. With little to keep her in London and no
other options, Margery followed Shields to Herne Bay.[32]

Shields was on the permanent staff of the regiment and had
a sleeping out pass. With Margery now settled in lodgings
with Shields' friend Ruth, a young widow, he spent the next

two weeks – or the nights at least – with Margery, returning to camp every day. Ruth found Margery not very talkative, but she did glean that she was separated from her husband and had been working as a film extra. She felt that Shields and Margery were very much attracted to one another. She was also aware that Margery had no money and when they left, it was Shields who paid the bill.[33]

After a couple of weeks, Shields tired of the daily journey from Tankerton to Herne Bay, so he arranged more convenient lodgings for himself and Margery with a Mrs Hambrook in Herne Bay itself. They were to stay here from early October to December of 1945. Shields and Margery signed in as 'Mr and Mrs Hamilton', but after a few weeks, Mrs Hambrook discovered that they weren't married and challenged Margery, living out of wedlock not being considered respectable at the time. Desperate not to be turned out of their lodgings, Margery explained that she had separated from her husband because of his drinking. He'd been pestering her to get back together again, but she had refused. She confided in Mrs Hambrook that when she had first met Daniel Shields, she had been destitute and that he had been extremely kind to her ever since. Margery may well have been overstating her financial peril to both Shields and Mrs Hambrook, as Mrs Wheat was sending her money via the Post Office at Herne Bay throughout this period. Mrs Hambrook allowed them both to stay. But, as ever in Margery's life, this moment of security was not to last for long.

At the beginning of November 1945, Shields was posted to Folkestone pending discharge from the army, but Margery wanted to stay on in Herne Bay. He continued to believe that his relationship with Margery was ongoing and was surprised when he returned one weekend to find her with a pilot who had been working on the jet plane record attempt at Herne Bay. The relationship with Shields deteriorated into recriminations about Margery's flirtations with other men. After a terrible row in Folkestone, Margery returned to London.

In the New Year of 1946, Margery bumped into Shields again in the Lord Nelson in Chelsea, where they had met the year before. Shields was anxious to have a suitcase returned to him that she had borrowed. Margery told him that she had lent it to her husband but would get it back from him. She also said that she had left some of her clothes at their lodgings in Herne Bay and wondered if he might collect them for her. Shields obligingly did so, collecting her belongings and even paying some money she owed to Mrs Hambrook. He met Margery at the Lord Nelson to give her her things. They then spent the night together in Notting Hill at the Connaught Hotel, Pembridge Square, booking in as 'Mr and Mrs Shields'. This was yards away from the Pembridge Court Hotel where she was to die six months later.

Margery's brother Gilbert was now twenty-nine and had recently been demobilized. Gilbert had joined the Territorial Army in 1939 and as a 2nd lieutenant had been sent to France with the British Expeditionary Force in April 1940. He survived the evacuation of Dunkirk and after two years of anti-invasion duties he had been sent to India. He later fought in the Burma campaign of 1944 as a platoon commander. He was then promoted to company commander and subsequently to intelligence officer at Divisional H.Q. after the capture of Mandalay.[34] It was while he was in Burma that Gilbert decided that he would not be returning to take up his position in the family firm as a solicitor. His father now deceased, the future of the business had fallen to him. But Gilbert's wartime experiences had led him to discover his true vocation as a teacher and in 1946 his old headmaster offered him a position at a prep school in

Derbyshire. In contrast to his sister, Gilbert Wheat was very much his parents' son, and even as a young man displayed a reserved and dignified character with a great sense of moral responsibility. Though very aware of his sister's frailties and temperament he was both supportive and kind to her and began to supplement her income with an allowance of £4 a week whilst she looked for the steady job that continued to elude her.

In the New Year, Gilbert travelled down from Derbyshire and visited Margery in her flat at 59 Earls Court Square. He found that she had only recently been discharged from St Mary Abbot's hospital and was recuperating from a miscarriage. Margery had previously told her mother that she was pregnant with Peter's child. Fortunately, Peter and his new girlfriend, Tiddles, had been present when Margery started to miscarry and had succeeded in getting her to the hospital.

After the miscarriage, Margery recovered and moved to Bramham Gardens, her final address, where her mother visited several times. At around this time, Margery confided to Mrs Wheat that she had a new boyfriend, but never revealed his name. She said that he was a 'nice quiet man who used to turn up for breakfast and bring her something to cook and he would sit with her in the evenings'.[35] In all probability, this was Peter Tilley Bailey, who had known Margery for about two years, but had only known her well since the beginning of that year. In January, they had bumped into each other at the Lord Nelson shortly after he had been released from prison having served his sentence for driving a stolen car along Knightsbridge. By June, Tilley Bailey was spending two or three nights a week with Margery at her flat in Earls Court Square and then at Bramham Gardens. He held a key to Margery's flat, where he was known by the landlady as 'Peter Gardner', but he was to offer a very fragile stability.[36] Though the relationship was exclusive on Margery's side, whether she was aware of it or not, Tilley Bailey continued to have relationships with other women.

Like many women in this period, Margery Gardner clutched at the sexual freedom that the war had offered, but then struggled with the harsh consequences – a hand-to-mouth existence with no security and little consistency in a period already fraught with hardship. Her last letters to her mother also suggest some sort of recurring gynaecological problem as well as an overwhelming sense of exhaustion and depression ('my nerves have gone to hell'). One of her friends, Iris Humphrey, observed that in the seven or eight years she had known her, she felt that Margery had 'changed':

> When I knew Margery some years ago she was a nice girl and I could not help noticing how she had changed in every way. She seemed to have become cheap and acted as if she would not have minded who she was with.[37]

Another close friend, Joyce Frost, offered a more compassionate understanding of her character:

> [Margery] was a very straightforward sort of girl with no harm in her at all, and very quiet, who never made male acquaintanceships for money. She was content to spend the night with a man after a few drinks for company.[38]

And perhaps this was at the heart of her erratic emotional life. She wanted company or, as her mother had said, 'a nice quiet man . . . to sit with her in the evenings'. Instead of which she crawled from pub to pub, night after night, living on hand-outs, cadging cigarettes and comfort from a series of feckless men.

From the perspective of the early twenty-first century, Margery Gardner seems very much a woman formed and defined by the times in which she lived. But she was also a woman ahead of her time. Like Tennessee Williams' Blanche Dubois,[39] she is revealed, in various witness statements and her own letters, to be a highly creative woman in challenging circumstances, emotionally needy, trying to locate a haven for herself in a broken, half-familiar world where she resorted – of necessity – to some pretty desperate choices; dependent if not on the kindness, then on the indulgence of strangers.

CHAPTER FOUR

Thursday 20 June 1946

.

Joyce Frost had been friends with Margery Gardner since the late 1930s, but had lost contact with her for a couple of years during the war. They had bumped into each other again at a Victory Celebration Party on the rain-sodden 'V' Day, 8 June, which had been organized by Peter Gardner in Kensington.[1] A few days later, they had seen each other again at the Trevor Arms in Knightsbridge. From thereon they had picked up their friendship, meeting at the Nag's Head in Kinnerton Street, a pub much frequented by guardsmen from the nearby Knightsbridge Barracks. When they met for drinks, Joyce noticed that Margery always drank beer, but she was almost always broke. Joyce was thirty-three, had been married, but was separated from her husband. She lived in a flat at 51 Ennismore Gardens near

Hyde Park. A lodger, Desmond O'Dowd, shared the flat with her.[2]

On Wednesday night, 19 June, Joyce was drinking in the Nag's Head at about eight o'clock with her lodger. She caught sight of Margery in the back bar of the pub, just inside the door. Margery was with two men at the time whom she introduced to Joyce as 'Ken' and 'Jimmy'.[3] The latter was undoubtedly Heath, fitting his description perfectly: '[Joyce] distinctly remember[ed] he had a caterpillar badge in the left lapel buttonhole of his jacket.'[4] As the group chatted, Heath told Joyce that he was attached to the South African Air Force and had his own plane. She commented on Heath's caterpillar badge and he was only too delighted to tell her, 'That's for baling out.'[5] It seemed that Margery had been introduced to Heath a few weeks before. He had only recently made the Nag's Head one of his locals as he had previously been stationed abroad.

That night, Margery left the pub at about 10 p.m., but not before sitting down with Joyce and her lodger again, with Heath standing near them. Margery excitedly told Joyce that 'Jimmy is going to fly me to Brussels or Paris'. The two women arranged to meet for lunch the next day.

Thursday 20 June was the last day of Margery Gardner's life.

Peter Tilley Bailey called round to see Margery for about ten minutes at about 11 a.m. in the morning, finding her still in bed. He had stayed over at Bramham Gardens on the previous Sunday evening, as well as another night that week. Margery told him that she had met somebody that she hadn't seen for some time. She didn't say who it was or when she was going to meet him – and she may well have been testing Peter, trying to provoke a reaction from him.[6] The status of the relationship between Margery and Tilley Bailey is hard to read. He retained his own flat in Coliseum Terrace in

Regent's Park, yet spent two or three nights of the week at Bramham Gardens. They were sufficiently close for him to leave his identity card with Margery,[7] but though she was in dire need of money, he doesn't seem to have offered to help her out financially.

Just before lunch, Margery met Joyce and her lodger for a drink at the Packenham Pub on Knightsbridge Green. From there, they headed to the Lido Café which was opposite another of their locals, the Paxton's Head. Joyce paid for Margery's lunch, as she was broke again. After eating they went over the road to the Paxton's Head for another drink. O'Dowd left, leaving the two women alone together. They each had a glass of beer and Joyce subbed Margery some ciga-rettes. Margery was dressed in the same clothes she had worn the night before – her pale grey two-piece suit, a greyish brown cape made of possum fur, 'very dark nail varnish' and an unusual pair of earrings made from flowery fabric. Margery complained of a stain on her right-hand skirt pocket and went to buy a bottle of 'Thawpit' from Barnes' the chemist next door. She told Joyce that the shilling she had just spent on the cleaning fluid was her last, but it'd be worth it as she wanted to look her best that night.

'Why do you want to look your best tonight? Are you meeting somebody particular?' asked Joyce.

'An old boyfriend. Haven't seen him in a while.'

'Anyone I know?'

'No.'

'And this mystery man – is he on a promise?'

'Absolutely.'

According to Peter Tilley Bailey, Margery had been faith-ful to him throughout their relationship, but perhaps she was beginning to realize that this was not reciprocated. Despite her fidelity, her relationship with Tilley Bailey had not resulted in any tangible support from him. If Margery was contemplating being wined, dined and romanced by her date that evening, it would be the first time she had done so since she had started her relationship with Tilley Bailey.

Margery and Joyce carried on from the Paxton's Head to Cooper's Stores on the Brompton Road where Joyce bought some food. They then walked on to Joyce's flat in Ennismore Gardens. On the way to the flat, it started to rain. Margery took her headscarf from her handbag – an RAF scarf – and covered her head from the shower. When they got back to the flat, they continued chatting for about a quarter of an hour. Margery remembered that she was supposed to see her lady doctor (the Dr Kelly that she mentions in her letters to her mother), but she'd have to put it off until the next day. Whilst at the flat, Margery asked if Joyce would mind if she drew her picture? Joyce thought Margery a very good artist and readily agreed. While she was drawing, they continued their conversation.[8]

'Will you be in the Nag's Head tonight?' asked Joyce. 'Desmond and I are going.'

'I might do,' said Margery, then asked, 'Do you know Jimmy's surname?'

'How could I? I only met him last night.'

'Flying abroad. Exciting, isn't it? His own plane as well.'

'Margy. Do you have any money for this date tonight? How about I lend you £1?'

'I'll be fine.'

'Take it. You said you spent your last shilling on the "Thawpit".'

'I'll be all right once I meet my date tonight.'

Margery's date was never identified, but she was very clear that he was nobody Joyce knew. In no way did she suggest that she would be meeting either Jimmy Heath or Peter Tilley Bailey. About a quarter past three, Margery stopped her drawing as time was getting on.

'I want to get back to the flat. I have washing and ironing to do before tonight.' Margery paused. 'Joyce . . .'

'Yes?'

'I don't suppose I *could* borrow a few pennies, could I?'

'Of course you can.'

'Just for my fare home.'

'How much do you need?'

'Fivepence?'

Joyce gave Margery the 5d. for her tube fare home to Bramham Gardens. She would never see her friend alive again.

The physical geography of the Earls Court and South Kensington areas that Margery lived and socialized in would have been very familiar to her today: terraces of tall, stuccoed buildings, graced with entrance pillars, and Edwardian red-brick town houses with leaded windows, all crouched in the shadow of the great cultural edifices on the Cromwell Road – the Victoria and Albert Museum and the Museum of Natural History. But the inhabitants of the area have changed dramatically since the mid-forties. Gone are the bedsits, boarding houses and bomb sites that Margery would have known, replaced by duplex apartments and day nurseries with clipped box hedging. Bramham Gardens itself is a shady garden square in Earls Court. The flat, at number 24, was in a slim, five-storey red-brick terrace. It is now part of a retirement home and retains an air of down-at-heel gentility; the brickwork dulled by years of soot and traffic, yellowing net curtains draped at windows permanently fastened by decades of paint.

Margery successfully managed to clean the stain from her skirt pocket with the 'Thawpit', as she wore the same outfit that evening. Leaving the flat, she put her door key in her brown leather handbag and walked out past the derelict house next door, uninhabitable since the Blitz, and made her way to the Nag's Head.

Often hurriedly grabbed at the first sound of an air raid, Margery's handbag offers a revealing and intimate snapshot of her life.[9] Amongst some pencils and a notebook bearing her name was a pair of imitation suede gloves. Her cigarette case contained eight cigarettes. Margery – not vain, but always trying to make the best of her appearance – wore glasses occasionally and in their red case, together with her spectacles, there was a cheque for £4, payable to her husband. She also had a pair of white-framed sunglasses for the sunny weather that June promised but never delivered that summer. As well as a powder compact, a powder puff, a box of eyeliner, two broken combs and a hair clip, Margery had another small make-up purse containing lipstick, cream and rouge. Knowing she was expecting her period soon she carried three Tampax sanitary towels just in case, as well as a tube of Gynomin tablets ('the scientifically balanced, Antiseptic and Deodorant Contraceptive Tablet').[10] In a black leather wallet, she kept a large volume of letters from her family and a variety of male friends as well as some personal photographs, including one of her young daughter, Melody, now two years old. In her bag, she also kept her identity card, which would later help the police to identify her body – as well as an application for the replacement of some clothing coupons to buy the new clothes that she so desperately wanted.

Three pawn tickets spoke of the unstable fortunes that Margery had suffered in the preceding months. She had pawned an overcoat in February of 1945, one of the coldest months of that year, a possum fur cape in April of 1946 (which she must have redeemed as she was wearing it that night), and a typewriter. At the bottom of the bag was a single pink handkerchief, clean and folded – perhaps even washed and ironed by her that afternoon – and bearing the initials 'M. A. B. Gardner'. In her purse Margery had a single silver sixpence and two coppers, a total of 8d. (a pint of Guinness cost 11d. at the time). Even as she stepped out of her door and into the streets of Earls Court, Margery's options on the night of 20 June were extremely limited.

By 6.30 that evening, Margery was in the Nag's Head, where she chatted to the landlady, Eva Cole.[11] She told Mrs Cole that she was waiting for a telephone call, which finally came after she had been there about three-quarters of an hour. A few moments after she put the phone down she walked out of the pub, saying 'Goodnight' to Mrs Cole. She didn't indicate who the call was from, but it may well have been her friend Trevethan Frampton, whom she then went on to meet. She walked to the nearby Trevor Arms, across the road from Knightsbridge tube station where she met Frampton, an art student with whom she had been friendly since the beginning of the year. They stayed together for about an hour and during this time were joined by a number of men, two or three of whom Margery had met before. One of these was Jimmy Heath.

Heath asked Margery if she would have dinner with him later that evening, but she told him that she had already arranged to have dinner with an army captain who was in the bar. Margery's friend Frampton left at 8.30 p.m. to go back to his hotel for dinner. He told Margery that if she was free later, he would meet her at the Renaissance Club in Harrington Road. He would aim to get there himself for about 9.30 p.m. Margery said she'd most likely join him later, after she'd had dinner with her date.

However, the army captain that Margery had arranged to meet that night had met an old school friend at the bar and left the Trevor Arms with him, leaving her alone. All that Margery had in her purse was small change – not enough to buy a drink and certainly not enough to buy herself a proper meal. Catching sight of her alone, Heath went to the bar and brought her over to some of his RAF friends, introducing her as a 'great little scout'. The four men and Margery drank on for a couple of hours during which some half-dozen further rounds were ordered. Seeing that Heath was apparently flush with cash, Margery saw an opportunity to salvage her evening – and her chances of dinner at somebody else's expense. She wondered if she *could* take Heath up on his earlier offer? She would love to have dinner with him. Heath by now was spending his way through the £30 (an average month's wages at the time) he had acquired earlier that day and seemed like he had money to burn. So it was that Margery, not wanting to be alone at the bar and not having enough money to buy her own drinks or dinner, effectively sealed her fate.

Heath and Margery then left the Trevor Arms and went to the Normandie Hotel for dinner. They left between 9.30 and 10 p.m. and popped in to the nearby Torch Club for a drink. They then decided to go to the Panama Club, which had a late licence, where Heath had entertained Yvonne Symonds only the weekend before. Heath signed the yellow Visitors' Form 'Lt. Col. Heath and friends'.

Heath and Margery went up to the main bar on the second floor, with Margery carrying her opossum coat over her arm. Almost immediately they bumped into Peter Tilley Bailey accompanied by 25-year-old Catherine Hardie, a nurse at Battersea General Hospital. Given that Peter had spent two of the previous four nights at her flat, Margery may well have been surprised to meet him so blatantly dating another woman. Margery and Peter curtly acknowledged each other, without introducing their companions. Margery said nothing, but there was certainly a frostiness at this meeting. When Catherine Hardie was later questioned about Margery's movements that evening, she claimed that she deliberately ignored her: 'When I am with a party of men, I don't look around, especially as Peter Bailey had passed the time of day with her.'[12]

Another of Tilley Bailey's party that evening, Ronald Birch, was also a casual acquaintance of Margery's. At one point, he noticed her in company with Heath at the bar. They were holding hands and though she seemed very attentive to Heath, he appeared 'slightly indifferent' to her. Birch later recalled: 'All the time she stood at the bar she appeared to be trying to promote [Heath's] interest, so rather obviously that I thought that she did it deliberately to annoy Peter Bailey.'[13]

Margery then ran into another friend of hers, Iris Humphrey, a civil servant who lived in Earls Court Square. She had known Margery for about eight or nine years.[14] They had been very friendly before the war, but had lost touch during it when Iris had been evacuated to Bath. Since Iris had moved back to London in April 1946, the two women had met in various pubs around Earls Court. Iris was sitting in the club room by the dance floor with her friend John Le Mee Power when Margery entered with Heath. Margery called 'hallo' over to their table. When Iris and Le Mee Power got up to dance, Iris went over to the table that Margery had sat down at with her handsome companion.

'Would you mind looking after my things whilst we have a dance?'

'Of course,' said Margery.

She took Iris' handbag and copy of *Vogue* and put it on the table in front of her. Iris and Le Mee Power went off to the dance floor before Margery could introduce them to Heath. After a short while, Heath and Margery got up to dance themselves. Iris and Le Mee Power left the dance floor and went to collect her bag and magazine. For the next hour, Iris observed Margery and Heath sitting at their table, holding each other's hands, smoking and drinking – with Heath rubbing his hand against Margery's leg. At the time, Iris commented to Le Mee Power that she thought that Margery's companion looked 'dissipated', with big bags under his eyes. She remarked, with terrible prescience, that 'Margery was in for a bad time' that night.[15]

Phyllis, the waitress, first noticed Heath and Margery at about 11 p.m. when she checked to see that nobody was drinking alcohol without a meal, in accordance with their licence. Phyllis had seen both Heath and Margery at the club before, hanging around with what she called the 'Chelsea Crowd', led by Peter Tilley Bailey. Heath pulled at Phyllis' apron string, which caused her apron to fall loose. Phyllis turned round and he said 'Repeat the order', so she went to get them some more drinks. When Phyllis arrived with the drinks, the couple were getting up to dance again and this time Margery told her 'Repeat the order'. When Phyllis came back for the money (6s.), Heath said, 'I owe you for the last one. Aren't I honest?'[16] According to Phyllis, the couple sat on their own table all night and didn't speak to anyone else. Iris Humphrey and Le Mee Power left about 11.30, leaving Margery at the club with Heath. The band stopped playing at midnight but members had twenty minutes drinking-up time. Peter Tilley Bailey and Catherine Hardie left the club about ten minutes after midnight, but couldn't see Margery to say 'goodbye'. Perhaps smarting from Peter's date with a younger woman, at some point during the evening, Margery consented to go back to Heath's hotel – possibly for a nightcap – just as he had suggested to Pauline Brees in February.

Outside the Panama Club, Harold Harter was driving his taxi eastwards along Old Brompton Road in the direction of South Kensington tube station.[17] About 12.20 a.m., Heath

was leaving the entrance to the Panama Club, talking with
Margery. He saw Harter's cab and started to walk along the
pavement to the corner of Thurloe Street, with his hand up,
hailing it. Harter stopped on the opposite side of the obelisk
in the middle of the road. The couple walked across the road,
Heath holding Margery's hand as she dragged slightly behind
him.[18]

According to Harter, Heath asked Margery where a particular address was, but she didn't seem to know. She was
currently living in Bramham Gardens in Earls Court, less than
ten minutes' walk away from the Panama Club down Old
Brompton Road. Given the convenience of her flat they
would have to be travelling for something specific to justify a
taxi ride. Heath's suitcase, of course, was at the Pembridge
Court Hotel with everything it contained. Heath then
directed Harter to Pembridge Gardens in Notting Hill, which
was just under two miles away. Harter observed that Margery
'seemed to be in a drunken stupor' and when Heath opened
the door of the cab for her to get in, she had walked to the
other side of him 'as if she didn't know where she was'. Heath
looked around for her asking, 'Where the hell are you?' Once
they were safely in the cab, Harter noticed that Margery was
lying back and Heath had his arm around her.

According to Peter Tilley Bailey, Margery had never spent
a night away from her flat since they had been together, so
this was the first time she was to do so. It was also the first
time she had been observed in an extremely drunken state –
this perhaps exacerbated by her feelings towards Tilley Bailey
as well as the large amount of cash that Heath had been
spending at the bar.

After about ten minutes, they arrived in Notting Hill and
Harter turned his cab into Pembridge Gardens.

'Whereabouts do you want?'

Heath told Harter, 'This will do.'

Margery said nothing and 'appeared not to notice what was going on and she did not seem to hear me'. Harter pulled up about fifty yards short of the Pembridge Court Hotel on the left-hand side. Heath got out of the cab first – his face illuminated by the light of the meter. He went to help Margery out of the cab. After about a minute, he got her out on the pavement where she stood 'as though in a stupor and had no interest in anything'. Heath left her and turned to Harter.

'How much is that?'

'One shilling and ninepence.'

With the precision of a very drunk man trying not to appear so, Heath slowly counted out 2s. and 2d. (a small tip), fumbling with his change under the meter light. Once he had paid the cab, Heath put his arm around Margery's waist and the couple walked the fifty yards ahead towards the Pembridge Court Hotel, effectively holding each other up. Harter watched from his cab as they disappeared through the gate outside the hotel and up the steps to the porticoed entrance. This was the last time that Margery Gardner was seen alive by anyone other than the man who killed her.

Earlier that evening, back at her flat in Bramham Gardens, surrounded by her own artwork, Margery had left an exercise book in which she had been writing (in pencil – she had pawned her typewriter) the first few chapters of a novel about a girl called 'Julie', not unlike herself – or at least, Margery's own vision of herself. Autobiographical in tone, the story poignantly articulated Margery's hopes and disappointments.

> Julie had not been with us more than a couple of weeks before she knew all the bars, all the cafes, all the clubs. She had green eyes and dark hair that fell on her neck and shoulders like a hood . . .
>
> People really liked her to talk to. She was fresh and vital

– different, amusing too, and she was innocent. She had girl
friends, although she got on better with men. She was bold
and reckless in those days, finding her feet and her own values
– and her mistakes.

Always new places, new faces, for Julie was out to conquer
the world. And she did conquer the world. At least she
conquered one bitter bit of London. It was that bit of London
by the river.

'What are you doing with your life?' She would open her
eyes and say, 'Enjoying yourself for the first time. Finding a
dream that is real.'[19]

But Margery Gardner's dream wasn't real. As with much in
her life, the story was never finished and like her existence
itself, brought to a tragic, abrupt end.

CHAPTER FIVE

Detective Inspector Spooner

At 3.15 p.m. on the afternoon of Friday 21 June, Divisional Detective Inspector Reginald Spooner was in his office at Hammersmith Police Station when he received a telephone call from one of his inspectors at Notting Hill, Shelley Symes. As soon as Spooner answered the telephone, the gravity of Symes' voice made it clear they had a serious case on their hands.

'Guvnor,' said Symes quietly, 'we've got one.'[1]

This call was to be the first step of a manhunt that was to extend the length and breadth of the country – even to ports and airfields – and which was to involve as many as 40,000 officers. Spooner's character and his skill as a police investigator were to be tested in an emotionally gruelling and intellectually demanding investigation, the success of which was to rely on thousands of man-hours, but would also pivot on the most extraordinary coincidences that would seem the preserve of fiction. Ironically, the case would also result in both pursued and pursuer becoming famous, indeed infamous – Heath as one of the most vilified criminals of the twentieth century and Spooner as the most celebrated detective of his generation. Spooner's superintendent, Nick Carter, later regarded him as 'the greatest detective this force has ever known'.[2] Years later, when Spooner wrote his memoirs, he started by writing about Heath, the case that defined his career.

Though they came from similar backgrounds – the respectable but financially anxious middle class – Heath and Spooner couldn't have been more different. The charismatic and seductive Heath was the antithesis of the cautious Spooner. Neville Heath was flamboyant and extravagant – a honey-tongued playboy spending his time and money in bars and nightclubs in the pursuit of pleasure and sex. Reginald Spooner (always 'Reg' to friends and colleagues) was a modest, precise workaholic who was extremely careful with money. In stark contrast to the womanizing Heath, Spooner dated only one other girl before becoming engaged to his future wife, Myra Newman, at the age of twenty-one.

Reg Spooner was a Londoner born in 1903 into the comfortable middle-class suburb of Upper Norwood and raised in Wood Green. He regarded himself very much as a cockney. His wife was 'my old woman', his boss always 'Guv'nor'. He prided himself on his in-depth knowledge of London, its dark hidden places and its people.

Spooner's early years were dominated by a series of personal crises that were to shape his attitudes in later life – particularly regarding money and security. These would preoccupy him throughout his working life and would ultimately guide him in his choice of career. His father, Jabez Spooner, worked for the family firm, a business transfer agency dealing with stocks and shares based in the Smithfield region of London. But Spooner's grandfather Alfred, who headed the family business, was known for his 'extravagant way of living'. Though successful in business, he had very little cash saved for emergencies. He never thought of the future. When he ran into a spell of bad luck on the markets, he realized he had nothing to keep the business or his family afloat; the business collapsed. In March 1904, Alfred was summoned to court over his mounting debts. He never turned up. Unable to cope with the shame of financial ruin, and the dire position into which he had placed both the family's business and their homes, Alfred Spooner shot himself in the head. The coroner recorded that he had taken his own life whilst temporarily insane.

Alfred's suicide left the family business – and Spooner's parents, Jabez and Blanche – in a financial crisis that initiated a domestic one. The family home in Upper Norwood, south of the river, had to be sold and the Spooners moved to a smaller, more modest home in Hornsey, north London. But the family hadn't seen the last of their worries. In 1911, at the age of thirty-four, Jabez became paralysed after having been involved in a fight. He died shortly afterwards, leaving his widow and her two young sons, Reg (8) and Rodney (6), without savings, insurance or security of any kind. As the widow of a professional man, Blanche didn't qualify for a widow's pension. Having neither skills nor training, and no means of income, Blanche was forced to sell the house in Hornsey and most of their possessions. Together with her sons, she moved to her parents' house in Elmar Road in Wood Green. At the age of thirty-five, Blanche Spooner, once a comfortable suburban housewife, became an apprentice embroideress. It was a humiliating fall. She would never let her young sons forget the value of money and the sheer struggle of life without it.

The Spooner brothers were educated at the local Lordship Lane School in Ellenborough Road, just a half-hour walk from their home. Class sizes were large (often of forty or more) and each class contained three age groups, as was the norm during this period. In 1917 in the midst of the First World War, too young to be called up for active service, fourteen-year-old Reg left school without qualifications. His priority was to bring in some money to help the household so his working life began as an office boy for the Hearts of Oak Assurance Company, based on the Holborn Viaduct. His pay, though only a few shillings to start with, eased the financial burden on his mother. Every week he would hand her his pay packet – unopened – and she gave him back a shilling to spend for himself. By application and study, Spooner rose to the position of clerk by 1923.

In 1924, Spooner applied to become a police officer. Though his maternal grandfather had been a police sergeant in the nineteenth century, it appears that his desire to join the police force was inspired by a need for security, rather than a desire to follow in his grandfather's footsteps. Even as a probationer, he would earn £3 10s. a week – 10s. more than he had been earning at the Assurance Company. But most importantly it offered a career with a regular income and a pension. Knowing that he would have to care for his future wife and family as well as his mother at some point in the future was critical in Spooner choosing the police as a career.

By the time he was twenty-one, Spooner was an athletic man, 6 feet 1 inch tall, with strong, handsome features and dark, thick, wavy hair. He was perfect force material. On 19 February 1924, he was summoned to Scotland Yard with sixty other candidates. Competition was fierce, with many ex-servicemen and guardsmen at the time also keen for the security of a police career and pension. By the end of the medical and academic tests, only nine candidates remained; Spooner was one of them. PC 475 'J' started on probation in Victoria Park, east London, on 7 March 1924.

From the start, Spooner set his sights on joining the Criminal

Investigations Department (CID) as a detective. After serving his time as a uniformed officer, which he disliked intensely (his girlfriend Myra never saw him in uniform once), he joined the CID in 1928, where he excelled. At the same time, Myra was training to be a Norland Nanny based at the Norland Training Centre in Hyde Park Gate. They were engaged on 9 March 1927 – Myra's twenty-first birthday. A two-year engagement followed whilst Spooner saved enough money for the wedding. He wrote to Myra explaining the reasons for his caution:

> It will be up to us during our engagement to save all we can so that we can meet all the initial expenses of our prospective home as soon as we get married. This will be much better than following the example of most other married couples who buy their homes a bit at a time.[3]

He was not prepared to borrow money, nor to buy on HP (hire purchase). Going into debt was anathema to him – a clear indication of the ghosts that haunted him from his family's past.

As a young detective, Spooner prospered and soon attracted the attention of his superior officers. He found that he had an amazing facility for remembering names, incidents and places; he became renowned for his 'card index' memory. He was a master of detail and took meticulous notes of everything, never throwing anything away. As his career continued he kept notebooks with newspaper clippings of every case he had been involved in. He was hugely industrious, putting in hours on the job beyond the call of duty (and these were already long – 9 a.m. to 2 p.m., 6 p.m. to 10 p.m.), much to the chagrin of his long-suffering wife. He had married Myra in 1929 and she had given birth to their daughter, Jean, a year later. With Spooner volunteering to work well into the night with only one day off, it was clear to Myra from the beginning of their marriage that family life would always come second. The landlady of his favourite pub in Limehouse, the Hole in the Wall, noted that Spooner 'never seemed to go home. I thought if I were his wife I wouldn't put up with a life like that.' Essentially, Spooner was married to the job. He continued to impress his superiors and received several commendations, including one for his part in the investigation of the 'Bow Cinema Murder', his first murder case that resulted in a conviction.

In the early morning of Tuesday 7 August 1934, 35-year-old Dudley Hoard, the manager of the Palace Cinema in Bow Road, had answered the doorbell to his staff flat above the picture house. On opening the door, he was attacked by an assailant armed with an axe. The two men fought in the entrance to the cinema balcony and after fourteen blows to the head, Hoard was left for dead and the takings cleared from the previous bank holiday weekend. The police investigating the crime couldn't work out how the intruder had gained entry to the cinema itself as it was protected by a locked iron grille. Despite the fact that the grille appeared to be securely locked, Spooner was convinced that this was the method of entry. He shook the grille until it came loose. It took a knack to open it. This, thought Spooner, together with the knowledge that the bank holiday takings remained on the premises, would only have been known to somebody who worked in the cinema. Spooner was led to nineteen-year-old John Frederick Stockwell, a cinema usher. Despite trying to cover his tracks with a suicide note, Stockwell was traced to Yarmouth where he was arrested. Despite an appeal, Stockwell was hanged, the first man Spooner was to send to the gallows. He would not be the last.

In November 1935 at the age of thirty-two, Spooner had been promoted as first class sergeant to 'Central One', commonly known as the 'Murder Squad', and transferred to Scotland Yard. Central One dealt not only with murders but crimes that involved several police divisions and government departments. Consequently Spooner gained a huge breadth of experience in a wealth of criminal activities including fraud, murder and assault. In 1938 he was appointed as Central One's officer in charge of pornography and in November of that year, he was promoted to detective inspector at Marylebone Police Station.

A considered, careful man, Spooner was also a heavy drinker and chain-smoker.[4] Even in this period when drinking and smoking 'on the job' was both common and universally tolerated in the force, Spooner's habits seem to have been extreme. Albert Pierrepoint, the public executioner during this period, became a friend of Spooner's and remembered that he always had a cigarette in his mouth, both on duty and off. 'There was always cigarette ash falling onto his waistcoat which he did not bother to brush off,' he recalled. Even in the 1930s Spooner was renowned for his smoker's cough.

When war broke out in 1939, Spooner and his family were on holiday on the Isle of Wight. They had barely settled in when a telegram arrived ordering his immediate return to London; all police leave had been cancelled. Spooner originally insisted that Myra and their nine-year-old daughter Jean should evacuate to the country, but Myra was reluctant for them to live apart for the duration, so they eventually settled in a house in Palmer's Green, also offering a room to Spooner's mother, Blanche, who was to remain with them for the next twenty-two years. Throughout the war, the correspondence between Spooner and his wife continued to be dominated by his anxieties about money, despite the fact that he was now earning a very healthy £11 a week. With a curious reticence, even up to his death in 1963, Spooner never told his wife how much money he earned.

He was not to see active combatant service during the war, but in June 1940 was seconded from the police force to MI5, the British Secret Service. He was appointed as Deputy Head of B57, a special anti-espionage and anti-sabotage unit that had been set up by Leonard Burt, a former boss of his.[5] The unit was based in a cell at Wormwood Scrubs Prison. Due to their top-secret nature, few of Spooner's investigations during the war were reported by the press, but it is recorded that he investigated a broad range of espionage crimes including sabotage in Barrow-in-Furness in March 1940, an attempt to sabotage the *Queen Elizabeth* in March 1941 and an attempt to sabotage warships in Scapa Flow later the same year.

After one trip to Stockholm during hostilities, Spooner returned home with a large paper parcel for his wife. He told Myra not to tell anyone that he had brought it back with him as, officially, he wasn't supposed to bring back gifts from abroad. Myra was thrilled at the prospect of some perfume or maybe a dress-length of material. She unwrapped the package excitedly, but was soon disappointed to find that he had bought her a vegetable colander.[6] Undoubtedly, with the privations of wartime, colanders were hard to come by, but Myra had hoped for something more personal, more romantic. But Spooner was nothing if not consistent. In his letters he always signed off 'Yrs Affect. Reg'. Myra later recalled that she longed for him to write something more loving, how he missed her, 'the sort of thing a woman wants to hear, but he never did'. Myra kept every letter Reg wrote to her, filing them in bundles according to the year.[7]

In 1945, as the war reached an end, and the Allies moved remorselessly through Germany, the search for spies and saboteurs changed to a hunt for traitors, both civilian and military. On 22 April 1945, Spooner was commissioned in the Intelligence Corps with the rank of captain and a week later flew to Paris. Though he admired the city, he missed English food and lamented the shortage of cigarettes, asking Myra to send him over a regular supply of 300 a week.

After the allied victory in May, Spooner travelled by car

further into mainland Europe in pursuit of traitors and deserters. Nothing could have prepared him for his first-hand sight of the devastation the Allies had visited on the enemy. In three days, he felt, he had 'lived a lifetime'.

> I always thought that people in London and other English towns knew what war was, but I have changed my mind. Nothing the people of London have experienced comes anywhere near what the people of Germany have undergone. The country – certainly the Western aspect – is literally devastated, and one wonders how it is all ever going to be put right. Aachen and Hamm for instance, are literally a shambles, *not one* single building remaining habitable, yet one sees a few – very few – people wandering aimlessly around, living goodness knows where and on Lord knows what . . . The more we drive East the more of the debacle of the German Reich we have witnessed.[8]

British Intelligence had provided Spooner with a list of many of the traitors he was seeking. The most important traitor that MI5 were keen to capture was William Joyce, commonly known as 'Lord Haw Haw'. Joyce had broadcast from Germany throughout the war to Britain and encouraged the British people to surrender. Though listening to these broadcasts was not illegal in Britain, it was officially discouraged. In 1940, Joyce had estimated that he had 6 million regular listeners in Britain and 18 million occasional listeners. Many ordinary people were keen to hear what the enemy was saying and how they were justifying their attempts to dominate Europe. Since wartime information in Britain was strictly censored, it was frequently possible for German broadcasts to be more informative than those of the BBC.[9]

The investigation into Joyce's crimes was led by Captain William Skardon of MI5, another former police officer.

Spooner helped Skardon build up the dossier of evidence about Joyce's life in Germany and his activities as Lord Haw Haw. When Spooner searched Radio Hamburg, he discovered a recording of what was intended to be Joyce's last broadcast. Joyce had made the recording whilst drunk, when British troops were less than twenty miles away from the city. In it he lamented the fact that Britain and Germany had not made the natural alliance that they should have done and warned of the looming power and influence of the Soviet Union. The recording was never transmitted.

Though he generally despised the wartime traitors he was pursuing, Spooner had some sympathy for Norman Baillie-Stewart, the 'Officer in the Tower' who had already, curiously, attracted the admiration of the young Neville Heath. 'I quite like him,' Spooner told his wife. 'He is not like the others.'[10] Baillie-Stewart was an ex-Sandhurst officer who had been court-martialled under the Official Secrets Act in 1933 for selling military secrets to foreign powers. Though not in danger of the death penalty at the time (as Britain was not at war), the ten crimes he was found guilty of carried a maximum sentence of 140 years in prison. However, Baillie-Stewart served only four, and when he was released from prison in 1937, he immediately applied for Austrian citizenship. When this was refused, he applied for German citizenship the next year, but because of complex red tape and the beginnings of the Anschluss, his application was not accepted until 1940. Baillie-Stewart had, however, been making pro-Nazi broadcasts from 1939 onwards – in fact he had begun reading Nazi-biased 'news' on the 'Germany Calling' English language service the week before the declaration of war. When he did so, he was still technically a British citizen and was therefore (again technically) guilty of treason, the penalty for which was execution, as was the case with Baillie-Stewart's more renowned successor, William Joyce. In 1945, Spooner arrested Baillie-Stewart on the charge of high treason. A very fair man, Spooner set out to actively save Baillie-Stewart from the gallows by interviewing all of his friends and acquaintances from the time he arrived in Austria and also uncovering the clerical delay in the approval of his citizenship. Due to Spooner's diligence, Baillie-Stewart avoided execution and served only five years in prison.

Spooner was demobilized from the Intelligence Corps with the rank of major on 4 March 1946. Much to the exasperation of his wife, who was keen to take the holiday that had been truncated by the outbreak of war, Spooner rejoined the police force the same day. With the current dearth of police officers and the booming post-war crime wave, his commissioner had told him how urgently they needed the return of qualified senior detectives like him. Spooner replied that he could start straight away; 'If you need me, here I am.'[11] Officially Spooner had already been a divisional detective inspector for two years but he had never actually worked in that rank. His promotion had come through in June 1944 while he was on loan to the Secret Service, so it was based on seniority rather than merit. Now forty-three, Spooner felt, like thousands of men his age, that the war had held back his career and he was now to be faced with competition from a wave of ambitious young men keen to prove themselves in the force once they had been demobilized.

But Spooner needn't have worried about being eclipsed by up-and-coming younger men – for his defining moment was just ahead. His experiences as a London-based police inspector before the war and his more recent achievements in the pursuit of the most agile and deceptive of traitors and saboteurs, together with his extraordinary memory and inherent tenacity, were to be the ideal qualifications for him to lead the most celebrated murder investigation of his career for which he would be remembered as 'Britain's greatest detective'.[12]

CHAPTER SIX

The Pembridge Court Hotel

21 JUNE 1946

At 9.10 a.m. on the morning of Friday 21 June, Elizabeth Wyatt, the manageress of the Pembridge Court Hotel, told her waitress, Rhoda Spooner, to go up to Room 4 and give Lieutenant Colonel and Mrs Heath a knock. Neither of them had come down to breakfast that morning.

Twenty-six-year-old Rhoda's duties were to serve breakfast to guests at the hotel from 7.30 a.m. until 11 a.m. seven days a week.[1] Though she never normally served meals to guests in their rooms, she had been instructed to make an exception by Mrs Wyatt on the previous Monday morning, when she had served tea and toast to Heath and his 'wife'. Rhoda had also chatted with the lieutenant colonel over the preceding few days. She had seen him in the hotel lounge on Wednesday morning where she had been serving. He'd asked her for a cup of tea and during the conversation he had mentioned that he was going away on Friday with his wife to Copenhagen and that 'Mrs Heath' had just left the WRNS.

So, on Friday morning, Rhoda went up to the first floor and knocked on the door of Room 4 as instructed. There was no answer. The door was closed, but not locked. Rhoda opened it and looked into the room. The curtains were drawn but there was sufficient daylight for her to see a woman asleep in the bed behind the door. This she assumed to be Mrs Heath (Yvonne Symonds) whom she'd last seen on Monday morning in bed with her husband when she'd taken up the tea and toast. The woman in the bed was covered up to her shoulders by the bedclothes. The other bed by the window was empty and didn't appear to have been slept in. Rhoda assumed that Heath had gone out and left his wife to have a lie-in.

'Will you be coming down to breakfast?' Rhoda asked.

There was no reply. She quietly closed the door, leaving the woman to sleep on. Downstairs she told Mrs Wyatt that she'd asked if Mrs Heath was coming down to breakfast, but had received no answer.

Later that morning, Barbara Osborne was attending to her morning cleaning rounds and knocked on the door of Room 4 at about 11.20 a.m. She received no answer either.

My duties as chambermaid are making the beds in all the guest rooms, sweeping the rooms, dusting the furniture and cleaning the wash hand-basins and generally to make each room clean and tidy. I start work at 9 a.m. and finish at 12 noon. And if I have attended to every room I just leave the house and go home, but should any of my work remain unfinished and I could not get access to the rooms, then I report it to Mrs Wyatt and the matter is left with her.[2]

Barbara entered the room. The curtains were still closed and the room in semi-darkness. She saw a woman whom she presumed to be Mrs Heath asleep in the bed nearest the door and noticed that her head was turned towards the window. The lady didn't stir when Barbara came into the room so presuming she was still asleep, Barbara left without speaking. She decided to come back later and went on about her business cleaning the other rooms. At midday, Barbara knocked on the door of Room 4 again. Receiving no reply, she opened the door and spoke to the lady lying in bed.

'Would you mind making the beds as I am going off duty?'

Again, Mrs Heath did not answer, so Barbara reported to Mrs Wyatt that she had been unable to clean the room. She finished her shift and went home, thinking nothing out of the ordinary.

By 2 p.m. that afternoon, Mrs Wyatt's daughter-in-law, Alice, who worked as assistant manageress at the hotel, went upstairs to Room 4. Mrs Heath may well have had a heavy night, but she surely wouldn't want to sleep on into the afternoon. Alice entered the room and drew back the curtains. Turning into the body of the room, she saw that there was no response from Mrs Heath to the daylight flooding in from the window. She approached the bed by the door, pulled back the bedclothes from the woman's neck and saw that she was dead. Alice replaced the bedclothes and hurried downstairs to find her mother-in-law. 'Come quick!' she called, 'I think this woman is dead.'[3] Mrs Wyatt accompanied her daughter-in-law back up to the room. The woman was clearly dead. Alice immediately telephoned the police.[4]

Sergeant Frederick Averill of 'F' Division, Notting Hill, arrived at the hotel at about 2.40 p.m. He was met by Alice Wyatt and shown up to Room 4. He noticed that the key was in the door on the inside but had not been locked. The bedclothes on the bed by the window had been roughly laid over the bed. The bedclothes on the bed near the door were pulled up to the woman's shoulders. He noticed that she had bruises to the left-hand side of her face. When Averill pulled back the bedclothes, the condition of the woman's body began to reveal the extraordinarily violent ordeal that she had suffered before she died. Averill then pulled back the bedclothes from the other bed and found the sheets beneath saturated with blood, with large clots in the centre of the bed. Averill called in the murder team.[5]

He was joined shortly afterwards by Dr Henegan, the deputy divisional surgeon, Detective Inspector Shelley Symes and Sergeant Frederick Anning of the CID. Henegan, a junior doctor, established that the woman had been dead for some time, but did not at this point look for the cause of death.

Reg Spooner arrived at the hotel at 3.30 p.m.[6] He alerted the pathologist, 39-year-old Dr Keith Simpson, whose reputation during the war had begun to eclipse that of the leading forensic pathologist of the pre-war period, Sir Bernard Spilsbury. Simpson had been lecturing that afternoon at the Police Training College in Hendon when he had a call from his assistant Jean Scott-Dunn to go to Notting Hill as soon as possible.[7] District Superintendent Tom Barratt also arrived at the hotel as well as the fingerprint division who carried out their tests and took the scene-of-crime photographs. The washbasin in the corner of the room bore traces of blood. It was evident that somebody had been attempting to wash something away after the murder. The side of the washbasin revealed one single bloody fingerprint.[8]

Spooner and Symes now took a closer look at the body of the woman on the bed near the door. She was completely naked, lying on her back. Her head was lying to the right-hand side of the pillow, turned towards the window, much as if she had been deliberately placed that way to look as if she were asleep. Her feet were tied tightly one over the other with a knotted handkerchief. Her right arm was pinned diagonally behind her back and her left wrist and left hand lay under the left side of the small of her back. The extraordinary position of the arms and hands, together with bruising on the wrists seemed to indicate that her wrists had been tied behind her back and the ligature later removed. There was a considerable amount of blood on the bedding, but the front of the body and the face were strangely free of it, as if she had been washed after her ordeal.

The cause of death was not immediately apparent. Spooner then tilted the body to see if there were any injuries to the woman's back. Across her back were several marks. The woman had been thrashed or lashed with a cane or a whip. There was also a trickle of blood from the woman's vagina, indicating some sort of injury there, but as her ankles were bound with the knotted handkerchief, it was impossible to establish what sort of injury this might be. Spooner and Symes noted that the bedding of the bed nearest the window was soaked with blood. This suggested that the woman had suffered her injuries on the bed nearest the window and had then been transferred to the bed by the door.[9]

Looking around the room, it seemed as if nothing had been disturbed. There was no sign of a struggle. On the mantleshelf was a white metal bracelet and on the dressing table were a pair of flowery earrings made of fabric. A large ornamental ring and two other rings were still on the dead woman's fingers. Her fingernails – varnished a very dark colour – were unbroken, although there were traces of blood beneath them. On a pillow on the bed nearest the window was a long, patterned, elongated mark in blood that suggested that a stick, a riding crop or whip had been struck or wiped across it. Keith Simpson arrived and examined the body at 6.30 p.m. and found it to be still warm. He estimated the death to have taken place at about midnight or in the very early hours of that morning.

A brown leather ladies' handbag lay on one of the armchairs. It contained all the personal elements of the woman's life including an identity card, which, together with several letters, confirmed that the woman was not 'Mrs Heath' at all. The dead woman was a Mrs Margery Gardner of Bramham Gardens, SW5.

Spooner interviewed the hotel staff and was informed that the room had been booked on the previous Sunday in the name of Lieutenant Colonel Heath. Mrs Wyatt was sure that she recognized the man's face and believed that he had stayed at the hotel before. When she later checked the register, she discovered that he had stayed there in November 1944 with a woman called Zita Williams. At the time he had been wearing a South African Air Force uniform and registered under the name of Armstrong. He had actually registered at the hotel twice before under that name.[10]

When interviewed, both Barbara Osborne and Rhoda Spooner were certain that the dead woman was 'Mrs Heath' because she had dark hair, but they had mistaken Margery for the dark-haired Yvonne Symonds whom they had both seen on the previous Monday morning. Importantly, Barbara also informed the police that she had thoroughly cleaned the washbasin as usual on Thursday morning, stating, 'I cleaned the washbasin and did so with a wet rag and Vim powder all around the inside of the basin and the edges. I have no doubt of that.'[11]

Curiously, despite the obvious violence of the attack, nothing untoward was heard during the night despite the fact that there were three other rooms off the first-floor landing. Alice Wyatt slept in the room directly opposite Room 4[12] and she had heard nothing after she retired to bed at 10.30 p.m. Of the residents in the hotel only a Mrs Thomas in Room 5 said that she had been woken in the early hours of Friday morning. She had heard creaking followed by the sound of the tap running in the bathroom on the landing. A little later on she heard the front door bang.[13]

When Spooner telephoned the Criminal Records Office at New Scotland Yard, he was informed that Lieutenant Colonel Heath was the name used by Neville George Clevely Heath who had a substantial criminal record and was said to be living with his parents at an address in Wimbledon. Spooner left Symes at the scene of the crime to supervise the examination of the body and made his way to Heath's parents' house in south-west London. After Simpson's examination at the hotel, Margery's body was removed in a cardboard coffin and taken to Hammersmith mortuary in Fulham Palace Road.

As the afternoon turned to evening, a *Daily Mail* journalist, Harry Procter, walked home past Pembridge Gardens and saw a 'small army of reporters' outside the hotel. Procter ran into a colleague of his, Sydney Brock, who said 'it looked like a murder, but it turns out to be an abortion'. Later that night, Procter met a police officer friend in his local pub, who presumed Procter was working on this latest murder case in Notting Hill. Procter had been told it was an abortion gone wrong. His police friend said, 'Then it's the queerest abortion I ever heard of', and told him that the dead woman had been tied up and beaten. Sensing a sensational story, Procter left immediately and headed for Hammersmith mortuary where he joined a growing crowd of reporters who had all been tipped off that an extraordinary investigation was under way.[14]

Across London, Spooner arrived at a comfortable, redbrick house in suburban Wimbledon. The house, standing proudly on the corner of Merton Hall Road, was a substantial three-storey semi-detached residence in a very respectable area, surrounded by avenues of trees and backing on to open playing fields. Spooner introduced himself to Mr and Mrs Heath, who were apparently a very decent couple in their fifties. William Heath was the manager of the Waterloo Station branch of Faulkner's, a chain of hairdressing shops, and his wife was a housewife. Bessie Heath told Spooner that her son had always been secretive, and was prone to being excitable which sometimes overcame him and made him sick. Heath's father told Spooner that Neville drank rather heavily, usually beer, but alcohol didn't seem to affect him. Neither of his parents had any information about their son's association with women, who he appeared to shun.[15] Though he was not unduly conceited, he was very particular about his appearance and bathed most mornings.[16]

After interviewing Mr and Mrs Heath, Spooner searched Heath's bedroom and took away some of his personal possessions including books, papers – and four whips.

He also took Heath's address book. This contained the names, addresses and telephone numbers of over 300 women.[17]

The post-mortem on Margery Gardner took place that night at 10 p.m., attended by both Spooner and Symes, where Simpson was able to make a more thorough examination of the body.[18]

Margery's breasts had been so savagely bitten that one nipple was hanging loose; the other was found, bitten off, under her body. Turning the body over, Simpson counted seventeen lash marks, many of them so severe that the diamond weave pattern of the whip and its ferrule-like metallic tip were imprinted on her flesh. Nine of the lashes were on her back and buttocks, six were on the right side of the body injuring the breast, chest and abdomen and the remaining two were on the head over the left and right brow. The

lashes were so clearly defined that Simpson was able to measure them with mathematical precision. The left-hand side of
Margery's face had been bruised by two blows or punches.
There was also a group of bruises under the chin consistent
with someone gripping it to prevent her head from moving.

The wound from which the blood had seeped when
Spooner tilted the body was a seven-inch long tear of the
vagina running four inches up the right wall and a further
three inches across the back. It had been caused by a 'tearing
instrument such as a whip or cane' being thrust into her and
savagely rotated. The actual cause of death was asphyxia due
to suffocation, though there was no indication of strangula-
tion. Speculating about the order in which the injuries might
have occurred, Simpson felt that the whip lashes took place
first, followed by the blows to the face. The assailant then
gripped Margery's jaw with his hand and then her arms. After
this he savaged her nipples with his teeth, then penetrated her
vagina with the haft of the whip. Finally he forced her face
into the bedding, ending her appalling ordeal by suffocating
her. Simpson also confirmed the telling detail that Margery's
face had been washed after her death.

Though the injuries had taken place before she died it was
not possible to ascertain whether or not Margery was
conscious during the attack. She may have been rendered
unconscious by the two blows to the head. She was certainly
made helpless by the knotted handkerchiefs around her legs
and wrists. She could also have been gagged, which may have
contributed to her suffocation. This would also account for
the fact that none of the nearby guests heard any screams
from the room, despite the excruciating pain Margery must
have suffered.

Simpson concluded that the injuries were the consequence
of 'a most violent and sadistic sexual assault'.[19] Having investigated the lash marks and the internal injuries to the vagina,

Simpson was convinced that these injuries had all been executed with the diamond weave whip. 'If you find that whip,' he told Spooner, 'you've found your man.'[20]

Another clue that the post-mortem yielded was the handkerchief that had bound Margery's feet together. This bore the name 'L. Kearns' handwritten in black ink and also had an embroidered 'K' in blue silk cotton in one corner. This clearly didn't belong to Margery as it was a man's handkerchief and she had a clean and pressed one bearing her name in her handbag. So, who was this man Kearns and how was he involved in Margery's death? At the time it seemed to Reg Spooner that the hunt was on for *two* men, both potential killers, both on the loose – and judging by the brutality of the attack on Margery Gardner – both extremely dangerous.

Given how clear the case against Neville Heath looked, Spooner issued a memo to the *Police Gazette* and to the press with a description and photograph of him as well as a request for information regarding the owner of the handkerchief. This memo was dispatched to every newspaper editor in the country and arrived on their desks on Saturday morning. But by Monday morning, Spooner had a change of heart. Though he needed the press to help trace Heath as swiftly as possible, he worried that the photograph might compromise a future court case. The taxi driver's identification of Heath as the last person to be seen with Margery alive would be crucial. If the defence could prove that the driver had already seen a photograph of Heath in the newspapers, his evidence would be compromised and it might make it impossible to prove his guilt.

Another memo was hastily issued by Scotland Yard, withdrawing the photograph from all newspaper publication. Any deviation from the police's directive would be followed by the full force of the law. Consequently, though written descriptions of Heath appeared in all newspapers, the photograph was completely withdrawn from circulation.

> In connection with the death of Margery Gardner at Pembridge Gardens on the night of 20/21 June the Commissioner of Police of the metropolis requests editors to kindly refrain from publishing any photograph of Neville George Clevely Heath as publication will seriously prejudice any subsequent court proceedings.[21]

In the months to come, this controversial memo was to lead to questions in the House of Commons. Within days it was to have a tragic, indeed fatal, impact.

PART TWO

Neville George Clevely Heath

CHAPTER SEVEN
Rake's Progress

6 JUNE 1917 – 12 JULY 1938

It is a difficult question, my friends, for any young man . . . whether to follow uncritically the track he finds himself in, without considering his aptness for it, or to consider what his aptness or bent may be, and re-shape his course accordingly. I tried to do the latter, and I failed . . . However it was my poverty and not my will that consented to be beaten. It takes two or three generations to do what I tried to do in one; and my impulses – affections – vices perhaps they should be called – were too strong not to hamper a man without advantages.

Thomas Hardy, *Jude the Obscure*, 1895

Neville George Clevely Heath was born at home in a Victorian bay-fronted terraced house at Dudley Road, Ilford on 6 June 1917. The world he was born into was dominated by war, violence and loss – themes that for him, and for many of his generation, would characterize and define their lives.

The newspapers that day headlined a further offensive in Belgium where the British army was still fighting for control of the city of Ypres.[1] Unseasonally wet weather had turned the battlefields into a sea of mud and by October that year, British casualties would mount to over 159,000. This, the 'most gigantic, grim, futile and bloody fight ever waged',[2] became known to history as the Battle of Passchendale. At home, southern England was also being terrorized by German raids. By this point in the Great War, Zeppelin airships had largely been replaced by a newer and much more powerful aircraft – the sinister Gotha Bomber. On the evening of 5 June a great battle took place over the Thames between the Imperial German Air Force and the Royal Flying Corps; bombs dropped across the south and east coasts and the inland south-eastern counties. The *Evening Standard* noted that picturedromes and tearooms quickly emptied as crowds sought to find a vantage point to watch the extraordinary air battle.

> Our gunners smashed their formation almost at a volley, scattered them like fluttering birds, sent cones of bursting shells over them, around them, straight at them. The Huns had the gaping six miles of estuary below them. They pelted bombs down. Many hit the water. Great columns of water surged up and the din was terrific.[3]

The German planes were driven away by Royal Naval Air Service pilots resulting in the loss of ten 'Hun' aircraft. German air raids continued throughout the month and 300,000 Londoners sought nightly shelter in tube stations, just as they would do a generation later.

Heath's parents later claimed that their son had been born in an air raid and that this ill-starred beginning must in some way have contributed to his complex personality. As early as 1938, when Heath was sent to borstal, his father was citing the air raid as the reason for his son's excitable and highly strung nature.[4] Reg Spooner, thorough as ever, examined records of enemy action and found that no air raids were recorded in Ilford on 6 June itself. But there is no reason to doubt the Heaths' testimony, as they are generally reliable and honest. It may be that Bessie Heath's labour started on the evening before – the day of the raid over the south-eastern counties. This is the first of the many confusions that occur throughout Heath's life and story. Three doctors and two nurses attended the labour and Heath's head was 'badly damaged by instruments at [his] birth',[5] suggesting a forceps delivery. This would have been necessary if Mrs Heath was exhausted or if the baby was becoming distressed. Air raid or not, Heath's birth was clearly traumatic.

After his trial, Heath's parents were at pains to search their memories for incidents from their son's childhood that might have affected his emotional or psychological development. Their well-intentioned attempts to uncover a forgotten clue or some inherent pattern that could justify his later actions might seem a little unscientific. Was there a genetic root to his aberrant behaviour? Bessie Heath revealed that her uncle, William Clevely, had been confined to a mental home for most of his life and had died, institutionalized, in 1938. 'He was quite small when he set his bedclothes alight and bedroom on fire – and the shock was so great that his brain never grew on normal lines again,' she stated.[6] She observed that her son had 'always been susceptible to shock' and her husband concurred in a letter to Heath whilst in prison, reassuring his son that 'any kind of shock has always been the thing to upset you most'.[7] As well as reiterating the damaging psychological effects of being born into a world at war, they searched for concrete physical reasons to justify their son's acts – a broken wrist or a fractured elbow in childhood, maybe? For surely, to commit such horrific acts, to cause such pain and suffering – there must *be* a reason? But perhaps these are the desperate questions that any parent in the Heaths' circumstances would ask themselves. Where did we go wrong? Are we, as parents, in some way responsible?

Heath's father, William, was born in 1890 into a respectable, hard-working, lower-middle-class family from Highbury, north London. William's father had trained as a copperplate engraver of maps and charts, but then set up his own business, running an hotel.[8] William himself worked as an assistant clerk with the civil service. Bessie Clevely was the daughter of a printer and had also been born in London, a little further north than William in Stoke Newington. In 1899, the Clevely family had moved some distance away to Ilford in Essex. This could be because the Clevelys had relatives there, as the whole Heath family, after the traumatic events of 1946, moved back to the area in the 1950s.

In April 1913, 23-year-old William Heath married Bessie Clevely at St Alban's, Ilford – a classic pressed red-brick church – just around the corner from Bessie's parents' house at 35 Dudley Road. This was to be William and Bessie Heath's first married home and where they would live with their extended family for the duration of the First World War. William Heath had been registered as a 'warehouseman' at the time of his marriage and as a 'soft goods traveller' at the time of Heath's birth, but it's very likely that he saw active service at some point during the war. The Military Service Act in January 1916 made conscription compulsory for single men between eighteen and forty-one. Married men like William were only exempt until May 1916. By the end of the war, 25 per cent of the total male population had joined the army, a total of 5 million men.

Of the many English towns that are the backdrop to Heath's story, Ilford seems to have changed the most – not only because of wartime bombing and 1960s urban planning – but because of post-war immigration. A large Asian community of Hindus, Muslims and Sikhs now resides in the quiet and ordered streets around the Heaths' first home in Dudley Road. Hindu temples have replaced Anglican churches, front gardens concreted over to accommodate people carriers. Only half an hour from London by train, it's not the first time in its history that Ilford has undergone a dramatic cultural change. For over 1,200 years, Ilford had been a small village in Essex, part of the parish of Barking. But after the first rail link from Liverpool Street was constructed in the 1870s, the entire character of Ilford changed, and the town evolved with great speed into a dormitory suburb. With the advent of the railway, it was a comfortable commuting distance from central London and would house the clerks, assistant managers, teachers and shop workers – like the Clevelys and the Heaths – who served the booming city of London at the zenith of its imperial potency. Developers bought up large areas of land specifically for housing developments with the intention of attracting the new breed of owner-occupiers. Thousands of homes were built to suit the budgets of blue- and white-collar workers, from domestic staff to managing directors. In many cases even the deposit was the subject of a short-term loan provided by the builders. Shops, swimming pools, theatres, cinemas and libraries all followed as Ilford developed into a sedate and self-sufficient satellite of the metropolis. The expansion of the area was extraordinary; in 1881 Ilford had a population of 7,645 – by 1911, it had rocketed over ten-fold to 78,188.[9]

By the 1920s, Ilford was established as a mature and fashionable suburb, but in 1922 the town was shaken by a story of sex and violence that took place on a politely ordered avenue and within an archetypal family that had come to define the comfortable but aspiring middle class that typified the area. This story – which was to wreck the lives of several local families – would anticipate the fate of the Heaths as well as touching their lives with an extraordinary, chilling coincidence.

Good-looking and sophisticated, Edith Thompson and her husband Percy were typical of the commuter families that had settled in Ilford. Edith was a professional woman who managed a hat shop in central London. Having married the dull and occasionally violent Percy Thompson, her head had been turned by a young man serving in the merchant navy, Frederick Bywaters, whom she had been introduced to by her younger sister, Avis. Looking for a room in the area when home from sea, Bywaters became the Thompsons' lodger. Nine years Edith's junior, he was handsome, virile and full of stories about his exotic travels abroad. Soon after he moved into the Thompsons' house at 41 Kensington Gardens, Bywaters and Mrs Thompson began an affair. When he was away at sea, Edith fuelled the relationship with a series of letters, heavily influenced by the romantic fiction she voraciously consumed, but also chronicling the journey of their own sexual relationship in intimate detail. She poured out her love for Bywaters and her desperate desire to be rid of her husband. She even suggested that she had dosed Thompson's food with poison and ground glass from an electric light bulb. This became the tabloid image of Edith Thompson – a 'Messalina of the Suburbs'[10] who used her age and experience first to seduce the naïve Bywaters and then to entice him to kill her husband. But this image proved to be a fantasy – a melodramatic attempt on Edith's behalf to keep Bywaters excited by the relationship during his time away at sea, whilst she remained at home, submitting uncomfortably to her husband in the bedroom. When Bywaters returned to England, Percy Thompson became aware of his wife's adultery and confronted the lovers, telling Bywaters to leave the house immediately. Bywaters did so, but insisted at the same time that Thompson should give his wife a divorce.[11]

On 3 October 1922, the Thompsons were returning home from the Criterion Theatre at Piccadilly Circus, having caught the 11.30 p.m. train from Liverpool Street, arriving at Ilford Station around midnight. Whilst they were walking along a part of Belgrave Road that was unlit by streetlamps, an assailant rushed past the couple and attacked Percy Thompson with a knife, pushing Edith aside. She cried out, 'Oh, don't, oh don't!' in 'a most piteous manner'. Percy collapsed against the wall. The Thompsons were only 54 yards from home.

Bessie Heath's older brother, Percy Clevely, was then living with his wife at 62 Mayfair Avenue, a few minutes' walk from the Thompsons' house. On the night of the murder, Percy had also been walking home from Ilford Station with a friend, Dora Pittard. Suddenly, Edith Thompson 'seemed to come out of the darkness', running towards them, hysterical and incoherent. She said that her husband had fallen down and was ill and that she desperately needed help. She wanted to know if they knew of a doctor? Percy Clevely and Dora took Mrs Thompson to a Dr Maudsley at 62 Courtland Avenue who said he would come and help. Mrs Thompson ran ahead and when Clevely and Dr Maudsley arrived, they found Percy Thompson propped up against a wall with his wife kneeling over him. Dr Maudsley struck a match and examined Thompson, but he was by then already dead. Percy Clevely asked Mrs

Thompson what had happened and she said that she couldn't say. Something had 'brushed' or 'flew' past them and then Percy had collapsed. When Dr Maudsley told Edith that her husband was dead, she asked, 'Why did you not come sooner and save him?'

Percy Thompson had died of stab wounds and both his wife and Bywaters were arrested and charged with murder. Percy Clevely was called as a prosecution witness to the Old Bailey on 6 December 1922.[12] He was cross-examined by Travers Humphreys who had appeared for the Crown in the trials of Oscar Wilde, Dr. Crippen and George Joseph Smith, the 'Brides in the Bath' killer.

Despite a lack of convincing evidence that Edith Thompson had in any way instigated the murder, both she and Bywaters were executed in January 1923 – with Mrs Thompson dragged, drugged and unconscious, to the gallows, causing mass protestations of her innocence and a strong lobby against the death penalty. This controversial case, essentially a miscarriage of justice, was to continue to fuel the debate for the abolition of the death penalty through-out the rest of the century. Such was the public fascination with the case, that later, when the contents of the Thompsons' home were put up for auction, the hedge in the front garden was completely stripped of its leaves by people wanting a souvenir.[13]

Edith Thompson's beautifully decorated, double-fronted Edwardian house – her pride and joy – was minutes away from the more modest Clevely family home in Dudley Road. But for the young Heaths and their little son, Neville, it must have seemed extraordinary that a murder could have taken place in the streets of Ilford – on their own doorstep. Bessie's brother Percy was in the papers – and not just in the *Ilford Recorder* and the *East Ham Echo*, but in the national press, too. This sort of scandal just didn't involve ordinary people like

William and Bessie Heath. But wouldn't it be a fascinating tale to tell their grandchildren by the fireside one day – the time when Uncle Percy was a witness in the most sensational trial of the age?

After Edith Thompson's execution, there was much local sympathy for her family who continued to live in the area. In the wake of such traumatic events, how did they find the resolve to face the world with such quiet dignity?

A generation later, William and Bessie Heath were to find out for themselves.

In about 1918 the Heaths had some studio photographs taken of their young son. Dressed in white, with long, golden curls, he looks girlish, as was the fashion of the day. His eyes are bright and lively and we know them to be a dazzling blue. In one photograph, he leans against his mother's head, his left arm resting on her shoulder, his baby teeth just visible as he and Bessie smile into the camera. His mother is an attractive woman, not yet thirty, with even features and dark hair. There's trust and love in the photograph. A proud and contented mother, an adored and beautiful child.

Possibly motivated by William's work as a manufacturer's agent in the textile industry, the young family left Ilford in the spring of 1920 and moved across London to Merton in south-west London. At the same time, Bessie had announced that she was pregnant again. The Heaths set up home in a corner property in a street of smart Edwardian houses at 1 Bathurst Avenue where, on 5 September, Bessie gave birth to another son, Carol William Clevely Heath – a younger brother and companion for little Neville. But tragedy was soon to cloud their lives.

Tubercular meningitis, popularly known as consumption, was an epidemic in the early twentieth century with no known cure. Feared by the entire population, it was known to be infectious and deadly. Children under four were most vulnerable as their immune systems were not sufficiently developed to fight the ravages of the disease which affected the lungs and resulted in lethargy, fever, weight loss and coughing – sometimes, distressingly, bringing up blood. Tragically for his family, Carol Heath soon began to exhibit symptoms. The disease was hugely contagious and both Bessie and William would have been vulnerable to it, but the family member at the highest risk of infection would have been Neville, who was six at the time. Many adults who developed the illness would be treated in sanatoria, effectively removed from society in order to prevent the spread of their disease, but Carol, being still a child, was cared for at home. Both parents would have been aware that his prognosis would be very bleak; in this period, the vast majority of individuals who contracted the disease did not survive. At the beginning of February 1923, Carol's condition deteriorated and he fell into a coma. He never recovered and died at home on 24 February 1923, his mother at his bedside. He was just two.

The Heaths were devastated by the loss of their son, but were particularly concerned about how it would affect his older brother, who was now 'grief-stricken'.[14] For the six-year-old Neville, without other siblings to console or distract him, Carol's death was deeply traumatic. His later relationship with his brother Mick gives an indication of how much Heath valued this fraternal bond. Heath's sole concern whilst in prison was to try to secure his brother's future. For Mick, too, this affection was reciprocal, even following his brother into the RAF when he was old enough, attempting to live out his brother's dreams.

After Carol's death, Heath had the upbringing of an only child. Mick would not be born until 1928 and it's very likely that Bessie Heath may have become pregnant in the

interim, but not succeeded in bringing more children to
term. The relationship between Heath and his parents was
very loving – as his letters from prison testify. He felt them
well suited to each other, with neither dominating the other
– always kind and possibly, he admitted, indulgent towards
him.[15] It's not surprising that the Heaths should have adored
their golden-haired boy given their loss, but even so, Heath
didn't think his mother was unusually possessive or
emotional. Though he never shared any personal difficulties
with his parents, he felt that if he were ever to do so, it
would have been with his mother.

As a young boy, Neville began to reveal an acquisitive
streak as well as a pronounced slyness. Though his mother
later dismissed his childhood misdemeanours as 'stupid and
unnecessary',[16] he was developing habits that he was to
continue to practise as an adult. On one occasion he had been
caught taking cakes from a confectioner and putting them on
somebody else's bill. When he was found out, his first instinct
was to run away. Tellingly, Bessie Heath noted that 'there was
no need to [steal] as he always had plenty at home'. On another
occasion, his parents found some cheap things in Neville's
pocket which he admitted he had stolen, but were of 'no use
to him'. None of young Neville's petty thefts were driven by
need; they were driven by desire. Subsequently, Bessie Heath
said that 'he was told how seriously wrong it was but [he] was
not harshly treated'. Even as a child, Neville Heath had a
growing awareness that he had a knack for getting away with
things unpunished. Certainly Spooner felt that Bessie Heath
had been an over-indulgent mother and that she had possibly,
in sparing the rod, spoiled her child.[17]

Though his parents were Church of England by faith, young
Neville was sent to Holy Cross Convent, a local Roman
Catholic school in Wimbledon. This, the Heaths felt, was the

only decent school in the neighbourhood and it's clear that from an early age his parents were ambitious for their son and wanted to give him the best start in life. Although kindly treated at the convent, he felt isolated with the other Church of England children, but he bore no lasting ill will towards the nuns who taught him in the three years he attended. He then proceeded to a local council school until he was old enough to go to a secondary school.

Significantly, even when he was discussing his past with a psychiatrist after his arrest, Heath insisted that he had actually spent this period at a private prep school. This suggests that Heath felt embarrassment or at least some anxiety about his background and education and, certainly, for the rest of his life he was to conjure a much more upmarket CV for himself than the modest reality.

By 1928, William Heath was still working in the textile trade, though now specifically as an underwear manufacturer. In the spring of that year, Bessie Heath found herself pregnant again and, perhaps wanting more space for two growing children, the family moved to 1 Melrose Road, a semi-detached cottage in a leafy, almost rural, garden estate. The house itself was around the corner from St Mary's in Merton – an ancient parish church where Lord Nelson used to worship. At Melrose Road, Bessie gave birth to another son, Michael Robert Clevely Heath, always known as 'Mick'. Despite the difference in their ages, the two boys were very close. Unable, at first, to pronounce Neville's name, Mick took to calling him 'Nen', a family nickname that stuck for the rest of Heath's life.

In 1932, the family moved house again, this time rising considerably up the property scale which presumably also increased their social standing. The Heaths' new home was a solid red-brick Edwardian villa, situated on the corner of Merton Hall Road, just outside Wimbledon town centre and in the same road that would house, from 1940, the Wimbledon School of Art. The house remains today – a five-bedroom property, typical of suburban London, with a garden looking on to playing fields at the back. It was a house of some comfort – certainly of no privation. Immediately the family moved in, Bessie took advantage of the extra rooms and offered them to paying guests, renting out rooms to as many as four lodgers at a time. At its most crowded in 1939, the house was home to seven adults plus the eleven-year-old Mick Heath. Several of these lodgers became long-term tenants including Lavinia Scoley who stayed with the Heaths from 1932 to 1938. There would continue to be lodgers at Merton Hall Road throughout the 1930s and for the duration of the war. The Heaths were never to live there alone and even in 1946 they had a single lodger.[18]

One of the reasons for taking in paying guests would have been that the Heaths had hopes of securing their sons places at the local grammar school, where the fees were £3 10s. per term.[19] Rutlish School was situated at the junction of Kingston Road and Station Road in Merton Park – a ten-minute walk from Merton Hall Road. Neville Heath's time there from 1929 to 1934 was typical of the period – a conservative haven of safe (if prosaic) middle-class values; a world of cricket teas, rugby XVs, Gilbert and Sullivan operettas, sports days and prize-givings.[20]

Rutlish, a typical suburban grammar school, had been set up in 1895. In 1921 an ambitious new headmaster, Edward Varnish, had taken over with an agenda for radical change. One teacher who had joined the school in the 1920s, remembered that he found the school 'undergoing a revolution':

[It was] filled with community spirit that I have never seen surpassed elsewhere and seldom equalled. It was clear from the first that Mr Varnish had in some way captured the imagination of boys and staff and made them believe that all belonged to a place that was unique and bound to succeed.[21]

Varnish promoted his ambitions, however, at the expense of the fabric and upkeep of the actual school buildings. In 1933, a school inspector recorded that the school was in an appalling state of squalor:

> The old premises are dark and dingy . . . There is no library, no changing accommodation, no waiting room. The hall is inadequate. No gymnasium. Several forms are not adequately housed. No manual room. No geography room. The cadet corps headquarters were makeshift. There was no dining room. Cloakrooms wretched.[22]

But Varnish wasn't interested in the physical aspects of the school – he wanted to change its ethos. His agenda in the 1920s and 1930s was very much focused on reforming the school along the lines of one of the great English public schools. The foundation of Varnish's plan was a House system to instil in the boys a sense of competition and belonging. On entering the school each boy was allocated to one of eight houses named after an ancient warrior race: Argonauts, Crusaders, Kelts, Parthians, Romans, Spartans, Trojans and Vikings, the house that Heath joined. Each of the houses was made up of about sixty boys with a housemaster and a captain. Over the school year, points would be awarded to each individual boy for sporting and academic achievements and these would be added to a house score at the end of the year. The winning house would be known as Cock House.[23] This fostered a sense of camaraderie within each house as well as a sporting sense of competition between them.

The ethos 'For King and Country' married to driving

ambition was firmly established at the heart of Rutlish tradition – even enshrined in the school song:

> *We are arming for the fight,*
> *Pressing on with all our might,*
> *Pluming wings for higher flight.*
> *Up! – and On!*[24]

Several of the younger masters had seen active service in the
First World War and ninety-eight Rutlish Old Boys were
remembered on the War Memorial at the back of the school
hall.[25] This environment was to engender a martial spirit in
the generation of boys like Heath who were educated at the
school in the period leading up to the Second World War.
In 1922, Varnish had initiated a Cadet Corps, which was
affiliated to the 5th Battalion of the East Surrey Regiment
Territorial Army. Though this was an attempt by the headmaster to follow an established public school tradition, it
was also very much a sign of the times, as the thirties
progressed and Germany's international ambitions were
becoming clearer. In the year that Hitler was appointed
chancellor, the Rutlish Cadet Corps – including Heath –
were the proud recipients of the inaugural 'Nation Cup',
which was established to acknowledge the most outstanding
Cadet Corps in Britain. The trophy was presented to the
Corps by the Prince of Wales in the garden of St James's
Palace in June 1933.

Varnish introduced a series of other innovations in order
to ape the public school system. They began to play rugby
rather than soccer and by the early 1930s Heath was playing
for the First XV. He was also appointed as a prefect, this
system also initiated by Varnish. As well as keeping order,
prefects were authorized to give canings as punishment.
These were always carried out in the presence of a witness

and entered into the Punishments Book.[26] By this period, such beatings were ubiquitous in British public and grammar schools to the extent that in France the act of flagellation had famously been dubbed 'the English vice'. Though there's no reason to suspect Heath of overindulging his authority as a prefect, in all probability his time at Rutlish will have been his introduction either as a witness or a participant to corporal punishment.

In *The English Vice*, Ian Gibson notes that for many flagellants, very often the first excitement in connection with beating takes place in early childhood when a whipping inflicted by an adult has been witnessed, undergone or read about. Freud and the German sexual psychologist Krafft-Ebing observed that several of their patients had remarkably similar case histories, dating their first awareness of sexual arousal from reading flogging scenes in *Uncle Tom's Cabin*.[27] There was also a very strong tradition of school stories in boys' fiction published throughout the Victorian period and many of these described canings, whippings and thrashings as a matter of course. This was carried on into the twentieth century in twopenny weeklies like *The Gem* and *The Magnet* as well as in annuals such as *Boy's Own* and *Chums*. A typical scene from the period Heath would have been reading appears in *Chums Annual* (1927–8):

[Chummy] was wondering how many strokes it would be, whether it would draw blood, whether he would cry in front of all the form!

Mr London picked up the ground-ash and pointed to a vacant desk in front.

'Bend over there,' he commanded.

Chummy put himself in position and put his handkerchief into his mouth.

Mr London brought the stick down with all his force, four

times, four deliberate, even strokes, and each stroke raised a
purple weal under Chummy's shorts ... and that is how
Chummy came to worship Mr London with all his heart and
soul.[28]

There's little difference, it would seem, between these
stories aimed at children and the seamier reaches of 'adult'
fiction.

But it is not only the casual sadism that these boys' weeklies
depicted that might have influenced the adolescent Heath.
George Orwell made a study of the culture surrounding these
comics, often (inaccurately) described as 'penny dreadfuls' in
his 1940 essay 'Boys' Weeklies'. He observed that 'nearly every
boy who reads at all'[29] went through a stage of reading one or
other of them. The most celebrated and the oldest were *The
Gem* and *The Magnet*, each of which promoted an idealized
view of life in public schools: St Jim's in *The Gem*, Greyfriars
in *The Magnet*. These are represented as ancient institutions
much like Eton or Winchester. The boys in the stories never
aged and remained perpetually about fourteen. The stories
were endlessly repetitive, focusing on horseplay, practical
jokes, ragging, fights, canings, football, cricket and food.[30]

Orwell notes that boys who did actually go to public
schools read the comics, but nearly always stopped reading
them at about the age of twelve. But boys at cheaper private
schools, like Rutlish, 'that are designed for people who can't
afford a public school but consider the council schools
"common"',[31] carried on reading them until they were fifteen
or sixteen. Orwell's point was very much about class. These
weeklies promoted a dated and conservative ethos that was
consumed by vast numbers of schoolboys, like Heath, who
felt excluded from some sort of paradisal boyhood promoted
in their pages.

One Rutlish old boy from this period remembered that

from his first day, two specific objectives were outlined: 'By the time you leave Rutlish School you will be able to swim and to speak the King's English.'[32] Another pupil felt the Varnish agenda was extremely simple: 'Get educated, talk proper and you will succeed in life.'[33] Elocution was pivotal to a Rutlish education and was drilled into the boys by Herbert Cave, an English master who had written a book on the subject in 1930, *Practical Exercises in Spoken English*.[34] The Governors' Report of 1933 particularly commended this – 'a successful attempt had been made to turn out boys with power to speak correct Standard English'[35] – by which they meant Received Pronunciation. This was to prove invaluable to Heath who was to use his accent and the assumption of a patrician manner to masquerade as a member of the upper-middle class throughout his life and career.

Given how frequently he was to attempt to pass himself off as a product of Eton and Oxbridge, it's clear that something of Varnish's social ambitions for his boys rubbed off on the young Neville Heath; his yearning for upward social mobility, his self-aggrandizement and snobbery was ignited by Varnish's public-school ambitions for his grammar-school boys.[36] J. D. Casswell, Heath's defence counsel, was later to identify this key element of Heath's character. He was, he said, 'a man never satisfied to remain in the station to which he had been called and for which he was qualified'.[37]

Far from accepting the rigid class divisions of pre-war Britain, Heath was to study them, learn the manners and language of his social superiors – ape them – then ruthlessly exploit them.

In the various books and articles written about Heath over the past six decades, several cite uncorroborated incidents from his school days that identify embryonic sadistic behaviour. Gerald Byrne in *Borstal Boy* reports the instance of a girl in Heath's class at school being beaten by him so hard with a ruler that she had to be sent home in a taxi. If true, this must have taken place before the age of twelve, as Rutlish was a school for boys only. Certainly, Bessie Heath denied that this incident ever took place: 'I do not know of this incident [and] neither does his headmaster, who has nothing but good to say of him. Surely I, his mother, would have heard of this, if it had happened?'[38]

This may well be the opinion of a mother blind to the faults of a much-loved son. But, in the wake of the huge publicity surrounding Heath at the time of his arrest, many of the tales about him may well be apocryphal. Like this story, none are verifiable by any sources. *Borstal Boy* was published immediately after the trial in 1946, written in great haste and with a tabloid audience in mind. Its author, Gerald Byrne, was a journalist with the Sunday newspaper, *Empire News*. He had met Heath casually in various pubs and during the trial had talked to many of Heath's associates. Though he doesn't cite any sources, some of the incidents he describes do have the ring of truth. He quotes one young woman, a friend from Heath's schooldays:

Even at the age of fifteen Neville Heath started to show his sway over girls. The girls at the local school I attended used to take turns arranging regular little parties at their various homes and we wouldn't have dreamt of having a party without Neville – it wouldn't have been complete. He was an unmitigated liar, show-off swank-pot and all the things that usually go to make an unpopular character, yet although all the girls knew his faults, he somehow managed to blend them into an unusual and charming personality, and we all liked him.[39]

Heath was to develop this persona as the likeable rogue, the young dandy, throughout his adolescence to such an extent that by the time he reached borstal, he was a self-confessed 'Raffles'.

Byrne cites another incident, uncorroborated at the time, but verified a decade later by Giles Playfair and Derrick Sington in their study of psychopathy, *The Offenders*. Having read of the incident in Byrne's book and uneasy about quoting unverifiable sources, they had tracked down many of the individuals involved.

One winter night, when he was about fifteen, the young Heath and a boy called 'Howard' attended a party at the home of a mutual friend, Elizabeth, in Wimbledon High Street. The two boys, who were in the habit of drinking quarts of beer together in the garage behind Howard's house, had purchased a considerable amount of alcohol from the off-licence in Sutton High Street. As well as the boys, Elizabeth had invited five of her female friends. Her parents were out for the evening and the young people were left to their own devices. After a while, it was suggested that they play 'Murders' and the group dispersed to various parts of the house. They successfully played the game twice. The third time, Heath and Howard persuaded a girl called 'Jeanette' to accompany them in their search for clues. The three young people climbed to the top of the house and entered a bedroom. Suddenly, Heath grabbed Jeanette and threw her on the bed, calling to Howard to help him.

'Come on Howard, let's make real love to her!' Neville held Jeanette down as she violently kicked and struggled. The two boys first tried to kiss her face but she moved her head from side to side to avoid their lips. Then – 'We'll soon show her what love really is!' said Neville.

Jeanette screamed, alerting the other girls in the house. She returned home, deeply shocked, 'with deep blue finger marks on both sides of her throat'.[40]

Gerald Byrne interviewed both Jeanette's father and Howard in 1946. Then, in 1956, Playfair and Sington attempted to have the assault verified by Jeanette's father, a former MP.[41] He confirmed that the story was true. After the incident, he had gone off in search of the two boys and caught up with them outside Howard's house. He reprimanded Heath and warned him that not only might he be expelled from school for such behaviour, but he might also be reported to the authorities. This, after all, was a violent attempted sexual assault and not merely adolescent 'horseplay' as Byrne has Heath refer to it. Heath was 'disarmingly apologetic, courteous and contrite' and managed to persuade Jeanette's father not to report him to Varnish or the police. This was to become a well-rehearsed strategy in Heath's life. Having committed offences, he would rely on his innate charm and good manners to side-step difficult situations. Together with the appearance of sincere contrition this usually led to Heath being let off the hook. Not only did this allow him to refine his skill in petty offences, but it also began to cement his attitude to those in authority.[42]

This incident is the first evidence of violence in Heath's life, and it's worth bearing in mind that he stated to a prison psychiatrist in 1946 that he had no knowledge of sex until the age of eighteen,[43] some years *after* this attack. But it's also significant that Heath had been drinking before the assault – the marriage of sexual aggression and alcohol already fused, even before he had lost his virginity.

Though adept at sport – especially at rugby, cricket and athletics – Heath did not excel at school, mathematics being the only subject he felt confident in. He sat the matriculation

exam but failed. He refused to take it again, despite appeals
from his mother and Mr Varnish. Without matriculating,
neither university nor a commission as an officer in the services were options for him. At the age of sixteen, on 9 March
1934, he started work as a warehouseman in the silk department of Pawson and Leaf, an established textile importer at St
Paul's Churchyard in the City of London, which had been
trading since the eighteenth century.[44] The building still
remains situated directly opposite the cathedral. This job had
probably been arranged for Heath through his father's
connections in the textile business and William Heath may
well have worked for Pawson and Leaf at some point himself.
Heath earned 25s. a week for general menial duties and
though the job was dull, he was buoyed by the social life.[45] In
the City, he made friends with several other young men who
were in the Territorial Army, specifically the Artists Rifles
whose ranks were generally filled with young businessmen
and public schoolboys. On 30 October, Heath enlisted as a
rifleman 'terrier' in the 28th London Regiment Territorial
Army at the Drill Hall, Duke's Road, just off the Euston
Road. By now, Heath had specifically set his sights on a
uniformed service career, commenting to a friend at the time
that 'it is the uniform I want'.[46]

The appeal of the uniform was fundamental to Heath's
psychology. For him it became a complex symbol which
accumulated power and significance as his career progressed
from peacetime to war – at once a signifier of status and class
as well as an indicator of bravery and heroism. From the mid-
1930s onwards, Heath would adopt various uniforms, only
some of which he was entitled to wear. When he was on
active service in Palestine in 1940, he lamented the fact that
his division did *not* wear uniform and were allowed to wear
'civvies'.[47] By a conspiracy of historical events, Heath would
reach his maturity when the world would be suddenly – and

rapidly – flooded with uniforms as it launched headlong into the Second World War.

Heath's ultimate aim was to be a Royal Air Force pilot. His tenure with the RAF was the apotheosis of his life – the fulfilment of a *Boy's Own* dream. His relationship with flight and flying was intense and he was later to state: 'I have always been crazy on flying. All my successes, and all my failures, are bound up with my history as a flyer.'[48]

The RAF had only been a force independent of the army or the navy as recently as 1918 and throughout the 1930s, with Germany re-arming and investing in her defences, they launched an extensive campaign to expand the service. From 1935, forty-five new air stations were ordered to be built throughout the British Isles, most of which were operational by 1939.[49] This was accompanied by huge investment in new aircraft designs with up-to-the-minute technology and a mass recruitment drive. The RAF increased in strength from 31,000 personnel in 1934 to 118,000 in 1939, backed by 45,000 reserves; an increase in manpower of 500 per cent in five years.[50] With extraordinary speed, the RAF had transformed from a small and exclusive elite into an ultra-modern combat service with the manpower and technology to lead the Allies in the new frontier of warfare; the air.[51]

Throughout the 1930s, the priority for the RAF was to publicize their fledgling service and to find a way of engaging a generation of boys who would become the core of the force during the Second World War. It was essential for them to explain to the public who they were, what they did and what they stood for, *per ardua ad astra* ('through adversity to the stars') – a suitably aspirational motto for the boy from suburban Wimbledon. From 1920 to 1937, an air pageant was held every summer at Hendon Aerodrome, which included races, mock battles and aerobatics. These events

– later named the Royal Air Force Air Display – attracted huge crowds and were reported throughout the media. At the same time there was huge popular interest in the Schneider Trophy, an international air race that encouraged advances in aerodynamics. The 1930s became very much the age of the plane – fast, glamorous and modern. Aviators like Charles Lindbergh and Amy Johnson were as famous as film stars and stories of their record-breaking achievements filled the newspapers. Consequently a whole generation of boys became fascinated with the mystery, romance and power of flight. As Patrick Bishop points out in his study of Fighter Command, *Fighter Boys*, many of these boys' first encounters with aeroplanes and airmen took on a dream-like or mythic aura and many of those that are recorded have a sense of a meeting with Destiny.[52]

This generation had been brought up on illustrated papers like *The Magnet*, *The Gem* and *The Modern Boy*, which celebrated the heroism of the fighter aces from the First World War like Captain W. E. Johns. In 1932 Johns himself made a huge impact when he published the first of his Biggles stories. Captain James Bigglesworth was both a figure fit to hero-worship as well as a role model that a generation of schoolboys – including 'Dam Buster' Guy Gibson – would follow into the air in less than a decade. Crucially, Johns didn't depict a hardened and experienced flyer – but a boy, just like them.

> [Biggles was a] slight, fair-haired good-looking lad still in his teens but [already] an acting flight commander . . . his deep-set eyes were never still and held a glint of yellow fire that somehow seemed out of place in a pale face upon which the strain of war, and the sight of sudden death, had already graven little lines . . . he had killed six men during the past month – or was it a year? What did it matter anyway? He

knew he had to die some time and had long ago ceased to worry about it.[53]

The Air Ministry even appealed directly to schools for recruits and advertised in flying magazines and newspapers. One front-page advertisement from the *Daily Express* stated that though the basic educational qualification was a school certificate, 'an actual certificate is not necessary'. What the service required was not qualifications but a particular sort of character, as the RAF, even in its embryonic stage, had begun to establish its own identity, attracting a very specific type of recruit distinctly different from the other services. They tended to be louche and eccentric about their dress, hence the iconic look of pencil moustache, flying jacket and silk scarf, now the stuff of easy parody but at the time very much regarded as a fashion of dissent. RAF officers treated the army and navy (the 'senior' services) and their traditions flippantly, priding themselves, for instance, on their lack of knowledge of horses.

As well as dress, pilots adopted, by army and navy standards, an extremely casual attitude towards drill and saluting as well as a tendency to hard drinking and prank-playing. This carefree culture was more reminiscent of a private flying club than a focused fighting service. Many of these young men, were, like Heath, barely out of school or university; immature, high-spirited and literally, care-less. They brought with them in-jokes and slang from English public schools and American movies which was soon to develop into a specific language of understatement, bravura and cheek, all of which contributed to a great sense of camaraderie and belonging. Cecil Beaton, who was hugely impressed by the 'matchless team spirit' he found within the RAF, attributed this to the service being 'surprisingly free from conventions'.[54] Junior officers addressed their squadron superiors as 'sir' on the initial meeting of the day, after which they always used first names.

Something about this ambience, the culture, the uniform, this sense of belonging to a new type of defence force based on up-to-the-minute technology completely entranced the young Neville Heath.

On 25 November 1935, Heath attended the RAF Training School at Desford in Leicestershire where he was given *ab initio* training – the very first stage of flying instruction. For many young pilots, first flights left an indelible impression, akin, as some would remember, to their first encounter with sex. And it is perhaps significant that Heath lost his virginity in the same year that he started to fly. One young pilot from this period, remembering his first flight years later, was still moved by the intensity of the experience:

> I still find it hard to find the words to describe my sheer delight and sense of freedom as the little biplane, seeming to strain every nerve, accelerated across the grass and suddenly became airborne.[55]

Heath was taught to fly by George E. Lowell and Sergeant Bulman in a De Havilland D.H. 82, a 'Tiger Moth' – the RAF's primary training aircraft at the time. Now that he had completed his flying training and with a very strong recommendation from his superior officers in the Territorial Army, Heath left his job at Pawson and Leaf on 10 February 1936 and was granted a short service commission for four years in the General Duties branch of the RAF. He had had to pass a written test and a strict medical and was questioned by a panel of officers who were looking for technical knowledge as well as some evidence of enthusiasm. An aptitude for sports was usually taken as a strong indication of the latter and Heath had distinguished himself as an athlete at school, if nothing else. On 22 March he started at No. 11 Flying Training School at RAF Wittering in Northamptonshire as an acting pilot officer.

At Wittering, Heath spent three months flying biplanes – the Hawker Hart and Hawker Audax – followed by three months in the Advanced Training Squadron flying Hawker Furies. Trainee pilots went through twenty-two exercises, beginning with 'air experience' – the first flip – through to aerobatics. These were actively encouraged by flying instructors in order to increase the young pilots' confidence – but also to prepare them for the realities and unexpected dangers of aerial combat.[56] Heath was then sent to the RAF Depot at Uxbridge for two weeks of drilling, training and familiarization with mess protocol. The young recruits would be measured for their uniforms and mess kit and given £50 to cover everything – not enough if, like Neville Heath, they preferred the better outfitters. Student pilots would live in the mess and dress for dinner every night except on Saturdays, a 'dress-down' day when blazer, flannels and tie were permitted.[57]

After successfully completing the first half of the course, pilots received their 'wings' – a badge sewn over their tunic pocket, 'the most momentous occasion in any young pilot's career'.[58] The chief instructor would then assess each trainee pilot's qualities and abilities and whether he should go on to train as a fighter or bomber pilot.[59] Heath was assessed as 'above average', displaying the necessary discipline and audacity to become one of the most glamorous figures in the mid-1930s – a modern-day hero at the helm of a Rolls-Royce engine; a fighter pilot.[60]

On 24 August 1936, Heath was posted to 19 Squadron at RAF Duxford, near Cambridge. He was sent on parachute and armaments courses as well as given instruction in night flying. He was paid 14s. a day, from which 6s. went on mess costs covering food, lodging, laundry and a personal batman. The rest went on cars and alcohol, the two being inextricably linked in the social lives of young pilots on air bases. Cars were often bought collectively by a squadron and groups of young pilots would club together the £10 to £25 needed to buy one. These would be used to get to local country pubs or occasionally on trips to London where they would call in at Shepherd's in Shepherd Market – a favoured haunt for RAF servicemen, also popular with high-class prostitutes. But drink and petrol were both expensive, with fuel costing 1s. a gallon and a pint of beer costing 8d.[61]

19 Squadron was the first to be equipped with the fighter plane, the Gloster Gauntlet, the fastest aircraft in the RAF from 1935 to 1937. They were also the first to fly the Supermarine Spitfire, which was to play a pivotal role in the Battle of Britain and thereafter became the backbone of Fighter Command. Heath was training at an extraordinary time in a force at the forefront of modern technology. He was promoted to pilot officer on 25 November 1936, the lowest commissioned rank in the RAF. At this time, he genuinely seemed to prosper – his commanding officer remarking that 'this man has the makings of a first-class pilot and should prove himself an officer of outstanding abilities'.[62] Technology, history, opportunity – Heath was in exactly the right place at the right time, one of the young men of the moment with huge possibilities, as well as challenges, ahead of him.

Around this time Heath got engaged to Arlene Blakely, a Wimbledon girl who lived with her parents Alan and Grace at 15 Manor Gardens, just off the southern end of Merton Hall Road. At last his life and career seemed to be fulfilling his great promise – and yet this is when his RAF career started to go awry.

The source of his problem was not his ability in the air, but his issues with money. Though he had become an RAF officer by gaining a short service commission, he had not come from one of the major public schools or universities like many of his brother officers, nor, crucially, was he cosseted by their private incomes. Having succeeded in entering the well-to-do world of RAF mess dinners with their class-ridden rituals and parties, Neville Heath, the grammar-school boy from Wimbledon, was challenged with the task of keeping up with his peers without the money to do so. His father estimated that Heath's service wage was £250 to £300 a year, which was clearly insufficient (for Heath anyway) to support the lavish officer lifestyle to which he aspired. Like Pip in *Great Expectations*, despite the veneer of gentility and his accumulation of upper-class manners and tastes, Heath was not and would never be 'the real thing'.

Whilst at RAF Duxford, Heath was frequently to be found in the various pubs around Cambridge and became acquainted with students from the university. One of them, Allen Dyson Perrins, was introduced to Heath around this time.

He joined my circle of friends and I saw him frequently for about three weeks. He was never more than a mere acquaintance. He appeared to be fond of the company of women and frequented public houses. He mentioned that he had been to Eton and Oxford and I had no reason to doubt this. On occasions he visited me to my lodgings . . . I missed three cheques from my cheque book which I had left on my desk and I suspected Heath of taking them. I later received a telegram from my bank regarding one of the cheques. It transpired that it had been presented for payment, and as a result he advised me to communicate with the Cambridge Police.[63]

Already, at the age of nineteen, Heath was lying about his background and stealing money from friends. But it is within the RAF that he was to find himself in more serious trouble. On 15 March 1937, Pilot Officer Heath was transferred to Mildenhall to join 73 Squadron. He was already living beyond his means and was worried about money. He had arranged a loan from Lloyds Bank in Pall Mall and even had an appointment to go and discuss his financial issues with them on 16 March, arranging to do this by telegram the day before. But despite this, two cheques of his were returned; one for £1 10s. paid to the mess secretary at Duxford and another for £3 to the Aviation Club. Investigating Heath's recently released court martial files, it's interesting to note the sequence of events here, as the outcome of this incident was to have a profound effect on the rest of his life. Most significantly, the whole scenario could have been avoided if Heath had simply come clean and told the truth.

He didn't.

RAF Mildenhall had played a celebrated role in aviation history in the 1930s, famously hosting the Royal Aero Club's MacRobertson Air Race from London to Melbourne in 1934. At the time, the air race stood as the longest race ever devised and attracted over 70,000 spectators to Mildenhall, including George V and Queen Mary. For young flyers brought up on *Flight* magazine and tales of the pioneering aviators of their time, a transfer to Mildenhall must have felt like an extraordinary privilege. With no warning, Heath's squadron were transferred to Mildenhall overnight.

On his arrival, Heath had a telephone call from his commanding officer at Duxford, Squadron Leader J. W. Turton Jones, who had an 'official and serious' conversation with him about cheques he had written to pay his mess bill and the Aviation Club. The bank had returned them. After the telephone call, rather than thinking the matter through rationally, Heath panicked. Needlessly so, as is indicated by the records of the RAF, who investigated the matter with his bank, and discovered that he had indeed arranged a loan to cover the cheques.

In view of the fact that the accused officer had on a previous occasion been granted by the Bank an overdraft to an amount greater than that which would have resulted from the honouring of either of these cheques, I am of opinion that the circumstances are insufficient to support charges under the Air Force Act in respect of these transactions.[64]

But next morning, when the squadron assembled on their first day at Mildenhall, Pilot Officer Heath had disappeared.

For Heath, this became his favoured response to difficult circumstances. Rather than attempting to explain, his instinctive reaction was to run away. He didn't want to have a discussion about his behaviour – but he did want to make a statement about it, so would frequently send a letter. Again, this became a recurrent tactic in his life – flight followed by explanation – but only on his own terms, in his own time and with the sole objective of justifying his actions. Before leaving Duxford, Heath had left a letter for Turton Jones, promising to honour the cheques. In another he tendered his resignation. 'I think it will be the easiest way out to save dragging the name of a decent squadron in the mud,' he wrote. 'I consider I have been a disgrace to the service which will be well rid of me.'[65]

He added that he was going to Scotland, but intended to go abroad in a fortnight. He wanted to keep the affair from his parents as his father was unwell, but he would settle all outstanding bills within the month. He gave no indication how he would be able to honour this. A postscript added that he could be contacted through the personal column of the

Morning Post (again, this detail of offering contact through the personal column of a daily newspaper became a regular tactic). If he had stayed at Mildenhall and the RAF authorities had confirmed the loan with Lloyd's Bank, everything could have been resolved. As it was, Heath compounded the problem by absconding, starting a whole series of complicated events from which it would be impossible for him to extract himself.

After leaving Mildenhall, Heath didn't go abroad – he didn't even make it to Scotland – but instead he went home to Wimbledon where he stayed for the next three months, living openly in Merton Hall Road with his parents. There was no sense that he was in any way on the run or in hiding. He even wore his RAF tie.

It wasn't until 22 June that the RAF service police arrived to arrest him on charges of desertion. Flying Officer Kerby went to Merton Hall Road and saw Heath running towards him.

'Are you Pilot Officer Heath?'

Heath initially denied it. He was surprised to see Kerby – confused even, but soon collected himself.

'All right. I won't run away.'[66]

Heath was taken to Debden Aerodrome near Saffron Walden to await court martial for desertion and fraud. He was kept under open arrest and allowed the freedom of the aerodrome, the RAF taking his word as an officer and a gentleman that he wouldn't abscond. Ian Scoular, who was stationed at Debden at the time, remembered Heath's time under arrest there: 'Twice a day he had to be escorted around the aerodrome for exercise, and if any members of 73 [Squadron] were airborne they would see how close they could land to him, sending him on his face in the grass.'[67]

For Heath had not been well liked by all quarters. Johnny Kent, the Canadian Flying Ace, met Heath in this period and thought him a 'strange and rather unpleasant young man,' finding Heath very moody.[68] But this may well be because of the pressures Heath was trying to manage at the time, knowing that the life and career he'd striven for was under threat.

Heath's word as a gentleman proved to be worth very little and in the early hours of 22 July, he further exacerbated his situation by running away again. He stuffed some pillows on top of his bed under a blanket, stole a car belonging to another officer and drove to London, abandoning the car in Waterloo Road. He had decided on a 'party in London' – threatening his whole career with the RAF for a night on the town. He was later arrested and on 20 August 1937 attended his court martial hearing at Debden. He was defended by H. L. B. Milmo, a civilian barrister who argued that Heath was guilty of escaping and stealing the car but not desertion. Heath made a rather disingenuous statement:

> Having sent in my resignation, I expected an answer, but I received no intimation that the resignation had not been accepted. Had I been notified, I would have returned to the squadron or communicated with the Air Ministry.[69]

Milmo reminded the court that this was Heath's first offence and that he should be treated leniently. His reasons for leaving RAF Mildenhall were 'due to a sudden impulse after experiencing financial difficulties'. He was a decent young man who had got into a scrape simply because of inexperience. He had admitted his mistakes and was both sorry and ashamed, as was indicated by his chivalrous letter sent to his squadron leader. As to the charge of desertion, Milmo was appalled at the thought. 'The charge is repulsive to an officer and a soldier. This "mere boy" has been a foolish fellow, but did not intend to desert,'[70] he claimed.

Heath was acquitted on the charge of desertion but was found guilty of the lesser offence of going absent without leave. He was also found guilty of escaping whilst under arrest and of stealing a superior officer's car without permission. The charges of fraud regarding the mess funds were dismissed when Heath's bank confirmed their loan. The court martial marked his first appearance in the pages of both the London and the national press: 'RAF Officer Not Guilty of Desertion' (*Evening Standard*),[71] 'Officer of 20 Did Not Desert from RAF' (*Daily Mirror*).[72]

Heath was dismissed from the service with effect from 20 September 1937. He had been an officer in the RAF for less than a year.

In 1946, when recalling this period 'when [he] really began to go astray', Heath remembered the events rather differently. He claimed that he had been arrested for 'a flying offence'. This incident he mentioned throughout his career and even to his defence counsel during his trial – that he had flown an aircraft, without permission, under a bridge, threatening his own life, public property and an expensive aircraft. There is no evidence that this incident took place. It might well be an early example of Heath's boastful and flamboyant deceit. But it's also exactly the kind of needlessly dangerous, devil-may-care prank that was typical of him. It's also true that young pilots were encouraged to take out planes on jaunts, as it gave them extra flying practice. Certainly, being arrested and dismissed from the RAF for such an act of daring makes a much better story than being arrested for signing a dodgy cheque. Already, Heath was altering the facts, heightening reality, embroidering his own myth.

After his dismissal from the RAF, Heath returned home to Wimbledon. He hired a car from a local garage and on

5 October he travelled by road to the Midlands, looking for a job. He also borrowed £18 from his fiancée, Arlene. This was the last time she would actually see him – or her money. On hearing that he had been dismissed from the RAF and with his name all over the papers, she broke off the engagement and despite his attempts to phone her, refused to take his calls.[73]

He first went to Cambridge, well known to him from his time at Duxford, and stayed at the Lion Hotel. He then travelled on to Nottingham and booked into the Victoria Station Hotel. On both occasions he left without paying the bill. From 15 October to 6 November, he continued to tender worthless cheques to shopkeepers and bought expensive clothes costing £47 8s. He then tried to buy a car worth £175 from the landlord of the Sherwood Inn, Nottingham, promising that he'd send a cheque in the post. Throughout this spree in the Midlands, the identity Heath used most frequently was that of 'Lord Dudley'.

Heath's adoption of this aristocratic identity is one of the more audacious fictions that he was to present. The Earl of Dudley had been a friend and confidante of the Duke of Windsor when he was Prince of Wales, so his name would certainly have had currency with the people that Heath met at this time, the abdication having only taken place in December of the preceding year. But there may be a more prosaic reason for Heath using Dudley as a pseudonym. Throughout his career he would use genuine names and addresses that would quickly come to mind, in order to give his stories a sense of authenticity. These names and addresses frequently did exist, as if he was keen to stay as close to the truth as possible; Dudley Road was the name of the street where Heath was born.

But local police soon tracked Heath down to an hotel. Detective Inspector Hickman of Nottingham CID approached him at the bar, where Heath was drinking, pipe in hand.

'Are you Lord Dudley?'

'Yes I am, old man.'

'Well, I am Detective Inspector Hickman of the CID.'

'Then, in that case, I am *not* Lord Dudley.'[74]

Heath was arrested and appeared at Nottingham Petty Sessions on 11 November 1937.

As well as attempting to obtain the car and money by false pretences, he was charged with eight other offences in Cambridge, Stafford and Peterborough. All these petty crimes had taken place in the three months since he had been dismissed from the RAF. He justified his actions at Nottingham by saying that he had been on a mad spree after the disgrace of his dismissal from the RAF. They were boyish pranks for which he was heartily sorry, particularly for the shame that it would bring on his family. Effectively he adopted the defence that he was to use throughout the rest of his life – that he was a good lad, high-spirited and foolish but not a felon: 'My parents want me home. I have learned my lesson.'[75] This tactic certainly worked at Nottingham; Heath was placed on probation – bound over on remand for two years and placed under the supervision of Mr F. V. Dale, a probation officer in Wimbledon. Again, Heath's misdemeanours were reported in the national press ('Ex RAF Man: "I'm Lord Dudley" – But Not If You're A Detective, Old Man'). Bessie Heath, interviewed by the *Daily Mirror*, was supportive, but weary of her son's behaviour:

I am afraid that Neville has been spoiled. By his last escapade he has ruined his father's business.[76] He is not a criminal. He is a really clean-living decent young fellow – a good sportsman. This will be a severe lesson to him and now he will have to find a job. His father and I are waiting for him to come back so that we can do our utmost to help him.[77]

He was lucky; this time he had got away with it. This sense of inviolability was to develop over the years – and with good reason – as Heath became more adept at side-stepping his way out of trouble. Despite his record of persistent offending, various authorities seduced by his 'hail fellow, well met' manner would continue to give this charming young man the benefit of the doubt, which can only have fuelled his confidence that he could get away with anything.

As he observed Heath's progress over the Christmas of 1937 and the New Year of 1938, Heath's probation officer noted the good relations he had with his parents, but was also concerned that Bessie Heath seemed to shield her son and excuse his conduct when he misbehaved. Mr Dale felt that this sort of indulgence was exactly the wrong way to force Heath to face his responsibilities.[78] Even by the beginning of 1938, Dale felt that young Heath was drifting into a 'slack and irresponsible mode of living'.[79] He reported regularly to the Court House in Queens Road in Wimbledon and he certainly gave Mr Dale the impression that he was settling down and making an effort to find work. He was always full of wonderful offers and opportunities that had come his way, but none of these ever materialized. And in February, Heath suddenly stopped reporting to Mr Dale and began a spree of petty theft and swindling, unprecedented in his career to date.

On 24 February, Mrs Maud Archdall of Woburn Sands, Buckinghamshire was rushing for the 4.10 p.m. train from Euston to Bletchley. Thinking she might miss her train, she flagged down a taxi to take her to the station. She made the train, but soon realized that she had left her handbag in the cab. In the bag were many personal items, some money and seven blank cheques. The next person to pick up the cab was Neville Heath. Broke, unemployed and desperate – this was too good an opportunity for him to pass up. He spent Mrs Archdall's cash and when that was all gone, he used the

cheques to fund a swindling holiday across the country –
from Sussex to Somerset, from Leicestershire to London.[80]

From 22 February, Heath had been lodging at 15 Oxford
Terrace in Paddington under the name A. J. Banham. The
day he moved in, he paid a visit to the gentleman's outfitters,
Moss Bros in Covent Garden, announcing himself as Pilot
Officer Banham. He walked out of the shop with £27 1s.
8d.-worth of new clothes; if he was really going to succeed
in his latter-day Rake's Progress, he would need to dress the
part. The real Officer Banham was later traced and the forgery
detected. But by now Heath's deceptions had developed into
an easy skill and, as well as his way with women, he was now
practised at exploiting the deferential trust that lower-class
shop workers placed in the officer class to which he confi-
dently appeared to belong.

When he left Oxford Terrace on 7 March, he paid the
landlady Mrs Bayley with one of the cheques that he had
stolen from Mrs Archdall's handbag. On 18 March, he bought
a wireless at Deaford in Leicestershire with another of the
cheques. The rest were cashed under a variety of pseudo-
nyms: J. Donaldson, J. R. Denvers, Richard C. Jeffries and
James R. Bulmar.

Out of the blue, on 22 March, Heath's former fiancée
Arlene Blakely received a letter from him with no address,
enclosing a cheque for £20. She had never believed that she
would see her money again. Surprised, but delighted, she
paid the cheque into her account at Chancery Lane Post
Office two days later. The cheque bounced. Given that she
lived so close to his parents, it is understandable that Heath
should want to repay the debt. But to make the grand gesture
of sending a letter and cheque to dispatch it, knowing that it
would bounce, seems perverse – particularly knowing how it
would further embarrass his parents. But Heath seemed blind
to the consequences.

At Deaford where he bought the wireless, Heath had accidentally left behind a sheet of paper with several names and
addresses scribbled on it. These seemed to be leads that he
was following up in pursuit of various jobs. One of the
addresses was for the Hoover shop in Regent Street which
trained vacuum-cleaner salesmen, hardly the obvious choice
for this swaggering young man about town. Other names at
Wardour Street and Gainsborough Studios suggested that he
might have been looking for work much more suited to him
as a film extra.[81] He does seem to have considered some sort
of film work, as when he arrived at borstal later that year, his
father wrote that his son was 'awaiting the results of these
proceedings before signing a film contract'.[82] This, of course,
wasn't true.

Another of the contacts from the Deaford list was particu
larly curious. Mrs Horace Ferguson of 31 Dover Street was
the proprietress of the 'SOS Agency'. The nature of her business was to 'provide Guide Escorts to ladies who wish to have
the company of a gentleman for dancing, dining, theatres,
racing, motoring, etc. The guide escorts are men of title,
ex-officers, public school and varsity men'.[83] When later
questioned, Mrs Ferguson was sure that Heath never actually
contacted her about employment with the agency. But it is
apparent that at this time he had decided to exploit, or at least
explore, his greatest asset – his looks.

A photograph from 1935 shows a smart and fashion-
conscious eighteen-year-old, pale-skinned, perhaps pretty
rather than handsome, but it's easy to see why magistrates
were convinced by this respectable-looking young man
and why women were also seduced by his sensitive features.
His good looks in conjunction with his charm were a
winning combination. Sydney Brock, one of Heath's early
biographers, felt that Heath's growing awareness of these
advantages resulted in a confidence that bordered on

conceit: 'He felt confident that his personality was so winning that he would be able to go on indefinitely making a mockery of the law.'[84]

Brock was clear what he felt was at the heart of this confidence and people's willingness to be taken in by him. 'If Neville Heath had been an ugly, unprepossessing fellow, would he have been treated so leniently? I think not.'

Having now evolved into a modern-day Macheath, the charming, audacious (but always gentlemanly) thief had developed a simple formula for personal advancement – robbing from the rich to give to himself. But at this point, with several constabularies on his tail, he made an effort to get back on the straight and narrow. He seems to have been encouraged by Mr Dale, his probation officer, 'who helped him in every possible way to get a job'.

Consequently, Neville Heath – wanted man, fraudster and swindler – secured employment as a lowly assistant at the John Lewis department store in Oxford Street. In doing so, he realized that he would need to deal with the long list of petty offences he had been committing since he had appeared at Nottingham. Again, he relied on the strategy he had utilized in the RAF when faced with a situation that was threatening to spiral out of control – he wrote a letter to the chief superintendent of the CID at Scotland Yard.

8th April 1938

Dear Sir,

Before you read this letter I would like to make it quite clear that not in any way do I mean it to be taken as either being frivolous or impertinent. In view of this I beg that you submit my request for the consideration of the proper authority.

During the last few months I have been living a criminal

existence. I fully realize the serious view taken of the crimes I have committed and will, for the rest of my years, do the utmost to make full reparation. I was practically forced into this life of crime by financial circumstances and the inability to secure employment. You, who know my history will surely understand the reflex action upon the mind after once having ruined a decent career. I most sincerely ask you to believe and understand that I am not by nature a criminal, nor do I enjoy leading the life it entails.

Today I have been fortunate enough to secure employment of a legitimate nature with a reputable firm and this is the reason I am asking you for leniency and understanding and a chance to make good. I am going to make a most unusual request but I am convinced that if there is a human side to justice and any truth in the saying that the police are to prevent crime and prevent the making of criminals, I am convinced you will grant my request.

I am going to request that you withhold the warrants which are issued for my arrest, until you see that I am serious and telling the truth.

I want to start work on Monday and from my salary I shall make payments to all hotels, etc. from whom I have secured credit and money by false pretences. I shall keep these payments up until all my debts are cleared.

I further promise that from this time of writing I shall undertake nothing dishonest ever again. In the event of your granting my request and in the event of my failing to keep my promise, I ask that this letter be produced and that my normal sentence when convicted be doubled.

Once again, sir, I ask you for human understanding, and in helping me to take this chance which may never come again, you will very effectively rid the world of one more criminal.

I have the honour, to be, sir
Your Obedient Servant,

Neville GC Heath

> *In the event of your granting my requests I should be obliged if an*
> *insertion could be made in the personal column of the 'Daily*
> *Telegraph', in which case I shall be only too pleased to refund the*
> *expense incurred.*[85]

The notion of Heath being 'practically forced into [a] life of crime' is laughable – his protestations, of course, always pointing the blame elsewhere or on circumstances beyond *his* control. And offers that he will never be able to keep ('I shall undertake nothing dishonest ever again') are both childlike and childish in their naiveté.

Heath was employed as an assistant in the fabric department at John Lewis on a wage of £2 per week, half what he had been earning with the RAF. But this sojourn as a respectable wage earner was not to last for long – thirteen days in all. It was soon apparent that his references were not bona fide, and nor was he. Heath was sacked – a substantial blow to his confidence; he couldn't even hold down a job as a shop assistant. Despite his recent claims that he was not 'by nature a criminal' and did not enjoy the life it entailed, he now embraced his former life with a renewed alacrity and an increased audacity.

In June, Heath was staying at the Royal Sussex Hotel in Brighton and ran into a friend of his, Percy Masters, who was spending a few days by the sea. Masters was a bank manager and lived comfortably in Edgware. Knowing that his house was now vacant, Heath couldn't resist. On 7 June he travelled up to Masters' house, 42 Penshurst Gardens, and smashed a window at the back. He opened the catch and let himself in. Whilst he was there, he entertained a girlfriend, wearing Masters' pyjamas and even sleeping in his bed. The intruders ate a meal of sardines and beer in the kitchen, the table laid with fish knives – a precocious touch. A newspaper dated 7 June was later found in one of the rooms. Heath had made himself very much at home, effectively taking a holiday in his friend's house. When he left he took with him a selection of 'playboy' booty – a revolver, golf clubs, binoculars, a camera and some jewellery. At the same time he stole various clothes: a dinner suit, two lounge suits and an overcoat. He even took some of Masters' favourite cigars.

When Masters reported the break-in to Detective Sergeant Driscoll of Edgware Police, Driscoll felt certain that this was the work of somebody who knew the house and its owner. He asked Masters if he suspected anyone who might be involved. Masters mentioned Heath's name and it didn't take long for Driscoll to check the Criminal Records Office where he noted Heath's appearance at Nottingham the previous November. Heath seemed a very likely suspect indeed.

On 13 June, the golf clubs and binoculars were traced to a pawnbroker in Tottenham Court Road and Masters went to identify them. The pawnbroker described the man who had surrendered the goods and identified him as a James Bulman.[86] 'Bulman' was traced to the Royal Sussex Hotel in Brighton. The Metropolitan Police called their colleagues in Brighton to arrest the suspect. Bulman, a.k.a. Neville Heath, was taken to London where he was charged with housebreaking and stealing property worth £51 11s. 6d. He was further charged with his fraud at Moss Bros in February. A total of ten other offences at Pevensey, Weston-Super-Mare, Leicestershire and London were taken into consideration covering a period from 19 February to 28 May 1938.

In addition to these crimes, Heath had also defrauded his own family. His uncle, Walter Barker, worked as a market gardener at Laleham. Heath had offered him a cheque for £55, saying that he had won a bet on a horse. But Barker had loaned money to his nephew before and Heath still owed him £50, so he only gave Heath £5. Needless to say, Heath's cheque bounced. At Weston–Super–Mare Heath had also taken £5 from an aunt, again offering her a dud cheque.

Heath had no scruples, and strangers, friends and family were all fair game in his desire for personal gain. Neither his uncle nor his aunt pressed charges, but cumulatively the other crimes amounted to a career of wrongdoing. Heath was to be tried at the Old Bailey.

The two murders apart, all of Heath's crimes followed a similar pattern, usually stealing money or property (frequently clothes) or pretending to be somebody else. None of the crimes he was actually convicted of before 1946 involved violence or threatening behaviour. He was a small-time crook, a con man with a relentless, acquisitive instinct for money and status. The gilded lifestyle he aspired to was in some contrast to the reality of his modest background – his father a hairdresser, his mother a landlady.

Whilst awaiting trial, Heath was held in Wormwood Scrubs Boys' Prison in west London. The court commissioned a series of reports to assess what to do with him and how to plan for his future. Having failed to meet his probation commitments, could he be trusted again? Did he require a custodial sentence, or was that overly harsh? How could they rehabilitate this obviously intelligent young man and direct him towards a useful and law-abiding future? One thing was clear – despite his obvious charm and steady upbringing, the boy was patently dishonest, a liar and a thief. The court assessment was wide-ranging and included contributions from the prison governor, his probation officer, his old headmaster Mr Varnish, his parents and even his old employers at Pawson and Leaf. Generally, Heath seemed to have succeeded in convincing the various authorities that he was a good lad at heart who had gone off the rails: 'A boy who has got himself into a hopeless mess owing to his own irresponsibility and bad management and needs a lot of help and guidance.'[87]

But amongst the general chorus of support, there was one dissenting voice in the assessment of the incorrigible but charming boy gone astray. The chaplain at Wormwood Scrubs saw right through the veneer of Heath's bonhomie. 'He says he was so completely in debt that he has become a "Raffles",' he wrote. 'He is as crafty as they make 'em and I wouldn't give much for his future.'[88]

But even whilst awaiting trial at Wormwood Scrubs, Heath was keen to turn the situation to his advantage. With extraordinary resourcefulness, he contacted the editor of the *Daily Mirror*.

Wormwood Scrubs Prison

15th June 1938

Dear Sir,

No doubt you are astounded to hear from me, but perhaps it will help to clarify the matter if I mention two articles concerning myself which appeared in headlines in your paper. Firstly the court martial of Pilot Officer NGC Heath RAF which took place somewhere around last August and the more recent impersonation of Lord Dudley last November. Now I am on remand at the above prison, awaiting trial on yet another charge.

After my trial and sentence is over, I am going to make known the most sensational story since the Baillie-Stewart Affair.

I am communicating with you because you may be interested in having the sole rights of the story. I have however definitely made up my mind not to say a word until after my trial and sentence. If you are interested perhaps you would like to send your reporter or come yourself to interview me at this address. I am allowed to receive visitors on any weekday so I'll expect your representative one day this week. I'll give you a rough outline of the situation and afterwards you will be able to please yourself. I should, of course, expect you to respect my confidence.

> *By the way, if your reporter would care to bring with him any*
> *fruit, chocolate or magazines they will be most acceptable.*[89]

But though his misdemeanours had indeed been reported in the press, the stories appeared on page four and beyond. Even as a criminal he couldn't make the front page. Not yet, anyway.

Heath appeared for the first time at the Old Bailey on 12 July 1938 before Sir Gerald Donaldson. In his defence he said, 'I have no excuse for what I have done.' Donaldson despaired of all the opportunities that the youth before him had been offered and yet had wasted so shamefully.

> This is a tragic record. There were such bright prospects but now you have spoilt it all. There is only one chance for you and that is your instincts to do right. I cannot believe that you have lost all of them at your early age.[90]

Even at this juncture, Donaldson had highlighted a fundamental issue — perhaps *the* fundamental issue — at the heart of Heath's personality. Did he have an instinct to do right? Or had he indeed lost all sense of moral compass?

He was given a custodial sentence of three years. At the age of just twenty-one, it seemed that the golden boy's luck had finally run out.

CHAPTER EIGHT
Borstal Boy

JULY 1938 – DECEMBER 1941

I shall always remember that year at Hollesley Bay Colony
and (I think you know it too) I was really happy there. It's a
great pity I did not remember the many lessons I learned
there, but unfortunately my memory had always been abom-
inably short, and I've usually paid dearly for it . . .

Letter from Heath to C. A. Joyce, 8 October 1946[1]

Within a fortnight of his sentence at the Old Bailey,
Heath was transferred from the grim surroundings of
Wormwood Scrubs to a newly opened borstal institution
near Woodbridge in Suffolk, Hollesley Bay.

Hollesley Bay is perhaps most renowned today for being
the open prison that Jeffrey Archer was sent to for pervert-
ing the course of justice in 2002. The press dubbed it
'Holiday Bay'[2] at the time, but even in the early months of

its opening in the 1930s it had garnered a reputation as a soft option, with critics feeling it was more like a rural public school than an institution for young offenders. Heath had landed on his feet.

The Irish writer Brendan Behan happened to arrive at Hollesley Bay shortly after Heath. At the age of sixteen, Behan had been arrested in Liverpool for agitating on behalf of the IRA, who had initiated a wave of terrorist attacks throughout 1939 in Manchester, Birmingham and London including bombings at King's Cross, Tottenham Court Road and Leicester Square tube stations. Behan recalled his time at Hollesley Bay in the period leading up to the outbreak of war in his memoir, *Borstal Boy* (1958), a title that had been used by Gerald Byrne for his biography of Heath published twelve years earlier.

The borstal colony, as it was called, was set in beautiful countryside, within sight of the Suffolk coast – Aldeburgh to the northeast and Felixstowe to the southwest. Much of the colony was given over to market gardens and orchards growing a rich variety of fruit and vegetables – plums, apples, cucumbers, tomatoes, greengages and even grapes and peaches, the coastal climate being favourable for more exotic fruits. There were also hives for collecting honey and grazing land for the flocks of sheep that were reared by the inmates – all the produce being later taken to market. The colony had only opened the previous May and Heath was one of the first boys to be sent there.[3]

Built at the end of the nineteenth century, the main buildings at Hollesley Bay were large and rambling, complete with dormer windows and a clock tower, all designed to resemble a great Tudor manor house. On arrival, the borstal boys, having travelled in chains, were unshackled and issued with a kit of blue jacket, shirt, shoes and shorts, finished with thick stockings and a woollen tie. Unexpectedly, they were also given half an ounce of Ringers A1 Shag tobacco and a packet of cigarette papers.[4] This welcoming touch was very much the tone of the institution which had been established by Hollesley Bay's enlightened governor, C. A. ('Jack') Joyce, a man of great integrity who was convinced in the ability of the borstal system to redirect the lives of young men who had gone off the rails, empowering them by teaching them self-respect as well as respect for others: 'While you are here, the first thing I ask of you is courtesy to each other, to the staff and to myself.'[5] Joyce stayed in touch with many of his former borstal boys, including Behan and Heath. Both found their experience at Hollesley Bay formative. From prison, Heath later remembered the profound effect that Joyce's regime had on him. 'You and . . . your ideals which we all worked so hard for once, occupy a very special corner in my long list of pleasant memories.'[6]

Much of the daily routine at Hollesley Bay aped the structure of a public school timetable. Four houses – St Patrick's, St Andrew's, St George's and St David's – accommodated about 100 boys, each with prefects and a housemaster. Most of the boys were between sixteen and eighteen but the colony would admit young men up to the age of twenty-three. Most were single, but some were married with children. The boys were regarded very much as delinquents rather than criminals, deserving of rehabilitation, rather than punishment. None of them were thought of as high risk and much of the time they were unsupervised and able to abscond. Few did though, so responsive were they to Joyce's methodology.

Though the manual work could be hard – sometimes nine-hour days harvesting fruit and vegetables in all seasons – the facilities at Hollesley Bay were very comfortable. Though the dormitories in which the boys slept were basic and unheated, there were several public rooms offering a variety of leisure activities: a games room to play table tennis, darts and billiards, a radio room to listen to the wireless, a gym, a library, as well as playing fields for football and rugby. There were frequent treats – Brendan Behan nostalgically remembered teas of bread and jam, treacle duff and sweet cake and Heath was regularly able to buy the *Daily Mirror,* the *Observer,* or his beloved *Daily Telegraph.* The centrally heated dining room was furnished not with refectory tables, but with sociable tables for four, each decorated with bowls of flowers from the Hollesley Bay gardens. The walls were hung with colourful prints of the colonies – a subliminal suggestion, perhaps, to the delinquents that in the future they could make a fresh start in one of the British dominions.[7]

The colony promoted a healthy, outdoor lifestyle that suited Heath and he certainly prospered there. Food was fresh and plentiful and the coastal breeze invigorating. At Wormwood Scrubs Heath had measured 5 ft 10 ¼ and weighed 152 lb. By the time he left Hollesley Bay he was 15 lb heavier and had grown half an inch.[8] His strategy whilst at borstal seems to have been to keep his head low and behave, in the hope of securing an early release. He did carting, cropping and general farm labouring as well as working with horses. He was most keen, though, to tend the colony's show sheep, regarded as a light job for a man of his athletic build and developing strength. This he did with Fred Sams, Hollesley Bay's shepherd.

> His sole job for months was to be my assistant and all he had to do was make sure the sheep did not fall into the sea. He would laze there, mostly lying on the bank of the saltings at the edge of the North Sea, dreaming and scheming and never working but to shoo the odd sheep back from danger.[9]

The colony provided Heath with a sufficiently easy life with the sort of public school or military structure in which he thrived.

But in the outside world, political events were conspiring to impact even on this sleepy corner of the Suffolk coast. On 30 September, Neville Chamberlain landed at Heston aerodrome and announced that war had been averted by the signing of the Munich Agreement. The increasingly acquisitive Nazi Germany had been appeased, with Britain, France and Italy agreeing to the annexation of Czechoslovakia's Sudetenland – an issue that had been causing international anxiety since Germany had annexed Austria in March of that year.

> We regard the agreement signed last night and the Anglo-German Naval Agreement as symbolic of the desire of our two peoples never to go to war with one another again.[10]

Arriving at Downing Street later that day Chamberlain (in)famously announced that he believed that this was 'peace for our time'.

Heath's housemaster, Mr Macfarlane, hadn't, at first, been impressed by his new charge. In the autumn of 1938, he worried that Heath was too conceited, showing off his superior education and culture to the scorn of the other boys who dismissed him as an affected snob. But by the following spring, McFarlane had completely revised his opinion and commented that Heath had settled into the colony's routine extremely well.[11] He was taking an active part in the community and was even appointed as captain of his house. On arriving at Hollesley Bay, the precocious Brendan Behan was introduced to Heath, noting how 'strongly built' he was, as well as the silver star he wore on his jacket – a badge of seniority and authority.

'My name is Behan,' said I.

[Heath] smiled and said in a mock Irish accent, 'An' it's aisy to say where you're from, Paddy.'

I smiled too, because it seemed to be meant as a kindness.

'Phwart paart of Tipperary, Paddy?'

'I'm not from Tipperary,' said I.

'Are you not, now?' said Heath.[12]

Heath advised Behan and the new 'receptions' to keep their heads down and to commit themselves to scrupulous, almost military self-discipline. Violence, boisterousness, even swearing was out of order.

'Look here, cock,' said Heath, 'as long as I'm here, you keep that kind of talk to yourself. I won't wear it, and if I get you or any other filthy bloody swine talking like that he'll know all about it.'[13]

It seems, as far as Behan and his contemporaries were concerned, that Heath was, if not one of the lads, certainly respected by the other borstal boys.

In February 1939, the first Anderson shelter[14] was built in London. By April the WRNS had been re-established, followed in June by the creation of the WAAF (Women's Auxiliary Air Force). The Military Training Act was introduced in April,[15] initiating conscription for men of twenty and twenty-one to take six months' military training. As the country watched the international situation darken and realized that Chamberlain's promise of peace looked more and more like naïve wishful thinking, Britain prepared for war. In May, eleven months into his sentence, Heath wondered if he might be eligible for discharge for military training, given his background in the services and his spotless behaviour since he

had arrived at Hollesley Bay. He had already made it clear to
Mr McFarlane that his ultimate ambition was to rejoin the
RAF. McFarlane told Heath he must be patient. By now he
genuinely admired Heath's 'persistent good humour and
common-sense adjustments' that had enabled him to fit in
with the other boys like Brendan Behan, 'without lowering
his own standards'.[16] More and more, Heath seemed like the
model borstal boy, his time at Hollesley Bay having moulded
a mature and responsible young man.

During his time at borstal, Heath acquired some very
useful friends in high places. As well as gaining McFarlane's
admiration and support, he managed to catch the interest of
Jack Joyce, the governor. Through him, Heath secured a
meeting with Mr Scott, the Head of the Borstal Association,
to discuss his future. These two friendships were to develop
throughout the rest of Heath's life with Scott and Joyce as
unofficial mentors, taking a genuine interest in Heath's
progress. When he first met Mr Scott in June 1939, Heath's
'consuming anxiety' was to find out if there was any hope of
his being accepted by the RAF on his discharge from borstal.
He argued that he had held commissioned rank as a pilot and
already had 200 flying hours under his belt. Surely he'd be
ideally placed to rejoin the service in a time of national emergency, even if it meant starting again in the ranks?

Scott was impressed by Heath's passion, his excellent
physique and superior intelligence and promised to help. In
Mr Scott, Heath had secured a very influential champion.
Later that month, Heath's father also visited Scott at the
Borstal Association offices in Victoria Street to discuss his
son's future. Again, the two men became very friendly,
united in their desire to try and help young Neville fulfil his
potential. Like the Heaths, Scott also lived in Wimbledon, so
he began visiting them socially in Merton Hall Road, always
curious to know how their son was getting on.

True to his word, throughout the summer, Mr Scott made a series of enquiries at the Air Ministry on Heath's behalf to see if there might be some chance of his rejoining the RAF. These appeals were all rejected. This can't have been surprising as Heath had been dismissed from the service only two years previously and since then had been in court twice, thereafter spending most of his time in borstal. There was also a rush by hundreds of thousands of young men to enlist. The RAF neither wanted nor needed him back.

From the end of the summer, Britain galvanized herself for war. On 23 August, the Soviets and the Germans signed their mutual treaty of non-aggression, the Molotov–Ribbentrop Pact. A week later, the Royal Navy manned their war stations and the evacuation began to remove children from major British cities to the countryside. On 1 September, the Germans invaded Poland. The British army was then mobilized and a blackout imposed across the British Isles. The international crisis had an impact even at Hollesley Bay; on 2 September, Heath was discharged under emergency regulations and sent home to Wimbledon. This wasn't special treatment, though, as approximately 1,750 borstal boys were similarly discharged on the same day. And though Heath had been released, he would remain on licence for another three years.

The day after Heath was released from borstal, the National Service Act was passed, introducing mass conscription for all men between the ages of eighteen and forty-one. The following day, Heath called to see Mr Scott at the Borstal Association offices in a frenzy of excitement. He burst into Scott's office with his arms waving and his eyes blazing, shouting, 'My God, sir, they're up and I'm not with them.' Knowing the boy and his history, Scott could understand Heath's passion, but he felt at the time that 'Heath's manner, appearance and expression disclosed lack of control and an excitability far from normal'.

Making full allowance for the excitement prevailing throughout the country on that day and for this ex-pilot's feelings of
frustration and impatience, he displayed unnatural excitement and loss of self-control. His eyes were wild, his whole
body shook with emotion and he could not sit down.[17]

For Heath the outbreak of war was both an opportunity to
put the past behind him, but also a fulfilment of his destiny.
There was no sense that he wanted to fight for King and
Country with the old Rutlish rallying cry, 'arming for the
fight, pressing on with all our might'. His objective seems
to have been a personal one – to embark on a great adventure which at this point he felt was being blocked by various authority figures for mistakes he had made in his
youth. He seems to have had no anxieties about actively
pursuing a role in a war in which he might forfeit his life.
This is very much the *Boy's Own* attitude to mortality
enshrined in *Biggles*: 'He knew he had to die sometime and
had long ago ceased to worry about it.' This became
Heath's maxim for life.

Heath trudged from one RAF recruiting office to another,
but was rejected by all of them. In a letter to Mr Scott, his
sense of frustration is palpable.

> *Life is full of disappointments. I was ready, packed and preparing to
> depart yesterday morning when I received a letter from the Recruiting
> Centre at Croydon telling me not to go. Apparently Uxbridge is so
> full (5000 over number) that yesterday's and today's draft of recruits
> had to be stopped.*
>
> *However, in spite of the letter, I went to Croydon complete with
> case, just in case there was an off chance of getting away. The
> Recruiting Officer was awfully sympathetic but said there was noth-
> ing he could possibly do.[18]*

Despite his efforts and his obvious commitment, the RAF would not take him. He was 'horribly disappointed', but, with some tenacity, refused to be defeated. With his favoured options closed to him, he enlisted as a private in the army, volunteering for the Royal Army Service Corps. His admission to the RASC was in stark contrast to his former status as an RAF pilot – glamorous, heroic, daring, modern. The RASC was a much more mundane facilitating corps providing services and support staff. Heath joined them as a driver. This role could not have underlined more clearly the downward trajectory he had been on since being dismissed from the air force. A modern Icarus, his was a literal as well as figurative grounding; from flying a fighter to driving a truck.

Based at Buller Barracks in Aldershot, Heath's strategy at this stage – and it certainly seems like a careful and deliberate plan – was to join up as a lower-status private and then to pursue his goals from within the service. He may well have been starting at the bottom again but he was determined not to stay there.

By December of 1939, though there had been attacks at sea, there had been no significant offensives by the major powers in the war. Heath was at home in Wimbledon, visiting his parents for Christmas. While at a dance at the Dog and Fox on Wimbledon Hill, he bumped into Peggy Dixon, a 24-year-old girl from Loxley Road in nearby Wandsworth. They had been introduced some years before at a twenty-first birthday party. Peggy remembered that Heath had been in the RAF at the time, or was just about to join. Heath told her that he was an army cadet now and Peggy told him about her work as a civil servant. The pair got on well, arranging to meet again. Peggy visited Merton Hall Road and was introduced to William and Bessie Heath and Heath was introduced to Peggy's parents, too. The couple had a lot in common and it seemed a very sensible match. Given Heath's recent history, his parents must have been relieved that their son was settling down at last, with a job, a girlfriend – a future. Everything was looking up for him.[19]

Early in 1940, Heath joined the Officer Cadet Training Unit, passing out on 23 March as a 2nd Lieutenant. He visited Mr Scott and proudly showed off his uniform. He had passed ninth out of thirty-four cadets. He told Scott that he had discussed his past history with his company commander who was 'awfully understanding and terribly nice about everything'. Neville Heath the rakish playboy seemed to have turned prodigal. Not only was he prospering in the RASC, but he was confronting his past mistakes, being upfront and honest about them. His commanding officer had approached the RAF on his behalf and had arranged for a transfer. He was to be drafted to the Middle East soon as a reconnaissance pilot attached to the Mediterranean Expeditionary Force on a 'special job'.

Mr Scott was hugely impressed by the extraordinary turnaround in Heath's fortunes. But little of the information he gave Scott was actually true. Though he was certainly scheduled to travel out to Palestine and might have *hoped* for some sort of flying role, there is no indication from Heath's War Office records that he was offered one.[20]

Like many romances of the time, the overseas posting intensified Heath's relationship with Peggy. He asked her to marry him and she accepted. On Saturday 13 April 1940, Heath and Peggy celebrated their engagement with a family party at her parents' home in Wandsworth.

The heroic young subaltern was waved off to war on the 18 April, leaving his sweetheart and his family at home, all bursting with pride.

On 10 June 1940, just as Heath arrived in Palestine, Italy declared war on Britain and France.

Mussolini had designs on the French and British colonies in North Africa with the intention of expanding Italian territories in the area, seizing the Arabian oil fields and controlling the Suez Canal. Italian forces would first have to drive through Egypt, which, though officially neutral, had agreed by treaty to allow British occupation forces if the Suez Canal was threatened. Almost immediately, the Italian air forces started bombing the strategic port of Tel Aviv and the oil terminal and refinery at Haifa.

Heath was stationed at Sarafand in Palestine and in July of 1940, he sent letters to Mr Scott saying that he was now with the Mediterranean Expeditionary Force, 'longing to have a crack at the Italians'.[21] He had also written to his parents indicating that he had been promoted to the rank of captain, but there's no mention of this appointment in his service records. These advancements and his tales of the war from the centre of the action were all fantasy. The reality was rather different. Despite the entry of Italy into the war, if Heath had been expecting to be thrown right into a *Biggles*-style adventure, he was to be extremely disappointed. As he wrote later in his life story in the press:

> I was very bored of the enforced inactivity [at Sarafand]. We would wear civvies and everything was just like peacetime. When Italy entered the war I applied dozens of times for a posting to the Western Desert but this was consistently refused.[22]

Norbert Gaffrey, an orderly room clerk with the RASC, noted that when Heath first arrived at Sarafand he had carried out his duties well. Working in the office, Gaffrey was also aware that Heath had applied for a transfer to the RAF. Gaffrey typed a copy of Heath's application and dispatched it with a letter from the commanding officer to the Supplies and Transport Force Headquarters in Jerusalem. According to Gaffrey, the application was refused and this had a marked effect on Heath's behaviour. He now became 'unmindful and careless'.[23]

On 13 September, Italian forces crossed into Egypt from their base in Cyrenaica in Libya, outnumbering British forces four to one. But the Italians only made it as far as Siddi Barrani, a town near the Mediterranean. By the end of the year, the Western Desert Force under General Wavell had launched a counter-attack, Operation Compass. This resulted in the defeat of the Italian Tenth Army and the repossession of all the Italian gains in Egypt and most of Cyrenaica. British forces took 130,000 Italian prisoners of war. Frustratingly for Heath, all the action seemed to be happening nearby, but beyond his reach. Despite this, he wrote letters home telling a very different story – placing himself at the centre of the action, 'giving the Italians hell and it's just too easy' In real ity, he was more likely to have been playing football on the beach at Sarafand.

On 20 February 1941 he wrote to Mr Scott claiming that his transfer to the RAF had been approved and that he would soon be with a fighter squadron. Again, this is a fantasy, Heath's application having been rejected. But he does seem to have seen some action in the Middle East, during the little-remembered Anglo-Iraqi war.

Rashid Ali, the former anti-British prime minister of Iraq, launched a coup d'etat against the Iraqi Regent. Once in power, he threatened two British air bases in Iraq, much to Churchill's chagrin. But after British forces launched a pre-emptive strike against the Iraqis, Rashid Ali fled to Persia and the pro-British monarchy was restored.

Heath claimed to have played a subsidiary role in this war, which lasted for twenty nine days in 1941. He was stationed away from the fighting at H4, the pumping station on the Haifa-Baghdad road that was a potential target for sabotage. But during the ongoing conflict, Fort Rutbah near to H4 had been seized by the Iraqis. Heath heard of a British raiding party that was to attempt to re-take the fort – and, like a *Beau Geste* fantasy, he was determined to be part of it. It's certainly true that Blenheim Bombers from Squadron 203 did attack the Iraqis at Rutbah on 9 May and they did fly from H4. But, as ever, it's difficult to know with Heath what is true and what isn't. But he was certainly not the sort of man to hang around when there was action to be had in the immediate vicinity. It's also true that many servicemen keen to see active service did join in raids without the permission of their commanding officer.[24]

Heath claimed that after the raid on Fort Rutbah, when he returned to H4, his commanding officer had noted his absence and ordered him back to Sarafand for deserting his post. Shortly afterwards he claimed that he had more trouble with his superior officers when he was working on convoy duty. He had sent 200 trucks to Syria, but by the time they reached Beirut, there were two trucks missing. A furious superior officer upbraided Heath. An argument ensued between the two men and Heath was again sent back to Sarafand – this time, under arrest. Heath's stories about his time in Palestine conform to a particular pattern: headstrong young man seeks adventure. Though there's probably some truth in his stories of insubordination in Palestine, records from the War Office give a much more prosaic reason for his arrest.

Heath had been in financial difficulties for some time – to such an extent that in April his commanding officer devised a scheme for the supervision of his financial affairs. Heath agreed not to cash any cheques without the consent of his commanding officer or adjutant until all his debts were repaid. But despite this, he carried on writing cheques that continued to bounce. However, all the time, he had been drawing money from the field cashier with a *second* Advance Pay Book that he had stolen – which effectively enabled him to cash twice as much money as any officer of his rank. Certainly, off duty, Heath would have enjoyed a luxurious lifestyle – sumptuous dinners in smart hotels and free-flowing alcohol. But given that he was living in a war zone, with most of his needs provided by the army, how had he got into debt so quickly and what was he spending his money on?

Paull Hill's *Portrait of a Sadist* was published in 1960, some fourteen years after Heath's trial.[25] Significantly, Hill was a lawyer and would have known that the material that he discussed in the book would not be publishable until the passing of the Obscene Publications Act in 1959.

During the war, Hill had been an adjutant on a troop carrier, SS *Mooltan*, where he had first met Neville Heath. How much of the story Heath told Hill is true is unclear. But it would certainly account for Heath's increasing issues with money during his time in Palestine, as well as anticipating his later sexual predilections. During off-duty periods, Heath left the tedium of Sarafand and spent much of his time (and most of his money) in Jerusalem and particularly, Cairo.

In the Middle East at the time, Cairo was the focus for the entertainment of Allied troops on leave or for those passing through to the various desert theatres of war. By 1941, Cairo's population of half a million was increased by 35,000 troops from Britain and the Empire. It offered a pre-war, colonial lifestyle of indulgent luxury. Noël Coward, who made a journey throughout the Middle East at this time, was stunned and slightly sickened by the sybaritic existence lived out in the foyers and restaurants of the Continental and Shepheard's Hotel – where, famously, stocks of champagne didn't run out until 1943.

The restrictions of wartime are unknown; people sat there sipping Gin-Slings and cocktails and chatting and gossiping, waiters glided about wearing Fezzes . . . There were uniforms everywhere of all ranks and nationalities . . . [indicating] that perhaps somewhere in the vague outside world there might be a war of some sort going on. This place is the last refuge of the soi-disant 'International Set'. All the fripperies of pre-war luxury living are still in existence here; rich people, idle people, cocktail-parties, dinner parties, jewels and evening dress. Rolls-Royces come purring up to the terrace . . . it [all] felt rather old fashioned and lacking in taste.[26]

The large department stores Cicurel's, Chemla's and Le Salon Vert carried on business as usual and Groppi's, the most famous café in Cairo, continued to serve its famous coffee accompanied by pastries rich in clarified butter. Even the corner shops of Cairo were packed with goods that had long since been rationed in England; butter, sugar and eggs as well as exotic local produce like oranges, dates, beans, maize and the huge cabbages and cauliflowers that thrived in the Nile Delta. Luxury goods like French wine, grapes, melons, steaks, cigarettes, beer and whisky were all easily obtainable. This abundance was an extraordinary vision of plenty for troops fresh from the desert and used to tinned British Army rations of M&V (meat and veg), fatty bacon, cheese, marmalade and bully beef.[27]

The Gezira Sporting Club was the focus for many of the social events for officers in wartime Cairo. Given to the British Army by the Pasha of Egypt, the club covered the entire southern end of Gezira Island and boasted gardens, polo fields, a golf course, a race course, cricket pitches, squash and tennis courts, croquet lawns and a lido. At the same time, the Turf Club swarmed with officers and a dozen open-air cinemas showed films every night throughout the city. But the entertainment for which Cairo became infamous during the Second World War was the sex trade.

The brothels in the red-light district of wartime Cairo have become legendary – dens of vice and iniquity providing an extraordinary variety of services for the most diverse taste, from pornographic films and cabarets to peep shows, prostitutes, rent boys and orgies. The majority of brothels were situated along the Wagh el Birket or 'the Berka' as it was known – opposite Shepheard's and the Continental Hotel. Prostitutes called down from hundreds of New Orleans-style balconies that overlooked the long, narrow street, touting for business from below. The incidence of murders and rapes in the area at the time caused such concern that British military police attempted to make the worst districts of the city 'Out of Bounds to All Ranks' by putting up circular white signs with a black 'X' across them. But with 90,000 clients a month,[28] it proved impossible to police the warren of backstreets and alleyways that stretched across the ancient city, and the legend of extraordinary sexual practices – including the spectacle of women copulating with a variety of animals, among them a donkey – continued to lure troops on leave in search of relief, or adventure. Graham Tylee, an army private during this period, offers a first-hand account of Cairo's vice trade in his memoirs, held in the Imperial War Museum.

Each brothel had a number, some were better patronized than others. Each had a 'Madame' in charge of the girls – usually a prostitute who had moved from the bed to the cash desk . . . whoever you went with you still ran the risk of 'copping a packet' despite the fact that army doctors regularly inspected the girls. To really lessen the risk of venereal disease it was advisable to visit the PAC (Prophylactic Ablution Centre) and take the necessary precautions, which consisted of squirting a solution of permanganate potash crystals up the penis. After this performance the customer collected a blue ticket on the way out which guaranteed him no loss of pay if he contacted gonorrhea or syphilis. [At the brothel] You went up the stairs and sat down in company with dozens of other customers and sightseers. Each girl had her own gimmick to attract custom. But the best gimmick was youth and beauty. Some girls resorted to particularly perverted practices: others would stand in front of you clad only in transparent nighties and the tiniest bikini briefs which they would pull down a shade to reveal pubic regions completely denuded of hair. [The Berka] was recognized officially by the army authorities but there was another area definitely off limits and this was known as the Black Berka. Once you got off the main streets of Cairo you found yourself in a rabbit warren of narrow streets and dark alleyways where vice in all shapes and forms reigned supreme. The only way into this labyrinth of evil alleyways was with a guide, usually a ragged youngster who furtively tugged at your shirt or pullover, whispering, 'You want to see exhibish?' If you were on your own and you had any sense you shook the youngster off or if he was still persistent, you belted him round the ear. For once in the quarter by yourself you stood a very good chance of being robbed and murdered.[29]

At the Continental Hotel, Heath became friendly with the barman and told him that he'd heard rumours that a certain house in the red-light district – most probably in the 'Black Berka' – provided not only graphic sexual 'exhibitions', as described by Graham Tylee, but also provided an exclusive place known as the 'Amazon Room' where 'you could do what you like and no questions asked'. The barman told Heath that the Amazon Room could provide him with girls who liked to be beaten – and boys too, if that was to Heath's taste.

According to *Portrait of a Sadist*, Heath was shown into a house deep in the red-light district. The place was decorated in the Arab style, with no tables and chairs, but carpets, cushions and low sofas arranged on the floor. Coffee and cigarettes were offered by the brothel keeper, as Heath negotiated what he wanted and how much it was going to cost. He was offered two Greek girls by the brothel keeper – one sixteen years of age, and the other, her fifteen-year-old sister. A night with both sisters ('do anything you like, but no blood')[30] would cost £50. This is at a time when a London prostitute would charge £1 for her services.

The room that Heath was shown into had no windows and was padded. The floor, walls and ceiling were all painted red, as were the electric light bulbs. A collection of whips, canes, woven thongs and paddles were arranged in a rack against one wall. Against another were some low sofas and some horizontal bars. From the ceiling dangled a variety of ropes.

The sixteen-year-old was sent to Heath first – in tears and shaking with fright. He tied her to one of the horizontal bars and chose a whip to beat her with. Shortly afterwards, her younger sister was sent into the room, half-naked. Her ankles were then tied with one of the ropes dangling from the ceiling. She was then pulled up, upside down, until she was about two or three feet above the floor – just able to touch it with her hands. She was then beaten with a whip. Hill goes on to say that Heath witnessed further sex acts, including rape, but that 'this sort of thing didn't appeal to [him]'.[31] Hill's story is extreme and reads like pornography but it's clear that whatever Heath did at the Amazon Rooms, it was no more extreme than any of the other customers – fetishistic rather than sadistic violence.

Whether these stories of the Amazon Room are true or not is open to question. Veteran crime writer Donald Thomas feels that Hill is a reliable source (a lawyer with a good memory for what Heath might have told him). But it might be Heath himself who inflated the tale, turning various brothel visits into a sexual epic, casting himself as an outrageous Don Juan. It's also unclear how developed Heath's sexual tastes were at this time. It seems unlikely that he would have been able to practise fetishistic sex at borstal or in the English county towns around the RAF and army bases where he had been stationed. What is certainly true is that sexual practices of this type did go on in Cairo during the time Heath was stationed in the Middle East and perhaps it is here that he first witnessed extreme sexual behaviour.

It was not long before Heath's financial misconduct and various other offences in Palestine were exposed. Taken individually, each of the issues could have been dealt with by his commanding officer, but it is clear that Heath had repeatedly flouted authority, his wrongdoing now habitual.

As well as his issues relating to money, Heath was also found to be absenting himself from his unit without permission. He had told his commanding officer that he was having an operation on 2 June 1941 at the military hospital in Jerusalem because he had tonsilitis. He then claimed that he needed further follow-up appointments. But he was lying. He had only been required to attend the hospital once. His service records indicate that he had also been admitted to hospital twice in September of 1940 and once more in January 1941. These medical troubles may well have been valid, but it seems that he was exploiting them as excuses to be absent from his unit so that he could indulge himself in bars, brothels, restaurants and nightclubs. In mitigation, Heath later said that he was a fully qualified flying officer and was anxious to take a more active part in the fighting. He had applied for a transfer to the parachutists and the RAF, to no avail. His absences suggest his frustration at not being at the heart of the action; he'd rather spend a few illicit days 'on a party' in

Neville Heath as a child, with his mother, Bessie, *c.*1918.

Vikings House, Rutlish School, October 1933.
Heath is in the second row, seventh from the left.

Neville Heath in his mid-teens and already a young man about town, *c.*1930.

Heath aged twenty in his RAF uniform, in the garden at Merton Hall Road, 1936.

Heath's wife, Elizabeth, and their son, Robert, Johannesburg, 1944.

19 Squadron at RAF Duxford, 1936. Heath is fourth from the left in the second row. Johnny Kent is standing second from the right. Squadron Leader J. W. Turton-Jones is seated, centre.

American Mitchell Mark II Bombers of 180 Squadron prepare for take-off from Melsbroek, Belgium, for a daylight attack on the bridges at Venlo in Holland, October 1944.

S18049.   STRAND PALACE HOTEL.   FOYER - VIEW OF BUREAU & ENTRANCE TO WINTER GARDEN

The art deco foyer of the Strand Palace Hotel, designed
by Oliver P. Bernard.

Celebrations in Trafalgar Square on 'V' Day, 8 June 1946. 'This beats
everything – the Coronation, the Jubilee and any of the cup finals.'

Yvonne Symonds hurries to avoid press photographers, summer 1946.

Exterior of the former Pembridge Court Hotel, 34 Pembridge Gardens, 2012.

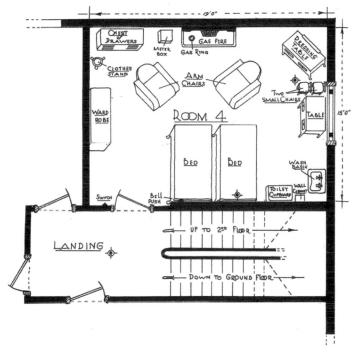

Police plan of Room 4 at the Pembridge Court Hotel.

The young Margery Wheat, mid-1930s.

Margery Gardner's identity card photograph, *c*.1940.

Jerusalem or in the Berka in Cairo than guard a static oil-pipeline in the middle of a desert.

Heath was arrested on a number of charges – for lying about his absences from his unit, for using the second advance pay book and for five bounced cheques. For the second time in his career, he appeared before a General Court Martial at Jerusalem on 17 and 18 July 1941. Found guilty, he was to be stripped of his rank and commission and ignominiously repatriated back to England. On 8 August, Heath wrote to his parents that he would be returning home soon, 'on leave'. Given the circumstances of his dismissal, how would he face his parents? What would he tell his fiancée?

He was held under close arrest from 15 August and was to be repatriated to Britain in October. Since Italy had entered the war, the passage home across the Mediterranean was closed, so he would be sailing by the much longer Cape Route via South Africa.

SS *Mooltan* was docked at Port Tewfik on the Suez Canal, loaded with troops, guns, tanks and stores. A former P&O Liner, she had been requisitioned by the RAF and was now painted a uniform grey as troop ship *W7*. Even at a speed of 17 knots, the voyage back to Glasgow – the final port of disembarkation – would take the best part of two months.

The *Mooltan* crew were repatriating 420 wounded British Army personnel from Crete, supervised by twenty-one VAD Nurses. Also travelling were 200 civilian refugees comprising friendly diplomats and their families as well as oil company representatives from the Balkans. Locked in the lower decks were thousands of Italian POWs. Sixteen officers who had been court-martialled were also on board. Some had been under close arrest for weeks – some, like Heath, for months.

Paull Hill was adjutant on the *Mooltan*. With the ship still docked, he called the sixteen cashiered officers together and told them that their sentences would now be officially promulgated. Heath was sixth or seventh in line in this process of sanctioned humiliation. First, he was sent to the Orderly Room to remove all decorations and insignia of rank from his uniform. Returning with them in his hands, he was told to place these insignia on the table in front of him, thereby reverting to civilian status.

Heath made quite an impression on Hill. Nearly six feet tall, with broad shoulders and slim hips, he seemed the least likely person to commit the offences he had been charged with. '[He was] a perfect specimen of young manhood – he was only twenty-four then – with blue eyes, fair curly hair and a carefree expression on his handsome face,'[32] Hill wrote in *Portrait of a Sadist*.

Hill took a keen interest in Heath throughout the voyage and on several occasions had to talk to him about various romances that he was having on board, particularly those with civilian passengers. It is during these discussions that Heath apparently revealed to Hill his adventures in the brothels of Cairo.

The *Mooltan* sailed south towards the Cape and docked into Durban's large lagoon harbour. Whilst taking on supplies for the rest of the voyage, it became apparent that the engines needed immediate attention. Essential spares would have to be found locally – or even flown in from England. The ship would be docked at Durban for at least a fortnight, possibly longer. Plans were made to transfer the POWs to a camp just outside Durban. The rest of the passengers would remain living on the ship, but would be allowed ashore during the day. Heath and the other court-martialled officers were subject to military law until the point of disembarkation, but having caused no trouble on the voyage so far, they were also permitted shore leave, on the condition that they were back aboard by 00.01 a.m. each night.

South Africa's ports and harbours, particularly Cape Town

and Durban, had become of global strategic importance since Italy had joined the war, making the route around the Cape of Good Hope a crucial artery in the Allied campaign. During the war years 45,000 ships would call at South Africa's ports – 400 convoys carrying a total of 6 million men. More than half of these ships would pass through Durban.

South Africa's geographical position meant that the war still felt distant. As in Singapore and Cairo, it was possible to live the classic colonial lifestyle of sundowners on the Durban Club terrace and polo at the Inanda Club. Even the currency reassuringly remained sterling, a legacy of the British Empire continuing to dominate the South African economy.[33] For clubbable (apparently), public-school men like Neville Heath, South Africa was a home from home, with few of the wartime disadvantages and much better weather.

Durban itself was a city of contrasts, an exotic combination of European and African cultures. A line of luxurious hotels and Art Deco buildings sat along the harbour rather like Miami in Florida.[34] There were handsome shops and elegant houses, impressive public buildings, cinemas, and an art gallery with fine English and Dutch paintings. Bernard Shaw's wife had claimed that Durban was the one city outside England that she could live in as it was 'so very English', but it was also very multicultural, with mosques and Hindu temples situated just off the main streets which were populated with Indians, Zulus, Muslims and Europeans. It was the perfect melting pot for Heath to be absorbed within and for him to indulge his hotel and bar-room lifestyle. It was also, for a young officer from dusty Palestine, a city of refreshing greenery with wide avenues and roads shady with flowering trees, flamboyants, jacarandas and bougainvillea,[35] that gave Durban a tropical air.[36] Alongside the tramcars and motor buses, the famous Zulu rickshaw boys ran barefoot along the tarmac, wearing head-dresses of bull's horns and feathers, coloured beads dangling from their neck and wrists. On the pavements, witch doctors sold the fat of the hippopotamus as a love charm, not fifty yards from the local chemist. Even in the suburbs, Durban exhibited an exotic fusion of modernity and elemental Africa as hundreds of monkeys played within sight of the newest apartment buildings.[37]

After a fortnight docked in the harbour at Durban, her engines now fixed, the *Mooltan* was ready to proceed on her voyage. But when Paull Hill tried to track him down, 2nd Lieutenant Heath was nowhere to be found. Returning to bombed-out Britain and facing an awkward and humiliating homecoming in Wimbledon, South Africa, with its colour and opportunities, must have seemed to Heath like an extremely tempting place to start a new life. When the *Mooltan* finally set sail for Glasgow, it left without him.

CHAPTER NINE
Lt. James Robert Cadogan Armstrong

DECEMBER 1941 – OCTOBER 1944

You don't know what it's like to feel frightened. You get a beastly, bitter taste in your mouth, and your tongue goes dry and you feel sick, and all the time you're saying – this isn't happening to me – it can't be happening – I'll wake up. But you know you won't wake up. You know it's happening and the sea is below you, and you're responsible for the lives of six people. And you have to pretend you're not afraid, that's what's so awful. Oh God, I was afraid tonight, when we took off and saw that [plane] on fire, I didn't think: There are friends of mine in that. I thought: That might happen to us.

Terence Rattigan, *Flare Path*, 1942

The Union of South Africa had joined the Allies in 1939 but only after a narrow vote when the nationalist and anti-British prime minister, James Hertzog, had been deposed following his attempt to promote South African neutrality in the war. Hertzog lost the debate by only thirteen votes and was replaced by his coalition deputy, the Boer War veteran, Jan Smuts. Smuts was very much pro-British and went on to acquire senior status within the Allied Commanders.[1] Given that his majority to commit South Africa to the Allied cause was small, there was to be no enforced conscription – the Union Defence Forces were to be bolstered by volunteers alone. At the outbreak of war there had been only 3,353 troops in the regular army with 14,631 territorials, so a vigorous recruiting drive was launched with posters encouraging prospective volunteers. 'Don't miss the greatest adventure of all time!'[2]

However, because of South Africa's race policies, there was a restricted pool of eligible whites from which to form a volunteer army. Black, coloured and Asian South Africans were, on the whole, committed to the Allied cause. They appreciated the dangers of Nazism and were well aware that supporters of the German cause in South Africa – led by the political opposition – were also the most vociferous advocates of segregation. A number of support corps providing cooks, drivers, stretcher-bearers and labourers were formed of black, coloured and Asian South Africans in order to release whites for active combat. Despite their much larger numbers, non-white South Africans were not allowed to fight because, in the convoluted logic of the prevailing ideology, they were not allowed to take arms against Europeans. At the end of the war 20,000 South Africans – of all races and creeds – celebrated a 'People's Day of Victory' in Johannesburg. At the same time, the government published cash and clothing allowances for discharged servicemen. Whites received £5 in cash and a £25 clothing allowance. Blacks were given £2 and a khaki suit.[3]

One of South Africa's greatest resources was labour. Before the war, industry in the Union was focused on the mining of diamonds and gold. In 1939 there was only one munitions factory in the entire Union. But within months of joining the Allies, South Africa converted much of her manufacturing power to wartime production, making shells, mortars, guns and a huge variety of equipment, including 32,000 armoured vehicles, 12 million pairs of boots, 5.5 million blankets and 2,435 million cigarettes. As a consequence, the number of South Africans in manufacturing, many of them women, rose by 60 per cent. Urbanization increased with great rapidity and by the end of the war many towns had doubled in size. In 1946, for the first time, there were more black Africans living in South Africa's towns than whites. Many settled in makeshift communities outside the major cities and though they had provided the essential workforce demanded by the war effort, this contradicted the segregationist principle that blacks should not become permanent urban residents. This legacy of the war was to play a direct part in the initiation of apartheid under the re-elected National Party in 1948.

In 1939, daily life in the Cape was barely affected by what seemed a distant European War. But shortages and restrictions did begin to appear in 1942 and towards the end of the war there were meatless days, a national loaf was introduced and petrol rationed, but the shortage of food and basic commodities was insignificant compared to the deprivations in Britain. Luxury goods like pins, toilet paper and cosmetics were frequently hard to come by – women finding lipstick frustratingly scarce. But the shortage most painful to many men was whisky. This was still being imported, but many freight ships had been torpedoed, driving up the price of remaining supplies. Before the war, branded whisky had been sold at a controlled price of 14s. a bottle (equivalent to £24 in today's money). After a black market for spirits developed, a bottle of whisky could cost anything up to £5 (£172 today).[4] Except for certain regions in the Cape, South Africa had always been a whisky-drinking country. Wine appeared only on formal occasions and it was common to drink several whiskies before dinner. A strange piece of legislation was introduced just before Christmas 1940, in order to curb excessive drinking amongst servicemen. This forbade anybody from buying a drink for anybody else in public. This ill-considered directive became known as the 'no-treating law'. Barmen, however, were quick to point out that it was impossible to enforce and the law soon fell into disuse.[5]

On 7 December 1941, the Japanese attacked Pearl Harbor, forcing America into the war. Two days later, South Africa declared war on Japan and immediately her long coastline and harbours felt vulnerable to attack. At the time, South Africa had only eight anti-aircraft guns and six searchlights throughout the entire Union. The Union Defence Force itself consisted of just 334,000 troops. In contrast, the Japanese had 1.4 million troops and 2,400 aircraft supported by a navy with 350,000 personnel. Like the south coast of England, attempts were swiftly made to fortify coastal areas from German and Japanese attack and to protect the Cape Route, the Allies' lifeline. Durban's south beach was cut off with barbed-wire fences, submarine nets were spanned across the harbour entrance and armed sentries patrolled the harbour gates.

Having jumped ship, Heath was now an illegal alien in a foreign country with few prospects and no money. But, ever resourceful, he posed as a Captain Selway of the Argyll and Sutherland Highlanders, awarding himself the Military Cross, one of the highest decorations for exemplary gallantry. As Captain Selway he procured £85 from Barclays Bank in Durban. Leaving the city, he went on to stay at a series of hotels in Maritzburg and Johannesburg – under different names – always moving on without paying the bill. From Johannesburg, he next travelled the thirty-five miles to Pretoria to the air base at Voortrekkerhoogte. On 22 December, he volunteered for the South African Air Force (SAAF).

Unlike the RAF, the SAAF had been little prepared for the outbreak of war with only 160 permanent officers and 1,400 ranks in 1939. Despite this, the Air Ministry would not recruit black or coloured volunteers. A concerted effort was made to dramatically increase training for the RAF, SAAF and other Allied flight services with the Joint Air Training Scheme (JATS). By 1941, there were thirty-eight Air Schools throughout South Africa and the SAAF had grown to a strength of 31,204 aircrew including 956 pilots.

Heath joined the SAAF as James Robert Cadogan Armstrong. The 'Cadogan' related him by implication to one of the wealthiest aristocratic families in Britain who were known for owning much of Chelsea. On his application form, he embellished his history with half-truths, fantasies and lies. Though he claimed he was born in Cape Town, he wrote that his family home was in England – Melton Hall, in Woodbridge, Suffolk – hence his English accent. Even in deceit, vestiges of Heath's real biography remained, 'Melton Hall' being a corruption of Merton Hall Road, the rather more modest home of his parents in Wimbledon. Woodbridge is indeed in Suffolk – the closest village to Hollesley Bay, the borstal colony that Heath had joined in 1938.[6]

Heath stated that he had been educated at Harrow and Trinity College Cambridge and that he had joined the Officers' Training Corps in both. He also claimed to have resigned his commission in the RAF in 1937 – lying again about his dismissal – and that he was a journalist by profession. He may have suggested that he had been a war correspondent and that this accounted for the fact that he had not joined the services before, given his useful training with the

RAF. In all official documents relating to his identity as Armstrong throughout his time in South Africa, Heath gave his date of birth as 6 June 1915, adding another couple of years to his real age.[7] This confusion might have been a simple ruse to cover his tracks if ever his record in the Middle East came to light. His application to the SAAF successful, he joined No. 62 Air School at Bloemfontein.

Bloemfontein, 254 miles from Johannesburg, was capital of the Orange Free State. Not a large city, its ground plan was based on the American rectilinear pattern – miles of streets in ordered parallel lines with distinguished public buildings of brick and local sandstone grouped around the central Hoffman Square.[8] It was a staid, sober town with a strong civic sense of order – a perfect setting for Heath to re-invent himself. From this point, both his career and his personal life improved with extraordinary speed. Within eight weeks of landing in South Africa he had met and married a very eligible young woman from one of Johannesburg's most respected families.

Twenty-two-year-old Elizabeth Hardcastle Rivers was the daughter of Charles and Aileen Rivers of Epping Road, Forest Town, a fashionable and leafy suburb in northern Johannesburg. Elizabeth was an attractive girl with 'sloe eyes and chestnut hair' coiffured in the Elizabethan style that was popular at the time. She had been educated in England at Roedean, the exclusive girls' school on the south coast and, like Heath, was very sporty – enjoying hockey, golf and skiing, which she had learned at a finishing school in Switzerland. She had come out as a debutante at one of the last pre-war Spring Balls and was very much part of Johannesburg's social elite.

Johannesburg in the 1940s was a city of opportunity. Only in existence since 1886 – when it had no buildings, only tents and a population of just fifteen – within sixty years it had transformed into a brash, modern metropolis of skyscrapers and neon. The reason for its vast and swift expansion was the discovery of gold. At the end of every street were golden pyramids, shining in the sunlight – dumps from the neighbouring goldmines. In a hastily built modern city of undistinguished architecture, the travel writer H. V. Morton felt that these goldmine dumps were 'what St Paul's is to London . . . a symbol of the city, its true coat of arms'.[9] Outside the city centre, what was once an arid, treeless veld was now covered with trees and houses built in a variety of styles – Spanish Colonial, Cape, Dutch and Tudor – which gave a Californian brilliance to suburbs like Forest Town. The surrounding gardens were full of flowering shrubs, pergolas, swimming pools and black servants moving noiselessly in spotless white uniforms. For Heath, Johannesburg offered an extraordinary opportunity to start a new life, with a new identity on a new continent; a golden lad in a golden land.

Heath wooed and seduced Elizabeth Rivers, but her parents disapproved of the match.[10] The couple had only just met and, besides, they knew hardly anything about him. But Heath, by now, was extremely confident of his charms with women. Elizabeth had fallen for him 'desperately' – for her, it was a 'beautiful dream'.[11] The pair eloped and on 12 February 1942 married in a small civil ceremony in Pretoria. None of her family were present. Heath married under the name of Armstrong, giving little thought, it seems, to whether this would invalidate the marriage. At the same time, he artfully extricated himself from his engagement to Peggy Dixon in England. He wrote and told her that he had been dismissed from the army, probably anticipating how she would react to the news. Peggy wrote back, breaking off their engagement, but kept her engagement ring.[12]

In Wimbledon, Heath's news from Johannesburg was met with some surprise. Shortly after the wedding, his father visited Mr Scott at the Borstal Association and told him

Neville's startling news. He was now training to be a flying instructor at the Central Flying School at Bloemfontein, had taken South African citizenship, had changed his name by deed poll and had married, all in the space of two months. Elizabeth had sent a very nice letter to her new parents-in-law in which she wrote that she hoped to visit England with 'Jimmy' to see them when the war was over. Heath also claimed that his father-in-law was interested in civil aviation, so it seemed that a career as a flyer after the war was assured. Mr Scott noted that though Mr and Mrs Heath were hurt about their son's change of name, they understood that this might have been necessary for him to make a fresh start.[13]

On 2 September 1942, Elizabeth gave birth to a baby boy, Robert Michael Cadogan Armstrong, so she may well have been pregnant at the time she and Heath were married. The naming of the child seems to have been all down to Heath who gave him the aristocratic (if bogus) 'Cadogan' where his own mother had given her sons the name 'Clevely' – Heath, with little irony, it seems, carrying on a family tradition, but without the family name. Sentimentally, he gave his son his younger brother's Christian names, reversed. In February 1943, the couple moved to Randfontein to be near No. 2 Air School where Heath was teaching trainee pilots to fly 1930s Tiger Moths. He was in his element.

> I loved it. They took me as a pupil pilot and gave me a test at once. My record for the years I was there shows I was right on top of my job. I was commissioned in March 1942, a month after I was married, and posted to the Central Flying School as an instructor. Even this period of non-operational flying instruction was enjoyable and I must have taught between 100 and 150 pupils to fly. These were the men who became part of the desert Air Force – as grand a bunch of men as there are in the world.[14]

Many of these trainee pilots were from Britain and the Empire as part of the JATS. South Africa's weather and clear skys were perfect for teaching them to fly over the broad open veld. Harold Guthrie, a pilot with the RAF, was taught to fly at Randfontein at the time Heath was teaching there. During his stay at the station, Guthrie remembered that Heath was exceedingly popular with everyone and was always an invited member of any party at which quantities of liquor were likely to be consumed. '[Heath] drank heavily and although he frequently appeared to be haggard in the morning, I have never seen him show any signs of alcoholic excess in any other way,' he recalled.[15]

Guthrie was aware that Heath was very well known in the higher social circles in Johannesburg and though he did drink excessively heavily, he always behaved in a perfectly gentlemanly manner, 'never speaking to women with anything other than complete respect'.[16] Heath and his wife often frequented the Inanda Polo Club where they would socialize with Elizabeth's old school friend and next-door neighbour, the actress Moira Lister, who was just starting her career in the theatre. Lister and her sister were both seduced by Heath's extreme good looks, wit and charm. 'Everyone,' remembered Lister, 'or all the girls at least, were vying for his favours.'[17]

For Heath, these sunny times in the heat, safety and abundance of South Africa were years of 'perfect happiness'. He was married to a beautiful young woman he loved, he had steered himself away from the dangers of his past and onto an even keel. He was a father now, with a healthy young son – and he was flying again. His life was contented and fulfilled. He even bought a dog. Only three years later, Heath remembered these times in a letter to Elizabeth with a sense of deep nostalgia:

Bloemfontein at [Central Flying School] *with that awful cold hotel — Greystones — the 'Rambles', with those enormous teas — The Bloemfontein Hotel and those early morning drives to the Aerodrome in that little open car which we both froze in so regularly — Randfontein and our house there. The chaps who used to come and stay with us — the parties we had there and at the Aerodrome* . . .[18]

It all seemed idyllic. But, as ever with Heath, his attempts to secure a golden future for himself and his family were to be thwarted by his past behaviour which, still unresolved, now came back to haunt him.

P&O, who owned the *Mooltan,* imposed a fine of £100 on anyone who absconded from troop transport. Since Heath had jumped ship at Durban, he was personally liable for the fine and had been pursued by the South African CID. They were also keen to trace him because of the money he had illegally withdrawn from Barclays Bank in Durban and the hotels he had defrauded before signing up with the SAAF. This meant that not only was his false identity exposed to the SAAF authorities, but the full extent of his past misbehaviour and dishonesty would now be known to his wife and to his in-laws. Heath had married Elizabeth under an assumed name, so the Rivers family were concerned that the marriage wasn't legal. An amendment to the marriage certificate was hastily arranged to make it valid. Heath had jumped ship without permission and was an illegal immigrant. His application to join the SAAF was almost entirely fiction and he had also lied that he had had no previous criminal convictions. Now that the full details of his court martial at Jerusalem were revealed, Heath's entire new life was held in the balance.[19]

The Immigration Authorities indicated that his continued presence in South Africa was entirely dependent on how the SAAF wanted to deal with his career of repeated deception. Due to the valuable work that he had done in training pilots at a time when the SAAF was rapidly expanding, the authorities discussed Heath's case at the highest level, even involving the director general of the service. Heath's commanding officer offered a glowing recommendation for leniency.

> He [has] carried out all his duties in the air and on the ground in a perfectly correct manner. He is keen and takes a great interest in the work he is now performing. His personal conduct has been exemplary.[20]

On 18 March, Heath himself wrote an impassioned and contrite letter from Randfontein to the director general of the Air Force in Pretoria. He outlined his commitment to the Allied cause and his usefulness as a pilot. He stressed that since joining the SAAF, he had not committed a single misdemeanour. He admitted that his former behaviour was simply due to his natural impetuosity. Desperate to make a fresh start for himself, he pleaded that if he were dismissed from the SAAF, it would ruin his life.

> *I decided to change my name and make a really serious attempt to change my character, the fact that I am now married has helped me — and my wife, who knows the whole story and has helped me — is shortly expecting a child.*
>
> *Proof that I have made this serious attempt at reformation is easily recognizable from my record during the past 15 months and by my present Commanding Officer's personal report. I can also produce the names of at least ten officers of Field Rank who would testify on my behalf.*
>
> *May I respectfully submit that my services be retained on probation. If I commit the slightest misdemeanour I shall have failed in my attempt to reform myself and then any action which may be taken will be entirely of my own manufacture. I can honestly promise that such a state of affairs will never come to pass.*

> *I have served as a fighter pilot for two years in the Royal Air Force in peace time and served with an International Fighter Squadron in Spain during the civil war. May I request that I may be retained in the SAAF on the above conditions and posted to one of the fighter squadrons on operations.*
>
> *I am convinced that if this request could be granted and a little trust placed in me by higher authority with regard to my future behaviour, I shall not fail.*[21]

There is no evidence that Heath fought in the Spanish Civil War nor did he have the opportunity to do so, given he was in the RAF when it started and at Hollesley Bay thereafter. It's doubtful, too, that Elizabeth was pregnant again, their son being only seven months old when this letter was written. But it's typical of Heath to risk lies such as these (one heroic, one sentimental) that could fairly easily be disproved. Fortunately for him, this gamble worked. Given his good record in service and apparent sincerity to reform his character, the director general of the Air Force thought he should be given another chance. He could remain in the SAAF on six months' probation on the condition that he repaid all his outstanding debts.[22] Heath's father-in-law reluctantly obliged. The Immigration Authorities would hold his deportation in abeyance. Once again, he was offered an extraordinary opportunity to rehabilitate and redeem himself.

Having successfully deflected these issues from the past, Heath might have embraced the strategy he had implemented at Hollesley Bay; to keep his head down for the duration and concentrate on training other pilots. However, on the international scene, the war was now moving in the Allies' favour. The Axis powers had surrendered in North Africa, British troops had landed on mainland Italy and the Italians had declared war on Germany. With a series of concentrated bombing raids on Germany beginning in February 1944 and the Germans heavily invested on the Eastern Front, Allied victory seemed a real possibility – a far cry from the situation when Heath had last been in England in 1940. It is at this point, Heath recognized in retrospect, that he made a fundamental mistake. Rather than settling for a safer, duller life in South Africa, he still wanted to go on active service and take part in the war.

One thing is certain, and it is that if I had I not left Training Command in South Africa to go on 'ops' none of this last eighteen months of hell would have occurred.[23]

Heath's desire to fly again with the RAF was intense. He had been trying for a secondment or transfer since 1940. His objective was not to work as part of support staff or in training, but to go on operations in one of the active theatres of war. He specifically wanted to return to Fighter Command, the daring, glamorous face of the RAF. In April 1944 he achieved his long-held ambition and successfully arranged a transfer, with the RAF presumably unaware that 'J. R. C. Armstrong' was actually 'N. G. C. Heath', who had been dismissed from the service in 1937.[24] Arriving back in England, he was sent to Dunsfold Aerodrome in Surrey to join 180 Squadron, part of the 2nd Tactical Air Force.[25] The squadron flew under the motto *'suaviter in modo fortier in re'* (charming in manner, forthright in deed), perfect for the golden-haired adventurer Heath.

On 27 June, Heath called at the Borstal Association wearing the uniform of a captain in the SAAF, bearing his wings and two ribbons on his chest. He told Mr Scott that he was now based in South Cerney in Gloucestershire working on Intruder Operations. This involved fighter planes making night attacks on German fighter bases, hoping to cause disruption to reduce the heavy losses that were being suffered by Bomber Command

at the time. However, whatever he told Mr Scott, Heath was
not flying in Fighter Command at all, but had been training to
fly bombers. This was a significant change for Heath as flying a
fighter and flying a bomber demanded very different skills of
their pilots and – some aviation experts would say – different
personalities. Much of the bomber's work was done before
they left the ground and flying over to Europe could mean
flights of seven, eight or nine hours. These journeys were
highly dramatic at take-off and landing, and particularly intense
over the target, but outside these peaks there were long periods
of boredom and fatigue. Heath had been used to flying up-to-
the-minute fighter planes like the Hawker Hurricane – sports
cars of the air. The Dam Busters veteran Guy Gibson likened
flying a bomber to driving a bus.[26]

As well as the different technical and intellectual demands
that flying fighters and bombers made on their pilots, one of
the crucial differences between Bomber Command and
Fighter Command was the number of fatalities they suffered.
Of the 125,000 airmen who served in Bomber Command
during the war according to one study, fatalities were as high
as 65 per cent. Two thirds would be expected to die. These
terrifying statistics would have been known to all bomber
aircrew. Air Chief Marshall Arthur 'Bomber' Harris, Bomber
Command's Commander-in-Chief later noted that:

> These crews, shining youth on the threshold of life, lived
> under circumstances of intolerable strain. They were in fact
> – and they knew it, faced with the virtual certainty of death,
> probably in one of its least pleasant forms.[27]

One nineteen-year-old flight engineer, Sergeant Dennis
Goodliffe, was told on arrival at his squadron: 'You're now
on an operational squadron, your expectation of life is six
weeks. Go back to your huts and make out your wills.'[28]

Yet, extraordinarily, even in 1944 when Bomber Command was suffering terrible losses, the supply of aircrew candidates never dwindled and the Air Ministry felt able to turn away 22.5 per cent of the volunteers who applied to join them.

Over several months of training, crew members would be taught in a particular role for which they had shown aptitude – pilots, navigators, engineers, wireless operators, air-gunners and bomb-aimers. But even in training the notion of death was never far from their minds as over 8,000 trainee aircrew died before they qualified – one seventh of fatalities that Bomber Command suffered throughout the duration of the war. These accidents in training often provided young crews with their first direct acquaintance with death, as many were still in their teens. The average age of an airman in Bomber Command was just twenty-two.

Heath was trained to fly American-made two-engined Mitchell bombers, the B-25. Having completed specialist training, pilots, navigators and bomb-aimers were given further advanced instruction before finally arriving at an Operational Training Unit where they would join the wireless operators and gunners, who had been trained elsewhere. It is at the OTUs that British trainees would meet their various counterparts from Australia and New Zealand who had been trained at the Empire Training Schools abroad. Crews were then put together in an extraordinarily unscientific process known as 'crewing up'. The requisite numbers of each aircrew category were put together in a large room or hangar and simply told to team up. Each potential aircrew member would need to make instinctive decisions, attempting to interpret a special chemistry between a group of complete strangers. Jack Currie, who reached his OTU in 1942, remembered that 'I had a strange recollection of standing in a suburban dance-hall, wondering which girls I should approach.'[29] And indeed, crewing up was a sort of mating ritual. Who would be calm, efficient, hard-working, reliable, great to have a laugh and a drink with and – most, importantly – who would be lucky? There must also have been some subliminal sense of attraction between the men who were drawn to each other. Heath was fit, good-looking and charming and it's easy to see how he would be able to attract an enthusiastic crew around him. The decisions that he and his fellow crew members had made in this casual, haphazard way were to be the most important decisions these young men would ever make, as it would dictate whether they – as a crew – would live or die.

Captain William Spurrett Fielding-Johnson was a hugely distinguished and much-admired flying ace, credited with five aerial victories in the First World War. He had been awarded the Military Cross in 1915 whilst serving with the Leicestershire Yeomanry. Following an injury in 1916 he had trained as a pilot with the RAF. In 1918 he destroyed four German fighters and a reconnaissance aircraft. He was exactly the sort of daring, heroic airman that Heath aspired to be.

Fielding-Johnson had volunteered for the RAF immediately the Second World War broke out and served as a squadron leader and aerial gunner. In 1940, at the age of forty-eight, he was the oldest rear gunner in the service and had been awarded the DFC. Having been wounded in June 1944, he was in recovery until September of that year, when he rejoined 180 Squadron as a squadron leader. He was responsible for the maintenance of aircraft armaments and assisting the commanding officer in observing the physical and mental wellbeing of the aircrews in his care.

As the Allies were forcing their way through Europe, 180 Squadron was preparing to move from RAF Dunsfold to Melsbroek in Belgium. The bulk of personnel, including ground staff, were sent to Belgium by road and sea, whilst the aircraft were flown over. Heath accompanied Fielding-Johnson with the land and sea party and this was the first time they came into each other's company. As the journey continued, Fielding-Johnson became aware of Heath's unusual behaviour, as he had 'periods of irresponsibility during off times and when he had a drink or two'. On more than one occasion, he took issue with Heath's behaviour – and despite Heath's ranking as a captain, Fielding-Johnson felt more and more that he was thoroughly unreliable. Once they had settled at the Melsbroek air station, Heath's behaviour continued to trouble him. When he had been drinking, Heath was like a completely different person; supremely arrogant, talking wildly about his past exploits and – in a most ungentlemanly manner – about his finances. Hugely knowledgeable about the pressures and strains that airmen had to cope with, Fielding-Johnson felt that Heath's behaviour was very similar to cases he had previously dealt with when a pilot's nerve had gone due to operational exhaustion or simply from the strain of flying itself. Effectively, he identified that Heath was in the throes of some sort of breakdown.[30]

In 1947, the Air Ministry commissioned a report, *Psychological Disorders in Flying Personnel of the Royal Air Force Investigated During the War 1939–45*. This study is a fascinating context in which to examine Heath's actions and behaviour at this point, exploring as it does the particular pressures that pilots suffered.

The physical fatigue of flying a heavy bomber is limited to the pilot who, as captain of the aircraft, has an added mental load. There was agreement that big men [like Heath] found these planes easier to fly than small men of slender build, and one station commander thought that there should be special selection for these heavy jobs.[31]

The report goes on to say, based on the evidence of flight
crews throughout the war, that the incidence of neuroses was
highest in Bomber Command, this being almost twice the
incidence in Fighter Command, and that the crew members
most affected were pilots of bombers. Psychologically, fighter
pilots had to concern themselves solely with their own safety.
Fighter planes were also both more agile and better armed
than bombers. Bomber pilots had a much less manoeuverable
aircraft, slower and more vulnerable to attack by enemy
fighters. Crucially, bomber pilots felt responsible not just for
their own lives but for the lives of the rest of their crew.

Flying for long distances, often in the dark, affected all
flight crews. Fatigue and frostbite were common and lack of
oxygen sometimes resulted in blackouts. It was not unusual
for a pilot to suddenly wake after a period of unconsciousness
in the air. A pilot staring for hours at his instrument panel
might also suddenly find everything he saw upside down –
normally the human eye sees objects inverted and the brain
corrects this, reversing the image. All of these symptoms were
brought on by changes in physical conditions during flights.[32]

The psychological neuroses exhibited by aircrew were
collected under six headings: anxiety, hysteria, depression,
fatigue, obsession and schizophrenia.[33] RAF neuro-psychiatrists
established that the most important cause of neuroses in aircrew
was, not surprisingly, fear.[34]

Many young airmen, paralysed with terror at the prospect
of their own violent deaths, were equally burdened with feelings of responsibility for the carnage that they caused in the
towns and cities of Germany. Frequently they would drown
their fears off duty in alcoholic binges and it's alcohol that
Fielding-Johnson identified as one of the causes of Heath's
abnormal behaviour, if not the root of it. But it's also true
that airmen had access to other stimulants that could be as
addictive and damaging. RAF medical officers regularly

distributed 'wakey wakey' pills to aircrew who were suffering from fatigue and who would need to keep awake for raids that could last for up to nine hours. This was the amphetamine known as Benzedrine. Officially doctors were only supposed to offer it to pilots, gunners and navigators on missions, but in practice it was readily available on RAF stations to aircrew, ground crew and even WAAFs. Airmen became accomplished at acquiring large quantities of the drug and storing it up for their own recreational use. They'd take the pills not only on operations when they needed to keep alert for several hours, but also at off-duty parties and drinking sessions. Joan Wyndham, a self-confessed addict, remembered the casual use of Benzedrine by WAAFs and aircrew: 'I really love the clear, cool feeling in my head and the edge of excitement it gives to everything you do.'[35]

Benzedrine usage was widely abused, and, like all amphetamines, highly addictive. It is the chemical base of the popular clubber's drug, MDMA (Ecstasy). The body quickly develops a tolerance of it, encouraging higher dosage. Side effects from long-term use of Benzedrine include hyperactivity, grandiosity, euphoria, increased libido, irritability, paranoia, aggression and psychosomatic disorders. The most severe symptoms of chronic amphetamine abuse can result in psychotic behaviour that can be indistinguishable from schizophrenia. Heath would certainly have had access to Benzedrine at the time and in combination with his alcoholism it might explain some of the more extreme behaviour observed by Fielding-Johnson.

Towards the end of October, 180 Squadron had made three daylight bombing attacks on the town of Venlo in Holland and were then ordered to make a fourth. Venlo had both a road and a rail bridge over the River Meuse and the Allies would make a total of thirteen attempts to destroy the bridges in order to cut off German supply lines and to block the retreat of German troops across the river. During the attacks on the bridges, from 13 October to 19 November 1944, 300 people were killed. Despite their best efforts, Allied attempts to bomb the bridges would fail and eventually retreating German troops would blow them up themselves in an effort to halt the Allied advance.

At this time, certain members of Heath's crew began to confide in Fielding-Johnson that they were not keen to go out with him at night off duty, though they would not give detailed reasons for their objections other than to say that he encouraged them to spend too much money. There were no complaints about his performance as a pilot. Fielding-Johnson took it upon himself to monitor Heath's behaviour from then on and actively encouraged other members of the crew to share with him anything that Heath might do or say which might be detrimental to their morale. This in itself was an extraordinary state of affairs as the tight fraternal bonds between bomber crews were thought to be crucial to their survival.

The fourth attack on the Venlo bridges was to take place on 29 October. Aircrews would hear after breakfast if they were due to fly that day. After the mission was announced, Heath's top turret gunner approached Fielding-Johnson and told him that he felt unfit. He didn't want to fly and had lost his nerve. This was known within the RAF as 'lack of moral fibre' (LMF), a bureaucratic euphemism for cowardice. It was recognized by senior officers that such cases had to be dealt with quickly as 'one really frightened man could affect the others around him'.[36] The threat of being branded LMF was used as 'little short of a terror tactic'[37] over all aircrew and many men carried on flying scared out of their wits because they were more frightened of being called a coward than they were of flying.

It wasn't so much the admission of fear and loss of self-respect that deterred men from going LMF, it was the awareness that they would be regarded as inadequate to the pressures of war in a country totally committed to winning the war. In this atmosphere, the man who opted out was a pariah, an insult to the national need. He was conscious of bringing shame to his family, and that most of his friends wouldn't wish to recognize him, or at best they would be embarrassed and awkward on meeting. Nobody cared about the explanations of the psychiatrists about stress-induced illness.[38]

On this occasion, as senior officer and an experienced rear gunner, Fielding-Johnson volunteered to take the gunner's place. Not only would the crew be able to take their part in the operation and the squadron could fly intact, but here was an ideal opportunity for Fielding-Johnson to watch Heath working under pressure.

The preliminary briefing took place a few hours before take-off in the briefing room hut. Some 120 members of the squadron filed into rows of chairs, having been checked in by RAF police. Cigarettes and pipes were lit immediately as the crews waited for the squadron commanding officer and the station commander. In some squadrons, a map of the target was propped on a stand, hidden by a blackout curtain to be dramatically revealed by the station intelligence officer, who generally led the briefing. In others, every available inch of the walls and desks was covered with large-scale maps and photographs – a mosaic of information about the 'target for today', for the attacks of the Venlo bridges were to be in broad daylight. The position of balloon barrages, ground defences and hostile fighter bases would be marked by blobs of purple ink. Threads stretched across the large maps to indicate the route the bombers were to take. The blinds were

then drawn as an epidiascope projected large images of the
target on the wall. On some stations, the padre would then
say a prayer before final preparations began – and a medical
officer would be on hand to distribute Benzedrine.

The squadron then headed to the mess for their pre-
operation meal, usually bacon and eggs, a luxury in days of
rationing. They were then sealed off from the outside world.
Phone calls to wives and girlfriends were forbidden as they
waited nervously to see if the weather was favourable,
chain-smoking and reading paperback books to distract
themselves. It is during these long hours of waiting that
Heath first began to read the adventure stories and thrillers
he liked so much: Peter Cheyney's Slim Callaghan novels,
John Buchan's Hannay books or James Hadley Chase's *No
Orchids for Miss Blandish*, a well-thumbed copy of which
seemed to be in every RAF mess. The sense of anticipation
and anxiety steadily grew from the time crews were briefed
until take-off. Guy Gibson felt that this period was the worst
part of any bombing raid: 'Your stomach feels as though it
wants to hit your backbone.'[39] Vomiting and diarrhoea were
common and men were prone to fly off the handle at the
slightest provocation. 'All this,' Gibson said, 'because you're
frightened, scared stiff.'[40]

When it was confirmed that the weather was favourable
and the sortie was on, ninety minutes before take-off the
crews got ready, pulling on their parachute harnesses, fasten-
ing life preservers ('Mae Wests') or adjusting the electric
tubes of their hot suits. The kit was awkward and bulky,
much of it to try and combat the freezing cold they would
encounter flying at such high altitudes – for every 1,000 feet
they climbed, the air temperature dropped 2.5 degrees and
after 8,000 feet, oxygen masks were needed.[41] They had a
whistle attached to their collar to call for help if they fell into
the sea, and dog tags stamped with their name and service

number made of a material that could withstand the most intense furnace. Many airmen carried some sort of lucky charm around the neck, or pocketed close to the heart, a rabbit's foot, or a rosary, letter, St Christopher, coin, photograph, playing card; anything to fend off the overwhelming fear of a violent and painful death.

The final briefing took place in the crew room where the meteorological expert gave up-to-the-minute information about the weather. Provisions were handed out for the trip – a thermos flask of coffee, energy pastilles, chewing gum, raisins, chocolate.[42] They were also given an escape kit in case they fell into enemy territory. These consisted of local money, phrase sheets and compasses as well as maps of France, Germany or Belgium printed on squares of silk. These could be secreted or sewn somewhere in their uniform. As a last precaution, all crew members then emptied their pockets and were given two different coloured pouches in which to put the contents. One of these would be sent to their next of kin if they did not return. The other would be sent to clandestine girlfriends.[43]

The aircrews piled into lorries, were driven to their waiting aircraft and assisted into them by the ground crew. Last cigarettes were smoked and many crew members urinated against one of the aircraft's wheels – a final ritual to bring good luck. Heath signed the F700, accepting the aircraft from the ground crew. He declared that all was in good order and handed the form back to the ground crew who then stood down. From a training that had now become instinct, each member of the crew busied themselves, cramped in their allotted action stations. The navigator of Heath's crew – a former teacher called Freddie Silvester – laid out his chart in preparation. Despite Fielding-Johnson's seniority on the ground, in the air, the pilot was always in command of the aircraft, so Heath was very much in charge. He checked the bomb load before ordering the bomb doors to be closed. He then started the port and starboard engines which gave the aircraft electrical power so the crew could carry out the rest of their checks. The Mitchell bomber was a safe and sturdy machine, but the engines were also extremely noisy. The sound was deafening as the engines began to roar. The wireless operator tuned up his set as the engineer checked the instruments. Heath then carried out a cockpit check. The wind from the power of the engines flattened the grass around the aircraft as the ground crew removed the vast chocks. Heath taxied into position for take-off. Mitchell bombers took off in pairs. Once a flight of six was in the air, they flew into correct formation and circled until the rest of the squadron had taken off. Then the whole squadron set course for the target and headed for Holland.

As pilot, Heath's role was to get the aircraft to the target, Silvester's job as navigator was to find it. However tense the approach to the target, nothing matched the terrifying minutes of the bombing run itself. The crew would steel themselves for flak if they were picked out by enemy guns.

Once they reached the bridges at Venlo, the bomb-aimer took over. He lay face-down in the perspex nose of the aircraft, exposing the full length of his body to the flak from the enemy bursting around him. When they were above the target, he ordered the bomb doors to be opened. A blast of freezing air filled the fuselage. Checking the lens of the bomb-sight, the bomb-aimer called corrections over the intercom to Heath, who was constantly holding the aircraft steady, all the time trying to avoid enemy fire. Finally the bomb-aimer pressed the button that released the bombs, shouting, 'Bombs gone!' The aircraft would then lurch and rise abruptly by 200 to 300 feet as 10,000 lb[44] of high explosive and incendiaries dropped on the target. Heath ordered the bomb doors to be closed. Though the mission was complete, the crew were still vulnerable as they made for home.

Flak from the enemy was excessive in the whole area around the bridges and as they turned back towards Allied lines, Heath's bomber was hit by two bursts underneath the fuselage and under the port wing. From Fielding-Johnson's position in the top turret he could see that they were in danger of losing all their fuel from the port tanks in seconds. He contacted Heath over the intercom, suggesting he should 'feather' the port propeller immediately to avoid risk of fire. Heath tried but the oil pressure had already dropped. Suddenly, the port engine burst into flames. As pilot and captain of the aircraft, Heath gave the order to bale out. The rear gunner and Fielding-Johnson got away quickly through the rear escape hatch, but Silvester the navigator struggled to get his parachute on in the very confined space as flames began to engulf the aircraft. As pilot, it was Heath's responsibility to bale out last, but time was running out – he couldn't control the bomber for much longer. Seeing that Silvester needed help, he got out of the cockpit and squeezed through the cramped fuselage of the burning plane. Having secured Silvester's parachute, he helped him out of the stricken aircraft. Finally, Heath parachuted out of the plane himself. Seconds later, the Mitchell crashed to the ground, bursting into a ball of flames.

Later, when Silvester took his two weeks' survivor's leave, he told his wife about the incident, praising Heath for his heroism and quick thinking. There was no doubt in Silvester's mind; Heath had saved his life. As far as Fielding-Johnson was concerned, Heath's behaviour in the cockpit had been exemplary. He had behaved calmly and quickly, and though they had lost the aircraft, all the crew had survived. They eventually got together on the ground and made their way to an RAF station in Holland. After they arrived, they had several drinks and a meal to celebrate their escape. The crew were now eligible to be members of the Caterpillar Club, the informal organization open only to airmen who had parachuted out of a disabled aircraft, entitling them to wear a caterpillar badge on their lapels. For Heath, he was at last a member of a small elite with membership not based on background, status or money but on the demonstration of his own character.

However, after Heath had been drinking for a while, Fielding-Johnson noticed that he was displaying the abnormal behaviour that had previously concerned him. Getting drunk was recognized as a natural reaction to the strains of flying in Bomber Command as well as a unifying way for crews to celebrate survival, so it took extreme behaviour to stand out. On this occasion, Heath's behaviour was particularly marked and caused Fielding-Johnson, as senior officer, considerable embarrassment, as the crew were all visitors in another mess. Though Fielding-Johnson did not describe Heath's behaviour in detail on this occasion, the South African writer Peter Godfrey recalls a similar incident in a bar in Johannesburg during 1944.

Godfrey was meeting Duncan Burnside, the South African Labour MP, at the Shakespeare Bar in the centre of the city. Burnside was known for his great conversation and extraordinary tales. One of his favourite stories – and one which he enjoyed improvising for the entertainment of his various friends – was how he had come to lose his leg. Godfrey had heard the story several times, but the facts were always different – the Homeric telling of the tale being part of the fun. When he arrived at the bar, Burnside was with a 'pleasant soft spoken man' in a SAAF uniform, who was introduced as 'Jimmy Armstrong'. Godfrey thought that Armstrong seemed cultured and had a sense of humour. He was drinking double whiskies and Burnside was drinking South African brandy with a Pilsener chaser. More people joined them to listen to Burnside's outrageous tales, but as the afternoon wore on, Heath became very quiet. One of the newcomers then asked Burnside how he came to lose his leg and he told a ludicrous tale about an encounter with a shark off the coast of Natal. The audience were very amused, all, that is, except Heath. Suddenly, he went into a frightening – completely unprovoked – rage, calling Burnside a 'bloody liar', grabbing a beer bottle by the neck and shattering the end of it. 'I'll give you some real scars to boast about!' he shouted. Heath lunged at Burnside's face with the broken bottle but was then grabbed by a couple of the other men until he let the bottle drop.[45]

Whatever occurred in the RAF station in Holland, it was sufficiently serious that when Heath's crew returned to London, Fielding Johnson discussed the matter with his squadron commander.

I felt obliged to do this as the peculiar moods in which I had seen [Heath] from time to time struck me as definitely abnormal as whilst in such moods he seemed to become an entirely different person and something quite different from merely a highly strung youngster who had taken a drink or two too many and this curious behaviour apart from undermining the spirit and morale of his own crew might influence other air crews.[46]

Heath would never fly for the RAF again.

CHAPTER TEN
Out of South Africa

NOVEMBER 1944 – JANUARY 1946

We shall drink on the seas and oceans,
We shall drink with growing confidence
And growing strength in the air.
We shall drink on our Island,
Whatever the cost may be;
We shall drink on the beaches,
We shall drink on the landing grounds,
We shall drink in the fields and in the streets,
We shall drink in the hills.
We shall never surrender OUR DRINK.

> Alterations to a poster of Churchill's speech,
> RAF Officers' Mess, 1944

After baling out of the Mitchell bomber following the Venlo raid, Heath took his two weeks' survivor's leave.

It is at this point, he later claimed, that 'the reaction occurred' when he first started to experience blackouts. One night, he woke up to find himself on the floor in a corner of his bedroom, brushing away imaginary flames and trying to pull his ripcord.

He was then admitted to the RAF hospital in Brussels on 29 November 1944 with sinus trouble, and both his *maxillary antra* (sinuses) were washed out three times. Discharged from hospital on 13 December, he returned to England and was admitted to an RAF hospital in Wroughton with *maxillary sinusitis* and *otitic barotrauma,* the blockage in the ears often felt on descending in a plane.[1] Untreated, both these conditions can be painful and lead to greater infection. Heath's mentor, Mr Scott, who was already alert to the possibility that Heath might be suffering some sort of mental illness, was to point out later that these physical conditions might be symptomatic of an underlying psychological problem.

> I think I am correct in suggesting that in the RAF sinus inflammation after considerable flying was frequently found to be the outward and visible symptoms of a neurotic state consequent on the strain of flying duties. At the time of this breakdown Heath had completed over 2,000 hours instructional flying, plus an operational spell.[2]

Just before Christmas 1944, Heath was categorized as temporarily unfit for duty and was granted twelve days' sick leave. In the New Year, he was found fit for discharge from hospital and returned to his unit in Morecambe. But the day after he was discharged, a letter from the Air Ministry to South Africa House confirmed that no further flying duties could be found for him and that his secondment with the RAF would cease before the end of January. It's unclear what the exact reason was for the Air Ministry's rejection of Heath at this point, as the war was still in process. But his spells in hospital and either formal or informal reports from Fielding-Johnson would have indicated that he was a pilot with many problems, both physical and perhaps mental. He was repatriated to South Africa, arriving there on 2 March. Rather than reporting to his unit, he went straight back to Johannesburg to see his wife and child. But his return was not the homecoming he had anticipated. As soon as he arrived, his wife told him that she wanted a divorce.

> I was absolutely shattered as we'd been extremely happy but she was adamant. I tried everything to make her change her mind and on the last evening I saw her I tried to shoot her and myself but I blacked out and became unconscious before this was accomplished.[3]

This statement was made after he was arrested in 1946 so it may have been an attempt to provide a reason (or excuse) for the murders. In an earlier statement from 1945, Heath described his return to South Africa in less detail, but still registering his extreme reaction to the notion of the divorce.

> Arriving home I discovered my wife asked me to give her a divorce, which was rather a blow and I am afraid I flew off the handle.[4]

Here he didn't mention either the blackout or the gun, but at this stage he was being tried for a series of other crimes, so presumably wouldn't have wanted to add to the trouble he was already in by mentioning them. When he sold his story to the *Sunday Pictorial*, Heath fleshed out the incident a little more:

> On my last attempt to dissuade her we stopped the car to talk. I felt my head go tight. Then it was half an hour later. I was

still in the car, in the same place, I was given to understand that I had tried to shoot my wife and myself but had collapsed. It was a blackout.[5]

Heath's return to South Africa is also discussed in an interview that his wife gave to the crime writer Peter Godfrey in 1947. She indicated that she had only once been witness to her husband's extreme behaviour – the night before he left her. 'I was lucky, I suppose. I managed to get away before things got too bad.' According to her, Heath's behaviour on this occasion was brought on by an excess of alcohol, particularly whisky:

To me there is no mystery about his various attitudes to the various women in the case. With Yvonne Symonds he must have been sober: with the others, very much the worse for drink.[6]

She agreed with Fielding-Johnson that alcohol made Heath a 'different person', a malevolent and dangerous Mr Hyde in contrast to the breezy and clubbable Dr Jekyll that she had fallen in love with. As far as the blackouts go, alcohol-induced amnesia *can* certainly result from the large amounts that Heath was known to drink, affecting the hippocampus in the brain and leading to varying degrees of memory loss. They may also have been induced by some sort of post-traumatic stress following his baling out over Venlo. That said, Heath was a fantasist and would use any excuse to try and negotiate his way out of trouble. It's also true that by the mid-1940s, film studios from Hollywood to Elstree had embraced the new science of psychoanalysis. Memory loss and blackouts dominated cinema melodramas of the time. In *Random Harvest*, Ronald Coleman forgets he is married to Greer Garson due to shell shock; in *The Seventh Veil*, Ann Todd plays a concert pianist traumatized by her Svengali (James Mason); and in *Spellbound*, Gregory Peck blocks out the memory of (accidentally) killing his brother as a child.

In 1946, Heath refused to discuss his marriage with his lawyers and psychiatrists. But several of the doctors who questioned him were convinced that the key to his breakdown and subsequent spree of murderous violence lay in his relationship with his wife – or at least in the breakdown of relations between them. The reason given for the divorce was desertion[7] and there is no suggestion from the brief interviews that Elizabeth gave at the time of the trial that Heath had been violent towards her. Indeed she went so far as to say that despite his drunkenness he was 'a big teddy bear'. It seems more likely that in his absence from South Africa, Elizabeth and the Rivers family had become aware of Heath's debts and possibly his dalliances with other women. Having raised their son alone for much of the war, and with the support of her family, she may simply have felt that she and her son were better off without him. But for Heath, the breakdown of his marriage was a shock, affecting him profoundly.

> I think my divorce broke me completely. I have never felt the same since it happened and ever since have acted in a peculiar way on occasions.[8]

With the end of the war in Europe announced in May 1945, the Allied nations celebrated the end of hostilities and the beginning of a new era. Men who had been lucky enough to survive the conflict would be returning home from all corners of the globe to their wives and families. The world was starting again with a new contract for peace. But Neville Heath had nothing. No home or wife to return to. The future looked bleak, empty and forbidding. Everything in his life – his health, his career and his marriage – had deteriorated. Despite the fact that he knew he was now absent without leave, he went on a spree, living in hotels in Cape Town, Randfontein and Durban. Perhaps he was attempting to relive memories of happier times with Elizabeth or he might simply have been indulging his depression in bars and brothels.

Heath checked into the Queen's Hotel at Sea Point, Cape Town on 14 June and introduced himself to the hotel clerk, Reginald Hoar, as Major Armstrong. He had promoted himself and had also awarded himself the DFC, the ribbon for which he wore on his chest. A week later he made a payment of £10 1s. 10d. in cash, so the hotel assumed that Armstrong was bona fide. This is exactly the assumption Heath wanted them to make. On 26 June, he cashed a cheque for £5. The next day he wrote a cheque for £20 to pay for his room. He then told Mr Hoar that he was flying to Pretoria but would be back soon. He didn't cancel the room and said he expected his wife to join him there. He left his suitcase behind, giving the impression that he'd be back shortly. In reality, he had no intention of returning. Nor did he go to Pretoria, instead making his way up the coast to Durban.[9]

On 3 July, Heath arrived at the fashionable Durban Club on the Esplanade, looking for a room. Guy Lomax, the secretary of the club, said he could be accommodated for six days. Again, Heath claimed to be a major in the SAAF and signed the register as a member of an affiliated club. Four days later, he went to the main branch of the Standard Bank of South Africa in West Street at about 10 a.m., claiming to be a Captain Gill. He wanted to cash a cheque for £15, which was duly processed by the bank manager.

It is while he was based in Durban during July that Heath claimed to have experienced another blackout. He had been to a dinner party and left in his car with a young woman he knew. He remembered nothing more until he found himself in bed back at the Durban Club. He later heard that he had violently attacked the woman, but said he had no memory of it.[10] This incident cannot be substantiated as no charge was brought against him and there is no report of the incident in the South African press at the time. Significantly, Heath only referred to these blackouts after he was arrested.

Heath left the Durban Club on 9 July, owing £37 7s. 1d., and gave his forwarding address as the Rand Club in Johannesburg, asking that the bill be sent on there. Just before he left, he cashed another cheque for £10 1s. 0d. All the cheques he signed in Cape Town and Durban bounced. He left a trail of bad debts and dud cheques throughout South Africa and it didn't take long for the various authorities to catch up with him. In the first place he was arrested by the SAAF police for being absent without leave and was told he would be facing a court martial. But before being disciplined by the military, he was handed over to the South African civilian police. In running away from the reality of his divorce, he had only brought more trouble on himself. But the debts and the divorce were not the only issues that were about to engulf him. He had left a combustive situation in England that was also threatening to catch up with him.

In September of 1944, though still apparently happily married to his wife in South Africa, Heath had got engaged.

Twenty-one-year-old Zita Williams was a respectable girl from Nottingham, the daughter of William H. Williams, an inspector of the Nottingham Co-operative Insurance Society and a chief inspector of the Nottingham City Special Constables. Zita had first met Heath, whom she knew as Jimmy Cadogan, at a dance at Steeple Claydon in Buckinghamshire, whilst she was serving with the WRNS at HMS Pembroke V and he was training at RAF Finmere, six miles away.[11] She saw a lot of him over a three-week period, during which time he proposed to her several times. As with

many of the women in his life, Heath swept the impression-
able Zita off her feet: 'I was told by a good many people how
lucky I was to merit Jimmy's attentions.'[12]

After he had baled out in Holland, Heath took the two
weeks' survivor's leave that was due to him and returned to
London. It is during this leave in November that he and Zita
stayed in a double room at the Pembridge Court Hotel. Like
Yvonne Symonds, Zita may have felt that she was 'unofficially engaged' to Heath before agreeing to sleep with him.
He had told her that he had been married, but assured her
that the divorce had been finalized the previous September.
Their official engagement was announced in the local paper
in Nottingham. All the preparations were made including the
purchase of Zita's trousseau. The church was booked, the
reception organized and the wedding cake ordered. Zita
looked forward to a perfect wedding and a wonderful life
together with her dashing and heroic pilot husband. However,
in February 1945, Heath told her that they would have to
postpone the wedding as he had to return to South Africa.[13]
He gave her a photograph of himself saying he would be back
in three weeks. She would never see him again.

Upon returning to South Africa, Heath wrote to Zita,
informing her that his wife would not divorce him. This was
a huge shock to her and the first indication she had that he
was not in a position to marry. When Zita replied by letter,
she told him that the situation was serious. Since he had left
for South Africa, she had discovered that she was pregnant.[14]
When he next wrote back, Heath said he wasn't getting a
divorce and advised her of a reliable clinic in London where
she could get an abortion. This is particularly curious as at
this time Heath's wife was telling him that a divorce was
exactly what she wanted from him. For whatever reason,
Heath didn't want to marry Zita Williams. In all probability
she was not the only young woman, either in England or

South Africa, to fall for Heath's extraordinary charm and to have gone through a fantasy 'engagement' in order for Heath to seduce her into bed.[15]

Zita's father immediately wanted to sue Heath for breach of promise. From what he had told Zita and her family, they had assumed him to be a man of some considerable means. Had he not told them that he was the nephew of the Hon. Edward C. G. Cadogan, KBE, of the Carlton Club in London?[16] Mr Williams' lawyers contacted the SAAF in an attempt to make Heath face up to his responsibilities, but to no avail. By this time, the authorities in South Africa had more serious issues to discuss with Heath than a jilted girl back in England.

Out of the blue, on 12 February 1946 – a year after he had left her to go back to South Africa – Zita received, given the circumstances, an extraordinary telegram from Heath saying:

> Just returned England. Staying Strand Palace. Meet me today. Telegraph by return stating time. Love, Armstrong.[17]

Zita didn't answer the telegram, nor did she go to London. Her father wrote to Heath at the Strand Palace Hotel and told him that Zita wanted nothing more to do with him.

Eleven days later, Heath would be caught in the same hotel having tied, punched and thrashed Pauline Brees. She was not to know it at the time, but Zita Williams had potentially had a narrow escape.

After Heath's arrest, Zita and her father were interviewed by the police and both were coy in their statements about her 'friendship' with him. They didn't mention that she had been engaged to him, nor did they mention the fact that she had been pregnant by him. Mr Williams was silent about his desire to sue Heath for breach of promise, perhaps stung by the social stigma that his daughter had incurred having been involved with such a man. By this time, whether she had lost the baby or had the abortion that Heath had coldly suggested, it seems that her child by Heath did not survive.

As a consequence of his treatment of Zita Williams, Heath also lost one of his greatest and most committed supporters, Mr Scott of the Borstal Association. Scott had been corresponding with Heath and his family throughout the war. Heath himself had written to Mr Scott, telling him about the relationship with Zita and the fact that she was pregnant. He also wrote that he had suggested that Zita should consult an abortionist. Scott felt that if Heath could behave so callously towards Zita and so cruelly to his own wife, then he would have nothing more to do with him. In a sad final note in Heath's borstal record, Mr Scott recorded a few last lines about Neville Heath, once his star borstal boy, now turned bad.

> A very disappointing end to what could have been an outstanding career. The war gave him his chance and the chance provided the atmosphere that proved too much for him. I fear his post-war career as a 'civvy' will come as too great a contrast to the life he has been living since 1940. It would not surprise me to hear him next in custody charged with F. P. [false pretences] or bigamy.[18]

Mr Scott was not to know that Heath was capable of much darker crimes.

On 27 July 1945, Heath sent a letter to Elizabeth – rather formal in tone and clearly meant to be referred to in future legal negotiations between them.[19] In it he stated that he would not be returning to her and that she may instigate divorce proceedings against him. In this letter he made clear that he had no interest in challenging her for the custody of their son. Three days later, he appeared at Durban Magistrates' Court charged with defrauding the Standard Bank in Durban and the Durban Club.

At his appearance at Durban he presented himself as a man who was not fully in control of his actions and he gave plausible reasons for his erratic behaviour. Estranged from his wife, he had nowhere to stay and knowing that his rank as temporary captain was not sufficiently senior for him to be accommodated at the Durban Club, where they only took senior officers, he pretended to be a major. He was unable to collect his pay from the SAAF because he was absent without leave and without any money, he couldn't pay his hotel bills.

> When I returned home I found my home was not a happy one so I decided to leave my home. Since I left home I have had this misfortune. I was boarded back from Holland with sinus trouble. I have had medical attention. It is still giving me trouble. I had this domestic trouble. I took it badly and lost my head . . . the normal person does not lose his head or get shot up.[20]

The magistrates at Durban found Heath guilty of fraud on both charges and he was given two sentences of hard labour or a fine. But sympathetic to the war-damaged officer before them, the court suspended both sentences for two years on the condition that he repaid the debts and didn't commit similar offences within that period. Elizabeth arrived at the courthouse and paid Heath's debts, so at this point, it seems that relations between him and his wife were at the least civil. Immediately he was released from the magistrates' court, he was once again arrested by the SAAF police on several counts, for being absent without leave, for masquerading as a major and for wearing the ribbons of both the DFC and – a new addition – the OBE.

At the beginning of August, Heath's lawyer sent a cheque to the Queen's Hotel at Seapoint, repaying the debts that he had incurred. But the legal process had already been set in motion and the hotel explained that the matter was out of their hands – but that Heath could come and collect his suitcase if he liked.[21] The debt to the Queen's Hotel must also have been covered by Elizabeth's family, so relations between them and Heath were still amicable. But shortly afterwards, Heath advised his lawyers that despite what he had agreed in July with Elizabeth and her family, he had changed his mind about his relations with his son. Though he was happy for Elizabeth to remain sole guardian of the child for the time being, he was not prepared to give up rights in the child 'for all time'. He stipulated that the reason for this was that he was sure that his wife would marry again and that he might not approve of her choice of husband as a suitable stepfather for his child – an extraordinarily unreasonable rider given his own extremely dubious career and criminal record.[22] This gambit may have been inspired by Heath's attempt to secure his own position by exploiting the Rivers family's desire to protect the child's future.

Elizabeth's mother, who Heath had little respect for – later accusing the family of dominating their daughter – then became involved in the proceedings. From the incomplete correspondence between Heath's solicitors and those who represented the Rivers, it seems that Heath eventually agreed to sign away all his rights in his child's future and upbringing if the family would stand his bail money and pay off his debts.[23] Despite Heath's later avowed love for his son, he used him at this point as a bargaining tool.[24]

At the end of August Heath appeared at Randfontein and was found guilty on another charge of fraud. Now that he had agreed to give up any say in his son's future, Elizabeth's family paid the debt and the £20 bail money. Heath was ordered to return to the court for sentencing in February 1946. He was released only to be sent to Cape Town to face the fraud charges in relation to the Queen's Hotel debts and was due to appear before the magistrates on 6 September.

Heath was under pressure from all sides. His marriage was over and he had effectively sold the rights to a relationship with his son. He had faced a litany of charges and fines from all parts of the Union and his military career looked set to collapse as he faced his third court martial in less than a decade. In England he had lied to his parents, alienated his most fervent supporters, detonated his relationship with his sometime fiancée and might even be facing a lawsuit from her father for breach of promise. His finances, his career and his personal relationships were all in free fall.

And yet, his next step was to turn a bad situation into, potentially, a disastrous one.

While awaiting his court martial hearing, Heath was held at the Youngsfield Army Base in Cape Town. He was billeted in a room next to Flight Lieutenant Chapman of the RAF.[25] On 5 September, the day before the court hearing concerning the Queen's Hotel debts, Heath accompanied Chapman and a Major Erick Donnelly of the SAAF on a trip into Cape Town, travelling there in a pick-up truck. Major Donnelly was also based at Youngsfield but was about to go on leave, so needed some money from his bank.[26] He came out of the bank with about £50 in cash, which he kept in a roll in his trouser pocket. The three men returned to Youngsfield and bought each other drinks in the mess of 62 Air School. As the bar closed early, they bought a bottle of brandy and a bottle of gin to drink in the lounge. Donnelly suggested that they go into town to a nightclub, but Chapman wasn't keen. Heath said he didn't want to go without Chapman and the idea was dropped. After five or six drinks, Chapman decided to go to bed and left

Donnelly and Heath in the lounge alone together, this being about 11.30 p.m. When he left, Chapman felt that Heath seemed merry but that Donnelly was getting drunk. The two men continued drinking and then left together for Donnelly's room where they had more drinks. By the end of the evening, Donnelly was so drunk that he fell over, so Heath helped him undress and put him to bed. Heath went back to his own room, which was in the same corridor as Donnelly and Chapman's.

In the early hours of the morning, Donnelly woke and checked his trousers, which were normally hanging from the peg behind the door. But when he looked, the wad of cash had gone. He went into Chapman's room, woke him up and told him he had been robbed. The next morning, he reported the matter to the military police.

That day, unaware of the drama back at Youngsfield, Heath appeared in the Cape Town Magistrates' Court and pleaded guilty to the charges of fraud. He submitted the letter from the Queen's Hotel saying that his debts had been paid by his family. Again, he made a plausible defence, claiming that the frauds he had committed were done at a time when his 'mind was disordered', highlighting the incident at Venlo and the state of his marriage as extenuating circumstances.

Due to this one month of folly I lost a certain amount of army rank and due to being absent without leave, I'm likely to lose quite a lot more . . .

I was at that time absent without leave and it was impossible to draw my pay. The divorce proceedings have already started. My wife was drawing half my salary. My mind did not seem to be working properly. I was fully aware of what I was doing.[27]

It's significant that Heath drew attention to this awareness of his actions – in conjunction with a feeling that his mind was

not working as it should – ten months before the death of
Margery Gardner. The issue was not commented on in any
of his civil court appearances or at his court martial.

He was once again given a suspended sentence of two
years. However, as soon as he left the courtroom, he was
cautioned and searched by the RAF police. They wanted to
question him about the £50 that had been stolen from Major
Donnelly the night before. Heath agreed to be searched –
and was found to have only £14 on him in cash.

However, given that Heath had a long history of dishonesty and fraud, the military police immediately began to
watch his movements. At 9 a.m. on the 7 September, he
sent a registered letter to himself at the base at Roberts
Heights in Pretoria where he had been staying. He then
sent *another* letter at about 5 p.m. The RAF police contacted
the Post Office and asked them to intercept the letters at
Pretoria.[28] One of the letters was intercepted and found to
contain notes in cash. Heath was arrested by the South
African Civil Police and questioned. Cornered, rather than
admitting his actions, Heath decided to front it out and
told the police an impossibly and unbelievably complicated
story.

He claimed that £50 had been cabled to him from England
and that he had cashed it at the Post Office in order to pay
the fines he thought he might be given by the Cape Town
magistrates on 6 September. As he was given no fines, he
found he had a large amount of cash on him. On the night of
the robbery, he had heard Major Donnelly through the wall
between his and Chapman's room, wondering where his
money had gone. He decided to say nothing as if there were
any enquiry made, he felt sure that he would be the one to
'get it in the neck'.[29] He set about trying to get rid of his
money as quickly as possible. The military police did not
believe Heath's story.[30] He was arrested and sent to Wynberg

civil prison. But despite the extraordinary evidence against him, when he appeared in court Heath was yet again given the benefit of the doubt and found not guilty.[31]

As far as Elizabeth and the Rivers family were concerned, the divorce between her and Heath was finally granted in the Witwatersrand Division of the Supreme Court on 23 October 1945. Heath wrote a letter to Elizabeth telling her that he would never contact her again. Having brought an end to the marriage, the Rivers wanted to draw a line under Elizabeth's relationship with Heath so that she could start a new life with her young son. Mr Friedman, the family solicitor, contacted the SAAF, outlining Heath's various crimes and misdemeanours – including his breach of promise to Zita Williams which Elizabeth and her family were now aware of – and pointing out that he had often claimed that he had no intention of staying in South Africa after the end of the war. Friedman requested that the military authorities encourage the Commissoner for Immigration and Asiatic Affairs to deport Heath as soon as the court martial proceedings were over. The family wanted Heath out of South Africa, and out of their lives, for good.[32]

At the beginning of December, Heath appeared before the court martial at Pretoria. There were eleven different charges including wearing military decorations without authority, conduct prejudicial to good order and military discipline and for being absent without leave. Ten of the offences related to his activities during July 1945.[33] Though he was not convicted of all the charges, he was found guilty of most of them. For the third time, he was sentenced to be dismissed from the service.[34]

Heath was placed in police detention and this time refused bail, pending arrangements for his deportation from South Africa as an undesirable alien. Even his departure caused a minor diplomatic spat. Given that he was an illegal immigrant, the Department of External Affairs in Pretoria suggested to the Office of the High Commissioner for the United

Kingdom that they should make arrangements for Heath's removal at their own expense. This was met with disdain from the British High Commission in Cape Town.

> It seems to us a bit hard that we should be expected to arrange and pay for the deportation of this man when the Union Defence Authorities deliberately kept him on in spite of knowing his previous history.[35]

It is not recorded who eventually footed the bill.

Heath sailed from Cape Town on the SS *Sumaria* on 17 January 1946, returning to England a changed man, sadder if not necessarily wiser. One night on the passage home, he found himself wandering around the boat deck of the *Sumaria* in his dressing gown, with no idea how he came to be there. He had lost his wife and forfeited his relationship with his son. He had no home, no job, no income and no prospects. The war was over. There was nothing to fight for. Endless civilian days lay ahead. Heath was just one of millions of men returning home in this period, trading a life of risk and adventure for a future of staid sobriety. Many would struggle to make the change, missing the camaraderie, excitement and danger of war. The *New Statesman* worried specifically about men – just like Heath – returning from the RAF:

> What are all these young airmen, with their highly specialized training, their terrific sense of adventure and their complete lack of earning power, going to do in postwar England?[36]

His only option was to return to Wimbledon – shame-faced and exhausted – a man of nearly thirty living with his mother.

CHAPTER ELEVEN
Thursday 20 June 1946

[He] walked home from Moorgate Station across the ruins.
Pausing at the bastion of the Wall near St Giles's, he looked
across at the horrid waste, for horrid he felt it to be; he hated
mess and smashed things; the squalor of ruin sickened him;
like Flaubert, he was aware of an irremediable barbarism
coming up out of the earth, and of filth flung against the
ivory tower. It was a symbol of loathsome things, war,
destruction, savagery . . .

Rose Macaulay, *The World My Wilderness*, 1950

To British servicemen returning home from the war,
London in 1946 presented a much-changed face; half
familiar, yet wrecked, ravaged and ruined.

Throughout hostilities, the city had experienced 1,224
bomb alerts – about one every thirty-six hours. It had been

raided 354 times by piloted aircraft and from 1944 was
targeted day and night by nearly 3,000 pilotless bombs, the
deadly V1 and V2s. A total of 28,890 Londoners had been
killed and another 50,000 injured. Many shops, businesses
and domestic dwellings were eradicated – 100,000 houses
had to be demolished. An estimated 1,650,000 sustained
some sort of damage.[1]

The worst losses had been in the City of London. Out of
the total of 460 acres of built-up land, 164 acres had been
destroyed. Eighteen churches were beyond repair, including
fourteen designed by Christopher Wren.[2] Ten had been
razed to the ground in a single night. Austin Friars, the Dutch
church that dated from 1253, had been a light Gothic building and was now little more than 'a rubbish heap'. St Giles
Cripplegate, which Rose Macaulay wrote of – where
Cromwell married and Milton was buried – was now a ruin.
The statue of Milton outside the church had been completely
blown off its pedestal. St Clement Danes in the Strand had
been decimated. St Mary-le-Bow was reduced to a shell, her
font destroyed and her famous bells irreparably cracked.

> [The churches of London] had suffered a disgusting change,
> a metamorphosis at first stupefying. How could these dear
> interiors, panelled, symmetrically murky, personal, redolent
> of the eighteenth century, filled with ornaments and busts,
> urns, tablets, organ cases, carved swags, pulpits and galleries,
> pews, hassocks, and hymn books, have been turned into dead
> bonfires, enclosed by windowless and roofless lengths of wall,
> with pillars like rotten teeth thrusting up from heaps of ash?[3]

Even the colour of the city had changed, whether it was
Victorian granite, modern concrete or even the 'tweed-
textured' walls of earlier buildings; all had been scorched umber.
Seventeen of the city's Company Halls – including the

medieval Merchant Tailors' Hall – were flattened; six others were badly damaged.[4] The Inns of Court had suffered several times including the Middle Temple Hall, which had hosted the first production of *Twelfth Night*, Shakespeare's bitter-sweet comedy of love and loss. The Guildhall, once the setting for major trials such as that of Lady Jane Grey and Thomas Cranmer, had been burned to the ground in 1940, just as it had been in the Great Fire of 1666. Though still operational, the Old Bailey had been hit twice and the Royal Courts of Justice several times. Hundreds of London's historic buildings had come under attack and now lay half-wounded or annihilated. The Tower of London, St Thomas' Hospital, County Hall, Lambeth Palace, Holland House, Buckingham Palace, the offices of *The Times* and the Tate Gallery had all been damaged in the Blitz. The British Museum had lost ten of its galleries and 150,000 books. Madame Tussaud's suffered a direct hit on the night of 9–10 September 1940 resulting in the loss of 295 male heads and 57 female heads. Only two occupants of the museum survived completely unscathed; Paul, the museum's white cat, was found safe after the bombing clinging to the figure of Dr Crippen, the only waxwork not to suffer any damage at all. Directly the war had finished, the figure of Hitler was moved from the gallery of contemporary politicians and placed in the Chamber of Horrors.[5]

Whitehall, the centre of government, had been frequently bombed. Montague House, the offices of the Ministry of Labour, had been hit on fourteen occasions, the Ministry of Health was hit thirteen times and the Foreign Office, ten. The Palace of Westminster itself had also been shattered. It had taken at least twelve hits in one night in May 1941 when an incendiary bomb had set the House of Commons on fire whilst another hit the roof of Westminster Hall – steeped in British history, having stood since 1097. As firefighters could not save both, all efforts had been focused on saving the more

ancient building. The Commons Chamber was left to burn
and was not rebuilt until 1950. The clock tower that housed
Big Ben also suffered. The glass from the south dial of the
clock face was blown out, but its mechanism was not affected
and it continued to keep accurate time.

There was complete devastation around St Paul's Cathedral
and a wide area extending north from the river towards
Cripplegate and what is now the Barbican. Despite several
attacks and severe damage, St Paul's miraculously survived:

> The Cathedral had become in these later years more than
> ever a symbol of the unconquerable spirit that has sustained
> the fight . . . None who saw will ever forget their emotions
> on the night when London was burning and the dome
> seemed to ride the sea of fire like a great ship lifting above
> smoke and flame the inviolable ensign of the golden cross.[6]

Pawson and Leaf's opposite the cathedral, where Heath had
spent his only successful tenure in civilian employment, was
still standing, but had also been damaged by bombing. Further
west in Oxford Street, the John Lewis store where he had
worked for less than a fortnight in 1938 was completely obliterated. Bombs had also reached the suburbs, including Pinner
and Kenton in north London and Wimbledon in the south-
west of the city. Number 21 Merton Hall Road, though
never directly hit, had been 'badly shaken by bombs'.
Bramham Gardens in Earls Court had three houses which
were beyond repair, one on the corner where the gardens
met Bolton Gardens, the others to the right of number 24
where Margery Gardner rented a flat.[7]

Once cleared, the bombsites had been quickly utilized as
car parks or colonized as playgrounds by children newly
returned from evacuation in the country. These gaps, open
spaces and derelict sites were soon taken over by several types

of opportunistic weeds and wild flowers that started to sprout up across the city, enlivening the ruins and rubble. Some 126 different species flourished in the freshly created nooks and crannies; groundsel, coltsfoot, Oxford ragwort and the rosebay willow herb. London rocket had flourished in the ruins of the Great Fire after 1666 and had only made a reappearance when the new city wildernesses first started to appear in 1940.[8]

In the centre of town, Trafalgar Square, a memorial to a more ancient war, suffered little, though one of Landseer's lions was damaged. A paw had to be replaced and in 1946, there was still a gaping wound in its stomach.[9]

On 12 February 1946, a week after arriving back in England, Heath checked into the Strand Palace Hotel. It is at this point that he contacted Zita Williams again, the girl that he had jilted and rejected the year before, suggesting they meet at the hotel, with Heath presumably hoping for a casual sexual reunion. Zita didn't respond to Heath's telegram and left it to her father to tell him to stop bothering her.

Eleven days later, Heath was asked to leave the same hotel after the incident with Pauline Brees.[10]

Later that month, the South African authorities notified Wimbledon CID that Heath had – incredibly, given his record – applied for various decorations that he had been specifically refused by the SAAF. He had applied for the 1939–45 Star, the European Air Crew Star, the Italy Star, the France and Germany Medal and the British Defence Medal.[11]

His application for these awards alerted Wimbledon police to his return and his various previous convictions involving fraud and false pretences. On the evening of 20 March, he was drinking at the Alexandra on Wimbledon Hill, kitted out in the uniform of a lieutenant colonel in the SAAF. He was noted by a local police officer, Detective Bilyard, who approached him and asked his name. Heath replied that his name was 'Armstong'. At 9.15 p.m. Bilyard arrested Heath for wearing a uniform that he was not entitled to, as well as wearing decorations that he had not been awarded, including the DFC.[12] He appeared at Wimbledon Magistrates' Court on 5 April and the case made the local paper: 'Masquerade of Ex-Public School Boy'. Heath pleaded guilty to both charges, but claimed that he had not been wearing the uniform or the medals in order for financial gain, but to help him get a job. Once again, the magistrates treated him leniently, fining him £5 for both charges, saying, 'We are ignoring anything that happened before you went into the South African Air Force because we want to try and help you.'

Heath then seems to have made a determined effort to plan his future. Throughout April and May he wrote to several air companies enquiring about work as a commerical pilot and his address book contained a long list of the various air companies he had applied to.[13]

On 12 April Heath wrote to the London School of Air Navigation asking for details of a 'B' licence flying course. This qualified a pilot to fly passenger and commercial cargo planes, as distinct from an 'A' licence which only qualified a pilot to fly solo or with a military crew, so he was certainly imagining a future as a commerical pilot. If he couldn't fly with the RAF, at least he could put the flying experience he had accumulated over the past ten years to some fruitful use. His father agreed to finance him until he passed his examinations and had become established as a civil pilot. Between February and June of that year, Mr Heath gave his son nearly £200, a substantial amount of money at the time, £42 of which he paid in fees for the flying course. At the same time Heath was 'liberally supplied with money, so that he should not have any worries whilst he was studying for his examinations'.

Originally given £2 a week spending money by his father, more often than not he was given £6.

Twenty-eight-year-old Ralph Fisher had left the RAF in November and, like Heath, was keen to work as a commercial pilot. He and Heath met as pupils at the London School of Air Navigation on 24 April when they registered for the five-week course. They both joined the Luton Flying Club and would each hire planes at £3 10s. an hour as they had to complete a certain number of hours' flying in order to qualify for their 'B' licences. At the same time they socialized together at weekends, with Fisher finding Heath a likeable, clubbable character, though he was 'inclined to brag and [Fisher] didn't believe all he said'. Fisher also noted that Heath drank 'freely' and that he didn't associate with one particular woman. He was to continue to remain on friendly terms with Heath throughout his trial and beyond.[14]

On Friday 26 April, Bessie Heath had a visit from a young woman she had never met before. The woman, about thirty years old, asked if Mr Armstrong was at home? Mrs Heath said that she didn't know of anyone by that name and then realized that the woman must mean her son, Neville. 'Oh, yes, his name is not Armstrong, it is Heath, but he is known as Armstrong in the RAF,' she said. Mrs Heath invited the young woman into the house. The woman introduced herself as Muriel Silvester, the widow of Flight Lieutenant Freddie Silvester. Freddie had been stationed in Belgium towards the end of 1944. When he had come home on survivor's leave in November 1944, her husband had told her that his plane had been gunned down over Venlo. He had struggled to get his parachute on and the pilot, Jimmy Armstrong, had raced down the burning plane to help him. Later, Freddie returned to Belgium to join a fresh crew, but, sadly, in February 1945 he had been killed. Muriel was very anxious to meet some of her husband's friends in the RAF and Armstrong in particular.

Mrs Heath invited Muriel to stay for tea; she was sure that Neville would be home soon. The two women talked about their experiences during the war, Mrs Heath telling her that even in Wimbledon their house had been affected by the bombing. Time wore on, Mrs Heath explaining that her son must be studying late at the Air School or flying at Luton as he was studying for his civilian pilot's licence. At 6 p.m., Muriel left Merton Hall Road disappointed not to have met Heath. She had so wanted to thank him personally for saving her husband's life.[15]

It is while he was flying at Luton that Heath met a young woman called Jill Harris. She was twenty years old and worked as a shorthand typist at Skefco, the ball-bearing works in the town, living just round the corner from the factory with her parents. She and Heath first met at the Royal Hotel in Luton on Saturday 11 May. He was standing at the bar with Ralph Fisher and two other girls, one of whom Jill knew by sight. Whilst she was waiting to be served, Heath asked if he could buy her a drink. She refused as she was with friends and was buying a round. During the chatter at the bar she overheard Heath say that he was going back to London the following day. That night, she saw Heath again at a fairground. He smiled and waved at her.

The next day, Jill was meeting a girlfriend at the Royal Hotel and was surprised to find Heath still there, accompanied by Ralph Fisher again. Heath said, '*Now* I can get you a drink?' So he bought one for her and her friend. Heath and Fisher invited the two girls to the Luton Flying Club that afternoon. How would they like a spin in the air? Heath took Jill up in a plane for about an hour and Fisher did the same with Jill's friend. They stayed at the club until about 10 p.m. Afterwards, Heath took Jill home and said goodnight on the doorstep. 'Beyond kissing [her] goodnight nothing happened. Heath behaved like a gentleman.'[16]

On Monday morning, Jill received a phone call from Heath at her office, saying that he had left his gloves with her. Later that day she met him at the main entrance of the factory to return them. She was delighted when he greeted her with some flowers. He said he was going back to London but would be back in Luton the following weekend. Though she was looking forward to seeing him he didn't arrive that weekend and only returned to Luton the following week.

On Tuesday 14 May, Heath and Fisher both took the Air Ministry flying test for their 'B' licence. But at the end of the third week of the course, Heath suddenly wrote saying he was ill in bed with flu and asked for some instruction books to be sent to him. The books were posted, but Heath never returned to the school. When he next saw Fisher, he said that he had taken his 'B' licence test on 5 June and had passed it.

According to his mother, Heath took more examinations between 7 and 11 June and this weekend was clearly a period of great anxiety and pressure for him. All his efforts and energy were focused on passing these examinations. At the same time, the whole country was gearing up for the celebrations for 'V' Day. This was going to be the party to end all parties.

Heath phoned Jill at her office in Luton on Friday 7 June and arranged to send a car to her home at lunchtime to take her to the Royal Hotel. Jill was in a celebratory mood as all employees at the ball-bearing factory had been given a share of a £10,000 'V' Day bonus in that week's pay packet. It's unclear from her later statement to the police whether she had sex with Heath that lunchtime, or simply had lunch with him. She met him again that evening and gleaned that he had been married before. He even showed her a photograph of Elizabeth. She assumed that since his divorce he had been dating a number of girlfriends.

The next day, Saturday 8 June, was 'V' Day itself. Heath called at Jill's home impressively dressed in the uniform of a major in the SAAF. They had lunch with her parents and then he took her to the Flying Club again. That evening they called at several pubs and after 10 p.m. they went back to the Red Lion where Heath was staying. After the manageress called 'time', Heath continued to try and order more drinks for himself and Jill. But the wily manageress thought that Heath's intention was to get Jill drunk and then take her up to his room. She saw to it that this didn't happen.[17] Heath was annoyed, so they left the hotel and went to a local park, Pope's Meadow, where despite Luton's austerity 'V' Day plans there was a £500 firework display. After watching the fireworks, they walked further into the park.

That night an incident took place between Heath and Jill. One paragraph of her statement remains classified[18] but seems to indicate either an attempted rape or some sort of sexual assault. After the incident, Heath walked Jill home in silence and left her outside her parents' house. She phoned him the next day, but didn't actually see him. She saw him at a dance on Monday 10 June, but he didn't speak to her. She was disappointed as he struck her as a 'very charming type of person until that evening in the park'.

Heath returned home and continued studying. He went to Luton again to take his second Navigation Test on Tuesday 11 June. Spooner records that on this day, Heath brought another young woman to a Marylebone hotel that he had also met in Luton and spent the night with her. They didn't have sex as the woman was menstruating at the time and according to her, Heath was not resentful.[19]

At around this time, Heath also ran into Moira Lister, his ex-wife's schoolfriend and neighbour, who had by then left South Africa and become a successful ingenue on the London and Stratford stages. She had recently secured a season with

Kay Hammond and John Clements' company at the St James's Theatre. Meeting by chance at the exclusive Milroy Club, Heath asked Moira to join him for a drink. When she asked how Elizabeth was, he told her that she had been killed in a car crash on the Pretoria Road. Moira was shocked by the tragic death of her friend but also bowled over by Heath and his 'ice-blue eyes':

> I can distinctly remember my reaction was, 'Well, you are so attractive and now a widower with a beautiful little boy – I wouldn't mind marrying you!'[20]

Heath took her contact details in his address book and said he would take her out to dinner one evening. Some weeks later when they met at the Bagatelle restaurant, Moira thought him 'charming, gay [with] absolutely nothing salacious about him'. He behaved 'impeccably' throughout the evening, drove her home and kissed her on both cheeks before saying goodnight. When she later heard about the murders, Moira couldn't believe that Heath was responsible.

> I still found it impossible to equate the savage abnormal sex murders he had done with the charming man who had taken me out on the town.[21]

The week following 'V' Day, Heath received some news that was to devastate him and might well have been the trigger for the events that would lead him to kill.

He was told that the fact that he had been previously dismissed from the RAF would make him ineligible for a 'B' licence. Though he had passed his exams and practical tests, he would not be able to receive his licence. Consequently, he would never be able to fly as a commerical pilot. All of his plans for the

future, the efforts he had put into his examinations and the
money his father had lent him had come to nothing. Desperate,
he wrote another of his impassioned letters to the Minister of
Civil Aviation begging, as ever, for one more chance:

> Should the licence be witheld it will mean utter ruin for myself and
> those dependent upon me, as I have staked everything on this one
> chance. Issuing or witholding the licence means the difference between
> a decent future or a future of poverty, misery and the continued
> payment for misdeeds of the past. Your decision, sir, will give me the
> one last chance I need to make good. This licence literally means
> everything to me. It means the chance to regain my self-respect and
> give my child a decent start in life. I can only prove my words by
> actions, but should this chance be given me I would pledge my word
> that I will commit no misdemeanour, however slight, in the future,
> and I should be everlastingly grateful . . . I have paid the penalty
> demanded by law for my misdeeds, which can hardly be described as
> criminal. Stupid and foolish, yes, but I submit that it would not be
> just should I have to suffer for the remainder of my life.[22]

The letter was typical of Heath – outlining his extenuating
circumstances, promising not to misbehave, claiming to be
foolish but not bad. But there was no reply from the Air
Ministry. Neville Heath, the golden-haired flyboy was finally
brought to earth. This time he was grounded – for good.

On Saturday 15 June, Heath was drinking at the City Club in
Raquet Court, Fleet Street where he met Harry Ashbrook,[23]
a journalist for the *Daily Mirror* and the *Daily Mail*. They had
been introduced by a mutual business acquaintance. Heath
said that he had recently been demobilized and was now
arranging to fly planes abroad. He had mentioned that he was
planning to fly to Copenhagen the next week to discuss the
purchase of some planes with the Flying Club there. By

coincidence, Ashbrook was also planning to travel to Copenhagen and was about to sort out his passage with Transport Command. Heath suggested that he could probably get Ashbrook there quicker and cheaper. He would need to hire a Procter plane from an air company that he knew well from his student days, Marshall's of Cambridge. Heath showed Ashbrook a copy of that week's issue of *Flight* magazine, which had an advertisement for Marshall's in the small ads section. The flight would cost £25 return, which Ashbrook thought was very reasonable.[24]

Heath mentioned that he had married but then divorced. He was now married again and his wife was living with her mother in Nottingham. Ashbrook noted Heath's caterpillar badge – he seemed a trustworthy, reliable character. But the whole negotiation was, of course, bogus, as Heath knew that he wouldn't be able to fly at all without a 'B' licence.

That evening, Heath met a young Wren who had only recently been demobilized at a dance in Chelsea.

Her name was Yvonnne Symonds.

On Sunday 16 June, Heath was at Merton Hall Road in the morning and went out to lunch with Yvonne at about 12.30 p.m., then spent the night with her at the Pembridge Court Hotel. After he had waved Yvonne off on the Worthing train from Paddington Station on Monday evening, Bessie Heath was sure that her son was in the kitchen at Merton Hall Road when she and her husband went to bed at 10.30 p.m. On Tuesday, she believed that he left the house about 8.30 a.m. to go and take the second part of his examination and to organize his passport for the flight to Copenhagen. This trip to Copenhagen he also mentioned to the staff at the Pembridge Court Hotel. He did not return to Merton Hall Road on Tuesday night.[25]

Heath rang his mother on Wednesday morning and said, 'I think I'll just nip smartly home and collect my laundry.' He returned to Wimbledon, having been to the Air Ministry, and told his mother that he had passed his 'B' licence. This must have been an extraordinary relief to Bessie Heath, as she knew that getting the 'B' licence represented hope for her son's future – a job, security, independence. It was only later that she discovered that this was a lie.

> People have said that in not telling me his application had been refused, Neville was just betraying those traits of cunning and deceit with which his character has been black-ened. That is not true. He lied because he did not want to hurt me by telling me of his failure.[26]

Following his rejection by the Ministry of Civil Aviation, Heath's parents' feelings were very much in his mind as they 'had sacrificed a great deal to give [him] this chance'.[27] He told his mother that he was going to the Air Ministry that afternoon to get his 'B' licence and his passport and was then going to pick up a Proctor plane which he was going to fly to Copenhagen. He had lunch and packed his suitcase. He was dressed in a grey double-breasted pin-striped suit that had been made in South Africa, with a cream shirt, brown suede shoes and a dark brown trilby. His brother Mick hailed a taxi for him from Wimbledon Station at about 2.30 p.m.

On the doorstep, for the last time in his life, he kissed his mother goodbye.

At Victoria the next morning, after having spent the Wednesday night at the Pembridge Court Hotel, Heath met Harry Ashbrook at the Grosvenor Hotel that joined the station platform and told him that he planned to pick up the plane from Cambridge on Friday. He would then fly to

Elstree from where they would expect to fly to the continent on Saturday or Sunday, if customs formalities could be completed. Ashbrook noticed that Heath carried his flying helmet and goggles. It was sunny in the early part of the day, so Heath wore a pair of RAF-issue sunglasses. At lunchtime, they went to the Cock Tavern in Fleet Street, which was famous for its good food. Here they bumped into an acquaintance of Ashbrook's, Leslie Terry. Terry, a restaurant owner, was also a petty criminal as well as a drinking companion of the journalist Gerald Byrne. He had sixteen convictions for shop-breaking, receiving stolen goods, larceny and for living on immoral earnings. In August 1946, he was also to receive a three-year sentence for the manslaughter of a woman.[28] Terry was typical of the shady characters that peopled the pubs and clubs of Heath's drink-orientated night time world. Heath wondered if Terry would do him a favour and lend Ashbrook some money?[29] Ashbrook needed to borrow £50 in all, £25 to pay Heath for the trip to Copenhagen, as well as another £5 that Heath wanted to borrow and £20 for Ashbrook himself. Terry phoned the nearby Barclays Bank in Fleet Street and arranged to cash a cheque for £50. He collected this at 4 p.m. and went back to the City Club where he gave the cash to Ashbrook. Heath was given his £30 and said he was going directly to Cambridge. He would contact Ashbrook when he returned on Friday. Ashbrook left. Heath immediately called for drinks at the bar.[30]

That day Terry had pulled off a big business deal and was in the mood to celebrate. Heath had something to celebrate, too, with £30 burning a hole in his pocket. When the pubs closed, Heath and Terry went to Anne's Club to continue drinking until it was opening time again at 5 p.m. They carried on drinking at the various ancient pubs along Fleet Street between the Law Courts and the decimated area around St Paul's: the Falstaff, the Cheshire

Cheese and the Cock Tavern. Heath drank beer steadily, though 'apart from a slight flush he showed no signs of drunkenness'. At around 7 p.m., the pubs in the area started to run out of beer – Heath's favoured drink. In order to carry on drinking, Terry suggested that they should drive over in his car to one of Heath's locals in Knightsbridge where, Heath said, they could get all the ale they wanted.

When they arrived in Knightsbridge at about 7.30 p.m., Terry drove past the Trevor Arms and suggested that they stop there 'for a drink. Once inside the pub, Heath introduced him to some RAF officers that he knew and they got into a round, Heath and the other officers drinking beer, Terry drinking whisky. After four rounds of drinks, Heath left the others and went to join a girl he recognized at the bar, Margery Gardner.

> I had not arranged to meet her . . . Margery was only a casual acquaintance. In the last two or three weeks I had seen her several times in the Nag's Head. Sometimes I saw her too at clubs I belonged to. Her friends seemed to be a very queer set – a bit 'arty'.[31]

Leslie Terry had noticed that Margery had been on her own at the bar for a while, so as it was his round, he offered to buy her a drink. Heath then introduced them. They remained together for about an hour, then Margery said she'd like to eat. Heath asked Terry if he would like to join them, but Terry said he had an errand to sort first, but where would they be later? Leaving the pub, Heath told Terry that he and Margery would be dining just down the road at the Normandie Hotel. Terry got into his car, but as he was driving, realized that he'd been drinking too much – they had, after all, been drinking solidly for seven hours – so he decided to go home.

Consequently, Heath and Margery dined together alone. They then went for last orders at the Panama Club. Heath realized he'd left his flying helmet at the Normandie, but would go back for it the next day.

It was after midnight when we left the Panama, taking a taxi to Notting Hill Gate. Margery Gardner was still with me when we reached the hotel, but I don't remember asking her to stay. The last thing I can recall is going to one of the rooms at Pembridge Court Hotel – number four – undressing and getting into bed. There were two beds, and Margery Gardner was in the one farthest from the window. I put out the light. I am not certain whether I remember waking when the light went on again. But that was my first thought – the light was on. I was sitting on the floor of the room. Of what had happened in that period I had no recollection. But I saw the result. There was the body of a woman on the bed.

I had no idea what to do. There were stains of blood on me, so I bathed in the bathroom on the next floor, going back to the bedroom to shave and dress. I was confused in mind but it would be wrong to say that I was panicky. I noticed particularly how steady my hand was when I was holding the razor. Packing a suitcase, I went by taxi to the Normandie Hotel, where I had left my flying helmet the night before and from there to Victoria. It was too early for breakfast but I got some coffee. My instinct then was to go away, anywhere. It was not flight exactly, for already I found it hard to connect myself with the sight I had just seen in the bedroom. Everything seemed like a dream or a nightmare. I wanted to get away where things were light and bright and different. So I went to Brighton.

I felt ill. After having some breakfast on the front I was better and went for a walk round the town. It was just an aimless stroll round places I used to know and eventually it took me back to the railway station. Then I phoned Yvonne Symonds. I had known her in London as a very attractive girl and I think she recently took a degree as Master of Arts. We had lunch together that day and the next; I spent the night at an hotel on the front.

By this time I wasn't thinking much about Pembridge Court. It was not a sudden shutting off of consciousness about it. All there was to remember was the wakening on the floor. It did not seem to be me in any way except that I had seen it. So I could still lunch and laugh and enjoy the company of friends, as I did at the Blue Peter at Angmering. An old friend whom I met at Worthing suggested spending an evening there and I took Yvonne. We met several RAF types who were known to me.

Next day I found my name staring from the pages of the papers. I thought more about it then.

I was not afraid but I wanted to get out of Worthing.[32]

Whilst Heath was awaiting trial, Leslie Terry was keen to benefit from his very brief association with the most wanted man in the country – selling his own story to the press and negotiating a deal for Heath himself. He lamented the fact that he had suggested that they should go looking for more alcohol once the pubs had run dry in the West End. '[Heath] certainly wouldn't have met [Margery] on that fatal night if we hadn't set off, at my suggestion, in search of beer,'[33] he said.

By the time Margery had met Heath at the Trevor Arms, Leslie Terry estimated that Heath had already drunk twenty-four pints of beer.

Heath and Margery had then gone on drinking for another four hours.

CHAPTER TWELVE
Rogue Male

22 JUNE – 7 JULY 1946

I suddenly feel I can't *stand* anything any more – the boredom – hopelessness. I miss the war . . . I need excitement, I
need things crashing against me, violence; the quiet will
kill me.

Elizabeth Taylor, *A Wreath of Roses*, 1949

At 3.47 a.m. on Saturday 22 June a telegraphic message
was expressed to all police divisions in England and
Wales stating that Neville George Clevely Heath also known
as James Robert Cadogan Armstrong was wanted for interview. 'He is particularly fond of the company of women and
is a frequenter of drinking clubs and bars.' The police were
also keen to trace the taxi driver who had picked up Heath
and Margery outside the Panama Club and driven them to
the Pembridge Court Hotel and they asked the press for help

in trying to trace him. Every cab rank in London was checked by the police.

At the same time, detectives kept a special watch on 21 Merton Hall Road in case Heath tried to contact his parents. They were also given a warrant from the Home Office to intercept any letters or telegrams that were sent to the house.[1] All hotel managers and boarding-house keepers in the London area were asked to keep a look-out for a man answering Heath's description, particularly anyone carrying a flying helmet or wearing RAF sunglasses. Across the capital, railway stations, bus and coach depots were under police surveillance. Because of Heath's flying abilities and his familiarity with airfields, Scotland Yard worried that Heath might have already flown abroad.

Journalists started to follow leads in the Chelsea and West End drinking dens frequented by Margery and Heath. A picture of the two protagonists quickly began to be consolidated in tabloid form – the handsome ex-RAF playboy and the bohemian artist/extra. These early stories printed in newspapers over the weekend were to dictate how Margery in particular was depicted throughout the hunt for Heath and his subsequent trial: 'Bound Film Extra Murdered in Hotel'; 'Police Watch House in Film Extra's Mystery Death'. Margery was presented very much as a Chandler-style vamp with the words 'film extra' or 'bohemian' used euphemistically for a woman of easy morals. Though Margery may only have worked as a film extra a few times and very much as a last resort, this image stuck.

Having read the *Daily Mail* that Saturday morning, in Sheffield, the Wheat family solicitor Ralph Macro Wilson rang the local police at 10 a.m. and told them that he thought that the murder victim was the daughter of a client of his.[2] The police immediately rang Reg Spooner at his office in Hammersmith and he advised the Sheffield police to interview the Wheat family as soon as possible.[3]

Margery's younger brother Gilbert was working at the time as a teacher at St Anselm's School in Bakewell, but he travelled to Sheffield to accompany his mother to the police station that Saturday evening. They were joined by Macro Wilson, who was not only their solicitor but also a trusted family friend and godfather to Margery's daughter. Mrs Wheat was extremely distressed and throughout the interview she was anxious not to discuss the more bohemian aspects of Margery's life, but Macro Wilson encouraged her to be as frank as possible. Gilbert also supported his mother through the gruelling three hours of intimate questioning.

Marjorie's on-off lover Peter Tilley Bailey and her husband Peter Gardner[4] were also interviewed by the police that Saturday. Like many of Margery's associates, as Spooner was discovering, both had criminal records[5] – and both had alibis. Gardner's record made reference to his unstable psychological state, which was confirmed by Mrs Wheat. Margery had frequently spoken or written of her husband's 'mental' behaviour. He told the police that he and Margery had split amicably because of her drinking but that they had never really argued. They continued to meet casually and he would occasionally (he claimed) lend her money. Much of what he said was at odds with Margery's letters to her mother and Mrs Wheat's recollections of what Margery had said about their dysfunctional relationship. Peter's statement reads very much as if he was attempting to distance himself from Margery; according to him they got on very well, there were no arguments between them, she did not associate with other men, and *she* had a drink problem, not him. In reality Peter was later to die of cirrhosis of the liver caused by his alcoholism. Many of Margery's associates confirmed that they had never seen her drunk.[6] Peter was very clear that he had a secure alibi for the night of her murder – drinking with friends in a pub. He was also aware that Margery had recently been associating with Peter Tilley Bailey.

Curiously, when asked by the police to identify her body, Margery's husband refused. Whether this is because he couldn't bear to see the body of the woman he once loved, or whether he felt a sense of guilt is difficult to judge. Gilbert Wheat and Mr Macro Wilson volunteered to go to London to identify Margery if necessary. Ultimately this duty fell to Macro Wilson, who would identify the body at 3 p.m. on Wednesday 26 June at Hammersmith Mortuary in Fulham Palace Road.[7]

Harold Harter, the taxi driver, also saw the story in a newspaper and came forward for questioning. He retraced his journey with the police from the Panama Club to the Pembridge Court Hotel. Several other witnesses from the Panama Club, including Margery's friends Joyce Frost and Iris Humphrey, as well as the staff at the Panama Club were also inteviewed. Staff and guests at the Pembridge Court Hotel also gave statements.

A clearer picture was beginning to emerge of the hours leading up to Margery's death. Heath had signed his own name in the hotel and Panama Club registers, there were dozens of witnesses to the fact that he and Margery had spent all evening together and the taxi driver seemed to confirm that Heath was the last person to be seen with Margery alive.

On Monday, after reading the description of Heath in that morning's newspapers, George Girdwood at the Ocean Hotel in Worthing went round the corner to the hotel annexe. When he knocked on the door of Heath's room on the first floor, there was no reply. Opening the door, Girdwood saw that though some of his belongings were still there, Heath and his suitcase had gone. Girdwood immediately rang Worthing police.[8]

At 9.10 a.m., Detective Inspector Eagle arrived at the hotel. Girdwood showed him the newspaper with the description of Heath. He had arrived on Friday and left the day before without paying his bill. He had not been seen since 9 a.m. on Sunday morning when he had been taken a cup of tea and said at the time that he would not require breakfast. Eagle found Heath's signature in the hotel register and asked if he could look at his room. As well as the five newspapers from the previous Saturday, Heath had left some clothes including his corduroy trousers, his suede shoes and some magazines. Screwed up in the waste paper basket he found a yellow ticket dated 20 June 1946 with 'Lt. Col. Heath and Friends' written on it. This was the entry slip to the Panama Club that Heath had used to sign Margery in on the previous Wednesday.[9]

Further questioning Girdwood and his staff, the police learned that Heath had been accompanied by a young woman and that later on Sunday, they had received a telephone call asking for Colonel Heath to ring Swandean 906. This local telephone number was checked and found to be that of Major J. C. Symonds of 'Strathmore' on Warren Road. Two police officers went to the house and met Mrs Symonds who seemed very reluctant to give any information except to say that her husband had gone to London that morning to see his solicitors, Pontifex, Pitt & Coy in St Andrew Street, Holborn. This information was relayed to Spooner, who rang the solicitors and requested that Major Symonds come to the police station for questioning. Symonds was duly interviewed at Notting Hill and outlined his daughter's brief relationship with Heath, giving the police the information Heath had discussed with Yvonne about his connection with the murder. At the same time, DI Eagle made arrangements for Mrs Symonds and her daughter to visit the police station at Worthing.

At the annexe, Eagle noted that the bed sheets were marked with bloodstains. Under the sheet on the right-hand side of the bed he found three iron nails.[10] The reason for the presence of these nails was never established. Yvonne had already lost her virginity to Heath the week before, so it's unlikely that there would have been hymenal bleeding during intercourse.[11] If Heath had succeeded in persuading her into any sort of extreme sex, Yvonne was subsequently unwilling to admit to it. At all times, Yvonne stated that Heath treated her with great gentleness and care. Yet the presence of the nails under the sheets does suggest a malign intent on Heath's behalf.[12]

At 3 p.m. Yvonne arrived at Worthing Police Station with her mother and made a statement regarding her association with Heath, focusing on the conversation they had at the Blue Peter Club about the Notting Hill murder. Yvonne also brought with her the two shirts that Heath had given her to wash. Any evidential value that the shirts might have revealed had now been washed and ironed out of them. The shirts and the other evidence from Heath's room was then sent to Spooner in London. Yvonne mentioned that Heath had two suitcases, one of which he had left at Worthing Central Station. When the police investigated the left luggage there, the other suitcase had gone. Yvonne was then sent away by her parents for a holiday with some friends. A police watch was put on the Symonds' house in case Heath tried to contact her.

A man answering Heath's description carrying a suitcase had been seen at Worthing Station at about 11.15 a.m. on Sunday morning, enquiring where he could get a taxi. He didn't state his intended destination, nor did he succeed in getting a cab. Further enquiries at the bus office and the railway station drew a blank as both were exceptionally busy that weekend. Heath had disappeared into the crowds.

The hunt for Heath now intensified along the south coast, focusing on Brighton and Hove, which Heath knew well. Aware that Heath would quickly spend his way through the £30 he had taken from Harry Ashbrook, messages were sent to all police stations along the south coast to report any attempt to borrow money or sell clothing or jewellery and particularly to investigate any complaints from young and attractive women.

Spooner now made use of Heath's address book that they had recovered from his room in Merton Hall Road. The book contained nearly 400 names and addresses throughout London and the provinces, all in Heath's handwriting. Most of these were women. Spooner thought it possible that Heath had made contact with one or other of the women in the address book, so he issued a circular letter to various police forces around the country to question all of Heath's associates. These included his former fiancées, Peggy Dixon and Zita Williams. Drawing a blank on the south coast, enquiries were made throughout the country – in Bedford, Portsmouth, Leeds, Jersey, Bristol, Bath, Luton, Manchester, Cornwall, Worcester and Wales. At its peak, 40,000 officers throughout the UK were working on the case. Many of the names and phone numbers led nowhere, with some women claiming not to have known Heath at all, or if they had, that they had only met him casually at a dance or in a pub. The police's job was made more difficult as many of the women were now married and not keen to discuss their wartime pasts. Added to this, several potential witnesses had been killed in the Blitz or on active service. Many of the addresses had been bombed and were now derelict, leaving no trace of their former tenants. At one point, police were rumoured to be watching 150 women across the country and the *Daily Mirror* correspondent claimed that the police were waiting for Heath to contact one of them.

In the end one of these women – and we are convinced that a woman is hiding him – will give us a clue to his whereabouts. Yesterday [a *Mirror* journalist] talked to a dozen women in the London area who have been friends with the 'Don

Juan' Heath . . . all were under observation by the police . . .
None would say a bad word against him. To an attractive
brunette to whom Heath proposed marriage only twelve
months ago [he] showed a photograph. 'The darling,' she
said. 'I still would love him always.'[13]

The knotted handkerchief marked 'L. Kearns' that had bound
Margery Gardner's feet was sent to the forensic laboratory at
Hendon, but despite a countrywide search the owner of the
handkerchief was never traced, though a second-hand car
dealer called L. Kearns was known to frequent the Nag's
Head in Knightsbridge, one of Heath's locals. What had
appeared at first to be a significant clue proved to be a red
herring in what was becoming an increasingly frustrating and
elusive investigation. The press scrutinized every development of the search, further inflating public fears that an
extraordinarily dangerous killer remained at large.

With Spooner's investigation focused on Worthing, but with
no real idea where Heath was, the police in London then
received an unexpected lead.

Superintendent Tom Barratt had been mentioned in
several of the newspaper reports over the weekend. On
Monday morning he received a letter at Scotland Yard.
Opening it, Barratt was stunned to find that it was a letter
from Heath himself.

22nd June 1946

Sir,
I feel it to be my duty to inform you of certain facts in connection
with the death of Mrs Gardner at Notting Hill Gate. I booked in
at the hotel last Sunday, but not with Mrs Gardner, whom I met
for the first time during the week. I had drinks with her on Friday

*evening, and whilst I was with her she met an acquaintance with
whom she was obliged to sleep. The reasons, as I understand them,
were mainly financial.*

*It was then that Mrs Gardner asked if she could use my hotel room
until two o'clock and intimated that if I returned after that, I might
spend the remainder of the night with her. I gave her my keys and told
her to leave the hotel door open. It must have been almost 3 a.m.
when I returned to the hotel and found her in the condition of which
you are aware. I realized that I was in an invidious position, and
rather than notify the police, I packed my belongings and left.*

*Since then I have been in several minds whether to come forward
or not, but in view of the circumstances I have been afraid to. I can
give you a description of the man. He was aged approx. 30, dark
hair (black), with a small moustache. Height about 5' 9" slim build.
His name was Jack and I gathered that he was a friend of Mrs
Gardner's of some long standing. The personal column of the 'Daily
Telegraph' will find me, but at the moment I have assumed another
name. I should like to come forward and help, but I cannot face the
music of a fraud charge which will obviously be preferred against me
if I should do so. I have the instrument with which Mrs Gardner was
beaten and am forwarding this to you to-day. You will find my
fingerprints on it, but you should also find others as well.*

N. G. C. Heath[11]

The fraud charge that Heath mentioned here is probably
related to the £30 that he had taken from Harry Ashbrook in
payment for the trip to Copenhagen. The whip that Heath
promised to forward never arrived. Heath deliberately impli-
cated 'Jack' who was either a figment of his imagination, or he
had given a description of the army officer whom Heath knew
Margery had arranged to meet on the night she was killed.

The letter was also full of basic errors (Heath met Margery
on Thursday, not Friday) and was at odds with the story he

had told Yvonne Symonds in Angmering in which Heath said that he had arranged for his friend to use his room at the Pembridge Court Hotel in order to entertain a prostitute. In the letter, it is Margery that Heath had supposedly been discussing the hotel room with. Perhaps with hindsight Heath had realized that he had been seen drinking, talking and dancing with her throughout Thursday night. He also suggested that Margery was a prostitute – an idea that the press picked up and continued to hint at. The alternative story that appeared less frequently was that Margery was 'sweet and refined with haunting eyes and rich black hair'. But somehow this version of the story did not appeal to the press, who were nurturing the case as that summer's media sensation.

As he continued to elude the police, Scotland Yard began to receive dozens of 'dud' 999 calls with sightings of Heath from Worthing to Wales, from Birmingham to Bognor.[15] Spooner called midnight talks to work through the mounting number of clues and leads.[16] Letters from members of the public, many scrawled and anonymous, suggested motives for the murder – for instance that Heath was at the centre of a white slave ring, seducing and exploiting defenceless young women. In the golden age of Agatha Christie, hundreds of armchair sleuths claimed sightings of Heath all over the country.

On Wednesday evening June 26th, in a 'bus' queue in the Strand at about 6 p.m. (outside Woolworth's) was a man who answered the description given in the newspapers . . . the man wore dark glasses which he took off on the bus . . . but the moral of this story is that if there were a picture of the man published, the writer of this letter might have known at once whether it was the wanted man or not.[17]

This concern about the lack of a photograph of Heath arose early in the investigation and was later proved to be valid.

During the night of 27 June a two-and-a-half-ton 'Dodge' truck was stolen from Rochester and found abandoned in Worthing the next day. The truck had been loaded with rolls of tarred paper but they had all been removed when it was found. In the cabin was a carton containing twenty-four jars of Brylcreem, a camera and twenty-four rolls of Kodak film. On the box of Brylcreem was a message:

The police thought they had got me but I am to clever for you, don't you agree. I warn you there is going to be another murder before very long you see.

J. Heath.

P.S. The silly police have got to hurry if they want me.

Though the handwriting was neat, the spelling ('to clever') didn't indicate a grammar-school education like Heath's. DI Eagle in Worthing passed the information to Spooner at Notting Hill but the clue turned out to be a red herring. It was clear that the longer Heath was at large, the more intense was the speculation about the possibility of him committing another violent murder.[18]

One newspaper, adding fuel to the fire, speculated that Heath might be carrying a gun.[19]

As well as questioning Heath's acquaintances, the police continued to investigate Margery Gardner's life and background. Her diary had been studied and copied and officers began to interview her friends and associates. It is at this point that the investigation into her death took a complex turn.

One witness, Trevethan Frampton, had known Margery

for about six months. They were both regulars at the same
bars and clubs. In his interview with the police, Frampton
gave an insight into Margery's character which offered an
alternative interpretation of the circumstances surrounding
her death.

> On occasions Mrs Gardner told me that she liked people to
> be rough when making love to her and also that her husband
> was invariably rough with her. From this I gathered that she
> was a masochistic. I am not very interested in this subject and
> never questioned her on it. I did discover though that she
> enjoyed the sensation of being at a man's mercy.[20]

If Margery had left the Panama Club with Heath knowing
what his sexual tastes were, had she allowed herself to be
tied by him in order to be beaten, just as Pauline Brees had
at the Strand Palace Hotel? Another witness who claimed to
know Margery well, a Mrs Smith, also attributed masochistic tendencies to her, but Spooner thought Mrs Smith was
'a borderline mental case'[21] and that her statement was
questionable.

Nearly seventy years on, the complexities of masochistic
behaviour are better understood and the subject is less covert
than it was in the mid-1940s. High-street chains like Ann
Summers sell a vast array of whips, handcuffs and ties aimed
at the female consumer and intended for the mutual explora-
tion of sexual dominance and submission. Though extreme,
none of the injuries that Margery had suffered would have
killed her, but Heath would only have needed to hold her
face down into the pillow for as little as thirty seconds in
order to suffocate her. Keith Simpson confirmed that
Margery's face seemed to have been washed after she had
died. Might this have resulted from Heath attempting to
revive her by splashing water on her face from the washbasin

in the corner of the room? Were the police looking at a sexual tryst that had got out of hand? And was this, therefore, a case of manslaughter rather than murder?

By the end of the first week of July, the investigation had been going on for sixteen days and despite several sightings, Heath had apparently disappeared. Maybe he was abroad by now or one of his women friends was hiding him somewhere in England? The police had drawn a blank.

On the evening of Saturday 7 July, Reg Spooner received a telephone call that was to accelerate the investigation, but was also to take it in an unexpected and harrowing direction. He was told that a man was being held at Bournemouth Police Station who was believed to be Neville Heath. This was the call that Spooner had been waiting for. He told the police in Bournemouth to keep the suspect at the station at any cost. He would be there as soon as possible.

Spooner instructed Detective Sergeant Frampton to fill a police car with petrol at Lambeth garage. Fuel still being rationed, Frampton drew three five-unit petrol coupons for the journey there and back.[22] At 10.40 p.m. Spooner and Shelley Symes climbed into the back of the Wolseley and raced the hundred miles down to Bournemouth.

PART THREE

Group Captain Rupert Robert Brook

CHAPTER THIRTEEN
Bournemouth

23 JUNE 1946

My learned friend quoted the great detective [Arthur Conan Doyle's Sherlock Holmes] who said that the curious thing about the dog in the night was that the dog did nothing in the night. Another great detective [G. K. Chesterton's Father Brown], known to my learned friend and possibly to you, once asked, 'Where does a wise man hide a pebble?' And the answer was, 'On a beach.' What better way of removing yourself from immediate notice at any rate, than to go and stay at a seaside place in the holiday season, taking on an identity and character which is not your own, and mingling with the seaside crowds, behaving as an hotel guest and an apparently ordinary person?

Mr E. Anthony Hawke, Counsel for the Crown[1]

Bournemouth is one of the few English towns one can safely
call 'her'.

John Betjeman, *First and Last Loves*, 1952

The contemporary view of Bournemouth is very much of
a place where one goes to die; a quiet place with a slower
pace. But this polite and ordered town stretching towards the
coast conceals a darker nature, perhaps even more sinister
given the sharp contrast between its sunny, holiday face and
the shadows haunting the villas and gardens that John
Betjeman observed in the early 1950s. It is curious to find, for
instance, that Mary Shelley, the creator of *Frankenstein* is
buried in St Peter's Church in Bournemouth, along with her
husband's heart, brought back from Italy after his death.[2]
Robert Louis Stevenson settled in Bournemouth and in 1886
wrote one of his most famous novels here – the definitive tale
of the dualities of the human personality, *The Strange Case of
Dr Jekyll and Mr Hyde*[3] – strange though it may have seemed
at the time that this polite English seaside resort should inspire
such a tale of corruption and horror. It is also in Bournemouth
– or Sandbourne as it is known in Hardy's Wessex – that Tess
kills her caddish seducer Alec D'Uberville at a 'stylish lodging
house' called 'The Herons' ('Tis all lodging houses here'),[4]
and where Mrs Brooks the landlady first notices D'Uberville's
blood 'drip, drip, drip' through the ceiling until the stain
resembles 'a gigantic ace of hearts'.[5]

The position of Bournemouth, about 100 miles south-
west of London, and its coastal situation had proved crucial
to the town's fortunes during the war. At the outbreak of
hostilities the town had been quickly prepared for invasion.
In 1940, Bournemouth and Boscombe piers had been closed,
blown up and stripped of their planking to prevent enemy
landings.[6] The sea front itself was closed to all but the military
and the beach, now a minefield, bristled with barbed wire.

Army vehicles had been positioned along the cliff tops to prevent possible invasion. Pillboxes, static water tanks and air raid shelters had been built throughout the town. All beach huts were removed and placed in their owners' gardens for the duration. Anti-aircraft guns were positioned on the flat roofs of the beachside cafes which once had swarmed with holiday crowds.[7]

Because of its peacetime occupation as a holiday resort, Bournemouth also had a unique resource to offer the war effort: accommodation. The town boasted hundreds of hotels from five star luxury to basic bed and board. As well as becoming a reception area for evacuees, many businesses and government offices from London including the Ministries of Agriculture and Education, the Home Office and the Board of Trade were transferred to Bournemouth and established in the main hotels. Consequently the town was flooded with hundreds of civil servants, all of whom needed to be accommodated as well.[8]

As the war progressed, the section of the coast both to the east and west of Bournemouth pier became crucial, not only as a defensive position, but as a practice area for military strategy. In February 1944, Studland Bay had been the scene of live ammunition beach rehearsals in preparation for the Normandy landings, supervised by Eisenhower and Field Marshall Montgomery. Nearby Poole Harbour was the departure point for many of the ships participating in D-Day itself. Thousands of service personnel from the Allied nations began to flood into the town in order to take part in these practice operations. At the same time, battle-weary survivors from the various theatres of war had been sent to Bournemouth on leave to recuperate.[9] Americans, Canadians, Czechs and – after D-Day – French servicemen were all billeted in Bournemouth's requisitioned hotels and guesthouses. By 1944 an Area Defence ban was in force creating an exclusion zone within ten miles of the coast and very few civilians were allowed within it. Bournemouth had become a garrison town.[10]

The large number of service personnel may well be one of the reasons that Bournemouth was bombed about fifty times throughout the war. It was targeted by 2,271 bombs, including incendiaries. Some 219 people were killed, 176 injured and 75 premises were completely destroyed. One of the most destructive raids took place on the night of 15–16 November 1940 when 53 people were killed and 2,321 properties were damaged. It is in this raid that Robert Louis Stevenson's house, 'Skerryvore', at the top of Alum Chine had been hit and damaged. Despite a public campaign to try and preserve it as a building of historic interest, the house was demolished the following year and by 1946 nothing of it remained.[11]

The most damaging attack on Bournemouth was a daring daylight 'hit and run' raid on Sunday 23 May 1943, when bombs were dropped in ten districts by Focke-Wulf 190s (known by the RAF as the 'butcher bird') and Messerschmitt 109s. These aircraft carried 500-kg high-explosive bombs and were light enough to fly above wave height, making them undetectable by British radar. Consequently, the town was not in a state of alert nor ready to defend itself when it prepared for lunch that Sunday. The Luftwaffe aircraft could fly so closely to their targets that survivors from the raid remember being able to look directly into the German pilots' faces.[12]

Among 3,481 buildings damaged in the raid, the Central and Metropole hotels were both destroyed. Beales' department store was completely demolished following a direct hit. Fortunately, this being Sunday, the shop was closed, but the hotel bars were busy with servicemen having drinks before lunch. In the Metropole Hotel alone seventy-seven people were killed. The attack took place exactly one week after the infamous 'Dam Busters' raid on the Mohne and Eder dams in Germany led by Guy Gibson and it may have been a revenge attack with the Metropole Hotel as a specific target, it being a Royal Canadian Air Force reception centre as well as a billet for Canadian, Australian and American personnel.

By the summer of 1946, many of the servicemen and women had left Bournemouth and a concerted effort was made to get the town ready to embrace its former identity as a holiday destination. German prisoners of war were assigned to remove barbed wire and landmines from the beach. The Russell-Cotes Art Gallery started to collect pictures that had been removed for safety from the various manor houses, rectories and churches to which they had been taken when war was declared. But the coastline around Bournemouth had deteriorated more than any other resort, due to heavy tides and coastal winds. The beach had almost disappeared leaving only a narrow strip of sand, so a great deal of intense work had to be done for the expected crowds in the summer. A gangplank was hastily laid across the skeleton of the derelict pier in order to give access to pleasure boats, but it was not to be fully restored until 1950.[13] Many buildings and hotels were still requisitioned by the military. The Royal Bath Hotel remained as the WAAF officers' mess until September 1946. The Burley Court Hotel had only recently been vacated by the Canadian Air Force in March, as had the High Cliff Hotel on the West Cliff.

The Tollard Royal Hotel was also situated on Bournemouth's West Cliff, just west of the pier and up an inclined slope from the promenade and the town's central gardens that lead down to the beach. The building remains – inevitably seaside apartments now – still commanding forty miles of uninterrupted views across the Channel. Slightly removed from the entertainments of central Bournemouth, the building continues to feel select, a little superior, perched above the town and facing the sea. Built in 1901, the Tollard Royal remained in use as an hotel until 1956 when it was divided into flats. But even today many of the original hotel features survive – the Art Deco fireplaces, mahogany doors with cut-glass panels, the grand internal staircase and even the revolving doors in the lobby.

The hotel had been requisitioned during the war as a leave centre for US service personnel but had been vacated in November 1945. After a period of refurbishment, it had reopened for guests in June and was keen to take advantage of the first post-war holiday season. It had been repainted inside and maintenance work that had been curtailed during the war had now begun again – some particularly urgent work being carried out on the roof that had been going on since March. The Tollard Royal was a smart hotel with 100 guest rooms, each having either a private bathroom or a sink with hot and cold running water. A Vita Glass Sun Lounge was 'flooded every evening and on dull days with health-giving Ultra Violet Rays'.[14] The hotel boasted two lifts, billiards, an American Bar and dances twice a week. Terms for the cheapest rooms were 5½ guineas a week – the tariff in guineas rather than pounds suggesting that the Tollard Royal was a select establishment, a cut above the rest, for the most discerning clientele.

On Sunday 23 June, a tall, bronzed South African with a military gait arrived as a chance visitor at the hotel. Violet Lay the receptionist signed him in at about 3 p.m.[15] He told her he would like accommodation for a week. His arrival was noteworthy only in that he was the sole guest to check in that day. He was allotted Room 71 on the first floor and gave his name as Group Captain Rupert Robert Brook.

The name might have raised a certain curiosity at the hotel. Rupert Brooke was the celebrated soldier poet who had died in 1915 on his way to Gallipoli. A classically educated Rugby and Cambridge man, he was distinguished by heart-stoppingly handsome features that had almost eclipsed his poetry in the mythology that developed after his death. W. B. Yeats thought him 'the handsomest young man in England'.[16] Brooke's poems were heartfelt, sentimental and patriotic. He effectively wrote his own epitaph with his most famous poem, *The Soldier*, which articulated patriotic sentiments that had become fashionable again in the war that had just ended.

Brooke had been a frequent visitor to Bournemouth before the Great War and a plaque on a house in Littledown Road commemorated the fact: 'Here Rupert Brooke 1888–1915 discovered poetry.' What a coincidence that the newly arrived group captain – as heroic and handsome as the poet – should also share his name.

Brook carried with him a single suitcase so was apparently not intending to stay in Bournemouth very long. Though he signed the hotel register, he failed to add the date of his arrival, nor did he surrender his ration book.

Like so many women before her, Miss Lay the receptionist had been seduced by the charms of the handsome group captain. He was quite the ladykiller.

CHAPTER FOURTEEN
Miss Waring

23–29 JUNE 1946

VERDICT ON BOURNEMOUTH
Two girls both of Birmingham commented: 'Been here a fortnight, nice for a rest, too little to do, queues for everything, should be more attractions on the beach and more to do on rainy nights, doubt whether local paper will print our views.' Four girls between 20 and 22 . . . None had been here before. All commented: 'Days very full, nights very dull.' Thought Pavilion booking system 'rotten'.
Considered there should be more amusements on the beach and said: 'Bournemouth is too classy for a really good time.'
Bournemouth Times, 16 August 1946

The newly arrived 'Bobbie' Brook was popular with the guests at the hotel, many of whom had recently been demobilized and were taking their first family holiday since being called up. He was equally popular with the hotel staff and spent much of his time ingratiating himself with them, talking about their mutual wartime experiences and about his career as a pilot. Ivor Relf had only recently been appointed as joint manager of the Tollard Royal and had been a former RAF officer himself.[1] Brook's engaging RAF manner, knowledge of aircraft and acquaintanceship with mutual air force colleagues convinced Relf that Brook was 'very definitely what he purported to be, that is a retired group captain in the Royal Air Force'.[2] Brook claimed he was to fly in a forthcoming air exhibition at Shoreham, but this was dependent on the weather. He obtained up-to-date weather reports with ease from various aerodromes including the meteorological station at Dunstable. Whenever he phoned for these reports, Brook used either the telephone in the dining room or the one at the reception desk. Consequently these conversations could always be (and may have been intended to be) overheard. So convincing was Brook in playing the role of the clubbable RAF gent that the staff trusted him absolutely. He was never given a bill for the full fourteen days he stayed at the hotel.

Arthur White, the head night porter, was charmed by the affable group captain, who often chatted to him about flying. White gathered that Brook was from Johannesburg and was now employed in Britain by the Auster Aircraft Company in Leicester. He thought that Brook had a 'wonderful personality and was a great hit with the ladies'.[3] Throughout Brook's stay at the hotel, White and another night porter, Frederick Wilkinson, noted that beyond several sports shirts and two or three pullovers, Brook had few clothes – no hat and no coat. He always wore the same pair of grey striped flannel trousers, a brown sports jacket and the same pair of brown shoes. On about 1 July, Brook asked Wilkinson to press his trousers, as they were the only pair he had.[4]

Peter Rylatt from Haywards Heath was an army captain who had served in South East Asia Command and had also arrived in Bournemouth on demobilization leave on 22 June, staying at the Burley Court Hotel.[5] He was thirty-one years old, 5 feet 10 inches, clean-shaven and had a complexion which a fellow guest observed had 'a yellowish tinge about it consistent with prolonged service in the Far East'.[6] He had mousey, brilliantined hair slightly receding at the temples and always wore dark horn-rimmed spectacles. His speech was 'rather quiet and low', the very opposite of the good-looking and gregarious Group Captain Brook, and yet the two men very quickly became firm friends.

Rylatt met Brook at lunchtime on Monday 24 June at the Royal Bath Hotel, which was still being used by the WAAF as an officers' mess. Brook explained that he was the chief test pilot for Auster's in Leicestershire and was down in Bournemouth to take part in the aerial exhibition at Shoreham. This was to take place on Saturday 29 June, but Brook claimed that he had come down a week earlier than he ought to have done, leaving him at a loose end.

Brook got on with Rylatt famously, to such an extent that he invited his new friend to lunch that day at the Tollard Royal. Rylatt gathered that this was Brook's first trip to Bournemouth, so together, they agreed to do some exploring. After lunch the two men walked along the cliff top to the right of the hotel and then went down the zigzag path to the promenade. The freshly sanded beach and newly reinstated beach huts were full of families taking advantage of the good weather. The pair walked towards Poole, passing Bournemouth's famous chines to their right. 'Chines' are deep, narrow, wooded ravines descending down to the sea. The word is peculiar to Dorset and the Isle of Wight, chines being very much a feature of this stretch of the English coast. Walking west from the hotel towards Poole, there was Durley

Chine, Middle Chine and Alum Chine – all in the Bournemouth area. At the head of Alum Chine were the ruins of Stevenson's house, 'Skerryvore'. Brook and Rylatt walked across the boundary into Poole and stopped by Branksome Towers' private beach and threw stones into the sea. Behind them was the most secluded of the chines, Branksome Dene Chine, known locally as a place for lovers' meetings. The two men then headed back towards Bournemouth Pier, the excursion to the chines and back having taken about an hour.

Over the six days that they were acquainted, Rylatt and Brook chatted about many subjects. Brook often told stories about his time as a pilot during the war. Rylatt commented on the unusual scarf that Brook wore around his neck. It was made of silk with a map of France and Germany printed on it. Brook explained that it was an 'escape map' carried on RAF operations and sewn into the shoulder of flying kit. During their various talks, Rylatt expressed great interest in the national hunt for Neville Heath, the man who was wanted in connection with the murder in Notting Hill. The case was in the papers every day – leads, sightings and speculation about his whereabouts. Brook told Rylatt that he actually knew Heath quite well and that he 'wasn't a bad sort of chap'. Rylatt later remembered that they discussed the case every day that they were together.

That Monday afternoon, after sitting in deck chairs in the sun for a while, Brook and Rylatt went to the Bournemouth Pavilion – an entertainment complex at the heart of the town, opposite the pier. When it had opened in 1929 the Pavilion was heralded as the 'biggest municipal enterprise ever created for the entertainment of the public'. It had a theatre, a concert hall and dining rooms such as the Lucullus Restaurant offering a bargain 3s. theatre supper. The ballroom was decorated in the Art Deco style and every day hosted tea dances between

4 p.m. and 6 p.m. for 1s. (tea included). Though Brook and Rylatt danced with various young women, neither took interest in any one girl in particular. The two men didn't join anybody's table, nor did they invite any ladies to join theirs. Rylatt had an engagement that evening, so they left the Pavilion at about 5.30 p.m. Knowing Brook was staying in Bournemouth alone, Rylatt asked if he would like to come on a trip to Wimborne the following evening. He had been invited to a cocktail party and was sure his hostess wouldn't mind if he brought a friend along. Brook said he'd be delighted to join him. Rylatt went back to his hotel and Brook returned to the Tollard Royal.

The next day, Brook met several other guests who were staying at the hotel, including Mrs Winifred Parfitt and her husband who were visiting for the week from Castle Cary. Brook introduced himself, telling the Parfitts that he was the nephew of Sir Alexander Cadogan, the permanent under-secretary at the Foreign Office. He also made the acquaintance of Major Phillips and his wife Gladys who were visiting from Llandaff in Wales. Chatting to Mrs Phillips, Brook mentioned that he had left the RAF in December and was now working for Auster's.

About midday on Tuesday 25 June, Brook met Peter Rylatt at the Tollard Royal. They went next door to the Highcliff Hotel where they had a drink in the cocktail bar. Here they met four 'rather working-class' girls from Wolverhampton and arranged to meet two of them after lunch at the tea dance down at the Pavilion. The two men lunched together at the Tollard Royal and then Rylatt waited in the lounge whilst Brook changed from his sports jacket and flannels into a double-breasted, pin-striped suit ready for their trip to Wimborne that evening. Rylatt was the only person to see Brook wear this suit and despite efforts by the police to trace it later, it disappeared. At some point between

26 June and 3 July, Brook must have sold or pawned it. The two men then went down to the Pavilion and met the girls they had seen earlier. Rylatt made a date to meet one of them the next day. Brook wasn't interested in either of them.[7]

At about 4.55 p.m., they then went back to the Burley Court Hotel, so that Rylatt could change for the party in Wimborne and then took a taxi to 'Moorings', the country home of a Mrs Comyns who was entertaining about twenty people for cocktails and dinner. Again the topic of the hunt for the Notting Hill murderer was hotly discussed over the martinis and gin slings. Rylatt got on particularly well with a Major Holford of the 12th Hussars and his wife, so he and Brook arranged to meet the Holfords for dinner in Bournemouth later that week. They took a taxi back to the Tollard Royal at about a quarter to midnight – Rylatt kept the taxi waiting as he had a nightcap with Brook before he took the taxi on to his own hotel, running up a fare of £2.

Earlier that day another new guest had arrived at the Tollard Royal. Peggy Waring was an attractive 37-year-old divorcée from London, a student of psychology and philosophy. She had come to the Tollard Royal to stay with a friend of hers, Anouska Symon. Peggy had only intended to stay for a couple of days but found herself staying much longer. That night, in the bar at the Tollard Royal Hotel, she met Group Captain Rupert Brook. He was to have a profound effect on her – and she on him.[8]

He told me his name was Rupert Robert Cadogan Brook. I was introduced to Brook by some acquaintances of Mrs Symon, Wing Commander and Mrs Wilkes. Wing Commander Wilkes said he had known Brook in the RAF where Brook had been a group captain. Brook himself told me that he had been demobilized from the RAF and was then a test pilot at the Auster Aeroplane Company.[9]

Both Peggy Waring and Peter Rylatt's statements are crucial in attempting to gauge Brook's state of mind during his stay in Bournemouth yet neither of their statements was discussed at the trial and neither of them was called as a witness. From their subsequent relationship, it is clear that Peggy Waring had a great influence over Brook, but in the extraordinary game of cat and mouse that developed between them in Bournemouth, what were his intentions towards her? Was he genuinely romantically fixated on her or was he grooming her for some darker purpose?

The next morning, Peter Rylatt was playing tennis with Wing Commander Wilkes and saw Brook at about 12.30. Brook claimed he'd had a heavy night and stayed up drinking until 2.30 a.m. Rylatt went to the Highcliff Hotel to meet the girls from Wolverhampton they had danced with the day before, but Brook said he wasn't keen to do so. Rylatt then lunched with him at the Tollard Royal. On each occasion they dined together at the hotel, Brook added it to his bill, telling the waiter, 'Put it on my crime sheet, will you?' Rylatt left him talking in the lounge with Wing Commander and Mrs Wilkes, Anouska Symon and Peggy Waring. From this point on, Peggy found Brook increasingly in her company, to an obsessive degree.

[He] attached himself to me, so much so that we were together most of the time. He drank excessively. On the day after my arrival he asked me to marry him. I refused and he then asked me to have an affair with him. This I also flatly refused but each day he pressed me to allow him to come to my room or me to his room. This I would not allow but my sympathies were aroused for him, particularly when he told me his wife had left him for another man in South Africa. As a consequence of this I decided to stay on and try and help him, and this is the reason I altered my original plan. I talked

The Tollard Royal Hotel, West Cliff, Bournemouth.

TOLLARD ROYAL HOTEL

(Street Plan : Square J5)

A few minutes' walk from Shopping Centre and Amusements
One minute from Cliff Lift
Beautiful Grounds overlooking Bay   GARAGE   PRIVATE BATHING HUT

VIEW OF 40 MILES OF SEASCAPE

ON THE WEST CLIFF PROMENADE

PRIVATE SUITES

Every Bedroom is exceptionally well furnished and has a Private Bathroom
or Hot and Cold Running Water

NEW RESTAURANT   MAGNIFICENT SOUTH LOUNGE
BALLROOM
TWO PASSENGER LIFTS   EFFICIENT NIGHT STAFF
MUSIC   BILLIARDS   DANCING

VITA-GLASS   Flooded every evening and on dull
SUN LOUNGE   days with health-giving Ultra Violet Rays

LICENSED BRIDGE CLUB ATTACHED.   AMERICAN BAR

TERMS from 5½ gns. weekly

For full particulars apply to Manageress

Telephones : Management, Bournemouth 3574 (2 lines)
Visitors, Bournemouth 6152
Bridge Club, Bournemouth 5969

Advertisement for the Tollard Royal Hotel, for its
first season since the end of the war, summer 1946.

Doreen Marshall, her father, mother and sister, Joan Cruickshanks,
in the garden at Woodhall Drive, summer 1946.

Bomb damage in Kenton Road, the Marshalls' former home, 28 June 1944.

Doreen Margaret Marshall.

Detective Constable George Suter.

Divisional Detective Inspector
Reginald Spooner (right)
with an unnamed assistant.

Police photographers take pictures of the scene of the crime,
Branksome Dene Chine, July 1946.

Violet Van Der Elst is arrested among the crowds gathered outside Pentonville Prison on the morning of Heath's execution, 16 October 1946.

A woman reads the notice of Heath's execution outside Pentonville, 16 October 1946.

Heath's waxwork at Madame Tussaud's in London, wearing a copy of the tweed jacket he wore to the pre-trial hearings at West London Magistrates' court.

Heath's effigy is groomed in the Chamber of Horrors at Madame Tussaud's, at some point in the 1960s. Here he wears a copy of the pinstripe suit he wore at his trial.

A Bournemouth newspaper headline reporting the murder of Doreen Marshall, 9 July 1946.

The cover of Sydney Brock's book, *The Life and Death of Neville Heath*, published in 1947. It promised a 'Sensational–Sadistic–Romantic–True Story'.

Heath returning from West London Magistrates' Court, August 1946.

to him of my religious beliefs and my belief in the goodness
of people to such an extent that he ceased drinking to excess
although he called me a 'bloody fool' and said I should think
of myself more and not so much about other people. He still
persisted in trying to have an affair with me and wanting to
marry me.[10]

That day another significant change took place; Brook
changed rooms. According to hotel records, this move was in
order to suit the management, as Room 71 had already been
booked.[11] Brook himself, despite later speculation to the
contrary, did not make a request for this change in order to
have a room with a gas fire, which might imply that at this
point he was contemplating suicide. His new (and cheaper)
room, number 81, was situated on the second floor to the
west of the building and faced West Hill Road, looking out
over the main entrance of the hotel and in the direction of
the Bournemouth chines.

Peggy Waring's arrival had certainly altered Brook's behaviour and was beginning to have an effect on his friendship
with Peter Rylatt. Brook and Rylatt lunched together again
on Thursday at the Tollard Royal and Brook complained
that he'd had a champagne party the night before until 3 a.m.
and was still feeling the worse for it. Rylatt had arranged to
meet the Holfords that evening whom they had met in
Wimborne. Perhaps in an attempt to clear Brook's head, they
walked along the promenade, past the private beach by
Branksome Towers, with Branksome Dene Chine to their
right – a stroll of about a mile. Rylatt was already feeling
peeved with Brook as he had not offered to contribute
anything towards the taxi fare from Wimborne. He had often
seen Brook pay in cash for rounds of drinks and cigarettes and
he invariably over-tipped the waiters, so money didn't seem
to be a problem.[12] They walked on to the next chine, passed

through the stone defence blocks in the car park and walked up the Chine Road, ending up on the main street at Sandbanks. They then returned to their respective hotels.

Later that afternoon, Brook rang Rylatt and said he was feeling ill and asked if he could be excused that evening's party. Rylatt told him that this would be extremely awkward and very embarrassing. Two young ladies had been invited specifically to entertain them. He insisted that Brook attend the party whether he felt sick or not. Brook refused. Exasperated and angry, Rylatt told Brook how difficult the evening would be without him. Brook didn't appear to care.

The next day, when they met outside the hotel, Peter Rylatt was still annoyed. The dinner party had been a failure, just as he had expected. Reluctantly, Rylatt had an awkward drink with Brook, Peggy Waring and Anouska Symon in the lounge, but refused the offer of lunch. At some point he commented that Brook's escape map scarf looked rather dirty. Peggy agreed that it could do with a wash. Relations between them still frosty, Rylatt wished Brook goodbye as he would be returning to London the next morning on the 8.20 a.m. train. He left Brook alone with Peggy in the hotel lounge.

With Peter Rylatt gone, over the next twenty-four hours, Brook's relationship with Peggy developed an unsettling intensity, with Brook apparently struggling to control himself in Peggy's presence.

I should say he was abnormal, inasmuch that when he even kissed me quite normally, his passions seemed to be so roused that he was compelled to become rough with me and then to control himself, he would immediately leave me. On other occasions when he has held my hand, I could tell the effect it had on him, because he would thrust it away from him.

Brook told Peggy that he was flying in the air display that Saturday and was eager for her to watch him, though she had already made it clear that she wanted to return to London. He was so keen, even desperate, for her to stay that he offered to pay her expenses at the hotel, but she refused. Though she had only intended to stay in Bournemouth for two days, she reluctantly promised that she would extend her stay, watch the air display and then go home immediately afterwards on the late train on Saturday night.

At about 8.30 on Saturday morning, her last day in Bournemouth, Peggy was dressing in her room when Brook whistled up to her from the garden. She waved at him. He went and stood on the opposite side of the road and pointed to the writing room of the hotel, meaning he would wait for her there. She joined him about an hour later. For the next hour Brook phoned to the meteorological station at Shoreham to see if it was possible to take a light aircraft up that day. Finally he told Peggy that it was too windy to fly – a great disappointment as he had been talking about the air exhibition ever since he had arrived in Bournemouth.

They were then joined by Lieutenant Colonel Tutt from Thurnham who was having a break in Bournemouth following the recent death of his mother.[13] The three chatted in the writing room until 12.30 p.m. when Peggy excused herself. She wanted to go for a walk, but promised to come back in time for lunch with Brook. But his insistent, obsessive behaviour was troubling her. At about 1.10 p.m. she telephoned him at the hotel and said that she wouldn't be coming back to lunch after all. Brook fired questions down the phone, wanting to know where she was, why she'd gone out alone, and where she was going. Peggy was vague and said – quite honestly – that she just wanted to be on her own. In fact, her afternoon couldn't have been more uneventful. She visited the Russell-Cotes Museum, just east of the pier, and took some notes about its celebrated collection of Victoriana. She returned to the hotel later that afternoon. Brook had apparently gone out with Colonel Tutt, so Peggy went up to her room. She was soon joined by Anouska Symon, who pleaded with her to change her mind about leaving Bournemouth that night as Brook seemed so distressed at the thought of her going. But Peggy had had enough of the constant strain of his intense and demanding behaviour. He was just too needy and jealous without reason. She broke down in tears.[14]

A few moments later, Brook himself knocked on Peggy's door and said he wanted to speak to her, so Mrs Symon left, leaving Peggy alone with Brook. He seemed very distressed and perspiration was pouring down his face. He asked Peggy where she'd been and said he couldn't be doing with being given cryptic messages. Peggy said that she had been to the museum. He said he didn't believe her. Exasperated, Peggy was in despair. Brook then begged her to stay on in Bournemouth. Once again she told him that she wouldn't sleep with him and she wouldn't marry him either, but she would like to be his friend. At this point she held out her hand to him and asked him to sit next to her. She wanted him to know that she cared about him. But this proximity to her just seemed to exacerbate his extraordinary behaviour. 'He seemed terribly distressed at the thought of being so near me and he shook his head violently and his face was contorted, at what I took to be emotion,' she later stated.

Brook then left the room telling her that she should rest and that he'd wait for her downstairs. Again, Peggy burst into tears, full of pity for Brook, but also feeling pushed to breaking point herself.

After about an hour, Peggy pulled herself together and went downstairs to join Brook and Colonel Tutt for tea. They then went for a walk, returning to the hotel in time for dinner. They sat in the lounge afterwards until Colonel Tutt left Brook and Peggy alone in the drawing room. This was the first time she had been alone with him since his extraordinary outburst that afternoon and Brook proceeded again to plead with her not to leave that night, doing so for another forty-five minutes. But by 11.00 p.m., Peggy was adamant. She was going for the 11.30 p.m. train as she had planned. Her luggage was packed and she was ready to go. Just as she was about to leave, he said to her: 'You have won yourself a magnificent victory. I only hope you congratulate yourself on Monday.'[15]

Leaving him behind, Peggy felt only 'pity and tenderness' for Brook. As a student of psychology, she cannot have hoped for a better subject to study at close quarters. The well-intentioned aim of her relationship with him had been simply 'to try and help him to believe in people'.[16]

After she returned to London, Peggy wrote Brook two letters, later to be found in his jacket pocket. He telephoned her at home in St John's Wood on Sunday and Monday, saying that he would be coming to see her in London on Tuesday 2 July; he did not arrive. Her steadfast refusal to give in to Brook's relentless demands may well have won her more than a 'magnificent victory' – it may even have saved her life.

CHAPTER FIFTEEN
Miss Marshall

3–4 JULY 1946

MURDER IN LONDON'S PARKS!
After a spate of gloomily psychological murder dramas, it is
a pleasant change to turn to *Wanted for Murder*, a new British
thriller which has been built around a case of schizophrenia
or dual personality, a straightforward thriller abounding in
hearty chills and thrills. Eric Portman gets one of the juiciest
roles in his career as a pleasant-mannered gentleman who
quite frequently strangles unwitting young ladies. This,
believe it or not, is due to a streak of sadism inherited from
his grandfather, who was the finest public hangman of his
day. His crimes take place in and around the familiar spots
of London, the police eventually catching up with him in
Hyde Park.

Film section, *Harrow Observer*, 13 June 1946

Twenty-one-year-old Doreen Marshall had served as a Wren during the war and was discharged from the service on Thursday 27 June. After a recent bout of measles and 'flu, her father suggested a holiday in Bournemouth; the sun and coastal breeze would do her good. The family had visited the town before, so it would be familiar to her. On Wednesday 26 June, Doreen and her father had bought two first-class return tickets from the Polytechnic Tours Office in Regent Street, each costing £1 13s. 2d.[1] Doreen's mother, Grace, wanted Doreen's older sister to accompany her on the trip, but for some reason, at the last minute, Joan had decided not to go. But with an independent spirit and a WRNS training behind her, Doreen was happy to holiday alone. Doreen herself sent a letter to the Norfolk Hotel in Bournemouth, making a booking for ten days from the Friday of that week. She arranged to return home on 8 July.

Just before leaving for Bournemouth, Doreen was at home spending the evening with her mother. The murder of Margery Gardner had been front-page news for days and the search for Neville Heath continued to dominate the papers. Mrs Marshall remembered:

> I was reading details of the Margery Gardner case in the *Daily Mail* and mentioned something about it to [Doreen]. Doreen was sitting opposite me and snatched the paper out of my hand saying, 'Don't read such things, Mummie.' She scanned the headlines before putting the paper down but didn't read Heath's description or the text of the story.[2]

This seemingly casual, apparently insignificant moment was to prove fatal. The newspapers, though permitted to publish a description of Heath, were forbidden to print any photographs of him. By the time the police had changed their minds and given a directive for photographs of Heath to be published, Doreen's own young life would have been brought to an end in an orgy of horrific, terrifying violence.

Like many men of his generation, Charles Marshall had seen the full horror of the Great War having fought in the front line at the Battle of the Somme – his feet giving him acute pain for much of his later life as a result of trench foot.[3] A salesman by profession, he had married Grace Merritt in 1913 – both of them having been raised in Hackney. After the war, they had two daughters, Joan Grace, born in Harrow in 1921, and Doreen Margaret, who was born in Ealing in 1924. Mr Marshall had a close relationship with both of his daughters, but a particularly strong bond with his older daughter, Joan. Joan's surviving daughter remembers Charles as a lovely, gentle man, in contrast to his wife who came across as rather stern, the inevitable impact perhaps of the loss of her daughter.

Joan Marshall had married Charles Cruickshanks of the Royal Navy Reserve just after Christmas, 1941 and as he was on active service she lived with her family for the duration of the war. The Marshalls had moved into a semi-detached house in Kenton Road in the newly built suburb of Kenton in 1930. Kenton had been developed to take advantage of the tube expansion into Metroland with the intention of attracting middle-income commuters just like Charles Marshall, now the director of his own company. The Marshalls' house, 'Kenilworth', was typical of the period; bay-fronted with an Ideal boiler for hot water, a Radiation gas cooker, three bedrooms, a bathroom and separate toilet. For thousands of families, houses like 'Kenilworth' were an achievable dream of modern comfort and convenience – all for an affordable £800.

In early 1943, like thousands of other young women, Doreen had followed her older sister into the Women's

Royal Naval Service ('Join the WRNS – and free a man for the fleet!'). Joan had worked at the admiralty decoding messages. Only seventeen, Doreen started two weeks' intensive training at the WRNS training depot in Mill Hill. All 'on shore' naval bases or 'stone frigates' were named after Royal Navy vessels and though it may have sounded grand, intimidating even, 'HMS Pembroke III' was, in reality, a disused cancer hospital. As a probationer, Doreen had been put through both medical and written tests in order to establish a suitable division for her experience and aptitude. In her first weeks, she was taught about the backbone of the service: discipline, routine and tradition. The Royal Navy was dominated by traditions and rules evolved over many centuries. These traditions, of course, had been evolved by and for the exclusively male intake who made up the 'Senior Service'. Women had briefly been able to join the service in 1917 but this initiative had been disbanded two years later. A further attempt to create a Women's Royal Naval Reserve had been mooted in the mid-1930s but after due consideration by the Special Sub-Committee of Imperial Defence, it was 'deemed not desirable'.[4] It had taken the darkening events in Europe in the late 1930s for the admiralty to accept that the need for a Women's Naval Reserve was pressing. Effectively, Doreen had joined a new and innovative organization of women that would have an impact not just on each Wren individually, but on a generation of young women who felt that being part of the WRNS in some way emancipated them from pre-war strictures and conventions.

The WRNS exposed young women like Doreen and Joan Marshall to a way of life a world away from their suburban backgrounds. They had to learn a completely different vocabulary relating their new, unfamiliar world to naval lore; a room was a 'cabin', the dining room was the 'mess' and the floor the 'deck'. All work was divided into 'watches' with 'divisions' held in the Assembly Hall and Holy Communion in a small chapel every day.[5] Crucially Wrens were forced to engage with other classes of women that they had never had the opportunity to meet before. For the first time in her sheltered middle-class upbringing, Doreen came face to face with women from a range of different backgrounds. For Doreen, her time in the WRNS was defining – the job, like the war, having spanned her adult life. She spent her career in the WRNS serving at various sites around the London area, mostly at accounting bases like HMS Pembroke III and HMS Westcliff. Much of her work was clerical, covering everything from submarines to post-hostilities planning and by 1946 she was working in Whitehall with senior figures in the admiralty at HMS President I.

Both Joan and Doreen's duties with the WRNS were very much office-based jobs with little chance of action. Ironically, the nearest they came to danger was at home in Kenton. At 8.10 a.m. on 28 June 1944, the peace of a typical English summer morning had been devastated by a violent explosion that engulfed the entire neighbourhood.

> Without any warning there was a colossal compression and explosion immediately followed by all kinds of crashes, bangs, screams, sounds of breaking glass and God knows what else.

The neighbourhood had been targeted by a V1 bomb – the deadly 'doodlebug'. Seconds after the blast, Newton Myers, a twelve-year-old schoolboy who lived at 5 Kenton Gardens, emerged from his family's Anderson raid shelter in the garden to witness a world in chaos:

> I clambered out of bed and through the door of the shelter, out through the back room door into what was left of our

hall. There was dust everywhere . . . and there were other yells, shouts and screams coming from other places. At this moment my father appeared staggering down the stairs which were still relatively intact. His face was a mask of blood and he was shouting 'this is the end, this is the end' over and over again. As we met at the bottom of the stairs he picked me up and rushed out into the front garden with me in his arms. Then he put me down and I rushed back into the house. I went into what was left of the front room. The mantelpiece had come away from the wall and was lying horizontal across the sofa. The bay window was halfway out into the garden. When I looked out and to the right all I could see were what appeared to be the roofs of our neighbours' houses. The only problem was that they were at ground level with no houses underneath them. Dust was everywhere, there were still screams and moans coming from the buried, dying and injured . . . Before long the rescue teams arrived and started the grisly task of recovering the bodies. I was unlucky enough to see one of my friends' sisters on a stretcher under a blanket being carried past me towards the ambulance. As the stretcher-bearer passed me, a doctor pulled back the blanket, I had the unpleasant sight of someone who had been completely flat-tened. Not a pretty sight . . . This whole incident had a disas-trous effect on my nerves. Up until now I had borne the bombing with typical British phlegm. However now I begged my father to take me out of London. I was panic stricken and absolutely terrified.[6]

Thirteen people were killed in the attack. The most severe damage was suffered by Kenton Gardens, but the whole area was reduced to rubble. Though their house was hit, Charles and Grace Marshall and their daughters were relieved to have escaped with their lives, Grace having often despaired during air raid warnings as Joan always refused to use the Anderson shelter in the garden. Significantly, though, Doreen did not escape the incident completely unscathed. From that morning onwards, a shock of grey began to appear in the dark curls of her hair, just above her right temple. This was very distinctive in such a young woman – a continuous reminder to her and everyone she met of the unspoken but continuing effects of the Blitz.

With 'Kenilworth' uninhabitable, the Marshalls moved four miles further to the northwest and rented a half-timbered, semi-detached house in Woodhall Drive, Pinner. The house had been built in the early 1930s, very much in the stockbroker Tudor style beloved by John Betjeman. In a conservation area today, it remains a hymn to Metroland – parquet floors and Bakelite door handles, manicured lawns, sculpted privet hedges and quiet avenues surrounding a village green; all the elements of comfortable pre-war middle-class life.

Living the first months of peace in the suburban comfort of Pinner, the Marshalls were well aware that they were very lucky to have survived the war with the family intact. A photograph taken in the garden at Woodhall Drive shows a happy, relaxed family group, the horrors of the war behind them – no inkling of the terrible tragedy ahead.

On Friday morning of 28 June, Charles Marshall drove Doreen to Waterloo Station and saw her off on the 9.30 train to Bournemouth.[7] Given the huge holiday crowds mixing with recently demobbed servicemen swarming around the station, Doreen and her father may not have even noticed Faulkner's, the busy hairdressing shop on the station concourse. The Waterloo branch was ably managed by a Mr William Heath but that day he was not at work, having pressing family issues to deal with at home.

Settling into her first-class carriage, Doreen checked her luggage, which consisted of two suitcases and her black suede clutch-style handbag. In the bag she kept a small pigskin notecase, four or five pounds in cash, her driver's licence, about sixty clothing coupons and the return half of her railway ticket. She also carried with her a key for the house in Woodhall Drive, keys to the suitcases, a lipstick, a comb and a couple of family photographs. She powdered her face with a blue and gold enamel powder compact, oblong in shape containing rouge, powder and a space for cigarettes. Though there was a crack across the mirror of the compact, Doreen kept it as she'd been given it by her sister Joan.[8] She also carried a small silver penknife in her bag, with a matching fountain pen. She had won them as a schoolgirl at an ice-skating competition at Wembley. The pen was inscribed with her name.[9]

Arriving at Bournemouth Station, Doreen took a taxi to the Norfolk Hotel on Richmond Hill. The hotel, one of the oldest in Bournemouth, was the only one not to have been requisitioned during the war years, so preserved a rather select reputation. The building still operates as an hotel today, opposite the Art Deco offices of the *Bournemouth Echo*, which had been built in 1932. Doreen was booked into Room 94 by the receptionist, Elsie Jones. She confirmed that she would be staying for ten days, as her letter had indicated. She signed the registration form and was shown to her room.[10]

That evening Doreen telephoned her father to say that she had had a comfortable journey and had arrived safely. She also had a chat on the phone with her sister and mentioned that she had talked to another guest at the hotel, an American antique dealer by the name of George Wisecarver.[11] Doreen phoned home again on Sunday and told her father that she was all right, but feeling a bit lonely, so she was looking through some books in her room.[12] Talking to her sister on the telephone, she mentioned that Mr Wisecarver had invited her on a trip to Exeter, but she didn't want to go. She rang home again on Tuesday 2 July and spoke to her mother. She also sent letters to her father and sister which arrived in Pinner on Tuesday and Wednesday morning, but in these letters – her last – she didn't refer to anybody she had met since she arrived in Bournemouth. She did write that 'unless I speak to somebody shortly I shall scream'.

For a young woman alone, there was plenty of entertainment for Doreen to occupy herself with at the local cinemas that week. The Electric in Bournemouth was showing the new Gene Tierney picture, *Leave Her to Heaven*. *The Blue Dahlia* at the Odeon starred Alan Ladd and Veronica Lake and the Astoria at Boscombe was showing Rex Harrison and Lilli Palmer in *The Rake's Progress*. But it was too hot to sit in a dark cinema during the day, as the weather that week was glorious.

> Summer came into its own yesterday [2 July] with a heat-wave which, though ideal for holidaymakers, left some office workers somewhat prostrate. Sea bathers increased in number at lunchtime by Bournemouth folk going down for a pre-prandial dip – for some, their first bathe of the summer. The temperature rose between 3 and 4 p.m. to 80 degrees, the highest recorded so far this year.[13]

On the morning of Wednesday 3 July, Doreen took a walk on the promenade, packed with families at the height of the holiday season. But having been in Bournemouth for nearly a week on her own, she was now feeling isolated, bored and lonely. In her mind she had already decided that she would return home early. She would take the train back to Waterloo tomorrow. Wednesday would be her last day in Bournemouth.

That morning, whilst stopping to watch a Punch and Judy show on the promenade, Doreen was delighted to meet an

engaging young man – tall, tanned, blond and handsome
with startlingly blue eyes made even more remarkable by the
backdrop of the sea and the cloudless blue sky above the
beach. She felt at ease with him and after several days of feeling rather sorry for herself, she was glad of his company. He
introduced himself as Group Captain Rupert Brook – but
she must call him 'Bobbie' or 'Bob'. He was extremely
charming, a real gentleman. He recalled his meeting with
Doreen some days later.

> I was on the promenade on Westcliff when I saw two young
> ladies walking along the front. One was a casual acquaintance
> I had met at a dance at the Pavilion during the latter part of
> the preceding week. (Her Christian name was Peggy but I
> was unaware of her surname.) Although I was not formally
> introduced to the other young lady I gathered her name was
> 'Doo' or something similar. The girl Peggy left after half an
> hour and I walked along the promenade with the other girl I
> now know to be Miss Marshall. I invited her to have tea in
> the afternoon and she accepted.[14]

Despite later attempts by the Bournemouth police to trace
'Peggy', she was never found. In all probability she never
existed and is one of several phantom figures that Brook
conjured in his various statements. Doreen had been very
open with her family that she was lonely in Bournemouth
and mentioned all of the few acquaintances she had made,
so it seems unlikely that she wouldn't mention befriending
another young woman if she had, indeed, met one. Brook
may have been attempting to suggest that his first meeting
with Doreen was more socially correct – an introduction
through a mutual acquaintance than the rather casual pick-
up that it was. The name 'Peggy' may have been inspired by
his recent acquaintanceship with Peggy Waring who had

only returned to London on the preceding Saturday. It seems much more plausible – and more consistent with his usual behaviour – that he noticed Doreen was alone and introduced himself. She might have stood out particularly to him because of the distinctive shock of grey hair above her right temple.

> I met her along the promenade about 2.45 p.m. and after a short stroll we went to the Tollard Royal Hotel for tea. It was about 3.45 p.m. The conversation was fairly general. She said she had served in the WRNS and mentioned she had been ill and was in Bournemouth to recuperate.[15]

Since the departure of Peggy Waring and Peter Rylatt, Brook had spent a considerable amount of time with some other guests at the Tollard Royal, Mr and Mrs Heinz Abisch, a German couple who lived on the Finchley Road in London. Brook would join them for drinks before lunch and dinner and for coffee after meals. That afternoon, Abisch and his wife returned to the hotel for tea where Brook was already sitting in the lounge with Doreen. Mr Abisch was amused to see Brook with yet another girl. He had had several mild flirtations with girls in the hotel – and Peggy Waring from whom Brook had seemed inseparable had only recently returned to London. Abisch smiled knowingly at him. At this point, Brook excused himself from Doreen and went over to buy a newspaper from the porter, passing Abisch. As he did so, he turned to Abisch and said 'in quite a nasty tone', 'I'll soon wipe that smile off your face.'[16] Brook then returned to tea with Doreen in the lounge and Mr and Mrs Abisch left the hotel. After tea, Brook suggested that they meet again that evening for dinner. With no other plans and nobody to answer to, Doreen said she'd be delighted. She left the Tollard Royal at 5.45 and returned to the Norfolk Hotel to dress for dinner.

Just before 7 p.m., Doreen went to the desk at the Norfolk Hotel and asked James Newland, the porter, to call her a taxi as she was going to the Tollard Royal for dinner. Newland rang Autax, a local cab firm. The car soon arrived and Newland saw Doreen into it.[17] After a few minutes, when the car arrived at the Tollard Royal, Doreen got out and paid the driver, Sydney Bush. He remembered a distinctive glass fob watch she wore on the lapel of her lemon-coloured coat. She gave him no instructions to be collected later.[18]

The events of the evening preceding Doreen Marshall's death read like the scenario for an Agatha Christie play; the lounge of a Bournemouth hotel, an assembly of witnesses, including a retired major and his refined lady wife (Mrs Gladys Davy Phillips). Even the weather was suitably dramatic, as the evening was dominated by a violent thunderstorm with vivid lightning and heavy rain. It began with Doreen's arrival at the hotel, as she had arranged with Brook that afternoon. Brook recalled her entrance:

At appoximately 7.15, I was standing outside the hotel and saw her approaching on foot.[19] I entered the hotel, went to my room to get some tobacco and came downstairs again just as she was entering the lounge. We dined at 8.15, sat talking in the lounge afterwards and then moved into the writing room. The conversation was again general but she told me she was considering cutting short her holiday and returning home in a day or two. She mentioned an American staying in her hotel and told me he had taken her for car rides in the country. She also mentioned an invitation to go with him to Exeter but I gathered although she did not actually say so, she did not intend to go. Another American was mentioned – I believe his name was Pat – to whom I believe she had unofficially become engaged some while before.[20]

Brook deliberately suggested that Doreen may have had other boyfriends and that, as a single girl on holiday and away from home, she had made the most of her freedom. Though a plausible story – Bournemouth was still full of American servicemen waiting to be repatriated – there's no evidence that Doreen had met any other men at all, let alone become engaged to one. Wisecarver, her American acquaintance, was a respectable antiques dealer and had already left the country. Doreen was also known by her family to be a 'quiet girl who didn't have boyfriends'.

Doreen had dressed smartly and stylishly for dinner. Under her distinctive fleecy lemon box coat she wore a plain black silk frock with matching black sandals. She was also wearing silk stockings and a pair of cultured pearl earrings matching her Ciro pearl necklace. On one of her fingers she had a three stone diamond ring, set in platinum, which was a twenty-first birthday present from her parents. Under her arm she carried her black suede handbag. She used her blue compact to powder her nose. As she did so, Brook noted that it was cracked. Doreen explained that she was clumsy: 'I'm always breaking things.'

Heinz Abisch and his wife returned to the hotel and went in to dinner at about 7.30 p.m. Shortly afterwards, Brook came into the dining room with Doreen and they sat two tables away. The dinner menu that evening offered a choice of two soups, trout or roast duck, cauliflower and cream sauce with boiled new potatoes. This was followed by raspberry ice or pear trifle. Brook ordered a magnum of champagne, though Doreen drank little.[21]

After dinner, he escorted Doreen into the lounge, where the Abisches were already settled. He took one of the armchairs and Doreen sat opposite on a sofa. Winifred Parfitt came into the lounge at about 8.30 p.m. to take her coffee after dinner and Brook introduced her to Doreen. He explained that Doreen was an old friend and that he had not seen her for some time, but had bumped into her on the sea front that morning. Doreen didn't contradict this statement, and she may well have felt it was less awkward to comply with Brook's social white lie. Brook also told Mrs Parfitt that Doreen had served in the WRNS. Mrs Parfitt had also been in service in the admiralty during the war so she and Doreen had a great deal in common to chat about.

Sitting only three or four yards away from them, Abisch overheard Brook call Doreen 'darling', and watched as she was introduced to Mrs Parfitt. Eavesdropping, he heard that Doreen was staying at the Norfolk Hotel, she was from Pinner and 'would be going home the next day'. Mrs Abisch was sitting on a sofa to the right of Brook, when he suddenly turned to her and said, 'Pull that skirt down. It makes me mad.' Both Mr and Mrs Abisch were puzzled by Brook's remark, as Mrs Abisch's skirt had not ridden up sufficiently to justify it.[22] Brook and Doreen were served glasses of port on the house by Wilkinson the night porter, but Doreen refused hers, saying she had had enough to drink. Brook drank both glasses. Mrs Parfitt noticed that Doreen had only one drink – a gin and orange – during the whole evening, but Brook had had several, mostly beer in pints. To Mrs Parfitt, Brook seemed 'in a very cheery mood – not drunk – just cheery.' According to the hotel rules, drinks served outside the dining room should be paid for when ordered, but Mr Parfitt recalled that Brook told the waiter, 'I haven't got a bean on me today. I meant to go to the bank this morning. Put it down, old chap, on my crime sheet.'[23]

As the summer evening turned to night, the weather began to change. After the intense heat of the day, a storm was on its way, rumbling from a distance at first, but by 10.45 it had developed into a dramatic electrical storm, with lightning cracking across the vast dark sky in front of the hotel.[24]

Brook then suggested that they might listen to some
dance music, so he, Doreen and Mrs Parfitt moved from the
lounge to the writing room where there was a portable
radio. That night John Reynders and his orchestra were
broadcasting on the BBC Light Programme from 10.30 p.m.
As the wireless played dance music, Doreen chatted some
more with Mrs Parfitt, telling her that she had been ill and
had come to Bournemouth to recuperate. Mrs Parfitt did
think that Doreen looked rather pale. Finding her sympathetic, Doreen confided that she had been rather lonely in
Bournemouth and her stay had not been particularly happy.
She complained that she was not feeling well and that she
felt dizzy. She supposed it was because she was feeling very
tired. She may actually have been feeling unwell as her sister
later confirmed that Doreen was expecting her period. She
asked Mrs Parfitt to persuade Brook to take her back to the
Norfolk Hotel.[25]

At about 10.45 p.m., Doreen visited the ladies' cloakroom.
While she was out of the room, Mrs Parfitt told Brook that
she thought Doreen wanted to go home, but he was flippant
– it was far too early. Mrs Parfitt then followed Doreen to the
ladies' as she thought she might be ill. When she got to the
cloakroom, Mrs Parfitt wasn't sure if Doreen had been sick in
the lavatory, but she was powdering her nose from her blue
compact and refreshing her lips with her American lipstick.
She seemed to be getting a little brighter after they went back
to the writing room. The wireless was now playing music by
Billy Ternent and his dance orchestra, accompanied by Ruth
Howard and Gerry Fitzgerald.[26]

Between 11.15 and 11.45 p.m., the party listening to the
radio were joined by Major and Mrs Phillips, who had been
out for the evening. Brook introduced them both to Doreen.
Mrs Phillips felt that Brook seemed rather the worse for drink
as when she refused to have a drink with him, he became

annoyed with her.[27] She noted that Doreen seemed sober and looked pale. Mrs Parfitt left to go to bed shortly after the Phillips' came in. Before retiring she asked Mrs Phillips if she would see about getting Doreen home, as she was clearly tired. Mrs Parfitt wished everybody 'goodnight' and told Doreen that she hoped they would meet again. Outside, it had started to rain. For some reason, Mrs Parfitt slept badly that night. When she woke abruptly from a fitful sleep, she could still hear the rain.

Shortly before midnight, Doreen asked Major Phillips if he would order a taxi for her as she wanted to go home. Mrs Phillips noticed that Doreen made this request 'in a rather appealing kind of way, touching his hand when he was about to depart for the taxi'. Major Phillips ordered a taxi from the night porter and then he and his wife retired to bed. Doreen would be back at her hotel within five minutes.

At some point during the evening Brook had said, done or suggested something that unsettled Doreen. Several witnesses commented on how pale and tired she looked, to such an extent that she was keen to go back to her hotel. Had he pressurized her to come up to his room, as he had done with Peggy Waring? Or had he gone even further? Brook had already been very open with Peter Rylatt about his acquaintanceship with the murderer, Neville Heath. Had Brook said something to frighten Doreen?

A minute or two after Major and Mrs Phillips retired to bed, Brook came out of the writing room and asked Arthur White, the night porter, if he had ordered a taxi.

'No, sir. I was just going to order it,' said White

'Cancel it,' Brook told him. 'The young lady will order it later.'[28]

Brook went back into the writing room to join Doreen.

The midnight chimes of Big Ben played on the wireless, followed by the national anthem. There would be no more dance music that night. Brook and Doreen left the writing room and went towards the doors that opened onto West Hill Road. Doreen collected her lemon-coloured coat from Arthur White's porter's box. He noticed that the coat had a label with a foreign name on the inside. The door had been locked, as usual, at 11 p.m., so Frederick Wilkinson unlocked it to let them out.

'I'll be back in half an hour,' Brook said to Wilkinson.

Doreen stopped to correct him. 'No – he'll be back in a *quarter* of an hour.'[29]

She didn't want the night porter – or indeed Brook – to get the wrong idea. Wilkinson let the couple out. As he closed the door on them, he noticed that Doreen put her arm around Brook's waist – comfortable, romantic, trusting.[30] They went out of the front door and turned left, walking towards the cliff top. The storm had ended and the rain had stopped. But it would not be the last of the bad weather that night.

They disappeared from view, walking into the dark.

CHAPTER SIXTEEN
The Tollard Royal Hotel

4–6 JULY 1946

LIGHTNING – THUNDER – HAIL – RAGING WIND
'Mixed-Grill' Tempest Over Wide English Area
One of the worst storms for many years – with terrific thunderclaps, brilliant lightning flashes, hail, rain and wind that sometimes reached hurricane force – swept South-East England in the night as a climax to the heat wave of the past few days . . . almost tropical violence and the lightning continued for hours . . . The Air Ministry described the wind which rose at 1 a.m. as a freak one. It went from calm to 38 mph and gradually died down to calm again. Tremendous squalls of hail lashed Hastings. Many holidaymakers and residents were awakened and remained up. After dying away, the storm returned with increased violence and remained until nearly dawn.

Bournemouth Echo, 4 July 1946

Between 4 and 4.30 a.m. on the morning of Thursday 4 July, Frederick Wilkinson the night porter was doing his rounds at the Tollard Royal Hotel. He had noticed that Group Captain Brook hadn't returned from escorting his guest back to her hotel and assumed that he had succeeded in romancing her, either at the Norfolk Hotel or on the way to it.[1]

During his stay at the hotel, Wilkinson felt he had got to know Group Captain Brook very well. Every night Brook would chat to him before he went to bed. The previous night was the first time during Brook's stay that they hadn't had their usual talk. Wilkinson quietly opened the door of Room 81 to find that it was already daylight, though the curtains were drawn. Brook was sound asleep in bed. He noticed that Brook had not left his shoes to be cleaned. As a rule, if he didn't leave his shoes downstairs to be cleaned he would leave them outside the door. Again, this was the first night that Captain Brook had not done so.[2]

The chambermaid, Alice Hemmingway, looked after half the rooms on the second floor of the Tollard Royal, including Room 81. Her daily duties were to clean the rooms, make the beds and to take guests their early-morning tea at 7 a.m. Just after this time on this Thursday morning, Mrs Hemmingway took a cup of tea to Brook's room to find him still asleep with the bedclothes drawn right up to his nose. Mrs Hemmingway apologized for being late. Brook asked what the time was and Mrs Hemmingway told him it was about ten past seven. She opened the curtains and, remembering last night's electrical storm, chatted about the weather before leaving the room.[3]

Frederick Wilkinson then returned to the room, taking in Brook's three daily newspapers. He was still sleeping and the tea which Mrs Hemmingway had taken up earlier was untouched. Wilkinson warned Brook that his tea would get cold and offered him the newspapers.

'Here's your papers, sir.'

'Ah! I done [tricked] you last night,' Brook said.

'How did you come in? Not by the front door.'[4]

He did not give an answer. But Wilkinson remembered the ladder just outside the bedroom window that was being used by the builders working on the roof. Given that he knew all the ground-floor windows and the front door had been locked, Wilkinson assumed that the only way Brook could have accessed his room was via the ladder. Added to this, a day or two before, Brook had teased Wilkinson, saying, 'I will get in one night without you knowing.' Clearly, this is what he had done. Whilst in the bedroom, Wilkinson noticed Brook's shoes near the bed. Round them, about half to one inch up the side, was a ridge of sand. From this, Wilkinson surmised that Brook had not taken Miss Marshall straight back to the Norfolk Hotel the night before, but had diverted their walk along the beach.

At 10 a.m. Mrs Hemmingway knocked on Brook's door but received no reply, so she entered the room to find him still in bed, and still well covered up. 'Can't drag yourself out this morning, sir?' she asked. He asked her to bring him some coffee, which she obtained from the second head waiter in the still room. He wondered if Brook had a fat head as he had ordered a bottle of champagne for dinner the night before?[5] Mrs Hemmingway took the coffee to Room 81. Later that morning, she knocked on the door again, keen to clean the room. Brook was in his dressing gown standing over the washstand, scrubbing his hands. He didn't look round, nor did he say anything. She apologized for intruding and left the room. At about half past twelve, Mrs Hemmingway had just finished lunch and passed Brook on the landing near his room. He asked her if she could bring him a piece of brown paper. She got some used wrapping from the pantry and took it to him. When she did so she felt that 'he was deliberately keeping his face away from [her]'.[6]

When Brook had finally vacated the room, Mrs Hemmingway went to clean it. In the fireplace was a fitted gas fire. The hearth had only recently been painted since the hotel had reopened in June. She then noticed a burn mark on the new paintwork. The mark was round and fairly large, about 10 or 12 inches across, but there was no debris or ash from whatever had been burnt. She was certain it had not been there the day before. She got some Vim to try and clean the mark off, but there was still a faint stain when she had finished. The mark wouldn't scrub away.

Mrs Hemmingway then swept the hearth and turned back the carpet. Underneath the carpet she found some sand and dirt. She prided herself on her work and was sure it hadn't been there yesterday. Somebody had swept the hearth without turning the carpet back, so the dirt had gone under it. She also noticed that the sink seemed grubbier than usual.

At about this time, Ellen Bayliss, a housekeeper at the Tollard Royal, found that one of the lavatories on the third floor was blocked with what she thought was a ball of paper. She tried to clear it by flushing, but was unable to get rid of it. She called the hotel carpenter, who dislodged the blockage with a plunger, but he felt that the obstruction was 'something hard and clean'.[7] The lavatory was on the floor above Brook, but the stairs leading up to it were directly opposite his room.

Having solved the problem, Mrs Bayliss was on her way downstairs when she saw Brook on the first floor close to the ladies' lavatories. His appearance made a vivid impression on her; his hair was disturbed, his manner agitated and he looked, according to her rather melodramatic description, like a 'hunted animal'.[8] Though manhole covers were later raised and the lavatory cisterns inspected, nothing significant was later brought to light, but it seems clear that on Thursday morning, Brook was keen to dispose of something. This was confirmed by Major Phillips, who at some point that morning was going to the garage on West Hill Road. He saw Brook carrying a brown paper parcel about 12' by 5' by 3', but didn't speak to him.[9]

At the Norfolk Hotel that morning, the last breakfast had been served and the head waiter noticed that Miss Marshall from Room 94 had not come down for her usual 9 a.m. breakfast. He phoned her room but there was no reply. The housekeeper confirmed that her bed had not been slept in but all her things were still in her room. She also had £20 locked in the hotel safe.

At the Tollard Royal, Heinz Abisch and his wife had gone for a walk after breakfast to Sandbanks, returning to the hotel in time for lunch. They were chatting about their walk when Brook asked which route they had gone. Abisch told him that they had walked along the cliffs and then through Branksome Chine. Brook commented that he 'didn't know you could walk so far'.[10]

Later that day Major Phillips asked if Brook had got the taxi he ordered for him last night? Brook said that he had walked Miss Marshall home and then walked back to the hotel. On the way back he had been caught in a heavy rainstorm and had got very wet.

That evening, at about 7.15 p.m., Robert Cook from East London was sitting in the gardens in Bournemouth town centre in front of Bobby's department store and the Lyons Tea Room. He was on holiday in Bournemouth with his wife and child. As he was sitting, a man approached him and asked if he would like to buy a new book of clothing coupons? When Cook refused, the man walked away, but after about 100 yards, he turned back, arousing Cook's suspicions.

The man was tall, blond and handsome with very blue eyes.[11]

Soon after he started his 8 p.m. shift that evening, Arthur White, the head night porter of the Tollard Royal, ran into Group Captain Brook.

'Do you know another way into the hotel?' Brook asked.

'Yes,' said White. 'But the way I know was locked. How did you get in last night?'

'I got up the ladder and got into my room that way. I thought I'd pull your leg.'[12]

Brook then joined Mr Abisch, Mrs Parfitt and Major Phillips in the lounge after dinner. Brook reminisced about his experiences during the war. He talked of the time he was station commander on an airfield in Belgium when the Germans made their last big raid on 1 January 1945, damaging eighty-eight British aircraft. The talk then turned to politics, Abisch noting that Brook was very conservative in his opinions. Brook then spent the rest of the evening with another young woman in the lounge before retiring to bed. White had noticed that Group Captain Brook always went to bed very late, drinking and chatting into the small hours, but on this occasion he retired unusually early. On his way up the stairs, he stopped to speak to White.

'Will you give my shoes an extra shine tonight?'

'We always do, sir.'

'Yes, I know, but I have been in sea-water in them.'

Brook left his shoes outside his door for cleaning. There was no longer a ridge of sand on them.[13]

Next morning, Friday 5 July, Brook went to H. J. Tuson's, a pawnshop in central Bournemouth. He was keen to pawn a ladies' three-stone diamond ring. The pledge was taken by the shop manager, Henry Burles. Brook gave his name as Mr Brook of Loxley Road, SW19.[14] When Mr Burles asked for the street number of the house, Brook said that it didn't matter as there were only two houses in the road. Burles gave Brook a loan of £5 in exchange for the ring.[15]

Around the same time that morning, Frank McInnes, the proprietor of the Norfolk Hotel, reported to the Bournemouth police that one of his guests, a Miss Doreen Marshall, had not been seen since the evening of 3 July. She had disappeared, leaving all her clothing and possessions, as well as some money in the hotel safe. Mr McInnes had been away for a short while so that he was not aware of Miss Marshall's disappearance until that lunchtime. He rang Detective Constable Suter at Bournemouth Police Station. Suter then rang Doreen's parents in Pinner informing them that their daughter was missing.

Later that day, Mrs Phillips had returned from the shops when she bumped into Brook at the hotel.

'What have you been up to?' Brook asked.

'Well, I've been shopping a bit and then went into the bank.'

'Funnily enough, I've been to the bank myself.'

And, indeed, Mrs Phillips had noticed that Brook paid for some drinks earlier that day with cash – £3 to £4 in notes – rather than putting them on his bill, as he usually did. It was then that Mrs Phillips commented on Brook's new shirt.

'Lovely new shirt, Captain Brook.'

'No, no. This is an old shirt.'

'But it looks perfectly new.'

'I assure you it's an old one.'

The new shirt stood out to Mrs Phillips, as on all other occasions Brook had worn a buff-coloured sports shirt.

'And what about your friend, Miss Marshall? Did she arrive home safely on Wednesday night?'

Brook didn't answer and Mrs Phillips didn't press the point. She then commented on the unusual scarf Brook was wearing around his neck. She hadn't seen him wear it before.

'What a funny scarf. May I see it?'

Brook took the scarf off and showed it to her – a thin silk square with a map printed on it – the 'escape scarf'. It was then that Mrs Phillips noticed that Brook had something on his neck, just below his right ear – three scratches: one long scratch and a couple of smaller ones. She made no comment.[16]

On Friday evening the manager of the Tollard Royal, Ivor Relf, took a telephone call from Mr McInnes, the manager of the Norfolk Hotel. McInnes explained that he believed that a lady – who had subsequently gone missing – had dined at the Tollard Royal on the previous Wednesday night. Relf told him he'd make enquiries and would ring him back. He consulted the head waiter's meal book and noticed that there had been two 'chance' diners that evening for dinner, but at this point he didn't connect Group Captain Brook's guest with the missing lady from the Norfolk Hotel. Brook had introduced Doreen to Relf as an old friend and hadn't mentioned where she was staying.

Late that evening, Doreen's father telephoned the Tollard Royal himself. Doreen had been missing since Wednesday when she had gone to dinner at the Tollard Royal. She had not phoned home, nor had she left any messages, so her family were extremely concerned. It just wasn't like her. Relf promised to investigate further. It's only then that he thought of Captain Brook's young guest in the fleecy yellow coat. He resolved to talk to Brook about the missing girl the next time he saw him.

The next day was Saturday and Relf saw Brook standing by himself in the dining room drinking coffee. Relf asked him if the guest he had entertained on Wednesday night was from Pinner and if she had been staying at the Norfolk Hotel? Brook replied, jocularly, 'Oh no, I have known that lady for a long while, and she certainly does not come from Pinner.'[17]

Relf suggested that Brook should contact the Bournemouth

police as the matter had become very serious. He had had a phone call from the manager at the Norfolk Hotel, and from the young lady's father who was terribly worried.

At 11.15 a.m. Detective Sergeant Stanley Pack was on duty when he had a call at Bournemouth Police Station from Bob Brook.

'I am speaking from the Tollard Royal Hotel. I understand a young lady is missing from the Norfolk Hotel. Can I speak to the officer in charge of the case?'[18]

Pack told him he'd need to speak to DC Suter who was not available at that moment but asked if he could take a message. Brook said, 'No it doesn't matter. I have a little information which may be of assistance. If you can tell me when the officer will be in, I will ring again.'[19]

At about 3 p.m., Brook joined Mrs Phillips and some acquaintances down at the beach. About a quarter of an hour later, he said he had to make a telephone call. He walked away in the direction of Poole. Half an hour later, DC Suter answered the telephone and spoke to Brook, who explained he was a guest at the Tollard Royal Hotel. Brook understood that Suter had been making enquiries about a young lady who had come to dinner at the Tollard Royal and said he might be able to help. Brook said that he was currently at Alum Chine enjoying the sun and wondered if Suter would like to join him? Suter declined and suggested that Brook come to the station at 5.30 p.m. that evening.

At around 4 p.m. Brook called into Freed's, a second-hand jewellers in the Triangle at the heart of the town. He wondered if they bought watches as he had one to sell. Brook showed Harry Berkoff, the manager, a lady's glass and metal fob watch. It was a quality piece – a Swiss movement with fifteen jewels. Brook wanted £5 for it, but Berkoff thought that was too expensive. He offered Brook £2. 20s. Clearly keen to sell it, Brook said, 'If you could make it a little bit more you can have it.' Berkoff eventually bought the watch for £3.[20] Brook returned to the party on the beach, having been away from them for about an hour. Brook then went with Mrs Phillips' party back to the Tollard Royal for tea. After tea, he left the hotel, heading for the police station on Madeira Road. He was dressed as usual in his sports jacket and was wearing his RAF sunglasses. This would be his last walk as a free man.

That afternoon, a short distance away from where Mrs Phillips' party had been on the beach, a group of schoolboys from the Russell Cotes Nautical School were walking along the cliffs from Bournemouth to Alum Chine. Whilst they were climbing, one of the boys, eleven-year-old Clive Miles, noticed something at the bottom of the cliffs, about seventy-five yards east of the entrance to the chine behind some beach huts.[21] When the boys climbed down to the beach, Clive went and picked up the object he'd seen behind a beach hut.

It was Doreen Marshall's black suede handbag.

CHAPTER SEVENTEEN
Detective Constable Suter

6 JULY 1946

> It was the policeman's nose, I suppose, but it just didn't tie
> up. The little bell was ringing.
> > George Suter, *Bournemouth Echo*, 5 November 1980

Sometime after 5.30 p.m., it was still bright and sunny and
the temperature still in the low seventies when Brook
arrived at Bournemouth Police Station, a 1930s brick-built
building, fronted by a low stone wall.

At the reception desk he introduced himself to Detective
Constable Suter.[1] At the age of forty, Suter was tall, bald,
square-jawed and broadly built. As a police officer, he had
been in a reserved occupation during the war, but had volunteered for the Rifle Brigade in the winter of 1943–4. In
February 1945 he had been at the crossing of the Rhine and
was amongst the first troops to liberate Belsen. Though he

never discussed his experiences with his family, they were aware that he had witnessed scenes of great horror during his time in the army. After the German surrender, his unit was based on the Danish border until he was demobbed in early 1946, at which point he went back to his pre-war occupation with Bournemouth police.[2] He had been back behind his desk at Madeira Road for a matter of weeks, mostly preoccupied with a spate of hotel burglaries that had taken place over the summer, before he became involved in the enquiry into the disappearance of Doreen Marshall.[3]

When Brook arrived, Suter showed him into the enquiry office on the ground floor of the station. Suter was puzzled from the start of the interview with Group Captain Brook. Brook wasn't wearing a tie, but had his shirt buttoned to the top, hardly in keeping with the dress of an RAF officer. Suter would have thought he'd wear a tie or at least a cravat. 'His dress did not tally with his station in life,'[4] he later stated. Also, granted the weather was still bakingly hot outside, but it did seem odd that throughout their conversation, Brook continued to wear his RAF-issue sunglasses.[5]

'I'm Brook from the Tollard Royal Hotel. Are you Suter?'

'Yes, sir. Now, I have been making enquiries about a young lady who was at dinner at the Tollard Royal Hotel on Wednesday evening.'

'Yes, I had a young lady to dinner with me on Wednesday evening.'

'Probably this was the same person about whom I've been making enquiries. Could you take a look at this photograph?'

Suter showed Brook a photograph of Doreen Marshall.

'That's her,' Brook said. 'Beyond a shadow of a doubt. She has a lock of grey hair here.' Brook indicated his own right temple. 'You can just see it in the photo.'

At that moment, there was some interruption in the office,

so Suter invited Brook upstairs into the sergeants' office where it was quieter. Suter asked Brook to carry on with his story.

'Will you tell me all about it from the beginning?'

'Yes. I met her on the beach on the Wednesday afternoon.[6] She was then with another girl named Peggy and I had previously met Peggy at the Pavilion. I gained the impression that it was a fresh acquaintanceship between the two girls. I asked Doreen to dinner at the Tollard Royal Hotel on Wednesday evening and she accepted. At about midnight – or just before – she said she was going home and she said she would walk. We sat on the front for a bit, then walked to the sea side of the gardens – near the Pavilion. Doreen said she would be busy for a few days but would ring me on Sunday and would be going back to London on Monday. She didn't want to go any further and she walked back to her hotel. That would be about 1 a.m. She did say she would be going back to London earlier and that she had been ill and felt a bit browned off. She told me about an American friend, that she went to Poole with him and for a ride to the country in a car and that he wanted her to go to Exeter with him but she did not want to go.'

'What was she wearing?'

'A yellow swagger coat, either black or dark blue frock. Carrying a handbag and wearing a string of pearls. She used a blue powder compact. With a cracked mirror. She told me she was always breaking things. The light streak in her hair was very noticeable.'

Brook had been upfront and honest and seemed to have nothing more to say, let alone anything to hide, so Suter wound up the interview.

'By the way, sir, I have not taken your full name or address.'

'Rupert Robert Brook, Thurmaston Aerodrome, Leicester.'

At this point, an extraordinary twist of fate began to draw Brook further into the hands of the police. As Suter's interview with Brook was ending, a clerk came up from the enquiry office and interrupted the conversation.

'Excuse me, sir,' he said, addressing Suter. 'There is a Mr Marshall downstairs waiting to see you.'

'That will be the young lady's father,' said Suter, who turned to Brook. 'May I contact you at the hotel if I need any further information, sir?'

'Yes – at any time.'

Suter led Brook downstairs to the enquiry office where they were met by Doreen's father. He was also accompanied by Joan, the missing girl's sister. Aside from Doreen's shock of grey hair, the two young women looked incredibly alike, dark-haired and petite. Suter had already met Mr Marshall and his daughter in the investigation of her disappearance and now introduced them to Brook.

'This gentleman had dinner with your daughter on Wednesday night.'

Brook repeated the story that he had already told Suter. Then, turning to Doreen's father, Brook assured him that he shouldn't worry about her.

'Doreen told me she would be busy for a few days. I wasn't expecting her to ring until Sunday. If there's any other way I can help?'

Mr Marshall thanked Brook for his concern. Brook went on.

'In all probability, she's with her American friend.'

But this reassurance didn't calm Marshall's worries. She wasn't the sort of girl to go off without telling anybody with a man she had only just met. Mr Marshall noticed that throughout the conversation, Brook didn't take his eyes off his daughter, Joan. Mr Marshall thought that Brook had a 'sickening conceit' and increasingly felt that this man was responsible for his daughter's disappearance.[7] Joan also had an instinctive feeling that Brook was involved. He had said he left Doreen at the Winter Garden near the Pavilion. It was after midnight and her hotel was only a few hundred yards from where he claimed they parted. Joan asked him directly, 'Why didn't you see her home?' Brook simply shrugged his shoulders. Joan had a dreadful sick feeling that her sister was dead and that the superficially charming man in the dark glasses had killed her.[8]

As Brook was talking to the Marshalls, Suter had the opportunity to scrutinize his handsome features at close quarters. Had his demeanour changed when he was brought face to face with Doreen's family – and particularly the girl's sister? Suter began to feel a growing sense of recognition about Brook's face. He had seen it somewhere before – recently. He recalled a photograph of a wanted man in the *Police Gazette*, pinned on the noticeboard upstairs in the CID office. Was there a similarity, or were his eyes playing tricks? Excusing himself from Mr Marshall and his daughter, Suter took Brook to one side.

'I think you must have a double, sir.'

'Oh really?'

'Yes. We have a photo of a chap who is wanted and you are not unlike him. Come up and have a look at the photo.'

Apparently bemused, Brook followed Suter upstairs to the CID office where Detective Sergeant Leslie Johnson was sitting behind his desk.[9] Johnson also noticed that Brook continued wearing his sunglasses. It was now about 5.45 p.m. Suter pointed to the noticeboard and showed Brook the *Police Gazette* photo of Neville Heath, wanted in connection with the murder of Margery Gardner at Notting Hill.

'You must admit there is a striking resemblance,' suggested Suter. 'Is that you?'

'Good Lord, no,' said Brook. 'I agree, it is *like* me.'

He turned decisively and walked out of the office. Suter followed him, but not before deliberately dropping his notes from his interview with Brook on the floor. With nothing said between them, DC Johnson picked up the notes[10] and immediately got on the phone in an attempt to contact Notting Hill police.[11] Suter and Brook returned downstairs to Doreen's father and sister where Brook jokingly said something about his similarity to the portrait. Everyone laughed.

At that point a uniformed officer joined Suter and told him he was wanted on the telephone. Upstairs DS Johnson told Suter that he had called Notting Hill Police Station in order to verify some details about Brook and to ask for a detailed description of Neville Heath. But with only an instinctive suspicion that Brook was not all he claimed to be, Suter had no reason to detain him. There was no evidence that Doreen Marshall's disappearance was sinister. Many young women disappeared for a couple of days at holiday resorts for their own reasons and then turned up again quite safe. Brook had also come to the police station of his own free will – extremely unusual in the case of a murderer on the run. All this put Suter in a quandary as he was now under pressure from his senior officer Inspector Gates to let Brook go. The group captain was clearly a gentleman and 'a gentleman's word should be accepted'.[12] But Suter was convinced the man was Heath and was prepared to stake his job on it. He went back downstairs where Brook was still in conversation with Mr Marshall and his daughter. After asking Mr Marshall where he could contact him, Suter wished the Marshalls goodbye and remained with Brook.

By this time, Brook had manouevred himself back outside the police station, leaning casually against the low front wall in the late afternoon sun, his eyes still shaded by his sunglasses. Freedom was imminent. Desperate to keep hold of him, Suter kept Brook talking about the wonderful weather, holidays and what his stay was like at the Tollard Royal. Shortly afterwards, they were joined by DS Johnson, who also entered into the conversation. Together, Suter and Johnson were determined not to let Brook go.

'I am a detective sergeant,' said Johnson. 'What do you say your full name is?'

'Brook. Group Captain Rupert Robert Brook. Why?'

'You answer the description of a man called Clevely Heath who is wanted for interrogation regarding a recent murder in London.'

'I know, he has said so,' said Brook, indicating Suter. 'Look, do you think I would come here if I was that man?'

'I don't know. You might. Have you any documents to substantiate your name to be Brook?'

'No,' said Brook, 'but I have at the hotel. Can we go there and I'll show you? I've got my "A" pilot's licence, identity card and letters.'

'No, for the time being I must ask you to remain here whilst enquiries are made. Firstly, what are you doing in Bournemouth?'

'I am here on holiday.'

'Where do you come from?'

'Leicester. Thurmaston Aerodrome. I'm stationed there, but you won't find anyone there on a Saturday.'

'Can you give me the name of anyone at Leicester who can vouch for you?'

'Yes,' said Brook. 'Any amount.'

'Who is your immediate chief up there?' Johnson was taking notes.

'Mr Walters, the chief test pilot for Austers.'

'I wonder if you would come back into the station, sir, whilst enquiries are being made?'[13]

Brook assumed an exasperated umbrage.

'Well, this is the last time I shall come to the police to give any assistance. By the way,' asked Brook, 'am I under arrest?'

'No,' replied Johnson, 'not at this stage.'

'That's all right then,' said Brook. 'By the way, when you are satisfied that I am not this man "Heath", will you give me a chit that I can show, if I am stopped again?'

'Yes, if you wish, and so soon as we are satisfied that you are not Heath.'

Brook, Suter and Johnson went back into the police station to the sergeants' office where Suter sat down with Brook. He kept the conversation to their wartime experiences – always bonding chat for men of their age at the time. Meanwhile, Johnson telephoned Scotland Yard again and was put through directly to Reg Spooner at his office in Hammersmith. Spooner outlined Heath's description and said he would verify Brook's story about his background in Leicester, but on no account must they let him leave the police station. Whilst waiting for Scotland Yard to get back to them, Johnson observed Brook sitting with Suter, chatting about the war. As he was watching, Brook dropped his pipe on the floor. As he bent to pick it up, Johnson noticed that Brook had an inch-long scratch on the right side of his neck showing half an inch and running parallel with the collar of his shirt. It was not fresh but had a thin scab for the whole length. Little by little the officers' instincts were feeling more and more justified. They now needed to play a waiting game as the Metropolitan Police verified that 'Brook' was the man they were looking for.

Brook's patience was now wearing thin and he said that he wanted to leave. Suter and Johnson referred him to their senior officer, Detective Inspector Gates. At about 6.35 p.m., Gates told Brook that he would need to be searched.[14]

'I understand that your name is Brook. Have you any means of identification with you?'

'No, I have nothing on me. But I have at the hotel. I have told your officers all about myself. My name is Rupert Robert Brook and I'm known at the Devonshire Club in London. I live in Leicester and have a banking account at the Westminster Bank there. Look, I admit that there is a resemblance to

Clevely Heath. I have seen the police notice, but I am not this man, Heath.'

Gates searched him. All he had in his possession was four £1 notes, 3s. 6d. in silver, two three-penny pieces, a pipe and tobacco pouch, some Churchman cigarettes, a box of Swan matches, five-pence halfpenny in copper, a handkerchief and his sunglasses.[15]

Brook asked if he could go back to the hotel and then come back to the station. Gates told him that enquiries were being made at the hotel by the police and he was being detained. Brook then said that he was feeling cold. Could somebody pick up his jacket for him? He had left it with the porter at the hotel, Harry Brown.

Gates arrived at the Tollard Royal at about 7 p.m. and sought out the porter. He handed Gates Brook's brown sports jacket. Searching the pockets of the jacket, Gates came across what was to become some crucial – and damning – evidence. In the right-hand pocket of the jacket he found one half of a first-class return railway ticket (number 10130), valid for travel from Bournemouth back to Waterloo, issued on 28 June 1946 – the day that Doreen Marshall had travelled alone to Bournemouth. There was also a 4d. railway cloakroom ticket (number 0800) issued at Bournemouth West Railway Station on 23 June – the day that Brook had arrived in Bournemouth.[16]

Just before 9 p.m., Gates arrived at Bournemouth West Station and interviewed William Gillingham, the chief clerk. Gates submitted the cloakroom ticket and took possession of a leather suitcase. Opening it, there was a soft hat, a mackintosh, a leather luggage-label holder bearing the name of 'Heath', and most significantly, a leather riding whip with a distinctive diamond-weave pattern – stained with blood.

There was now absolutely no doubt. They were holding Neville Heath, the most wanted man in the country.

★ ★ ★

Back at Bournemouth Police Station, DS Johnson received a call from Scotland Yard. It was exactly the information he had suspected. Nobody had ever heard of Group Captain Brook at Thurmaston. His entire story was false. Spooner told Johnson to detain Brook at any cost. He wanted them to go to the Tollard Royal and search Brook's room for anything that might confirm his identity, but that there should be no further searches in order to preserve any evidence. Johnson returned to Brook, who was still talking with Suter.

'Enquiries have been made from the particulars you have supplied about yourself and I am satisfied that they are false. You are *not* known at Leicester to the Auster aircraft company. No person by the name of Brook as test pilot is known to them. Nor do they know a Mr Walters. You will be detained pending further enquiries as to your identity since I believe you to be the man, Clevely Heath. Is that your name?'

'Well, I am not Heath,' said Brook.

Johnson replied, 'Would you care to furnish any further particulars regarding your identity? You can if you wish. If you still maintain you are not Heath, someone will shortly be able to come to this station and confirm that.'

'I do not want to give any other particulars. If someone is coming down here who knows this man Heath, that will be sufficient proof. Surely it's no criminal offence to give false particulars of identity?'

'Yes it is. If false particulars are entered into an hotel registration book.'

'How do you know that I have? Have you been up there?'

'Yes.'[17]

Stumped by the cold, hard facts, Brook made no further comment. At 9.15 p.m., Gates arrived back at the police station and approached Brook, who was with DS Johnson.

'From my enquiries I am satisfied that you are Neville George Clevely Heath. Wanted for interview by the

Metropolitan Police in connection with the murder of
Margery Gardner during the night of the 20 June 1946. You
will be detained until officers arrive from London.'

Heath simply replied, 'Oh. All right.'

Johnson now began to enter Brook's details onto the
charge sheet and asked Gates what name he should write.
'Should I enter the name of Brook?'

Gates advised, 'He *says* his name is Rupert Robert Brook,
use that unless he prefers his proper name.'

Johnson asked what name the suspect himself would prefer
to be entered on the charge sheet?

'Oh. Heath. Neville George Clevely-Heath. The surname
should be hyphenated.'

At 10 p.m. Johnson took Heath's trousers to check for
evidence and gave him a substitute pair. Gates then presented
Heath with the return half of Doreen's railway ticket.

'This ticket was in your jacket pocket. Can you tell me
how you became possessed of it?'

Thinking quickly, he said, 'I found it in the lounge at the
Tollard Royal Hotel.'

'When and where?'

'On a seat in the lounge on Thursday last.'[18]

It was a plausible answer – he'd admitted he had sat with
Doreen in the lounge on Wednesday and she might have
simply dropped the ticket from her handbag.

At about 10.30 p.m., Gates asked him whether he would
be able to make a statement regarding Doreen Marshall's
disappearance. Heath replied that he would. In some contrast
to his earlier off-hand attitude, he started writing this statement with great care at 11.50 p.m. and was still writing and
examining his statement when Spooner's car arrived at
Bournemouth at 1.30 a.m. the next morning.

Leaving him to finish the statement, Spooner and Symes
were greeted by several members of the Bournemouth police

including Gates, Suter and Johnson. They were handed the
suitcase which Gates had recovered from the railway station.
Examining it, Spooner found three leather luggage labels
with the names *Capt N. G. C. Heath, Major N. G. C. Heath*
and *Captain J. R. C. Armstrong.* The latter had *N. G. C.
Heath London* written on the reverse.[19] As well as the blood-
stained whip, there was a blue woollen scarf with traces of
blood and nasal slime as well as a blue neckerchief, also blood-
stained – both of which had been used for tying.[20]

Spooner and Symes went directly to the Tollard Royal and
searched Room 81, going through all Heath's belongings.
Significant among his possessions were his flying helmet and
an escape scarf that had been used as a tie. Some khaki
webbing straps with no obvious purpose were also found.
Spooner and Symes also recovered an extraordinary number
of handkerchiefs – forty-nine in all. Most of these were
womens' and bore traces of lipstick.[21] Many were mono-
grammed. In the middle drawer of the dressing table, Spooner
discovered a handkerchief that had been tied into a knot and
had recently been cut with a knife – on it were traces of
blood and soil, as if it had been dragged across the ground.
This bore the letters A. R. M., the first three letters of Neville
Heath's South African alias, Armstrong. Also in this drawer
were two pieces of string that had been freshly cut.[22]

At 3 a.m. DS Johnson met Spooner in the CID office and
gave him Heath's jacket. From the left-hand pocket, Spooner
recovered some things that hadn't been noticed before – a
caterpillar badge and a single artificial pearl, as if from a ladies'
necklace.[23] Once Heath's statement about the disappearance
of Doreen Marshall had been completed, at 5.20 a.m., Reg
Spooner finally came face to face with the man who had
filled his days and sleepless nights since 21 June.

'You are Heath?'

'Yes.'

'I am investigating the murder of Margery Gardner in your room at the Pembridge Court Hotel on the night of the 20–21 June last. I think you are in a position to give me some information about it.'

'Yes, I will make a statement after I have had some sleep. I was there but I am not admitting I did it.'

Heath was allowed to sleep until 8 a.m. They were then driven back to London, with Heath sitting in the back of the Wolseley between Spooner and Symes, speaking very little and occasionally dozing. When he did speak, Heath addressed Symes, the more junior officer to whom he was handcuffed. He never spoke directly to Spooner. Arriving in Notting Hill at 11.25 that morning, Spooner reminded Heath that he had said he would make a statement about the murder of Margery Gardner. Heath said he was willing to make a statement, but wanted time to think the matter over. At 3 p.m., Spooner challenged Heath with the letter he had sent to Scotland Yard.

'Did you write this letter to Superintendent Barratt?'

'Yes.'

'In it you refer to the instrument used on the woman Margery Gardner and you say you are forwarding it to the Yard. Did you do so?'

'No.'

'Where is it?'

'It's in one of my cases. I'll get it later on.'

'I will get it for you so you can see if it is the one you mean.'

'There's no need, it is the one.'

Spooner fetched the whip and presented it to Heath.

'That's it.'

'Do you wish to continue with your statement?'

'I am still thinking about it and I'm tired.'

Spooner left, returning later that evening. He wanted

Heath to account for his movements during the night of 20–21 June, but after co-operating for a while, Heath said he realized the gravity of his position. He didn't want to say more until he had taken legal advice after he had been charged – and he was certain now that he would be charged. Spooner left him at 8 p.m. Throughout the day, Shelley Symes had been taking notes of everything Heath had said. Heath looked through this statement repeatedly, paragraph by paragraph. Finally he signed it.

At 12.30 on Monday morning, Heath was led into the billiards room at Notting Hill Police Station by Inspector James Stone and placed in an identity parade with eleven other men of similar age, height and build. He was allowed to take any position and chose to stand sixth from the right. Spooner and Symes were also present, as observers only.

Harold Harter, the taxi driver, was asked to take a good look at all the men, and then to touch the man he had picked up with Margery Gardner outside the Panama Club.[24] Without hesitation, Harter went straight to Heath and touched him on the chest with his right hand. Stone asked if he had any doubt, but Harter was clear: 'That is the man.' Harter was then escorted out of the building. Stone asked if Heath would like to change his position before the next witness arrived, but Heath just shook his head. Solomon Josephs, the receptionist of the Panama Club, was brought into the billiards room and again, Stone asked him to touch the person that he recognized in connection with the case. Again, with no hesitation, Josephs walked directly to Heath and touched him on the chest. Immediately after Heath had been positively identified by Harter and Josephs, Spooner approached him again.

'You know who I am. I am now going to charge you with murdering Margery Aimee Brownell Gardner at the Pembridge Court Hotel during the night of Thursday to Friday, 20 to 21 June 1946.'

Spooner then cautioned him. Heath simply said, 'I have nothing to say at the moment.'[25]

At West London Magistrates' Court, the matrimonial court that was in session that afternoon was cancelled and the courtroom opened to the public. Crowds were already gathered around the court building when Heath arrived in a police car, handcuffed to Shelley Symes and smoking a pipe. He appeared before Paul Bennett, and was charged with the murder of Margery Gardner. He was remanded until 23 July. Asked if he required legal aid, he refused, saying, 'I think I can manage it, sir.'[26] After the hearing he fumbled for his pipe and puffed on it composedly as he was driven through the crowds back to Brixton Prison.

Early that evening, Reg Spooner sat down to write to his wife and daughter. They were currently away on the aborted family holiday that he had promised they would take together when he was demobilized.

> *At last success has come in this job and only two hours ago I charged Heath with the murder of Margery Gardner. I have just returned from the police court after seeing him remanded. It has all been a tiresome and worrying business and what with the sudden dash to Bournemouth for him and other things my last night's sleep was the first since Friday night. Anyway, I daresay you have read about it all in the press. There is still an immense amount of work to be done in it, but at least we have the satisfaction of having got Heath – and there is more in it than is generally known although this morning's papers were making inferences. The job has done me quite a bit of good and I am getting congratulations from high and low.*
>
> *The press say it is one of the best stories for years.*[27]

With Heath under arrest, it was clear that the disappearance of Doreen Marshall was now a murder enquiry. Bournemouth police announced that they were not looking for anybody else

in connection with the case. With no admission from Heath
and Metropolitan Police enquiries focused on the murder in
Notting Hill, they concentrated on searching the sea-front
cliffs west of the Tollard Royal Hotel and the wooded chines
leading down to the beach. Digby, Scotland Yard's famous
bloodhound, was also engaged 'in the greatest hunt which the
world-famed organization has ever known in its history'. But
even Digby failed to sniff out any leads and gave up the chase,
withdrawing 'in shame' to his home near Winchester.

> 'For the first time, I whipped him,' said his dispirited mistress,
> Miss Nina Elms, who, however, hopes that Digby will re-
> establish his fame as England's most foremost bloodhound.[28]

In London, wary of compromising the case against Heath,
newspapers implied a connection between his arrest and
Doreen's disappearance without actually stating it, with
stories appearing side by side on the front page. But five days
after she had last been seen, the whereabouts of Doreen
Marshall's body eluded the police. With Heath now suspected
to be a double murderer, the story of the blood-lust killer
ignited the public's imagination and fuelled their hungry
desire for sensational details of the case. But even the most
hardened followers of the story cannot have been prepared
for the shocking revelations soon to come.

CHAPTER EIGHTEEN
Branksome Dene Chine

7–8 JULY 1946

We generally describe the most repulsive examples of man's cruelty as brutal or bestial. Implying by these adjectives that such behaviour is characteristic of less highly developed animals than ourselves. In truth, however, the extremes of 'brutal' behaviour are confined to man; and there is no parallel in nature to our savage treatment of each other.

Anthony Storr, *Human Aggression*, 1968

Kathleen Evans was a cake-maker who lived with her parents in Pinewood Road, one of the well-to-do avenues at the top of Branksome Dene Chine.[1]

At about midday on Sunday 7 July, she took her dog for a run through the chine, aiming as usual for the beach. She entered the ravine through the Pinewood Road entrance, then adorned with an exotic Dragons' Teeth Gate, and walked half way down the main drive. She then branched over to the left, going down the steep steps into the chine itself. The ravine was densely covered with large pine trees and an undergrowth thick with rhododendron bushes, furze, bracken, heather and grass.

The spaniel then ran a long way ahead of her until she lost sight of him, but eventually she caught him up at a sandy cliff to the left. Miss Evans called the dog to her and carried on along the footpath towards the beach, coming to a spot with some bushes to the right and a hole in the ground to her left. The pathway began to narrow and it was at this point that Miss Evans noticed what she thought, at first, to be a swarm of bees buzzing around a bush of rhododendrons. Looking closer, she saw that the swarm of insects were not bees at all; they were flies.

Thinking that there must be 'something objectionable' in the bushes, she hurried on past, but noticed what seemed to be a dead fir bough propped against the bushes to her right. She thought no more about it.

However, on Monday morning, Miss Evans read the newspapers, which were full of Doreen Marshall, the 'girl in the dinner gown' who had 'vanished in the dark'. That evening, Miss Evans told her father about the swarm of flies she had seen in the chine the day before and asked if he would go with her to investigate.

Kathleen retraced her steps into the sloping ravine. The flies were still buzzing around the rhododendrons and Mr Evans peered into the bushes. Looking to the left, he couldn't see anything, but on the right he saw what appeared to be some clothing. Most distinctly he saw part of a yellow coat – just as had been described in the newspapers. Mr Evans and his daughter went to the telephone box at the mouth of the chine and called the police.

Given that Branksome Dene Chine was just outside

Bournemouth but within the Poole boundary, officers from both stations were sent to the chine, led by Detective Sergeant Bishop of the Dorset Constabulary, based at Poole Police Station. Approaching the chine from the beach, concrete steps led to a sandy footpath up the centre of the ravine. To the west was a refreshment pavilion with a hard road leading up to Pine Wood Road, north-west of the chine. The footpath led up the side of the valley to wicket gates at Cassel Avenue at the north end of the chine. Bishop entered from the promenade entrance, guided by Miss Evans and her father; together they walked about 150 yards up the central path from the sea. Bishop was led to what appeared to be a natural alcove, about 22 feet wide, enclosed on three sides by rhododendron bushes. A fir bough and some branches had been deliberately placed in front of the alcove. Hidden behind them, under the spur of rhododendrons forming the east side of the alcove, Bishop could clearly see a body.[2]

As it was now 8.40 p.m. and the light was already beginning to fade, Bishop decided to leave the body where it was until the next morning. The chine was closed to the public and a police guard was maintained throughout the night.

The next morning, several officers including Bishop visited the chine with Dr Crichton McGaffey, a pathologist from Somerset who practised in Taunton. Drawing back the fir bough and cutting away parts of the bush, the body was exposed to full view. The sight that met the police's eyes was so shocking that some officers vomited.

Doreen Marshall's body was in a grotesque position and had been horrifically mutilated. She was naked apart from her right shoe, lying on her left side with her head thrust forward. Her right arm was extended over her head and her left arm underneath her body. Her right leg was twisted over her left. A week since she had been killed, dried black blood covered her body, now crawling with thousands of maggots which had eaten deep into her wounds.

The body was to the right of the natural alcove formed by the rhododendrons. On the left, about seventeen feet away from the body, were two bloodstains twenty-six inches apart. This appeared to be the scene of the crime itself, just next to the pathway that led through the chine to Pinewood Road. Outside the bushes there were two similar bloodstains, also twenty-six inches apart, as if the body had been moved there, before Heath decided to further conceal the body beneath the rhododendrons. Near these bloodstains, Bishop recovered twenty-seven pearl beads that had been torn from a necklace. These were to match the single pearl that Spooner had discovered in Heath's jacket pocket.

By the stains under the bushes he found a stocking ripped in two. Near the body was the left shoe and fifteen feet away from it, Bishop found a handkerchief. Piled on Doreen's body were her clothes – her black evening gown had been pulled inside-out and her lemon-coloured swagger coat had been placed on top with the lining showing. A brassiere was on Doreen's shoulder. Underneath the coat was a corset belt, a sanitary towel and a pair of cami-knickers which had been torn. Another stocking was found in the bushes, about seven feet above the ground. Further towards the beach, Bishop came across a blue powder compact, the mirror slightly cracked – the gift from Doreen's sister.

The police continued to investigate the chine for clues, using axes and machetes to cut back the dense vegetation in the growing summer heat. Many officers were veterans of the Burma campaign and the work recalled their days in the steaming jungle.[3] Thirty yards from the body, the police recovered what they presumed to be another gruesome clue – a bunch of human hair. It had been permed, so had clearly come from a woman's head, and there was a substantial amount of it, perhaps three-quarters of a woman's head of hair. Some had been cut and some had been violently pulled out. Sent to Scotland Yard, the hair would not match Doreen Marshall's, leading the police to suspect that there may be another body hidden somewhere in the chine. Could this be the remains of 'Peggy', the girl Heath had mentioned in his statement, but who had so far not been traced? Press reports would ghoulishly hint that another woman's body lay in the chine — and that she had been scalped.[4]

As early as 7.30 a.m., holiday-makers, 'the majority of them women', in shorts, swimwear and sunhats crowded around the police cordon on the beach in the hope of glimpsing some of the horrors that rumours indicated had taken place in the chine. Children with buckets and spades also wandered up to the chine to see what the fuss was about. Later that morning, when Doreen's body was removed, the crowds lost interest in the murder scene and went back to sunbathing, eating ice-cream or making sandcastles on the beach.

Doreen's body was taken to Poole where her father identified her in the mortuary there. At 2.30, Crichton McGaffey proceeded with the post-mortem in the presence of Constable Bishop. The injuries that Doreen had sustained before and after her death indicated a frenzied sex attack of shocking brutality. Though she had fought bravely for her life, at only 5 feet 3 inches and with a small frame, she had been overpowered by Heath's powerful physique.

Doreen's throat had been savagely cut just above the larynx right to the back of her neck. The left carotoid artery was completely severed, but the knife — the size of a fair-sized pocket knife — had been stopped by the spinal column. A second cut just above the first was not so deep and stopped short at the midline of the girl's throat. Both these cuts were inflicted whilst Doreen was still alive and had resulted in her bleeding to death. But there was a catalogue of other terrible injuries that had been caused both before and after her death that revealed an appalling level of violence.[5]

There were a number of bruises to the back of Doreen's head and her left temple, as well as some abrasions to her right cheekbone, as if she had been battered about the head and punched in the face. She had been gagged and bound. There were nail imprints and bruising around both wrists where they had been tightly tied together. Her fingers had a series of V-shaped cuts that indicated that she had fought desparately to fend off a knife attack by grabbing hold of the blade. These wounds cut right down to the bone.

Above the soft parts of the larynx where the knife later cut through, there was a swelling that had been caused by pressure from a soft instrument, such as the penis. In all probability, like Yvonne Symonds, Doreen had been a virgin, but Heath had extended her none of the sensitivity that Yvonne had been fortunate enough to receive. There was a bruise on the right shoulder and an area of redness above and below the left collarbone, denoting some pressure, probably from Heath's knee. Some of her ribs had been broken and splintered, puncturing her left lung. These injuries might have resulted from Doreen being forcefully pinned to the ground and her squirming under Heath's considerable weight of 171 lb as he raped her, undoing the gag in order to force himself into her mouth, pinning her down with his knee.

There was a large area of abrasion of the skin between the two shoulder blades. On the left side of the back, below the shoulder blades there were horizontal abrasions and corresponding abrasions at the back of the left arm. These were possibly due to Doreen being dragged across the ground, naked, whilst still alive.

Having dragged her further into the undergrowth, he then released her hands, cutting the handkerchief at this point with the knife — possibly with the intention of forcing her to do further sexual acts under duress.

At the back of the neck were two stricture marks. These were horizontal, about an inch apart, as if an attempt had been made to strangle her, possibly with the webbing straps or lengths of freshly cut string that had been found in Heath's possession. Doreen had suffered all of these injuries before Heath had slashed her throat and killed her. The final moments of her life in a dark and lonely woodland by the beach must have been terrifying.

After she had been killed, Doreen's body had been subjected to a series of mutilations of animal savagery. The right nipple had been bitten off. There was a deep cut extending diagonally across the right breast below the nipple, sloping down towards the middle. A second cut above the nipple joined the first cut below. There were similar injuries to the left breast, the left nipple having been savaged and torn until it was hanging off. Most shocking of all was a long deep cut running vertically up the front of the body, starting below the genitals from the inner thigh upwards. The blade had reached deep into the muscle one and a half inches from the surface of the skin. The cut extended up to a line joining the nipples. This long cut was done in four brutal strokes with Heath positioned by Doreen's left shoulder. There were also injuries to the genitals. The vagina and anus had been perforated and the skin between them had been torn to a depth of three inches from the surface. These injuries had been made by a rough instrument — possibly a branch — with extreme brutality.

The police puzzled how Heath had managed to persuade a sensible, respectable girl like Doreen to such an isolated spot in order to carry out his intentions. At the Tollard Royal, Doreen had been very clear that she wanted to go straight home, but somehow Heath had succeeded in coaxing her to walk down the zigzag path in front of the hotel and down to the beach. The lights of the pier — and safety — were only a minute away to the east. But Heath persuaded Doreen to walk a mile in the opposite direction from her hotel towards the Bournemouth chines. It is clear from Yvonne Symonds' statements that Heath was extremely persuasive (she recalled that he 'over-persuaded' her to sleep with him) and he may well have resorted to this tried-and-tested strategy, suggesting to Doreen that they get married. This impulsive romantic suggestion in the middle of the summer night may have convinced Doreen to accompany Heath towards Branksome Dene Chine — an area he knew from his walks with Peter Rylatt. The chines nearer to Bournemouth and closer to the Tollard Royal were more developed and less suitable for lovers' meetings. Having failed to persuade Doreen to go up to his room at the hotel (as he had failed to do with Peggy Waring), Heath's objective may well have been to seduce Doreen in the chine. Having walked her along the beach, he then suggested that they go into the chine. In doing so he had either lied that it was a shortcut back to Bournemouth or he had already succeeded in persuading her to have sex with him.[6] Even today in daylight the chine feels dark and isolated — in the middle of the night it must have seemed extremely forbidding to Doreen, but she had her air force pilot to protect her.

Most of her clothes were later found undamaged, so either she removed them herself or Heath had done so. As with Pauline Brees at the Strand Palace Hotel, he might have battered Doreen about the head to stun her, then stripped her, pulling her dress inside-out as he did so, ripping her cami-knickers and discarding the sanitary towel. He had then stripped himself naked. He bound her hands tightly, probably with the handkerchief that Spooner had found in the dressing-table drawer of Heath's hotel room. At the same time he had gagged her in order to prevent her calling for help.[7] He then dragged her further into the dense undergrowth of the alcove and further away from any possibility of escape.

Having killed Doreen and mutilated her body, Heath then set about trying to hide it. Nearby a match was found; it seems Heath may have smoked after he killed her, reflecting on what he had done. Not satisfied with his first concealment of the body, Heath then moved it seventeen feet to the east of the alcove. Before doing this he took the diamond ring from her finger and the fob watch from her coat. He then covered her body with her clothes and concealed it with branches of pine and rhododendron.

After the murder, Heath was covered in blood. Still naked, he bathed himself in the sea to wash the blood away, perhaps drying himself with his shirt and underwear, which he would later try to burn in the grate of his room at the hotel. At this point he may have dropped the murder weapon in the sea, as it was never recovered. He then picked up Doreen's handbag and hurried from the chine, leaving behind him the handkerchief that he had gagged her with. Fifty yards towards the beach he opened the bag to search it, discarding the blue powder compact, possibly because he saw that it was cracked and worthless. He proceeded along the promenade as far as Alum Chine. Here he took out Doreen's pigskin wallet containing her money and clothing coupons, her fountain pen and penknife. Pocketing these, he threw the handbag over the beach huts where it was later discovered by the schoolboy.[8]

By the time he had reached the foot of the zigzag path leading up to the Tollard Royal Hotel, he had second thoughts about keeping Doreen's possessions, so he dropped the penknife. He then climbed up the ladder outside his room and went to bed where he was discovered at 4.30 in the morning sleeping deeply as if he had nothing to disturb his dreams.

What had triggered Heath's murderous frenzy in Branksome Dene Chine that night? Not every sexual relationship he had with women ended in sadistic violence. He had slept with Yvonne Symonds *after* the death of Margery Gardner and she claimed he only ever treated her gently. He had been drinking on the night he killed Doreen – brandy and a magnum of champagne – but nowhere near as much as he had on the night he killed Margery Gardner. Heath's own version of events, like his version of the events of 20 June, offer no clue to the inspiration for the attack.

> I have no recollection of going anywhere near Branksome Chine. The next thing I recall is lighting a cigarette. As I was flicking the match away I saw blood on my hands. I knew I had left the hotel with Doreen Marshall. But I did not know where she was or what had happened. Something dreadful, I was sure. I was at the lower end of the promenade, on the soft sand. I stood still and tried to think what to do. I had her watch and some other things in my possession. How late it was I did not know. But everything was quiet. I must have walked towards the hotel. Looking up at a window with a light in it I saw a woman standing there in her nightdress. I had washed my hands with seawater but I did not feel like talking to anyone, even the companionable porter. So I climbed a ladder to get into my room by the window. Again I felt the cold and calculating feeling I had felt while shaving at Notting Hill Gate.[9]

The police in London were now considering if the death of Margery Gardner could be explained as a drunken sexual tryst gone wrong. If this was not the case, then her death seemed completely without motive. But how to explain this second, even more brutal murder, committed when Heath knew he was wanted all over the country?

> If you had read such things in fiction you would throw the book aside, would you not, and said, 'That is impossible. It does not happen. If a man has once committed a crime like this he does not go straight off and commit another crime of a similar and even more awful character at a time when he knows that the police are hunting for him, when he has seen his name in the paper day after day.'[10]

Why had Heath killed Doreen when he had spent all afternoon and all evening with her in front of dozens of witnesses?

Almost immediately her death was reported, the *Daily Mirror* suggested that Heath did have a very clear motive in killing Doreen.[11] Had he deliberately sought out a victim as a potential defence for the murder of Margery Gardner? The extraordinary brutality of the second murder could establish him as mentally unbalanced and enable him to make a plea of 'guilty but insane' at his trial. Had he consciously set out to butcher Doreen Marshall – conjuring images of Jack the Ripper – in order to save himself from the gallows?

Throughout his life, even from his early childhood, Heath had committed a series of crimes and misdemeanours that he had succeeded in getting away with unpunished. He was given the benefit of the doubt on countless occasions by his parents, the police, magistrates and senior officers, all of whom had been seduced by his infectious charm, his good manners and his handsome face.

Was the killing of Doreen Marshall the biggest gamble of Heath's life – an audacious attempt to get away, this time, with murder?

PART FOUR

The Twisting of Another Rope

CHAPTER NINETEEN

3923

9 JULY – 23 SEPTEMBER 1946

Brixton Prison

9th July 1946

My dear Mother,
I cannot express how I feel about the sorrow and misery which I must have caused you all. For my own part I don't care what happens. I have never really cared since I lost Elizabeth and Rob. I got interested in life again a few months ago but that was quickly squashed by the fact that having made a few slips the Air Ministry refused to let me forge ahead again and refused to grant me my 'B' licence. I'd worked damned hard for that licence and was disappointed by their decision.

Newspaper reports are all very inaccurate and quite amusing. The one of my arrest was priceless. I was supposed to be in the Botanical

Gardens sniffing the roses — like Ferdinand the bull. Actually I walked into the police station to see them quite voluntary on a very different matter and they almost didn't recognize me.

They've kept all my money and clothes at the police station with the usual rash promise that they'll be sent on later. I'd be grateful if you could send me some cigarettes and tobacco and matches and some money to buy a few things. I'm in the hospital here which is quite comfortable. Had the offer of legal aid from the court but refused it. I've no intention of accepting charity and I've no intention of paying for any counsel.

I'm prepared to give an exclusive story to any one newspaper in return for their briefing counsel on my behalf and paying me a certain amount of money. Such a course of action would enable me to pay all my debts and it is the only manner in which I'll accept any legal aid so don't employ a solicitor on my behalf. The newspapers print anything and everything so one of them might just as well have an authentic version. If you can enquire whether the 'Mail' is at all interested. I would be pleased should they accept my offer. I shall be prepared to make a statement to Det Insptr Spooner of the Yard and to a representative of the newspaper at the same time. I feel Spooner will be pleased to have the statement as there is an awful lot he doesn't know. I think I know where the missing link is too so they may like to know something about it. But if the newspapers wish to write me up they may as well pay for the privilege. I want £500 and legal aid. That sum will just about clear all my debts. I've no objection to Insp Spooner being informed of this by you. He'll be at Notting Hill Gate Police Station I expect. Don't worry too much about me it isn't really worth it. Concentrate on keeping Mick on the straight and narrow. Please don't come to see me — I know you'll hate it.

All my love as ever,
Yours truly,
Nen[1]

Heath, now Prisoner Number 3923, sent this letter to his mother the day after Doreen Marshall's mutilated body was found in Bournemouth. As Heath's letters were being intercepted by the Home Office, Spooner was subsequently sent to visit him in Brixton Prison, accompanied by Shelley Symes. Heath had made no admission about the murders and Spooner was keen to hear what he had to say.

When Spooner arrived he met, for the first time, Heath's newly appointed solicitor, Isaac Near of Raymond, Near & Co., a firm based in Holborn. Near had been recommended to Heath by one of his flying colleagues, most probably Ralph Fisher. He had been practising as a solicitor since 1932 and had bought the firm Raymond's in 1936. In 1939 he had been called up to the Royal Navy Volunteer Reserve and thereafter found it a strain keeping the practice afloat, particularly after 1944 when his offices in Warwick Court had been destroyed by enemy action. Near proved to be a reliable and trustworthy ally throughout the trial and beyond. A rogue very much cut from the same cloth as Heath, in 1951 he would be struck off for 'conduct unbecoming a solicitor', having embezzled some of his clients' money.[2]

When Spooner was taken to the interview room to meet him, Heath affected surprise.[3] He said he hadn't asked to see Spooner at all. Spooner emphasized that the only reason he had come to Brixton was because Heath had specifically suggested that he wanted to talk to him. Heath demanded to know where Spooner had got this information from, but Spooner told him he wasn't at liberty to say – given that Heath's letters were being vetted and censored, with copies of everything he wrote and received sent to the Home Office and the prison authorities. Heath refused to discuss the matter further and Spooner left Brixton bemused.

The letter also caused anxiety amongst the prison authorities and the Home Office.[4] Heath was not allowed to sell his life story and it had already been explained to him that legal aid was available if he needed it. This Heath refused to accept. In the end his legal fees were met by his family, with the help of the money he eventually secured for selling his story to the press. Almost as soon as he arrived at Brixton he was contacted by Leslie Terry, whom he barely knew, having only met him on the day of Margery Gardner's death. Terry visited Heath several times and volunteered to find somebody to pay for his defence, but Heath was well aware that Terry would need something in return; his life story to sell to the newspapers.

> I don't care two hoots whether I'm defended or not, but I am prepared to give any newspaper the full facts in exchange for certain payment . . . if they agree to my terms they can have anything from me that I can give them. If they don't, well I couldn't care less . . . I'm not prepared to argue or bargain, I'm much too tired . . . I honestly don't give a damn what happens to me. I have faced death too often in the past six years to worry about it. Anyway, I've nothing left to live for since I lost my wife and child.[5]

Heath wanted £400 for his story – and no haggling. The police were aware of Terry's criminal background ('a most undesirable person')[6] and observed his negotiations with Heath carefully. Heath said he particularly wanted the money to pay back his outstanding debts to his father.

On 16 July, on narrowly lined war standard paper he wrote two pages, outlining his life story, the blackouts he had suffered in South Africa and the breakdown of his marriage.[7] The document was clearly intended for publication. But when Near visited Heath in prison to collect the document, it was confiscated by the warder. Near then challenged the Home Office to return the document as he argued that it was essential for Heath's defence. Theobald Mathew, the Director of Public Prosecutions, advised the governor at Brixton that they couldn't very well withhold the document, but that Heath and his legal team must be warned that it was not to be published.[8] In the end, a deal was brokered by Leslie Terry for Heath's story to appear in the *Sunday Pictorial*, as Heath's favoured option, the *Daily Mail*, weren't interested.[9] Though he never made a full statement, he managed to tell much of his story in a series of letters to Terry and his other friends. These letters formed the basis for the story that appeared in the *Sunday Pictorial* over three weekends after the trial was over. The document Heath wrote in prison was to surface again at a contentious point during the trial itself.

As a prisoner on remand, Heath was presumed innocent until proven guilty, so was allowed certain privileges. As well as his legal team, he was allowed visits from his family and friends and met them in a room 12 feet square, but always supervised by warders. Generally he got on very well with the staff at the prison and called the governor 'the boss', just as if he were back in an RAF mess. He was lodged in the prison hospital on a ward he shared with ten other prisoners. His day began at 7.30 with breakfast served in a mess room next to the ward. He was then shaved by the prison barber, inmates not being allowed to shave themselves with cut-throat razors. Afterwards he took an hour of exercise in the flower-bordered hospital grounds. He could send and receive censored letters[10] and corresponded with dozens of his friends and family as well as with his solicitor.[11] The letters are generally upbeat, full of RAF slang, banter and self-deprecating humour, not at all the tone of a man whose life was in jeopardy. He received one letter from Doreen Marshall's parents in Pinner, but didn't respond to it.[12] He was also able to keep in touch with life in the outside world with an allowance of two newspapers a day, which he hungrily scanned for articles about himself. He was also an avid reader of novels and maga-zines — society glossies and flying journals that were sent in by friends like Ralph Fisher and Leslie Terry.[13] He particularly requested copies of *Esquire, Life, Tatler* and the *Illustrated London News*. Though the prison library was good, he thought many of the books were too serious or American, 'which grates a bit'. He preferred one-shilling paperback novels: 'light stuff', adventure stories, mysteries and thrillers. Any books he was sent from friends were vetted by the prison chaplain. All but one of the books he requested – with titles like *Bring the Bride a Shroud* and *Call the Lady Indiscreet* – were banned. Mostly he chain-smoked, smoking 200 cigarettes (Players, Churchman or Players No. 3) and half a pound of tobacco a week. Time went by very slowly for him at Brixton and in many of his letters his primary complaint was boredom: he was 'browned off with inactivity . . . It's all this waiting that is so depressing. And wearing prison clothes doesn't do one's morale much good.'[14]

But the mundane routine at Brixton was broken up by his various appearances at West London Magistrates' Court. He appeared five times throughout July and August, travelling to and from Brixton in a Black Maria. Throughout the hearings, Heath said nothing but doodled on prison notepaper as he heard the events in Notting Hill and Bournemouth described. At his appearance on 29 July Heath was formally charged by Detective Sergeant Bishop from Poole of the murder of Doreen Marshall. He said, 'Nothing to say.' On 13 August, witnesses were called from both Bournemouth and Notting Hill, including Charles Marshall. One by one, Doreen's possessions were handed around the police court. Heath looked on as his defence counsel held up the penknife and showed it to Doreen's father.

'Are you sure about this knife?' he asked.

'Yes. Certain,' replied Mr Marshall.

'Why are you so sure?'

Mr Marshall explained to the bench, 'I know it so well. It

was a prize for ice-skating. She had a fountain pen to match it. Her name was inscribed on the fountain pen, but not on the knife. I am quite sure that knife is the one.'[15]

There was a moment's silence. Mr Marshall and the man who had murdered his daughter stared at each other for a second across the court. The last time they had met was at Bournemouth Police Station when Heath had reassured Mr Marshall that there was nothing to worry about, that his daughter would be found safe and well. Heath dropped his gaze quickly and shuffled uneasily on the fixed seat.

At these preliminary hearings only the case for the prosecution was heard with Heath reserving his defence. This meant that all the shocking details of the two crimes were now public knowledge and reported feverishly in the press, months before Heath would appear at the Old Bailey to offer his defence. Unable to publish the most graphic details of the killings, most of the reporters on the press bench laid down their pencils and stared ahead of them in stunned silence. Heath carried on doodling.[16]

At every appearance at the police court, large crowds queued for hours in order to get a glimpse of him.

As with so many crimes of violence, especially where the coarser and darker aspects of the sex-motive are concerned, the court-rooms were thronged with onlookers, mostly women, many of them 'teen-agers'. Outside the Police Court were mobs of eager sensationalists, elbowing and jostling, and some standing on walls, or tops of air-raid shelters: a trenchant manifestation of modern times and manners.[17]

Extra police were drafted in order to deal with the crowds. When a police officer refused admission to one woman, she began to cry and shouted, 'I must see Heath. I have come all the way from Golders Green!'[18]

During Heath's appearances at West London Magistrates' Court, Bernard Tussaud, the great-great-grandson of the wax museum's founder, spent three weeks observing Heath in the dock. As neither photography nor sketching was permitted in the court, he had to draw Heath's image after each court hearing from memory. The wax figure would take six weeks to make. If Heath were found not guilty or reprieved, the figure would be melted down and the wax used again.

As he prepared for his trial at the Old Bailey, Heath was very keen to get a 'decent suit'. He sent magazine cuttings of the suits he liked and took his own measurements as he wanted it to be a good fit. In the end, friends bought him an off-the-peg suit for £20 with a grey chalk stripe and some new underwear – all with Heath's clothing coupons.

Isaac Near then instructed the esteemed defence KC, J. D. Casswell, to defend Heath. Sixty-year-old Casswell had been born and raised in Wimbledon, not far from the home of the Heath family, and had come to prominence professionally in 1913 in the case of negligence brought against the Oceanic Steam Navigation Company (the parent company of the White Star Line) by relatives of several passengers who had perished on the *Titanic*. The jury found the captain to be negligent and each of the relatives received £100 compensation. Casswell then saw action in France during the First World War, but was invalided out of the army in 1917 with an eye condition. He had defended several high-profile murder defendants – forty by the end of his career – only five of whom were subsequently executed. In 1935 he had defended Percy Stoner in the murder of Francis Rattenbury in Bournemouth. Stoner was reprieved following an appeal. Perhaps most famously in 1944, he had defended Elizabeth Marina Jones, the eighteen-year-old waitress who had accompanied US Army deserter Karl Hulten on a spree of violence culminating in the murder of a taxi driver on the

Great West Road. The case became known as the Cleft Chin Murder – a sensation at the time and the story that provoked George Orwell to write his essay, *Decline of the English Murder.* Though Hulten was executed Casswell managed to secure a reprieve for Jones. She was released from prison in 1954.[19]

Casswell was known for his charm, imperturbability and doggedness and had some of the rhetorical gifts of Marshall Hall, 'the great defender', with perhaps an even better knowledge of the law. Before taking the brief, Casswell discussed the case with an eminent psychologist colleague who declared on the basic facts that Heath was 'mad as a hatter from a doctor's point of view'. But Casswell worried from the start, that though this might be true in medical terms, he was not sure that it could be proved that Heath was as mad as a hatter in the terms of the law. This astute comment was to prove true and the sole debate at Heath's trial was focused on this issue.

When Casswell was shown into the interview room at Brixton to meet his client for the first time, he immediately mistook the man he was presented with for a member of the prison staff, thinking to himself, 'What good-looking chaps they're recruiting as warders these days.' Casswell thought Heath a 'good-looking young man with a splendid physique and an attractive and charming manner . . . he certainly looked the opposite of the popular image of a sexual maniac.'[20] After Casswell had introduced himself, Heath's first question was directly to the point.

'Why shouldn't I plead guilty?'

'You've a father and mother and brother, all alive. Do you want it said that a man in his right mind could commit two such brutal crimes?'

Heath reflected for a moment.

'All right,' he said. 'Put me down as Not Guilty, old boy.'[21]

Casswell felt from this first meeting that Heath was

indifferent to whether he lived or died. Whatever the press speculated, Casswell dismissed any suggestion that Heath had murdered Doreen Marshall deliberately in order to try and secure a life sentence in Broadmoor. If anything, Heath seemed to have a death wish and his half-hearted attempts to engage with a medical enquiry Casswell felt were purely for the benefit of Heath's family.

At the same time, the Director of Public Prosecution was instructing the case for the Crown. Anthony Hawke, a 51-year-old senior Treasury counsel and veteran of several murder trials, was appointed as leading counsel for the prosecution. Under the terms of English law, Heath could only be tried for one indictment at a time. It was up to the prosecution to decide which murder he would be tried for first. In discussion with Theobald Mathew, Hawke felt that there was more chance of getting a conviction if Heath were tried for the murder of Margery Gardner. The murder of Doreen Marshall looked like the savageries of a lunatic and might give the defence the opportunity to plead insanity.

During his time on remand, as Casswell and Hawke prepared their cases, Heath was questioned by several medical officers, including Dr William Henry de Bargue Hubert, who was to be called on behalf of the defence. Dr Hubert Young, the senior medical officer at Wormwood Scrubs and Dr Hugh Grierson, the senior medical officer at Brixton were to be called as expert witnesses for the prosecution.

Dr Young had various meetings with Heath whom he found very polite and personable, being particularly proud of his flying career and claiming that he had a 'fighter pilot temperament'. He was completely unwilling to discuss the charges. He didn't dispute the facts and didn't see how he possibly could. He said that he had originally decided to give himself up to the police, hence the letter to Barratt about sending in the riding whip, but then changed his mind. When he was arrested he had at first intended to plead guilty and though Casswell had persuaded him not to, he told Dr Young that he was still unsure if it was the right decision. He admitted that for some time before the murders, 'he had been conscious of an impulse to react in a certain way in his sexual relationships'.[22] He wouldn't divulge to Dr Young what this impulse was due to, but said he had tried to explain it to Dr Hubert in strict confidence after they had been talking for three hours. Young felt that the reason for Heath's unwillingness to discuss the crimes had something to do with his marriage.[23]

Dr Grierson from Brixton had interviewed Bessie Heath who admitted that her son was highly strung as a boy but that he was a kind, not a cruel person, fond of children and animals. She thought he had been particularly upset in the RAF after seeing an airman have his head cut off by a propeller. In her opinion, her son wasn't insane but she thought that 'his brain must have gone'.[24]

Heath told Dr Grierson that he didn't want to talk about the charge and denied any abnormal state of mind at the time of the murders, adding – as he had done with Dr Young – that he could, if he so wished, give an account of all his actions but he didn't wish to do so. He didn't explain why he was unwilling to discuss it, either. Though he seemed unemotional it was evident to Grierson that Heath kept his feelings under strict control. He denied any abnormality in his sex life or of ever having performed any unnatural sex acts. When Grierson specifically questioned him about any sadistic impulses, in spite of the evidence of the two killings, Heath denied that he ever had any. This was supported when Reg Spooner interviewed many of the women that Heath had slept with, none of whom 'spoke of perverse conduct'. Mr Friedman, Heath's wife's solicitor, also confirmed that as far as Elizabeth knew, Heath had never shown 'any sexual or violent tendencies'.[25] When asked about the incident in the Strand Palace Hotel with Pauline Brees and her claim that he had said 'I hate women', Heath had nothing to say. Grierson felt that he was continually on his guard, even about matters not directly concerned with the charge. When Grierson attempted to discuss Heath's sexual relations with his wife and whether this might have had an influence on his later conduct, Heath was particularly unforthcoming.

Throughout his time on remand, the issue of his wife and child in South Africa played heavily on his mind. 'I'd rather not defend the charge at all than have them undergo any publicity,' he wrote in one letter. 'Look at it logically, and you'll see that any publicity of this nature will ruin the child's life.'[26]

He took a keen interest in how the case was reported in the South African press and even threatened to take legal action against those that he felt misreported the story. Following his appearances in the police court, Elizabeth and her son were soon pursued by the press in Johannesburg. Journalists began phoning her home in Forest Town twenty-four hours a day in the hope of getting an exclusive story.

> I am tired of living this haunted existence. I am tired of dodging photographers and being tracked down by reporters; tired of offers to sell my life story. I am a normal person who has done nothing to merit notoriety. What happened in my life was something over which I had no control. I had only two months of married life, so there really is nothing for me to tell. Ninety per cent of our marriage and divorce we were apart.[27]

Elizabeth and her son left Johannesburg with her new fiancé, to a secret address 'somewhere in the heart of the big game country near the Portuguese Mozambique border',[28] where they would stay until the furore surrounding the trial had died down.

In the heaviest Old Bailey calendar for years, Heath's trial was announced as Case No. 72[29] and was scheduled to take place in the week beginning 23 September. It was expected to last four days.

One of the witnesses called on behalf of the defence was William Spurrett Fielding-Johnson, Heath's former squadron leader. His testimony, recorded by Isaac Near, discussed the breakdown Heath had in 1944. But Fielding-Johnson was never to appear at the Old Bailey. Days before he was to give evidence, he had a heart attack. He was rushed to hospital and though he survived, his evidence was never heard.

The trial would continue without it.

CHAPTER TWENTY
Mrs Armstrong

14 SEPTEMBER 1946

Number 3923 Name N. Heath

Brixton Prison

Mrs Elizabeth Armstrong
15, Epping Road,
Forest Town
Johannesburg
Transvaal
South Africa

Elizabeth, my dear,
I said that I would never write to you again, but under the circum-
stances I hope you will read this last letter.
  I cannot explain what has happened — you will undoubtedly

know as much as I do about it – and the South African newspapers have printed many (untrue) reports and covered themselves with the word 'alleged'.

In the face of the evidence I cannot deny these two offences, but to me it still seems fantastically unbelievable. By the time you get this letter it will all be over and I do sincerely hope that I am awarded the maximum sentence.

It was originally my intention of forwarding no defence, but now it has been impressed upon me that I should tell the true story for my family's sake, if nothing else. I am assisted by the finest counsel obtainable in the country.

I am certain in my mind what the sentence will be, but my object in offering a defence against the charges is not to get a lighter sentence – I should hate that – but to make it abundantly clear, for the sake of the few people for whom I have a deep regard, that I did not set out to cold bloodedly commit two vile murders. That I am responsible, I shall never deny and I'm quite prepared to pay the piper.

A letter or word from you whilst I have been here, would have meant more than anything else to me, but I can quite understand your point of view in not writing.

I have reason to believe that the current opinion in Johannesburg is that I deserted you and then blackmailed your father into a divorce for sums varying from £2,000 upwards. All of this as you well know is complete and absolute nonsense and I shall never believe that you started this vile rumour. I have my own views as to the source, but have asked my solicitors, through their Johannesburg agents, to make a thorough enquiry. I, personally, can find a great deal of ironic humour in the report, when I think of those days when I begged you not to leave me. One thing is certain, and it is that had I not left Training Command in South Africa to go on 'ops' none of this last eighteen months of hell would have occurred. Anyway, what is done is done and nothing can repair the harm now. I blame nobody except myself.

Liz, my dear, do you remember the last time I saw Rob? I don't think you ever realized – or will ever realize, just what that moment meant to me. I always had some hope that you would not go through with the divorce and that you would return to me. On that day I must have realized that you were so completely under your family's domination, that nothing would change your mind or alter your decision. From that time onwards, nothing was clear to me and I could view nothing in its true perspective. Hate, animosity, revenge, a hundred and one feelings completely alien to my real self consumed my entire being. Life without you and Robby was just empty. Now, thank God, it is almost over. Since we parted, I know I've laughed a lot and been on parties etc, but the whole time there was that terrible feeling of hollow mockery in the background which made my entire existence miserably unbearable.

Always, across my mind, there has been a vision of you, or a blurred picture of Robby playing so happily in the garden with the dogs and then that frightening feeling of emptiness and frustration when I realized I should never see either of you again.

Life for me during the last eighteen months has been plain hell and I shall be glad when it's over.

Now, at last, I can look back upon those years of perfect happiness with you. Bloemfontein at [Central Flying School] *with that awful cold hotel – Greystones – the 'Rambles', with those enormous teas – The Bloemfontein Hotel and those early morning drives to the Aerodrome in that little open car which we both froze in so regularly – Randfontein and our house there. The chaps who used to come and stay with us – the parties we had there and at the Aerodrome – The way you cried the night before you first went to Yvonne Kotze's to meet the other officers' wives – the day we were invaded by all those puppies and chose Baron – all these memories and countless others are indelibly printed upon my mind and will stay with me whatever happens.*

Lastly let me say this, very simply but sincerely. You are the only person with whom I have ever been in love – I still am, and shall remain so until the end. Nothing can change that. It is just

*an established fact which in recent months has given rise to a great
deal of wishful thinking, but even now, that very simple fact, has
given me a sense of happiness, and it is just about the one thing
nobody can take away. That is the reason why, although pressed
to do so by several doctors, I have never discussed you or our
marriage in any way.*

*Goodbye now, my dear, and I wish you the very best of luck and
all the happiness in the world.*

*I'll end this letter with the familiar style which may help to bring
back a few of those memories for you.*

With all my love, darling, always,

Forever your own,

Jimmy

*Should your mother commandeer this letter I ask her to pass it on
without comment, with respect for my last wishes, if nothing else.*[1]

CHAPTER TWENTY-ONE
The Old Bailey

24–26 SEPTEMBER 1946

> Nowadays the thrill has gone out of most murder trials . . .
> The normal cut and thrust of advocacy takes on an added
> significance when one knows that a man's life is at stake.
> J. D. Casswell, *A Lance for Liberty*, 1961

In spite of warnings from the police that all-night queues were banned, crowds gathered outside the Old Bailey at 8 p.m. on the evening of Monday 23 September in order to get a chance of sitting in one of the thirty seats in the public gallery of Court No. 1 the next day.[1] Many brought blankets to keep out the autumnal chill and slept outside the building overnight. One smartly dressed woman from Bristol refused to give her name to the press: 'I wouldn't want my friends to know I was doing such a silly thing.'[2] Extra police were on duty overnight to deal with the anticipated crowds for the opening day of the trial. The next morning, a young couple, both students at London University, successfully secured seats in the gallery of the oak-panelled and glass-roofed court-room. Once settled in their seats the girl took out twelve rounds of toast, marmalade, a knife and a teapot from a shopping basket. The young man took the teapot, pushing his way through the crowds and asked a court usher, 'Can I get some boiling water in the building?'[3]

At 10.32 a.m., Heath made his appearance into the glass-panelled dock, smartly dressed in his new chalk-stripe grey suit, a shirt, pullover, brown suede shoes and his RAF tie – a new white handkerchief in his breast pocket. His blond hair was pomaded and his nails were said to have been manicured for the occasion.

The judge, Mr Justice Morris, wore a grey wig and scarlet robe finished with a black sash. He sat in a chair to the left of the Sword of State which pointed upwards on the wall behind him. Morris was fifty years old and this was his first big murder trial, having only been appointed as a high court judge the previous December.[4] A Welshman by birth, he had been educated at the Liverpool Institute and Cambridge. During the First World War he had served as an officer in the Royal Welsh Fusiliers and had been awarded the Military Cross for bravery.[5] When he spoke, he had a soft, 'almost apologetic' voice.[6] The jury of ten men and two women – Rosemary Tyndale-Briscoe and Emma Selling – were then sworn in.

Given the extremity of the evidence in the case and the dramatic countrywide hunt for Heath, the three-day trial was very considered – as if deliberately distanced from the violent and emotive material. In meticulous longhand, 'which slowed the pace of the proceeding almost to dullness',[7] Mr Justice Morris took precise notes of the evidence. One newspaper reported that 'only the facts – the bruised, slashed, beaten,

suffocated body of the girl – defied the scrupulous understatement of the presentation'.[8] On this first day, Anthony
Hawke opened with one of the shortest speeches on record
for a major trial. For thirty minutes, Hawke addressed the
court conversationally, as if he was 'leaning over a garden
fence explaining how to bud a rose'. He was precise, quiet
and clear, quickly establishing that he intended to dismiss any
possible defence of 'partial insanity'.

Hawke then called the witnesses for the prosecution,
including several police officers who had investigated the
Notting Hill murder. Harold Harter, Solomon Joseph and Dr
Keith Simpson were also called. Tension mounted in the
courtroom on only a couple of occasions – when the leather
riding whip was held aloft by the court usher and again when
a grimy pillowcase, spotted with dried blood, was presented
to the jury. The dramatic highlight of the day was the appearance of Yvonne Symonds, who had come to court accompanied by her father. She wore a dark pin-striped suit and close-
fitting multi-coloured hat, carrying with her a brown leather
handbag. When she was called, there was a sudden hush in
the courtroom.[9] Anthony Hawke said he would have liked to
spare her the ordeal of reliving her experiences with Heath so
publicly, but her evidence was crucial to the case. Throughout
the questioning, she spoke with long pauses between her
muted replies. Concerned that she might be feeling unwell,
Mr Justice Morris gallantly offered her a chair and a glass of
water.[10] She looked at Heath only once. 'You have met this
man, here?' Hawke asked her, with a gesture towards the
dock. Yvonne raised her eyes to the man whom she had
introduced to her parents as her future husband. 'Yes,' she
murmured and turned her head away.[11]

After being cross-examined, Yvonne was released from
the courtroom. She didn't give any interviews to the press,
though a couple of snatched photographs of her were taken.

Her family left their home in Warren Road in 1947. Yvonne left the country, not wanting her association with Heath to colour the rest of her life. She settled abroad and never returned to England again.

The first day of the trial ended with Detective Inspector Gates of Bournemouth police telling of the discovery of Heath's suitcase at Bournemouth West Station and how he told Heath that he was to be detained for the murder of Margery Gardner. He confirmed Heath's casual, careless answer, 'Oh, all right.'

On Wednesday 25 September, Casswell opened the case for the defence. He began by telling the jury that a few days earlier he had received an anonymous letter from a woman who had noted that three 'gentlemen' (she had stressed the inverted commas) were prepared to defend 'that inhuman monster Heath'. She placed Casswell and the defence team in the same category as Hitler and hoped that their consciences would haunt them for the rest of their lives. Casswell discussed the letter because he wanted to draw attention to the fact that despite the many 'unusual, disgusting [and] morbid details' of the case that had been discussed in the press at great length and in great detail, Heath was entitled to a defence and was entitled to be tried on the evidence put before the jury and not what they had read in the newspapers.[12] Many of the jurors, if not all of them, would already have read of the details of both murders in the newspapers in the preceding two months and must surely have already formed preconceived ideas about the case.

> Why have the press taken such an interest in [this case]? They have taken an interest in it because they think it will appeal to the public who are their readers. Why then have the public taken such an interest in this case? Why? Is not it because two

terrible and apparently motiveless crimes have been committed by the same man within the short space of a fortnight? Not a man, you know, who is unintelligent, but a man who has seen a good deal of the world, a man who has been commissioned three times. That is the sort of man with whom you have to deal; and yet you find that within the short space of a fortnight, these two astonishing and apparently motiveless crimes have been committed by him . . . Is it not almost unimaginable?[13]

Casswell explained to the jury that he would not be calling Heath to give evidence, as they would not believe a word he said. He was concerned that Heath might seem too intelligent and that he seemed so composed that the jury would never believe that he could be the victim of a mental disease.

Casswell's personal view was that Heath had committed both murders as the result of an irresistible sexually inspired impulse to kill, but he could not concede that in court, as to do so would have automatically taken Heath out of the protection of the M'Naghten[14] rules, the statute that was to dominate the debate at the trial.

In 1843 Daniel M'Naghten had attempted to assassinate the prime minister, Sir Robert Peel, but by mistake, shot dead Peel's secretary, Edward Drummond. M'Naghten was clearly mentally unstable, but was his mental condition such that he was not responsible in law for his actions? Lord Chief Justice Tindal directed the jury that if M'Naghten was in such a mental state as to have been incapable of knowing the difference between right and wrong, then he was not culpable for his actions. Guided by Tindal, the jury brought a verdict of 'Not Guilty'. As there was no provision for mentally ill criminals, such as Broadmoor, in this period, M'Naghten was released.

The notion of a murderer being set free caused a public

outcry, so the House of Lords asked a panel of judges what they felt about the Lord Chief Justice's directive. In essence the judges agreed that in order to establish a defence on the ground of insanity it must be proved that at the time of the act, the accused was labouring under such a defect of reason that he did not know the nature and quality of the act he was doing, or if he *did* know it, he did not know what he was doing was wrong. Despite advances in the study of psychology since the turn of the century, the M'Naghten Rules remained the statute by which all insanity cases were assessed.

Casswell was to call only four witnesses. Usually the defence would be at pains to prevent the jury from hearing about any other crimes relating to the accused, but in a departure from normal practice, Casswell referred to Heath's chequered history in some detail – his thefts, frauds and court martials as well as introducing the details of the murder of Doreen Marshall. Casswell stated that the case for the defence was that of 'partial insanity' and suggested that in view of the fact that the injuries inflicted on the second victim were far more severe than those inflicted on Margery Gardner, Heath's was a case of 'progressive mania'. He tried to make clear that there would be no inconsistency in the jury finding that the charming and self-possessed young man in the dock was capable of insane behaviour at the time of the two murders when normal restraints had given way. He called Dr Crichton McGaffey to discuss the nature of the injuries to Doreen Marshall and requested that the jury examine the distressing scene-of-crime photographs: 'Rather unpleasant, I'm afraid.'

Casswell also called Frederick Wilkinson, the night porter from the Tollard Royal, to indicate how normally Heath had behaved after committing the murder, climbing into bed and falling asleep. The onus was on the defence to

prove that Heath was insane, rather than for the prosecution
to prove that he was not. Though he felt that his case was
weak as far as the law went, Casswell believed that he might
be able to persuade the jury of Heath's partial insanity, if
their star medical witness could convince them from the
witness box.

Dr William Henry de Bargue Hubert was a major authority in the world of psychiatric medicine and seemed an
extremely credible witness. It was to be on his evidence that
the case for the defence – and Heath's life – would rest. In
discussion with Casswell in preparation for the trial, Hubert
said that he was prepared to say that Heath ought to have
been diagnosed as a mental defective from an early age and
that at the time of the murders he probably knew what he
was doing, but was so mentally abnormal that he didn't know
that what he was doing was wrong. From 1934 to 1939 Dr
Hubert had worked as psychotherapist at Wormwood Scrubs
and had collaborated with the respected Dr Norwood East in
a psychological study of the prevention of crime for the
Home Office in 1938.[15] Hubert was also the assistant psychiatrist to St Thomas' Hospital for Children and had previously
been psychotherapist at Feltham Prison and Broadmoor.
During the war, he had served in the army as a specialist in
psychological medicine and latterly as adviser in psychiatry to
the Middle East with the rank of lieutenant colonel. He
seemed the ideal expert witness and was certainly more experienced and better respected than the two doctors that the
prosecution were to call.

However, what was not known at the time was that Hubert
was a drug addict. This affliction was to prove disastrous.
When he arrived at the Old Bailey that day, Hubert told
Casswell that he had been involved in a taxi accident, so was
in an extremely nervous state. But shortly afterwards, having
taken the drugs to which he was addicted, Hubert appeared

confident, happy and on 'a cloud of drug-induced euphoria'. He was then ready to enter the witness box.

Initially questioned by Casswell, Hubert stated that he had interviewed Heath several times and that he was, in his view, certifiably insane. Throughout his evidence, which was to last an hour and thirty-three minutes, Hubert was hesitant in manner and paused frequently, 'sometimes for quite a long time', already giving the jury the impression that he was unsure of his own opinion. But it was his confused and inconsistent performance under cross-examination that Casswell thought 'quite ghastly'.

Anthony Hawke, with his 'customary bland courtesy and softly spoken voice', dramatically undermined Hubert's testimony with biting irony, alerting the jury to the weaknesses in Hubert's testimony by the repeated use of the killer phrase 'with great respect'.

'I take it from your evidence that at the time Heath murdered Margery Gardner he knew that he was doing something that was wrong?'

'No.'

'May I take it that he knew what he was doing?'

'Yes.'

'That he knew that he had bound and tied a young woman lying on a bed?'

'Yes.'

'That he knew when he inflicted seventeen lashes on her with a thong that he was inflicting seventeen lashes with a thong?'

'Yes.'

'He knew all those things?'

'Yes.'

'But he did not know that they were wrong?'

'He knew the consequences.'

'I did not ask that, you know, with great respect.'

'He did not consider it wrong, no.'

'*Did not consider* is not the question I asked, with great respect. I asked you whether he knew.'

'No.'[16]

Hubert argued that Heath felt that his sadism was an expression of his sexuality and that he therefore felt it right to practise it.

'Are you saying, with your responsibility, standing there, that a person in that frame of mind is free from criminal responsibility if what he does causes grievous bodily harm or death?'

'At the time, yes.'

'His criminal responsibility does not arise at a particular time. I asked whether, with your responsibility, you say that a perverted sadist who knows perfectly well what he is doing when he satisfies his perverted instinct is free from criminal responsibility because he finds the necessity to satisfy it?'

'My answer is "yes", because on questioning sexual perverts they appear to show no regret or remorse quite frequently.'

'Would it be your view that a person who finds it convenient at the moment to forge a cheque in order to free himself from financial responsibility is entitled to say that he thought it was right, and therefore he is free from the responsibility of what he does?'

'He may think so, yes.'

'Do you say that the person who has been proved to commit forgery for the purpose of improving his financial stability is entitled to claim insanity within the M'Naghten Rules as a defence?'

'I think he does it because he has no strong sense of right and wrong at all.'

'With great respect, Dr Hubert, I did not ask you what *he* thought. I asked you whether *you* thought he was entitled to claim exemption from responsibility on the ground of insanity?'

'Yes, I do.'[17]

Hubert had fallen straight into the trap that Hawke had carefully laid for him. He had forgotten that he was supposed to be arguing that Heath didn't know what he was doing was wrong. In the end he had admitted that Heath could just not help himself, the doctrine of 'irresistible impulse' that was completely unacceptable in law. This point was not lost on Heath himself. Throughout the trial he had been sending notes to Casswell (twenty-two in all), observations and questions about the witnesses. At this point he sent a note to Casswell via the court usher:

> It may be of interest to know that in my discussions with Hubert, I have never suggested that I should be excused or that I told him I felt I should because of insanity. This evidence is Hubert's opinion not what I have suggested he say on my behalf.[18]

Hubert had posited an indiscriminate licence to commit crime. If the criminal thought his acts were right – however modest or extreme – then they must be so. Years later, in his memoirs, Casswell detected a note of special pleading in Hubert's testimony. In seeking to justify Heath's behaviour in this way, perhaps he was attempting to exonerate himself for his own sins? Less than a year after the trial, Hubert was found dead in the bathroom of his house in Old Church Street in Chelsea. He had taken a lethal cocktail of barbituric acid and chloral hydrate. Whether his suicide was related to his performance at Heath's trial was never confirmed.

Under further cross-examination, Hubert suggested that Heath might be suffering from 'moral deficiency' or 'moral insanity'. The prosecution was quick to pick him up on this. Was he saying that Heath was a 'moral defective'? Hawke was keen to push this line of questioning as he was about to bring up a point of law. In the Mental Deficiency Act of 1927, a 'moral defective' must have exhibited criminal propensities before the age of eighteen. Asked if Hubert knew of any evidence from Heath's youth in which he had displayed vicious or criminal traits, Hubert said he had none. Hawke concluded that in that case, Heath could not possibly be a moral defective as outlined in the law. Outmanoeuvred, Hubert was stumped, admitting, 'It is difficult to prove.'[19]

Casswell was relying on Hubert to introduce evidence from Heath's past that might have relevance to the indictment. If Hubert raised the incident with Pauline Brees at the Strand Palace Hotel, the jury could be made aware that Heath had previously practised consensual sado-masochistic sex with no serious consequences. By doing so, he might also have raised the issue that the incident with Margery Gardner might have been consensual, too. When Hawke asked Hubert if he had any evidence that Heath had exhibited any cruelty in the past, Hubert said that there was.

'What evidence?' asked Hawke.

'That similar acts without such consequences have occurred before, yes.'

'When?'

'At different dates in the past.'

'Could you give me them?'

'No.'[20]

Though he was certainly aware of the incident at the Strand Palace Hotel, Hubert seemed to have forgotten all about it. After re-examining him, Casswell declared that that was the case for the defence. Anthony Hawke then called two medical witnesses in answer to Hubert's testimony. Dr Grierson and Dr Young were both respected in their field as senior prison medical officers at Brixton and Wormwood Scrubs respectively, but neither had the qualifications and clinical experience that Dr Hubert had and neither were specialists in psychiatric medicine. But with the destruction of Dr Hubert's testimony by the prosection, far from being debated, proved or disproved, the issue of Heath's insanity was barely even discussed.

On the third day of the trial, there were few witnesses left to question. As it appeared that a verdict would be expected later that day, Heath chose not to wear his RAF tie 'at the last "knockings"' – as if wearing it whilst the death sentence was passed would in some way be an insult to the service. At the beginning of the day, Rosemary Tyndale-Biscoe, one of the two female jurors, submitted three questions that she felt had not been raised so far. The questions were very perceptive and give the only indication we have (the jury's discussion process being completely private) of the debate that took place within the jury room. None of the issues raised by these questions had been touched on in the trial. Was Heath financially embarrassed? Had he been drinking on the night of the two murders? And, crucially, was there anything in Heath's present mental condition that might have affected his brain recently?[21]

The questions were perfunctorily dealt with, Mr Justice Morris attaching little importance to them. But each of these issues was extremely relevant to Heath's behaviour in the days before the murders. With no money he had conjured the scheme to fly Harry Ashbrook over to Copenhagen – a journey he surely had no hope of making. He then proceeded to drink his way through his £30 fee until he was paralytically drunk. Each of these steps surely indicated that Heath had reached the end of the line. He didn't care what happened to him. He had developed psychological problems throughout the war years, exacerbated by baling out of his plane over Venlo and brought to the fore by his divorce. Fielding-Johnson's evidence had

Sean O'Connor

not been heard;[22] consequently there was no probing investigation of Heath's past and how it might have had an impact
on his actions.

Cross-examining Dr Grierson, Casswell suggested that he
had failed to secure Heath's trust when interviewing him
and that as a consequence, Heath had held back his true
feelings. He suggested that Heath might have felt distrustful
because he was aware that a document headed 'Confidential
and Medical' had been confiscated by the prison authorities
– the document he had written about his past life which
referred to various losses of memory and the incident at the
Strand Palace Hotel. Casswell may well have been trying to
introduce the contents of the document as evidence, but
when Grierson was presented with it, he said he'd never
seen it before and simply handed it back. Warning Casswell
as politely as possible, Justice Morris made clear that he was
not permitted to submit any new evidence as the defence
had already rested their case. Consequently, the incident
with Pauline Brees at the Strand Palace Hotel was completely
lost on the jury in a series of cryptic references and Heath's
claim to losses of memory and blackouts was never aired in
court at all.

In his closing speech, for the first time, Casswell touched,
almost in passing, on the issue that might have been one of
the root causes of Heath's violent behaviour – his experiences
during the war.

He is one of thousands of young men who has taken his life
in his hands and risked one of the most painful of deaths, by
burning, on your behalf and mine. You may think that the
life which has been led by a young airman is just the sort of
life that might bring to the surface a defect of reasoning which
had been hitherto hidden in his life. That is the only reason I
refer to that. The human frame was not built to fly in

machines and be fired at. The human frame and human people have had to put up with shocks and risks and dangers which were unknown up to the present generation . . . The human frame and the human mind were not intended to meet with such awful shocks as they have had to meet with in the past few years, and it may be that they have not yet evolved such an immunity as to leave them normal after they have gone through those sorts of experiences. You may yourselves come to the conclusion that that kind of experience may have something to do with the outburst, the admitted outbursts, of sadism in this man after the war was over.[23]

In his closing speech for the prosecution, Anthony Hawke recognized that, to judge from Heath's actions, what he had done – how he had behaved before and after his crimes – *seemed* mad.

No one suggests that this is a normal person with whom we are dealing. I'd venture, most respectfully, to say that it might be entirely a wrong way to approach this case by saying, 'Oh, well, anyhow, nobody in his sober sense would do a thing like this. After all, the man must be mad. Let us forget all about what the doctors have been saying and what these men in wigs and gowns have been saying to us. Let us forget all that special pleading and just say, as common-sense people, that nobody but a maniac would behave like this man.' Members of the jury, with great respect, that is not the way to approach this.[24]

Madness – whether it was a moral or medical state – was not synonymous with insanity, which was a legal and not a clinical term. He reminded the jury that they were to establish whether Heath was responsible for his own actions purely in terms of the law. This was further stressed by Mr Justice

Morris in his summing up. Speaking for ninety-nine minutes
with simplicity and charm of manner, Morris guided the jury,
weaving a clear path through the intricate evidence. His view
was very plain: despite the confused and confusing semantic
debate between the defence and prosecution about partial
insanity, moral insanity, moral deficiency or moral degener-
acy, the legal position was clear; the laws of insanity were not
to be used as a 'get out of jail free' card.

> Strong sexual instinct is not in itself insanity; a mere love of
> bloodshed or mere recklessness are not in themselves insan-
> ity; an inability to resist temptation is not of itself insanity;
> equally, the satisfaction of some perverted impulse is not,
> without more, to be excused on the ground of insanity. The
> plea of insanity cannot be permitted to become the easy or
> the vague explanation of some conduct which is shocking
> merely because it is also startling. The law of insanity is not to
> become the sole refuge of those who cannot challenge a
> charge which is brought to them.[25]

After Morris's summing up, at 4.35 p.m. the jury retired.
Heath was taken down to the tiny cell below the dock and
waited, reading the scrawled messages that murderers of the
past decade had written on the walls. Very much a betting
man, having listened to the summing up, he made his odds
'thirty to one'. Casswell went home to Wimbledon, leaving
his junior Mr Jessel to take the verdict, a commonly exercised
privilege of leading counsel once their main duties were over.
However, the press, quick to manufacture a story out of very
little, claimed that Casswell had collapsed from the strain of
the trial.[26] This he dismissed as 'absolute nonsense'.[27]

At exactly 5.34, with less than an hour of deliberation
following this complex trial, the jury filed back into their
box. The autumn afternoon was getting dark, so the electric

lights were switched on.[28] Heath hurried up from the cells, snapped to attention and for the first time in the trial, lifted his head to look up. The silence in the courtroom was intense and for half a minute there was no sound.[29] Standing straight and firm, his hands clasped behind his back with the 'slightest twitch of the mouth',[30] Heath waited to hear his fate, his chest rising and falling. Two police officers stood either side of him in the dock as the judge and then the jury filed back into the courtroom. The clerk asked the jury, 'Members of the jury, are you agreed on your verdict?' The foreman, dressed in morning coat and hard white collar,[31] stood up and answered in a loud voice, 'We are.'

'Do you find the prisoner, Neville George Clevely Heath, guilty or not guilty of the murder of Margery Aimee Brownell Gardner?'

Another pause. The foreman cleared his throat and answered in a voice which reached every corner of the courtroom, 'Guilty.' There was no recommendation to mercy. The death sentence was passed and Heath was asked by Morris if he had anything to say. The garrulous airman had rarely had such an attentive audience. With all eyes on him, here was his opportunity to leave the trial with a flourish. All his life he had sought the limelight, a matinee idol at the centre of his own drama. But now there was no protestation of his innocence, no admission of guilt, no remorse or apology. Faced with death, words failed him. His only response to Morris's question, a suitably nihilistic, empty: 'Nothing.'

He left the court at 5.41, the gamble for his life rolled and lost in seven short minutes.[32]

Maggie Blunt was in her mid-thirties, a university-educated publicity assistant reluctantly working for a metals company near Slough. That night, she wrote in her Mass Observation Diary how ordinary people like her responded to the news of

Heath's sentence, not with confident cheers, but with an anxious ambivalence.

> So Heath has been sentenced to death. I have been following this case in the press all agog and aghast. The news of his death sentence came a long way down on the BBC bulletin tonight and I found Mrs S waiting for it, as I was. I wonder how many other people were doing the same.
>
> I can't see that it makes much difference whether he was 'insane' or not. He was obviously dangerously abnormal and had committed shocking crimes. N was arguing about it when she was here – that you couldn't condemn a man who was mentally imbalanced. This is a case that will be remembered and discussed in the far future when more is known of psychology.
>
> Where does one draw the line for a person being responsible for his own actions?[33]

CHAPTER TWENTY-TWO
Wednesday 16 October 1946

If ever there were a criminal quite obviously mad, such a one is Heath. It does not take a knowledge of psychiatry or long pondering the hair-splitting of expert witnesses to reach that conclusion. Not merely the circumstances of the crime, but the conduct of the murderer before and after it admit of no other answer. If that behaviour is not mad, then the word has no plain commonsense meaning.

> A barrister, *Daily Worker*, 28 September 1946

This weather is quite amazing, don't you think? For, although the days are quite cold the pleasant sunshine reminds one of any country except England. I've no doubt, though, that the fog and rain will not be far off now.

> Heath in a letter to his mother,
> 13 October 1946[1]

Taken to Pentonville in a Black Maria, Heath was introduced to the prison governor, Mr Lawton, and the medical officer, Dr Liddell, who asked if he would like some medication to help him get over the ordeal of the death sentence. But Heath was indifferent. He was taken to a cubicle and made to remove his smart civilian clothes and given the special uniform reserved for men convicted of murder – a rough grey suit, devoid of buttons or anything that might enable him to do himself an injury. He was now registered as Prisoner No. 2059 and shown to Condemned Cell No. 2. No. 1 was already being occupied by Arthur Boyce, who had been convicted of the murder of his fiancée, Elizabeth McLindon, the housekeeper to the exiled King of Greece. Whilst much of the country was celebrating that summer, Boyce had shot her at the king's Chester Square home on 'V' Day, 8 June.[2]

Most convicted murderers remained in a state of complete collapse for anything up to forty-eight hours after the death sentence was passed upon them, but as soon as he left the Old Bailey Heath began to chat casually with the warders on the 'death watch'. Traditionally, three Sundays would have to pass before the execution was carried out – which would be the week of 13 October. Under the Criminal Lunatics Act of 1884 the home secretary had the power to appoint two doctors to examine a prisoner under sentence of death. The time allowed for lodging an appeal was fourteen days after the trial. But after discussion with Casswell and Near, Heath decided against it, but did allow the medical enquiry to go ahead, though he didn't expect it to make any difference.

I am not optimistic about the result, neither am I unduly anxious, for in my opinion, the possible alternative may well prove far worse than the present situation.[3]

The fact that he refused to appeal and was to take little interest in the medical enquiry that might save his life was at odds with the assumptions printed in some newspapers that the death of Doreen Marshall was an extraordinary bid by Heath to prove that he was insane and thereby escape the gallows. Casswell thought this 'wholly unwarranted by the facts'.[4] Immediately the death sentence had been passed Heath was reconciled to it.

> *I have very little to say I'm afraid, except that I think I would rather have things this way than spend the remainder of my life behind bars. Even now it all seems like a bad dream and except for what I've read and heard I know extraordinarily little about the whole affair. God alone knows what must have happened but it is certain that I am responsible legally and therefore must pay the penalty.*[5]

During the trial, as the defence had effectively admitted that Heath was responsible for the murders, there was no necessity to fully debate the crimes and the motivation behind them. He was certain to be convicted and his only hope of escaping execution was Dr Hubert's testimony that had gone so disastrously wrong. The fact that Heath wasn't tried for the second murder also meant that many witnesses were not called and their testimony never examined. Effectively the jury had only heard a part of the story. It seemed the function of the trial was not to reveal the truth but to get a conviction. Even Heath himself claimed to have no knowledge about the motivation behind what Casswell had repeatedly called these 'motiveless' crimes.

> *Morally* [Heath wrote] *I don't feel I am guilty because I could never have set out to commit two such vile deeds in cold blood. I don't expect anyone to believe my story – except a few friends who have*

been terribly understanding – but without going into any details I want you to know that it wasn't the 'real me' who was the author of these acts.[6]

For Margery and Doreen's families, there was no explanation, no sense of closure. Other than the knowledge that Heath was to pay for his acts with his life, there was to be no satisfaction for them, nor was the public's curiosity about the case sated either.

Now that Heath was under sentence of death, the press were able to print any of the stories they had collected about him, whether they were true or not; a condemned man would not survive long enough to pursue a libel suit. Details of the case were embroidered or guessed at, including the particularly unpleasant detail that Heath had stuck empty cigarette packets in Doreen Marshall's wounds (he hadn't), the feeling being, perhaps, that Heath was such an inhuman monster that he must be capable of any depravity – as if the two murders he was responsible for were not, in themselves, horrific enough. The press hinted that Heath might have been guilty of other murders and sexual assaults. But as the trial was being prepared, Spooner had already investigated any unsolved crimes that Heath might have been responsible for. A member of the public had alerted the police to the fact that Heath might have killed Vera Page, a ten-year-old girl who had been found raped and strangled in west London, a mile away from her home.[7] Spooner also investigated the death of nineteen-year-old Louisa Steele from Blackheath who had been found strangled, raped and mutilated. Both murders had taken place in 1931 when Heath would have been fifteen, but nothing was found to connect him to either murder. On 26 October 1944 Florrie Porter, a 33-year-old nurse, had been murdered near RAF Finmere, where Heath had been stationed when he was seconded to the RAF. There was some similarity between the injuries sustained by both Florrie Porter and Doreen Marshall. But Spooner, scrupulously fair as ever, ascertained that Heath could not possibly have been involved in the death of Florrie Porter as he was on operations in Belgium at the time.[8] Despite rumours and assumptions in the press in Britain and South Africa, there is no evidence that Heath was involved in any other murders or assaults.[9]

The press also became bolder in their references to Margery Gardner's character and lifestyle. Somehow Trevethan Frampton's claim that Margery liked to be dominated by men reached the newspapers, which hinted at it when the trial was over. There was an increasing presumption by the press (and possibly by the police) that Margery was in some way culpable for her own death, that having known Heath's tastes, she had put herself in danger. Throughout the reporting of the trial, both victims were discussed in Hollywood style clichés – Margery Gardner cast as the vampish femme fatale and Doreen Marshall the innocent virgin – as if women could only conform to one of two extremes. Certainly, Margery had been promiscuous but it was Frampton – a man she had only known for six months – who assumed that she was 'masochistic', rather than Margery herself telling him that this was the case. When Spooner questioned Margery's friends and lovers, including her husband, they all agreed that Margery 'possessed no such trait'.[10] Peter Tilley Bailey, who had known Margery intimately in the six months preceding her death, confirmed that 'she has never shown any abnormal tendencies to me'.[11] Assuming that she had such tendencies certainly made the circumstances of her death more comprehensible (a sexual tryst gone wrong) and provided a further salacious development for the press to exploit. But was it actually true?

Given that Heath stated several times that he would rather

hang than spend the rest of his life in Broadmoor, he cannot have planned the murder of Doreen Marshall as a ploy to avoid the gallows. But if that was not the motivation for her murder, how could it be explained?

Having failed to establish what the motives for the two murders were at the trial, there was much speculation in the press as to what they might actually be. But a series of errors, inaccuracies and mistakes quoted at the trial and in the newspapers began to obscure this issue in a cloak of confusion.

Early in Spooner's investigation in June, both Leonard Luff and Thomas Paul of the Strand Palace Hotel were shown photographs of Margery Gardner and identified her as the woman Heath had been with at the hotel in February.[12] This, of course, was not true. It is clear that the woman at the Strand Palace who had submitted to Heath was definitely Pauline Brees. But she was not called as a witness at the trial and her evidence was never heard. Once Luff and Paul had made their mistaken identification, the story began to appear in the press, repeated as fact – that Margery Gardner had spent the night with Heath before and had escaped a beating.[13] In this scenario, she would *definitely* have known the danger she might be in and therefore must have knowingly succumbed to him at the Pembridge Court Hotel.

When Pauline Brees was finally interviewed by Spooner on 27 July and it became clear that Margery was *not* involved in the Strand Palace incident, stories suddenly appeared indicating that there were *two* similar incidents in *two* different hotels which *might* have taken place in March. Or was it May? These errors were repeated at the trial itself and even resurfaced in the memoirs of Josh Casswell and Keith Simpson.[14]

In reality, there was no evidence from any witness or in any police file that Margery had ever spent a previous night with Heath. Placing her at the Strand Palace Hotel was a mistake. Heath had only recently begun to patronize the same pubs and clubs that Margery did, possibly only a week or two before they met on the night he killed her; she didn't even know his surname. Consequently, despite what was reported in the press and then repeated in books and articles about the case ever since,[15] Margery may have had no idea at all what Heath's sexual tastes were when she agreed to go back with him to Notting Hill. In all probability, all that Margery might have expected at the Pembridge Court Hotel was straightforward intercourse with Heath. If this is the case – and taking into account the witness statements which have recently become available – a much clearer motivation for both murders becomes apparent and both crimes can be explained more simply and more plausibly.

Heath had lost everything; his wife, his home, his son, his career. Rejected from the Air Ministry, he stated several times that he had nothing left to live for. On the day of Margery Gardner's death, he was given £30 by Harry Ashbrook that he knew he wouldn't be able to pay back. Nor would he be able to supply the service that he had said he could – the trip to Copenhagen – as he had failed his 'B' licence. He had also lied to his mother that he had received the licence, which she would very soon find was not true. On 20 June, he wasn't even thinking a day ahead and proceeded to drink to great excess – a fact completely ignored at the trial.

Whilst seconded to the RAF, Heath's behaviour had been so extreme that he was never allowed to fly again and his senior officer, well versed in psychological problems in pilots, identified that he was suffering a breakdown. Following this he seems to have suffered some sort of post-traumatic reaction after he baled out over Venlo.

At the same time, Heath also admitted that he had been conscious of an impulse to 'react in a certain way' in his sexual relationships. Having lost all power and control in every other aspect of his life, was he now able to feel in control solely during intercourse?

Margery Gardner, like Pauline Brees, had certainly consented to sleep with Heath. She undressed and removed her earrings. But it may only have been at this point that Heath made it clear that he wanted some sort of extreme or sadistic sex with her. He might have assumed that Margery would consent, given her bohemian reputation. But had he been wrong-footed when Margery reacted in exactly the way that Pauline Brees said she had done? Had Margery rejected him? The incident at the Strand Palace Hotel was not discussed at the trial, but in their investigations, both police and psychiatrists fixed on Heath's comment to Pauline – 'I hate women' – as if it were an indication of Heath's misogyny. But what was more telling was his subsequent comment to Pauline: *'I'll make you do exactly what I want you to do.'*[16]

Could Margery, drunk as she was, have refused to submit to the more extreme acts that Heath desired, just as had occurred at the Strand Palace Hotel? Drunk, fuelled by rejection and sexually aroused, had he then knocked Margery unconscious (the bruises on her cheek), lost all control and gone beserk?

In his relationship with Peggy Waring, she noticed that Heath exhibited physical symptoms at the thought of rejection ('He seemed very distressed and perspiration was running down his face . . . His passions seemed so roused that he was compelled to become rough with me and then to control himself he would immediately leave me').[17] He had also shown these extreme physical reactions years before when he was confronted with the fact that the RAF did not want to take him ('He displayed unnatural excitement and loss of self-control. His eyes were wild, his whole body shook with emotion and he could not sit down).[18]

It's intriguing that these displays occurred when Heath

was unable to pursue the two great passions of his life, sex and flight.

Having killed Margery, in the cold light of the next morning, he was appalled at what he had done and what he was capable of. He went to Worthing and met Yvonne Symonds, sleeping with her on more than one occasion, but didn't harm her.[19]

When he wined and dined Doreen Marshall, just as he had done with Yvonne Symonds, had he 'over-persuaded' her to go up to bed with him? Hence Doreen's increasing anxiety during the evening and her desire to go home. Having failed to seduce her at the Tollard Royal, perhaps Heath had hoped to do so on the way back to her hotel. In order to secure her trust, he might have suggested they get engaged (just as he had done with Yvonne) as they walked towards Branksome Dene Chine.

By the time they reached the chine, Doreen might have agreed to have sex with him[20] or he may have suggested that the route through the chine offered a shortcut back to central Bournemouth. After having persuaded her into the isolated chine in the pitch dark, again, it may only have been at this point that Heath revealed his intentions and Doreen, like Margery, rejected his suggestion of extreme sex acts. Again, he knocked her unconscious (the bruises on the cheek), stripped and bound her – his desire merging with rage once more.

Both women were beaten in the face, both were tied and gagged, both had their nipples bitten and both their bodies were savaged by terrible genital injuries. So both murders may have been inspired by a similar chain of events rather than being the two very different scenarios they have hitherto been regarded as. This outline of events follows Spooner's thinking at the time:

> It might be assumed that Heath has resorted to violence and
> sadistic acts where his advances have been repudiated and so
> resulted in his use of physical force which accentuated his
> perversity.[21]

As is clear from Heath's whole life and career, he was very
much a creature of habit. He'd commit a crime and then
attempt to salve it with a letter. He would do wrong, then
run away before rationally thinking about the consequences.
He would propose to a girl solely in order to get her into bed.
His life was a fabric of repeated patterns and much of the time
he would be condemned to make the same mistakes and
never learn from his experiences. With the statements of
Pauline Brees and Peggy Waring, it's now possible to see the
pattern in two murders that have previously seemed to be
related but inexplicable acts; both women brutally murdered
by a man whose charm and good looks had fostered an arrogance and conceit that baulked at the idea of any woman –
whether vamp or virgin – telling him 'no'.

In the condemned cell at Pentonville, Heath was only
allowed ordinary prison food and none of the special treatment he had been afforded on remand. Asking why he was
only allowed to eat with a spoon and not allowed a knife
and fork, it was explained to him that from now on all his
food would be cut up for him by the warders. He was no
longer allowed to receive tobacco, though every day, due
to an archaic ruling, he had an allowance of tobacco and a
pint of beer. He was no longer allowed to be sent books,
magazines or newspapers from outside and was reliant on
the 'awfully good' prison library. Despite not having access
to newspapers, he was still concerned about how his story
was being presented, having been informed of this in letters
from home ('I see no reason why the press should be

permitted to print quite blatant lies').[22] Unlike his stay at
Brixton, the time at Pentonville seemed to pass 'very pleas-
antly', playing chess and card games. He read *The Thirty-
Nine Steps* twice; the story of a man on the run accused of
murder, desperately trying to prove he is innocent.

The sentence initiated a new wave of stories in the press relating to the case, including great concern about the police's
holding back of Heath's photograph from the public. Several
headlines appeared on the subject: 'Ban on Picture Cost Life of
My Doreen',[23] 'The Heath Picture: the Facts'[24] and 'Doreen
Marshall; Should She Be Alive Today?'[25]

The picture had been embargoed by the police for twelve
days whilst Heath had been at large and only released on
30 July when he was already in custody. It had not been
issued to the press who were warned that any publication of
the photograph would 'seriously prejudice' Heath's trial. But
Doreen's father could only see that the ban on the picture
had allowed a killer on the loose to kill again.

> We fully appreciate that publication of the picture of a man
> wanted for questioning might embarrass the police if he was
> afterwards found innocent. But in this case because normal
> procedure was followed it has cost my daughter's life. I am sure
> she would have recognized Heath from pictures she would
> have seen in the newspapers we take, but for the Scotland Yard
> request that newspapers should not print this picture.[26]

Doreen's mother concurred, recalling the night when Doreen
had grabbed the *Daily Mail* from her and told her not to read
about the Notting Hill murder.

> If there had been a picture of Heath she would have seen it
> automatically and the chances are she would have recognized

him later. Even if she felt she could not read such details a picture might have caught her mind and made all the difference.[27]

On Thursday 10 October, Norman Bower, MP for Harrow West, challenged the home secretary in the House of Commons about the embargoed photograph. Mr Chuter Ede took the opportunity to rebuff the question once and for all. Whatever the Marshall family felt, the police had followed the correct procedure.

The circumstances of the murder of Mrs Gardner did not afford any reason to suppose that her assailant would commit a second murder, and I am satisfied that the police were right in asking that the press should not take a course which might have prejudiced the due course of justice.[28]

As well as recriminations against the police, there was also a certain uneasiness from some quarters about the death sentence. Several newspapers ran comparisons between Heath's case and that of Ronald True – another ex-airman who had been tried and convicted of murder in 1922 under the M'Naghten Rules.[29] True's appeal failed, but the home secretary had intervened and the sentence of death commuted to life in a psychiatric hospital. True was still living in Broadmoor in 1946 and would remain there until his death in 1954. Given the similarities between the two cases, some commentators felt that Heath should be sent to Broadmoor rather than sentenced to death.[30]

On 7 October, as a contribution to the medical review, Heath's solicitor sent a copy of Fielding-Johnson's statement to the home secretary together with a letter from Bessie Heath outlining the difficulty of Heath's birth and the fact that her uncle had been sent to a mental institution. Heath also suggested to his mother that she tell Near about the 'Johnstone' episode when he was at school (possibly a reference to the incident with 'Jeanette') as well as 'several other events of a similar nature which you may be able to recall'. Heath was not keen to pursue it, but told his mother it was 'entirely up to you'.[31]

The medical enquiry had been automatically put in process by the Home Office. This was headed by Dr Hopwood, the superintendent of Broadmoor, and Dr Norwood East who was president of the Psychiatric Section of the Royal Society of Medicine, lecturer on crime and insanity at the Maudsley Hospital and co-author of *The Psychological Treatment of Crime*, which he had written with Dr William Henry Hubert. The doctors visited Heath at Pentonville on the afternoon of 9 October. Heath himself didn't see the point: 'My bet is that they are quite happy wth their present verdict and I'll lay you five to one that they don't alter it.'[32]

Hopwood and East consulted a broad variety of experts including the governor at Pentonville, the chaplain, Reverend G. W. Cleavely and Dr Liddell the medical officer, as well as Dr Grierson, Dr F. H. Taylor from Brixton and Dr Young from Wormwood Scrubs. They also interviewed the six warders who had supervised Heath twenty-four hours a day since his conviction. They had two prolonged interviews with Heath himself and studied the case documents. Again Heath said he had little memory of what had taken place at the time of the two murders. The doctors felt that this was not due to any sort of mental disease or defect. They thought that it may be that the details of the crimes were so horrific that Heath had effectively shut them out of his consciousness. Hopwood and East saw no reason to stop the execution on medical grounds.[33]

On the same day as the medical review, Rosemary Tyndale-Biscoe, one of the two female jurors at the trial, wrote a letter to the home secretary, Mr Chuter Ede, enclosing a petition voicing the concerns of several members of the jury who had served on the trial with her. She suggested, 'You might give consideration to the law of Insanity 1843, to bring it more up to date with regard to modern knowledge and conditions. We found the responsibility of finding the verdict extremely hard. May I please add my petition for the future abolition of the death penalty?'[34]

On 11 October, Chuter Ede wrote in green ink across Heath's file, 'The law must take its course.'[35] This was telegrammed to Mr Lawton, the governor at Pentonville, who then informed Heath that Mr Ede would not intervene with the process of the law; he would be executed at 9 a.m. on Wednesday 16 October.

Reading of the results of the medical enquiry in the newspapers, Mrs Tyndale-Biscoe wrote to Chuter Ede again, further outlining her concerns, not just about Heath's case, but highlighting how the law in its present form was unable to properly assess cases which focused on psychiatric issues.

I now read in the public press that Heath is not to be reprieved. In my view the law urgently requires review in the light of modern psychological science, and as a juror carefully following the trial and medical evidence and also the discussion by the jury after it and before verdict, I feel Heath's case comes within the category of cases requiring such review.

Though as the law now stands it was no doubt my duty to concur in the verdict, I feel and I believe there is a widespread feeling among the public, that reconsideration of the law is overdue and meanwhile this man should be reprieved pending such reconsideration.[36]

The letter was acknowledged, but the sentiment ignored. Mrs Tyndale-Biscoe then sent an anonymous letter to Heath in Pentonville. 'Whether under the regulations he will ever see it, I do not know. But I shall go on praying for him.'[37]

The days before the execution were filled with almost ritualistic preparation, much of it behind the scenes, with the public as well as Heath unaware of the process. On 14 October, a messenger from the Home Office left Whitehall with a small box containing a rope specially made for executions by John Edginton & Sons in the Old Kent Road. The rope was signed for by the governor of Pentonville, Mr Lawton, and then kept in a safe until 4 p.m. on the afternoon before the execution. Two ropes were always supplied, a new one and a used one. Most hangmen favoured the used ropes as there was less stretch in them and this resulted in a more accurate drop.

Heath's solicitor drew up his will, with two of the 'deathwatch' guards acting as witnesses. In a letter to his father, Heath particularly requested that after he died, he wanted any remaining money to be given to his brother to help get his 'A' licence. Like his brother, Mick Heath had recently failed his matriculation exams and Heath felt that the focus on him must have been the reason. His beloved caterpillar badge, which would be forwarded with his effects from the police, he left to his mother. Despite pressure from them, he persisted in refusing to see either of his parents before he died.

> *I want my mother to remember me as she last saw me outside. I do not want her to see me as a man condemned to death for murder. I hope she will always remember me as the son she knew some years ago, and will forget the situation in which I now find myself.*[38]

Albert Pierrepoint, the hangman and his assistant, Harry Kirk, also arrived at 4 p.m. the day before the execution. This time of arrival had been designated in the days when hangmen would get drunk the night before the execution and either made mistakes in their work or didn't turn up. Pierrepoint had served as an executioner since 1931, his father and his uncles having served in the same role; it was almost a family business. From the mid-1940s Pierrepoint would become something of a celebrity. As well as executing several British murderers – including Evans, Christie, Haigh, Derek Bentley and Ruth Ellis – he also executed over 200 Nazi war criminals in the autumn of 1946.

Pierrepoint was given Heath's statistics, but also looked through the 'Judas Hole' in the door of the condemend cell, so that he could assess Heath's physique. The execution shed was just next door, a small room painted green with trapdoors set in the floor. These trapdoors had two hinged leaves that were bolted on the underside. To one side of the doors was a lever; when this was released, the bolts were drawn back and the trapdoor opened. A cotter pin acted as a security device to prevent the lever being pushed by accident. A set of stairs to the side of the execution chamber connected it to the pit below.

Pierrepoint tested the equipment, using a sandbag to calculate the drop using the 'Home Office Table of Drops'. He adjusted the length of the drop tailored to Heath's weight and stature. The sack was left overnight to stretch the rope.

That evening, Violet Van Der Elst arrived at Merton Hall Road in her cream and black Rolls-Royce and told Bessie Heath, 'I've come to make a last effort to save your boy.' Mrs Van Der Elst was the daughter of a coalman but had become a successful businesswoman by developing Shavex, the first brush-less shaving cream, amassing a huge personal fortune in the process. As well as standing three times, unsuccessfully, as a Labour MP, she was a vehement opponent of capital punishment and had campaigned against the death penalty for years. After talking to Heath's parents she drove to the Home Office and insisted on speaking to the home secretary. When she was told this was not possible, she left him a note outlining the incident at Venlo and the difficulty of Heath's birth. She also stated that his parents did not appear at the trial as Heath had told them that if they did, he would plead guilty.[39]

Isaac Near tried one last time to persuade Heath to see his parents before he died, but he was adamant. He didn't want to see them because he didn't want to break down at this stage. Near felt that Heath didn't seem worried by the prospect of his own death and was resigned to his fate.[40] A gambler to the last, he spent his last hours playing poker with the guards for imaginary stakes, as he wasn't allowed any money.[41] After Near left him for the last time that night, Heath sent him a note to thank him for his professionalism and his friendship.

> *I don't know what time they open where I'm going, but I hope the beer is better than it is here.*[42]

Next morning, Pierrepoint was woken at 6.30 by the warder who shared his quarters and checked that the rope was in the correct position at the right height for Heath, 5 feet 11 inches. The sandbag was put in the corner of the pit, where there was also a stretcher to be used after the execution was completed. Pierrepoint drew a 'T' in chalk to mark where Heath's shoes would be aligned. He edged out the cotter pin so that it was only just in place – this would only save a fraction of a second, but it all helped to make the job faster. Throughout all their preparations, Pierrepoint and Kirk barely spoke, and if they did, only in a whisper, as Heath was in the condemned cell next door, unaware that the execution chamber had been right next to him since he had arrived in

Pentonville. The door was hidden behind a wardrobe.
Pierrepoint took great pride in his professionalism and attention to detail:

> [The] job had to go to a perfect rhythm, with full under-
> standing all round, as silently and well timed as a team of
> commandos hijacking a German general from his own HQ.
> That is craftsmanship.[43]

Pierrepoint and Kirk then went for a breakast of bacon and
eggs.

That morning there was a crowd of 3,000 people outside
Pentonville, mostly women 'with shopping baskets and children in prams'. There were also eighteen press photographers. Extra police had been arranged to deal with the
expected crowds. The 100-yard drive between the main road
and the prison was cordoned off by the police. At 8.55 a.m.
Mrs Van der Elst arrived in her Rolls-Royce. Dressed in
mourning clothes, she distributed handbills urging the abolition of the death penalty. Headed 'The Fresh Evidence', Mrs
Van Der Elst's leaflets claimed that Heath was not responsible
for his actions. She had visited Mrs Heath the previous
evening and had been told that when he was born, Heath's
brain was 'terribly injured' and that his parents thought he
would not survive. Mrs Van Der Elst claimed that 'this man
was a possessed madman and should have been sent to
Broadmoor'.[44] The leaflets were snatched by the crowd and
flung high in the air, falling 'like a snowstorm' on the crowd
which swarmed around her car. The car in conjunction with
the crowd then started to cause a traffic jam, so a police
inspector, Thomas James, told Mrs Van Der Elst that she was
causing an obstruction and must move on.[45]

In the condemned cell, unaware of the commotion outside,

Heath had risen early and was permitted to dress in the new grey, chalk-striped suit that he had worn for his trial. The prison around him continued its normal routine and the other prisoners carried on with their regular tasks, the prison authorities doing their utmost for the execution to take place as discreetly as possible. Prisoners normally occupied near the execution shed were given additional exercise in a yard remote from it. The prison clock was disconnected for the hour of nine.[46]

Just before 9 a.m., Pierrepoint and Kirk waited outside the condemned cell with Harold Gedge, the deputy under-sherriff, Mr Lawton the governor, two senior prison officers and the prison chaplain, Reverend Cleavely. Seconds before 9 a.m., the door was opened quickly and Pierrepoint went straight up to Heath, putting his hands behind his back and strapping his wrists as another door in the cell was opened to the execution chamber for the first time. On this occasion Pierrepoint used a special strap made of pliant pale calf-leather that he only used about a dozen times when 'I had a more than formal interest in this particular execution'.[47] He told Heath, 'Follow me.'

Heath walked seven paces into the execution chamber with the noose straight ahead of him. The two prison officers gently stopped him on the 'T' marked on the trapdoors so that his feet were positioned across the division between them. As Harry Kirk tied Heath's legs with the ankle strap, Pierrepoint looked him in the face, eye to eye, 'that last look'.[48] Pulling the white cap from his breast pocket he drew it over Heath's head. He then reached for the noose, pulling it over the cap. The noose was not knotted, but the rope ran through a metal eye. In seconds, Pierrepoint tightened the noose to his right, pulled a rubber washer along the rope to hold it and darted to his left, pulling out the cotter pin with one hand and pulling the lever with the other. There was a snap as the falling doors opened and Heath's body dropped into the pit. His neck was thrown back and his spinal column was severed instantaneously.

His body hung lifeless, swinging to stillness. Pierrepoint estimated that the average time it took from entering the condemned cell to pulling the lever was twelve seconds. But he had done it in seven.

The notice of execution with declarations from Harold Gedge the deputy under-sherriff and Dr Liddell was posted outside the prison gates at 9.25 a.m. Mrs Van Der Elst turned to a police officer near her and shouted, 'You swine. I remember you. You do your damnedest. Why did they hang that young man? You do not care a damn.'

She was charged with obstruction to boos and jeers from the crowd. Police officers forced her back in the car, one officer stepping on the running board and directing her chauffeur to Caledonian Road Police Station to be formally charged. At the station she was asked if she had any other witness to call on her behalf, to which she replied, 'Yes, my chauffeur.' Asked the chauffer's name she couldn't remember. After some time, she said, 'Jackson.' She was charged £2 for obstructing a public highway. She emphatically denied that she had sworn at a police officer.

Twenty minutes after he was hanged, Madame Tussaud's opened and Heath's wax figure was already on display in the Chamber of Horrors. The figure was dressed in sports jacket and flannels, similar to the ones he had worn at the police court hearings, but Bernard Tussaud, an ex-RAF serviceman himself during the First World War, would not permit the model of Heath to wear the RAF tie that Heath himself had worn in court for the first two days of the trial. A blue and white striped tie was found from the stocks at the museum.[49] When the museum opened its doors that morning, Heath's body was still hanging within the precincts of Pentonville Prison.[50]

The body was left hanging for over an hour. There was no reason for this last ignominy, it was a directive left over from the time when bodies were publicly exposed on a gibbet. This practice was not to be outlawed until 1949. Pierrepoint himself 'had no heart for it', nor did he approve of having to measure Heath's body after death, carefully logging in the official register the dimensions of the distortion of his body. With the spinal cord now severed, Heath's neck had stretched by two inches.[51] After the allotted time, Pierrepoint returned to the execution hut.

I stared at the flesh I had stilled. I had further duties to perform, but no longer as executioner. I had been nearest to this man in death and I prepared him for burial. As he hung I stripped him. Piece by piece I removed his clothes. It was not callous, but the best rough dignity I could give him, as he swung to the touch, still hooded in the noose. He yielded his garments without the resistance of limbs . . . In London there was always a post-mortem, and he had to be stripped entirely and placed on a mortuary stretcher. But in common courtesy I tied his empty shirt around his hips. [Harry Kirk] had fixed the tackle up above. I passed a rope under the armpits of my charge, and the body was hauled up a few feet. Standing on the scaffold with the body now drooping, I removed the noose and the cap, and took his head between my hands, inclining it from side to side to assure myself that the break had been clean. Then I went below and [Kirk] lowered the rope. A dead man, being taken down from execution is a uniquely broken body whether he is a criminal or Christ, and I received this flesh, leaning helplessly into my arms, with the linen round his loins, gently with the reverence I thought due to the shell of any man who has sinned and suffered.[52]

At 11.45 that morning an inquest was held within the walls of the prison chaired by the St Pancras coroner, Dr Bentley Purchase. Ten jurors were sworn in. James Liddell, the medical officer, stated that Heath's death by judicial execution had been instantaneous, his neck severed between the second and third vertebrae.[53] After a short consultation with his fellow jurors, the foreman then requested if they might view the body. Even in death people were curious to look at him, to see if they could read any clue in his handsome features to the horrors he had committed. Repelled by this request, Dr Bentley Purchase informed the jury that this would not be necessary.[54]

Thorough to the last, in the final act of their relationship of hunter and quarry, Heath's body was identified by Reg Spooner. He was then buried in an unmarked grave within the precincts of the prison with no ceremony.

At lunchtime, Spooner met Pierrepoint in a bar near Leicester Square.[55] After a few drinks, Spooner turned to him and asked, 'How did he go?' Pierrepoint was quite startled. Ever the professional, Spooner had never asked before (and would never ask again) what had happened during the last moments on the gallows. Pierrepoint said that Heath had faced death bravely with no fuss. He had walked calmly to the scaffold, like a pilot facing what he himself might have called a 'one-way Op'.

When the governor asked if he had any last request – perhaps a shot of whisky – Heath said that he would like one. As Mr Lawton turned to organize it, Heath, a player to the last, added, 'While you're about it, sir, you might make that a double.'[56]

CHAPTER TWENTY-THREE
Mrs Heath

THE *PEOPLE*, 29 OCTOBER 1946

I had a son called Neville, but he was not the man who was responsible for two brutal murders. I have read that my boy was a fiend, cold-blooded and calculating. I have heard him described as a monster. I do not believe it.

He did murder, I know that. He himself knew that he committed both crimes although he could never understand how he had come to do so. To him, everything connected with those poor girls was hazy, their deaths occurred while he was mentally 'blacked-out'. I am absolutely convinced that the Neville Heath who committed those awful crimes was a different man from the handsome, laughing son of mine who used to carry me off to the pictures or tease me gaily about my new dress.

The last time I saw him was in Brixton prison when he was awaiting trial. I still cannot believe that was the same boy. To me, my Neville was the joking young man, always ready for a prank, who was yet in deadly earnest about getting his 'B' licence to fly a plane. His failure to get the licence helped to turn his brain – of that I am convinced. Up to that moment he may well have been wild and he may have made foolish mistakes, but he would not have wilfully harmed anyone.

He rang me up that Wednesday afternoon, I remember. 'I think I'll just nip smartly home and collect my laundry,' he said. And he told me he had won his 'B' licence. People have said that in not telling me his application had been refused, Neville was just betraying those traits of cunning and deceit with which his character has been blackened. That is not true. He lied because he did not want to hurt me by telling me of his failure. And, on the doorstep, he kissed me goodbye.

He was always like that – kind and considerate to both his father and me. I remember once, when he was about twelve, his father was in hospital undergoing an operation. I took Neville to the cinema to keep his mind off the matter, because I could see that he was unusually upset and obviously worrying. Suddenly, in the middle of the film, he burst out crying and I had to take him home. He had been worrying over his dad and keeping that worry to himself until it was too great for him to bear any longer.

As a child, he was as normal as any other small boy . . . full of fun and ready to play a childish prank. He would do 'stunts' on his bicycle and he was wrapped up in sport. The mile record he set up at his school has still not been broken.

Yet, despite his natural dare-devilry, he was a wonderfully kind youngster. Never once did he forget a birthday and always I could be sure that he would turn up with some little present, bought from his own pocket money, which he knew I particularly wanted.

I never carried a glass mirror in my handbag and Neville

as a schoolboy knew this. On my birthday he presented me with a steel mirror contained in a leather case. 'There you are, Mum. You won't be afraid of breaking that.' Even when he was in prison awaiting trial he remembered my birthday and sent me a telegram. He also wired on his father's birthday.

It has been said that as a small boy he was cruel to animals and that he once attacked a little girl so badly with a ruler that she had to be taken home in a taxi cab. Frankly I do not know of this incident and neither does his headmaster, who has nothing but good to say of him. Surely I, his mother, would have heard of this, if it had happened.

When he was about eight, he longed for a puppy. One day I bought him Doodle, a mongrel, for half a crown. He came rushing in from school that day. 'Mum, did you get me that puppy?' he asked excitedly. I can still see his blue eyes alight with anticipation as he flung his schoolbooks aside and tore up to me. I had the puppy hidden under a pile of mending in my lap and told him that I had not been able to buy it. His whole face fell . . . until the puppy wriggled out and he picked it up and cuddled it in his face.

I do agree with certain statements about my boy and those are in his attitude towards pain and fear. He would not show fear and though he hated the mere thought of inflicting pain – either mental or physical – on others, he was not afraid of it for himself. One day he came home from school with his wrist bandaged. When I asked him what was wrong, he replied airily: 'Oh, just put my wrist out a bit, that's all.' Then he ate an enormous lunch and went off without even mentioning that he had a broken wrist and was going to hospital to have it set. He was always like that – cool and contemptuous of his own feelings, and considerate towards others. Once, I remember Mick, his young brother – who adores him still – excitedly demonstrating a rugby tackle on

Neville who was then about sixteen and pretty hefty. The
pair fell in a heap on the drawing-room floor. Neville was up
in a flash and almost in tears because he thought that Mick, in
tackling him, had hurt himself. The death of little Carol, the
brother between Mick and himself, affected Neville considerably. He was only about six at the time, but I remember
how grief-stricken he was. When Mick was born, he was
delighted because he now had a young brother to look after.

My son did wrong in the eyes of the world, but the world
also did him much wrong. He adored his young wife and
baby son, and was deeply affected when they parted. Though
his school record was not brilliant, he worked hard when he
had to and his friends have never ceased to speak well of him.
Even his days at borstal were coloured by happy memories
because there he was loved and respected by all. The fact that
he returned during the war to speak to the boys has been
mentioned as an example of his arrogance. That is ridiculous
– not only was he invited to speak but the governor during
his time wrote to me only this month to say how much he
appreciated Neville's help at Hollesley Bay.

It was his wish to die, knowing the only alternative was to
be confined and watched over for the rest of his life. And
both his father and I are still proud of him because we know
that he died bravely and, to the end, tried every way to spare
us suffering. In one of his last letters he wrote, 'As I see it, this
last journey is just one more Op. This time it's destination
unknown and Method of Travel Uncertain.' Those are the
things I remember about my son – the good things that every
mother remembers.

Everyone was more than kind to us in our trouble. I have
nothing but praise for the kindness shown to me by both the
police and the prison authorities. Our friends stood by us.
We have received hundreds of letters expressing sympathy
from complete strangers, and people in the district whom I

hardly knew have crossed the road to tell me how they believed in Neville.

In the Bible we learn that Christ cast out devils and I believe that at the time my son did those awful deeds, he was, in the true sense of the phrase, possessed by a devil. I can only hope and pray that soon the psychiatrists will have learned how to do as Christ did – and cast out devils from other unfortunate young men.

Mrs Bessie Heath[1]

AFTERWORD

The return of the soldier is a potent myth.

In 1946, many men returning to Britain from the various war-scarred parts of the globe had been changed by what they had witnessed and what they had done. At the same time many of the homes and families that they had idealized in their dreams throughout years of separation and suffering were now no longer intact; everything was in a state of flux, everything changed. Added to this, the whole concept of Churchillian 'victory at all costs' was tempered by revelations of genocide, mass rape, starvation, torture and the deadly power of a devastating new bomb.

Approximately 60 million people were killed in the Second World War[1] and at least as many who survived were bruised and shattered by it, servicemen and women, their spouses and their children. Many lived with the legacy of this trauma for years to come – and some continue to do so, though their number now dwindles year on year.

To date, the story of Neville Heath has been the preserve of sensational and often lurid true-crime anthologies. It has been consigned to history as a sex crime, in the tradition of Jack the Ripper and paving the way for Haigh, Christie and later horrors. But examined in the context in which they happened, perhaps the murders are uniquely a product of their time and place – not a simple tabloid tale of sex and sadism, but a much more complex story of class, aspiration and damage; of damaged individuals in a damaged world. In this light, Heath might also be counted as a casualty of historical forces beyond his control – shaped, defined and broken by his experiences in the war that had just ended. In turn, Margery Gardner and Doreen Marshall became further casualties, in Heath's hands, of the early days of peace.

After the death of her mother, Margery Gardner's daughter Melody had been formally adopted by her grandmother in Sheffield and given her mother's maiden name, in order to protect her from the extraordinary interest that the case elicited at the time. Mrs Wheat was also determined that Melody's errant father should have nothing to do with her upbringing. Two weeks after Heath was executed, Peter Gardner married Kathleen Wyard. But this marriage was to be short-lived; Peter died from cirrhosis of the liver on 1 May 1947, the inevitable outcome of his alcoholism.[2]

As a young girl, Melody accepted that she was an orphan like many children of her generation who had lost parents during the war. She and her grandmother lived together in Sheffield at Oakholme Road, with her uncle Gilbert visiting in the holidays from the various schools where he was teaching. But as she grew to maturity, Melody became more and more curious about her mother and began to ask her grandmother questions. Why was her name different, for instance, than her mother's that was carved on her gravestone in the local cemetery? Mrs Wheat and Gilbert, with the best of intentions, tried to protect young Melody from the truth for as long as possible. They had done their best to put Margery's death behind them, never giving interviews and never discussing it at home. Eventually, having been repeatedly pestered by Melody, Mrs Wheat broke down in tears and told her the story of her mother's tragic death. Now that she knew, Mrs Wheat hoped that that would be the end of the matter. But Melody was by then a curious adolescent and desperate to find out more about the mother she barely remembered, but missed intensely.

In 1960, Melody was sixteen years old. One weekend she was staying with a school friend in Sussex and the two young women decided to go to London to see the sights. Arriving at Victoria Station, Melody happened to be browsing the railway bookstall and picked up a book with a garish cover, *London After Dark* by Fabian of the Yard, full of salacious crimes of sex and murder. Flicking through the book, she read, for the first time, the story of her mother's death in graphic details gleaned from police gossip and tabloid newspapers, much of it inaccurate:

> It was known to police observers on the West End scene that Marjorie [*sic*] Gardner was by no means unacquainted with such brutal and humiliating activities. Something went amiss, and Heath carried his indulgences too far. Marjorie Gardner died of haemorrhage, stabbed internally with the haft of a hunting whip.[3]

The girl was devastated. Not just by the extraordinary brutality of her mother's death, but to read of her in this context stunned her to the very core. This was not the image of her dearly missed mother that she had imagined so often. Still in shock, her friend suggested that they carry on and look at the sights – Buckingham Palace, Trafalgar Square, Harrods, Madame Tussaud's. It might take Melody's mind off things.

At Madame Tussaud's, the girls entered the Chamber of Horrors, and whether she knew she was actively seeking him out there or not, Melody came face to face with the wax figure of Neville Heath, the man who had murdered her mother. She stared into his blank blue eyes. For Melody, the whole experience was deeply traumatic and one from which it would take her years to recover.

Returning home from the weekend, Melody went upstairs alone and locked herself in the bathroom. She filled the bath, feeling that all she wanted to do was slip under the water, relieve herself of this extraordinary, heart-aching pain and die.[4]

After Doreen Marshall's death, relations between her family were never the same again. Grace Marshall couldn't forgive her surviving daughter Joan for not accompanying Doreen down to Bournemouth that summer. Worse still, Joan couldn't forgive herself. She divorced her husband Charles in 1947 but went on to marry again in 1948 to a divorcé from Harrow, Reginald Adams, the father of three young sons. In 1954, she was delighted to have a child of her own, a girl she named Julia. But now a frail and nervous woman, Joan suffered from anxiety for the rest of her life. Throughout Julia's childhood, Joan stifled her daughter – always checking on her, making sure she was safe. As Julia grew into her teens during the sixties, her mother's controlling behaviour seemed suffocating. The world was rapidly changing and yet her mother wanted to keep her cossetted from it, wrapped in maternal cotton wool. It was only in her twenties that Joan revealed to Julia that the reason that she worried about her so intensely was that her sister had been murdered years before.[5]

Charles and Grace Marshall moved out of Woodhall Road,

with all its terrible memories, to a house in Stanmore. Grace died in 1967 and her husband in 1973. They were both cremated at Breakspear Crematorium in Ruislip. Tragically, Joan lived with the self-imposed burden of responsibility for Doreen's death for the rest of her life, over half a century. She died in Wycombe General Hospital on 14 August 1998.

Doreen is the only member of the family to rest in Pinner Cemetery. The grave, no longer tended, has weathered and declined over the decades. At the head of the grave there is a small bird-bath with a little stone bird, set there to encourage sparrows to drink from it, chosen perhaps by Doreen's parents wishing their daughter some company. At the foot of the grave, an inscription quotes the American poet, James Whitcomb Riley, from a poem perhaps read at Doreen's funeral, 'She Is Just Away'.

In 2012, the grave was registered by the Commonwealth War Graves Commission and will be tended by them if it falls further into disrepair.

In 1954, Reg Spooner had served thirty years in the police force with a series of celebrated convictions behind him, but none better remembered than his arrest of Neville Heath. That year he was appointed head of the Flying Squad and became one of the most recognized officers in the force. In 1958 he was appointed deputy commander. But after years of chain smoking, he was diagnosed with lung cancer in 1962. Knowing he was dying, Spooner carried on working as best he could. A former Scotland Yard colleague of Spooner's said that 'everyone knew that his work was his whole life. He had no other real interests. Retiring him because of ill health would have hastened his end.'[6]

Spooner finally died at St Thomas' Hospital just before midnight on 18 September 1963. When the night sister telephoned his wife to give her the news, she gently asked if they might have the cornea of his eyes to give sight to a blind

person. 'Oh, yes,' said Myra, 'Reg would have liked that.'
More than one thousand police officers of all ranks attended
his funeral.[7]

According to his wife, Spooner always talked with great
sympathy about the ordeal that Heath's family had experienced during and after the trial. As his brother had wished,
Mick Heath joined the RAF in January 1947 but found his
time in the service uncomfortable as corporals in primary
training would ask, 'Any relation to Neville?' as soon as
they heard his name. On a trip to Blackpool, he also went
to a wax museum and found himself staring at a figure of his
brother standing amongst a collection of ghouls in the
Chamber of Horrors. At night, when his RAF colleagues
went off to meet girls, Mick stayed behind in the barracks,
worried that he too might have inherited some element of
madness that had affected his brother.[8] He was discharged
from the RAF in 1949. In 1955, he married Irene Lovejoy,
a widow, some years older than him. William Heath died of
heart disease in 1956. Subsequently, Mick, his wife and his
mother moved back to Ilford together where Mick worked
as a telecommunications engineer. In 1982 Bessie Heath
died at the Mayflower Hospital in Billericay at the age of
ninety-one. Mick died of cancer two years later at St Bart's
Hospital in Smithfield.

In South Africa, Elizabeth Armstrong rebuilt her life,
taking a job as a dentist's receptionist and planning her
marriage to her fiancé. Following Heath's execution, she
expressed no bitterness towards him for she felt that 'there
[was] so much good in him'.[9]

> He came into my life and went out again, leaving me slightly
> bewildered. It seems like a beautiful dream that turned
> suddenly into a ghastly nightmare. I loved him desperately
> when I ran away and married him against my parents' wishes.

But at all costs little Robert must never know the truth.
Every photograph I had of Neville I have destroyed. Every
letter I have burned . . . I pray that all the tragedy of the past
may be buried in the passing of time.[10]

In 1947, Elizabeth married a young widower with two young
children of his own. He had a distinguished war service and
had spent three years in a prison camp in Germany having
been captured at Tobruk. Together he and Elizabeth put the
past behind them and never discussed her former husband.
They enjoyed a long and happy marriage until Elizabeth's
death in 1990. Her son by Heath went on to have a successful
career and a happy marriage with children and grandchildren
of his own, the horrors of 1946 a dim, distant memory; a
world away in a different country, another century.

In 1939, when Gilbert Wheat was going off to war, he
discussed with his mother all his hopes for the future if he
were fortunate enough to return: to marry, to settle down
and (he was very specific about this) to have four children.
    After the end of the war and the subsequent loss of his
sister, Gilbert committed himself to life as a schoolmaster and
went on to run his own school. He was a kindly, inspirational
figure who combined an irreverent disrespect for petty rules
with strong, traditional values. His mother, Mrs Wheat, died
in 1963 and his niece Melody married an army officer some
years later. With no wife or children of his own, when she
was later widowed, Gilbert took Melody and her children
into his home and they remained a close-knit family for many
years. In the absence of his sister Margery, Gilbert selflessly
committed himself to help raise Melody's four children,
fulfilling his own prophecy of a generation before. He died in
2010 at the age of ninety-three.

★ ★ ★

Despite the brutality and violence that dominates the story of Neville Heath, it is the seemingly insignificant details that seem most profoundly to articulate the sense of loss, that break through the patina of sixty-odd years to pierce our hearts: a leopardette coat, a powder compact with a cracked mirror, a caterpillar badge.

Fragile, precious and fraught with danger, 'life depends on a silken thread'.

Sean O'Connor
London, 2013

APPENDIX
Heath's Last Letters

Pentonville Prison

Tuesday, 15th October 1946

My dear Dad,
Very many thanks indeed for your letter.

I saw Near yesterday afternoon and understand that he told you the news [about the failure of the medical review]. *He also tried very hard to persuade me to see you. With regard to this, I know you'll understand how I feel about it and I think it far better if we just make a clean break without farewells etc. I've always hated being seen off on journeys and this I regard as just another journey, to somewhere I don't know and by a method of transport that I don't understand. To my very limited intelligence it is nothing more than that — just another 'op' — and like all 'ops' it may prove to be quite exciting.*

I'm taking with me many pleasant memories of a very crowded thirty years. Into my crowded hours I have crammed much. A lot I regret bitterly and a lot I am thankful for – but probably the outstanding thing of all is the unselfish love and loyalty of my parents. You, who have both suffered so much, have been splendid and I can only say – thanks!

I have instructed Near to send you £60 which is for Mick. You know what I want him to do with it if it is possible. The thought that I can make that possible and the knowledge that you will carry out my wishes will make me very happy and satisfied.

I have made a new will today leaving everything to Mick with you as Trustee. This is just in case any one decides to prove an old will of mine in South Africa.

Near has my instructions and a note of authority as well, so he will not prove this will unless the other one is produced.

Any money that mother has of mine will of course, go to Mick, and my personal effects from here will be sent to you and you will hand them to him. There should be about £10 from here. I think mother has about £30 so he should have a little more than £100. I don't know much about law, but I've instructed Near to send that money off now, before my death, as a gift.

One other thing, and this I am most sincere and firm about. I was painted as black as the Ace of Spades in court and you will possibly get several accounts rendered you by smart Alecs who hope to get them paid by your kind-heartedness.

You are not, in any way, and have never been responsible for any of my debts. Apart from this money which I am giving away now, I shall not leave a halfpenny. You will please not pay any outstanding accounts of mine. Once again – you are not responsible for my debts.

Well, I think that is about all, except to thank you both from the very bottom of my heart for all you've done for me and to thank you for giving me all the golden opportunities that I have so shamelessly wasted.

The very best of luck to you always, and don't let Mick make my mistakes. Goodbye and bless you both.

Always yours,

Neville

Pentonville Prison

Tuesday, 15th October 1946

My dearest Mother,
You now know the news so there is very little for me to say. One thing I feel certain of is that Near did all in his power to get the verdict altered. The sentence, I don't give a damn about. I've written to Dad and shall write to Mick. Everything has been said, but I'd like you to know how terribly grateful I am for your never-failing love, loyalty and devotion. It has always been of such a quality that no other parents could hope to equal.

Both you and Dad are unique in the way of parents and to me your honesty, simplicity, faith and sheer guts stand out like a brilliant star. My only regret at leaving this world is that I have been so damned unworthy of you both.

I'm not religious – I never have been and I'm not going to start now (at least I'm no hypocrite) – but if there is any God, and I know you believe in that sort of thing, you both deserve all the love He can bestow on you.

Let Mick profit by my mistakes. Help him to get airborne and make a success of it. If there is anything he wants to know Ralph will help him. His address is First Officer Fisher, BOAC, Central Flying School, Aldermaston, Nr Reading, Wilts.

I've nothing else to say except cheerio and thanks for all you've done for me.

In spite of Near's pleadings, I have decided not to see either of you. Please understand won't you? My thoughts are with you and you have all my love always.

Let's carry this thing through to the end with the quiet dignity
that we've shown all through.
Goodbye and bless you darling Mother,
Always yours,

Nen

Pentonville Prison

Tuesday, 15th October 1946

My dear Mick,
Just a short note to let you know for the last time that your writing
is abominable and your spelling even worse.

I won't be seeing you again but perhaps in the days to come you'll
feel a friendly Gremlin ease your aircraft out of a sticky position. You
may recognise the touch.

You'll shortly be going into a damn good service. Your future is
up to you. Don't make the mistakes that I've made. If you get any
urges in the wrong direction just say to yourself 'Christ, I've seen the
result of those' and open your throttles and go round again. You
know what I mean.

Use King's Regulations and Air Council instructions as your
Bible and stick to it. If you do that you won't come unstuck. I'm
more qualified to give advice than anyone else I know because
I've learned all the lessons — and how! Now you take advantage
of them. Ralph will always help you, never be too shy to ask
him, so will any other Air Force pilot who knew me. You'll find
Air Force friendships mean something and they're not easily
broken.

Get your 'A' licence and go ahead. You can do great things, it's
in you and it's up to you to do something to make Mother and Dad
proud of you. By doing that, you'll be helping me as well.

Cheerio Mick and very many happy landings. Don't you bloody well let me down or I'll haunt you, and I've a feeling I can be a most unpleasant ghost.

Ever yours,

Nen

                                                            Pentonville Prison
Tuesday evening, 15th October 1946

My Dearest Mother,
First of all very many thanks for your cable and also for Mick's. I've written several letters to my friends and one more to Elizabeth, but I'd like the last to be written to you. I can't say more than I said in my previous letter but I meant it wholeheartedly.

I shall probably stay up reading tonight because I'd like to see the dawn again. So much in my memory is associated with the dawn — early morning patrols and coming home from night clubs. Well, it wasn't really a bad life while it lasted, and I've lots to think about.

Please don't mourn my going — I should hate it — and don't wear any black. I really mean that. Just wear your gayest colours and refer to me quite normally — that is the easiest way to forget.

So now I'll leave you. Cheerio, my dear, and very many thanks for everything.

All my love is with you both always.

Forever yours,

Nen[1]

ACKNOWLEDGEMENTS

I would like to thank the staff at the libraries and archives around the United Kingdom and in South Africa who have assisted me in my research. I am particularly indebted to the staff at The National Archives in Kew who have responded with patience and diligence to my many requests to have the various files relating to the case made available to study for the first time.

I am grateful to the London Metropolitan Archives, the London Library, the British Library, the British Newspaper Library at Colindale, the staff at the Archives of the Imperial War Museum, the RAF Museum at Hendon, the Museum of Wimbledon, Melvyn Foster at the Association of Wrens, Charlotte Burford and Julia Collins at Madame Tussaud's, Professor John Moxham at King's College Hospital, Martin Hayes at Worthing Library, Jonathan Oates at Ealing Library, the Lincolnshire County Archives, the Nottinghamshire County Archives, the Sheffield Local History Library, the *Sheffield Telegraph*, the *Harrow Observer* and the *Bournemouth Echo*. Peter Kazmierczak at Bournemouth Library provided guidance and provided photographs from the local history archive. Hazel Ogilvie was particularly helpful at the Local History Library in Harrow, researching the movements of the Marshall family during the war. Matthew Piggott at Surrey History Centre helped to investigate the archives of Rutlish School. I'm grateful to Graham W. Mills, a governor at Rutlish and the current headmaster, Mr A. Williamson, for allowing me access to the school archive. Peter Elliot at the RAF Museum in Hendon very kindly read and advised about the RAF sections.

In South Africa, I am indebted to Anne Clarkson, who accessed a large volume of new material relating to Heath's marriage and his tenure with the South African Air Force in the archives held in Johannesburg, Pretoria and Cape Town.

For access to the remaining evidence from the case at the Crime Museum – including Heath's suitcase, his 'escape scarf' and whip – I am indebted to Paul Bickley and Camilla O'Hare at New Scotland Yard. Crime historian and researcher, Keith Skinner, has been extremely helpful and encouraging as well as being a mine of information and contacts. He has generously shared his own documents and research about the case from his archive.

Donald Thomas, who wrote the last major study of Heath twenty-five years ago, shared his insights into the case and his memories of the period. Dr Paul Addison, Juliet Gardiner, Roger Hollinghurst, Alwyn Liddell, Matthew Lloyd, Don Minterne, Tim McInerny, David Pirie, Martin Ridgwell, Geoff Sherratt and René Weis all offered help and advice at various stages in the inception and writing of this book, for which I'm very grateful.

Despite the horrific nature of Heath's story, several people have welcomed me with great enthusiasm to the many buildings where significant events took place. Early on in my research, Jay and Lucy Dowle invited me to visit them at the Heaths' former home at Merton Hall Road, as did Julie Williams, who allowed me to visit the Marshall family home in Pinner. Liliya Guzheva, Jamison Firestone and Robert Field generously allowed me to visit the scene of the crime at the former Pembridge Court Hotel. In Bournemouth, Nick the caretaker at Tollard Court, allowed me to spend time in the former Tollard Royal Hotel where many of the interiors in the public spaces of the building have remained unchanged. I was also welcomed to the Norfolk Royale Hotel (the former Norfolk Hotel) by the current manager, Simon Scarborough. I'd like to thank Matt Evans who accompanied me on a trip to Bournemouth to visit the scene of the crime at Branksome Dene Chine. David McRae, the manager of the Strand Palace Hotel, showed me Room 506, which still remains, as well as providing photographs from the hotel archive.

Michael Suter kindly shared memories of his father with me. Julia Young, the niece of Doreen Marshall, has been hugely generous with her recollections of Doreen's parents and her sister, Joan. I am indebted to the remaining members of Neville Heath's family who, despite their reluctance to explore a difficult area of their family history, agreed to meet me to discuss it.

Jackie Malton has offered support, insight and practical help from the start of this venture for which I am very grateful. I'm also indebted to Sarah Waters for her help and advice. My agent, Judith Murray, has championed this book since she read my first tentative pages and I am grateful for her encouragement and support throughout. Mike Jones at Simon & Schuster enthusiastically embraced the idea and I have been greatly supported by Jo Whitford and Lindsay Davies who have worked with me on the text.

Rob Haywood has been patient, supportive and encouraging throughout the gestation and realization of this book for which I'm hugely grateful.

My greatest debt, though, is to Melody Gardner, who has not spoken publicly about her family history for nearly seventy years. Despite the painful material, Melody has embraced the revelations I have put before her with extraordinary fortitude and open-mindedness. She has offered unique insights into three generations of Sheffield women: her redoubtable grandmother, Betty Wheat, her mother Margery Gardner and, indeed, her own life. She has encouraged the writing of this book, whilst always retaining distance from it. For me, enabling Melody to read her mother's story from original documents, rather than filtered through biased and erroneous newspaper reports, has been a great privilege. I hope she feels that her mother's tragic story has been told honestly, fairly and – at last – with understanding and compassion.

FURTHER READING

Original documents relating to the investigation and trial held at the National Archives (TNA):

HO 144/22871
HO 144/22872
DPP 1/1522
DPP 1/1524
CRIM 1/1806
MEPO 3/2664
MEPO 3/2728
P COM 9/700

In South Africa, the files relating to Heath are held at the Cape Archives and Record Service and the National Archives Repository in Pretoria, as well as at the Offices of the Master of the High Court in Cape Town and Pretoria.

Books about Heath or which discuss the case:

Brock, Sydney, *The Life and Death of Neville Heath*, Modern Fiction Ltd, 1947

Byrne, Gerald, *Borstal Boy: The Uncensored Story of Neville Heath*, Gerald Byrne, Headline, 1946

Critchley, Macdonald (ed.), *The Trial of Neville George Clevely Heath*, Notable British Trials series, William Hodge, 1951

Hill, Paull, *Portrait of a Sadist*, Neville Spearman, 1960

Selwyn, Francis, *Rotten to the Core: The Life and Death of Neville Heath*, Routledge, 1988

Adamson, Iain, *The Great Detective: A Life of Deputy Commander Reginald Spooner of Scotland Yard*, Frederick Muller Ltd, 1966

Bennett, Benjamin, *Why Did They Do It?*, Howard B. Timmins, Cape Town, 1954

Bixley, William, *The Guilty and the Innocent*, Souvenir Press, 1957

Casswell, J. D., *A Lance for Liberty*, Harrap, 1961

Fabian, Robert, *London After Dark*, The Naldrett Press, 1954

Hoskins, Percy, *The Sound of Murder*, John Long, 1973

Morland, Nigel, *Hangman's Clutch*, Werner Laurie, 1954

Phillips, Conrad, *Murderer's Moon, Being Studies of Heath, Haigh, Christie and Chesney*, Associated Booksellers, 1956

Pierrepoint, Albert, *Executioner: Pierrepoint*, Harrap, 1974

Playfair, Giles, and Sington, Derrick, *Crime, Punishment and Cure*, Secker & Warburg, 1965

Playfair, Giles, and Sington, Derrick, *The Offenders: Society and the Atrocious Crime*, The Windmill Press, 1957

Root, Neil, *Frenzy! Heath, Haigh and Christie: The First Great Tabloid Murderers*, Preface Publishing, 2011

Simpson, Keith, *Forty Years of Murder: An Autobiography*, Harrap, 1978

Thomas, Donald, *Hanged in Error?*, Robert Hale, 1994

Webb, Duncan, *Crime Is My Business*, Frederick Muller, 1953

Britain at war (and after):

Allport, Alan, *Demobbed: Coming Home After the Second World War*, Yale, 2010

Beaton, Cecil, and Pope-Hennessy, James, *History Under Fire: 52 Photographs of Air Raid Damage to London Buildings, 1940–41*, B. T. Batsford, 1941

Beevor, Antony, *The Second World War*, Weidenfeld & Nicolson, 2012

Bigland, Eileen, *The Story of the WRNS*, Nicholson & Watson, 1946

Calder, Angus, *The People's War: Britain 1939–45*, Jonathan Cape, 1969

Costello, John, *Love, Sex and War*, Collins, 1985

Drummond, John D., *Blue for a Girl: The Story of the WRNS*, W. H. Allen, 1960

Edington, M. A., *Bournemouth and the Second World War*, Bournemouth Local Studies Publications, 1999

Faviell, Frances, *A Chelsea Concerto*, Cassell, 1959

Fussell, Paul, *Wartime: Understanding and Behaviour in the Second World War*, Oxford, 1989

Gardiner, Juliet, *The Blitz: The British Under Attack*, Harper Press, 2010

Gardiner, Juliet, *Wartime 1939–1945*, Headline, 2004

Garfield, Simon, *Our Hidden Lives*, Ebury Press, 2004

Hodgson, Vere, *Few Eggs and No Oranges*, Dennis Dobson, 1976

Kent, William (ed.), *An Encyclopaedia of London*, J. M. Dent & Sons Ltd, 1951

Kent, William, *The Lost Treasures of London*, Phoenix House Limited, 1947

Kershaw, Robert, *Never Surrender: Lost Voices of a Generation at War*, Hodder & Stoughton, 2009

Kynaston, David, *Austerity Britain 1945–51*, Bloomsbury, 2007

Lloyd George, David, *War Memoirs*, Ivor Nicolson & Watson, 1934

Lofthouse, Alistair, *Then and Now: The Sheffield Blitz, Operation Crucible*, ALD Design and Print, 2001

London Evening News, *Hitler Passed This Way: 170 Pictures from the London Evening News*, 1945

Longmate, Norman, *How We Lived Then: A History of Everyday Life During the Second World War*, Arrow Books, 1973

Malin, A. M., *The Villager at War: A Diary of Home Front Pinner 1939–1945*, The Pinner Association, 1995

Marley, David (ed.), *The Daily Telegraph Story of the War*, Hodder & Stoughton, 1944

Mathews, L. W., *Chelsea Old Church 1941–1950*, Buckenham & Son, 1957

Nicholson, Virginia, *Millions Like Us: Women's Lives in War and Peace, 1939–1949*, Viking, 2011

Plastow, Norman, *Safe as Houses: Wimbledon at War 1939–1945*, The Wimbledon Society, 2010

Price, Alfred, *Blitz on Britain: The Bomber Attacks on the United Kingdom 1939–1945*, Ian Allan Ltd, 1976

Priestley, J.B., *Britain Under Fire*, Country Life, 1941

Richards, E. M., *The Bombed Buildings of Britain*, The Architectural Press, 1947

Scott, Peggy, *British Women in War*, Hutchinson & Co, 1940

Turner, Barry, and Rennell, Tony, *When Daddy Came Home: How Family Life Changed Forever in 1945*, Pimlico, 1996

Waller, Maureen, *London 1945: Life in the Debris of War*, John Murray, 2004

Wyndham, Joan, *Love Is Blue: A Wartime Diary*, Heinemann, 1986

Ziegler, Philip, *London at War 1939–1945*, Pimlico, 2002

Zweiniger-Bargielowska, Ina, *Austerity in Britain: Rationing, Controls and Consumption 1939–1955*, Oxford, 2002

The Royal Air Force:

Beaton, Cecil, *Winged Squadrons*, Hutchinson, 1942

Bishop, Patrick, *Bomber Boys: Fighting Back 1940–1945*, Harper Perennial, 2008

Bishop, Patrick, *Fighter Boys: Saving Britain 1940*, Harper Perennial, 2004

Clark, Denis, *Tail End Charlie*, Lutterworth Press, 1946

Dahl, Roald, *Over to You: Ten Stories of Flyers and Flying*, Hamish Hamilton, 1945

David, Dennis 'Hurricane', *My Autobiography*, Grub Street, 2000

Falconer, Jonathan, *RAF Bomber Crewman*, Shire Publications, 2011

Francis, Martin, *The Flyer: British Culture and the Royal Air Force, 1939–1945*, Oxford University Press, 2008

Hastings, Max, *Bomber Command*, Michael Joseph, 1979

Kent, Gp. Capt. J. A., *One of the Few*, William Kimber & Co, 1971

Minterne, Don, *The History of 73 Squadron, Part 2: July 1937 to August 1939*, Tutor, 2000

Nichol, John, and Rennell, Tony, *Tail End Charlies: The Last Battles of the Bomber War 1944–45*, Viking, 2004

Simpson, William, *I Burned My Fingers*, Putnam, 1955

Wells, Mark K., *Courage and Air Warfare: The Allied Aircrew Experience in the Second World War*, Frank Cass, 2000

Wilson, Kevin, *Men of Air: The Doomed Youth of Bomber Command*, Phoenix, 2008

General:

Aulier, Dan, *Hitchcock's Secret Notebooks*, Bloomsbury, 1999

Behan, Brendan, *Borstal Boy*, Hutchinson & Co, 1958

Benton, Charlotte, Benton, Tim, and Wood, Ghislaine (eds), *Art Deco 1910–1939*, V&A Publications, 2003

Bournemouth, Ward Lock Red Guide, Nineteenth Edition, *c*.1950

Brock, Colin, *Rutlish School: The First Hundred Years*, Rutlish School, 1995

Brooke, Rupert, *Collected Poems*, Sidgwick & Jackson, 1918

Browne, Douglas G., and Tullet, E. V., *Bernard Spilsbury: His Life and Cases*, Harrap, 1951

Bryant, Margot, *As We Were: South Africa 1939–41*, Keartland Publishers, Johannesburg, 1974

Carswell, Donald, *The Trial of Ronald True*, Notable British Trials series, William Hodge, 1924

Cave, Herbert, *Practical Exercises in Spoken English*, Harrap, 1930

Chapman, Pauline, *Madame Tussaud's Chamber of Horrors*, Constable, 1984

Cooper, Artemis, *Cairo in the War 1939–45*, Hamish Hamilton, 1992

Coward, Noël, *Middle East Diary*, William Heinemann Ltd, 1944

Coward, Noël, ed by Payn, Graham and Morley, Sheridan, *The Noël Coward Diaries*, Weidenfeld & Nicolson, 1982

Crisp, Quentin, *The Naked Civil Servant*, Jonathan Cape, 1968

Eddleston, John J., *The Encyclopaedia of Executions*, John Blake, 2002

Farndale, Nigel, *Haw-Haw: The Tragedy of William and Margaret Joyce*, Macmillan 2005

Gibson, Ian, *The English Vice: Beating, Sex and Shame in Victorian England and After*, Duckworth, 1978

Gibson, Perla Siedle, *Durban's Lady in White: An Autobiography*, Aedificamus Press, 1991

Gunby, Norman, *A Potted History of Ilford*, published privately by the author, 1997

Hardy, Thomas, *Tess of the D'Urbervilles*, Osgood, McIlvaine & Co, 1895

Hollis, Christopher, *The Homicide Act*, Victor Gollancz, 1964

Honeycombe, Gordon, *Murders of the Black Museum*, John Blake, 2009

Inwood, Stephen, *A History of London*, Macmillan, 1998

Jones, Nigel, *Rupert Brooke: Life, Death and Myth*, Richard Cohen Books, 1999

Kerridge, Ronald, and Standing, Michael, *Worthing*, Black Horse Books, 2001

Lister, Moira, *The Very Merry Moira*, Hodder & Stoughton, 1969

Macaulay, Rose, *The World My Wilderness*, Collins, 1950

Morton, H. V., *In Search of South Africa*, Methuen & Co, 1948

Orwell, George, *The Collected Essays, Journalism and Letters of George Orwell*, Secker & Warburg, 1961

Orwell, George, *Inside the Whale and Other Essays*, Victor Gollancz, 1940

Procter, Harry, *The Street of Disillusion*, Revel Barker Publishing, 2010 (first published by Allan Wingate in 1958)

Read, Simon, *In the Dark: The True Story of the Blackout Ripper*, Berkley Books, New York, 2006

Reader's Digest, *Illustrated History of South Africa: The Real Story*, Reader's Digest Publishing, 1988

Scott, Sir Harold, *Scotland Yard*, Andre Deutsche, 1954

Spoto, Donald, *The Dark Side of Genius: The Life of Alfred Hitchcock*, Plexus, 1983

Walker, Eric A., *A History of Southern Africa*, Longmans Green, 1957

Weis, René, *Criminal Justice: The True Story of Edith Thompson*, Hamish Hamilton, 1988

Weisbord, M., and Simmonds, M., *The Valour and the Horror: The Untold Story of Canadians in the Second World War*, HarperCollins, 1991

Wells, A. W., *South Africa: A Planned Tour of the Country Today*, J. M. Dent & Sons, 1947

Wheat, Gilbert, *The Wheats of Sheffield*, B. A. Hathaway Press, 1996

Worthing, Ward Lock Red Guide, Eighth Edition (Revised), 1939–40

Young, Filson (ed.), *The Trial of Frederick Bywaters and Edith Thompson*, Notable British Trials, second edition 1951

Studies in Psychopathy:

Baron-Cohen, Simon, *Zero Degrees of Empathy: A New Theory of Human Cruelty*, Allen Lane, 2011

Cleckley, Hervey M., *The Mask of Sanity*, Plume Books, 1982

Hare, Robert D., *Without Conscience: The Disturbing World of the Psychopaths Amongst Us*, The Guildford Press, 1993

Hibbert, Christopher, *The Roots of Evil: A Social History of Crime and Punishment*, Weidenfeld & Nicolson, 1963

Ronson, Jon, *The Psychopath Test: A Journey Through the Madness Industry*, Picador, 2011

Storr, Anthony, *Human Aggression*, Pelican Books, 1970

Fiction inspired by Heath:

Hamilton, Patrick, *Mr Stimpson and Mr Gorse*, Constable, 1953

Hamilton, Patrick, *Unknown Assailant*, Constable, 1955

Hamilton, Patrick, *The West Pier*, Constable, 1951

La Berne, Arthur, *Goodbye Piccadilly, Farwell Leicester Square*, W. H. Allen, 1966

Mallanson, Todd, *Ladykiller*, Weidenfeld & Nicolson, 1980

Taylor, Elizabeth, *A Wreath of Roses*, Peter Davies, 1949

ENDNOTES

Foreword

1. *Daily Mail*, 28 September 1946.
2. *News of the World,* 29 September 1946.
3. From Detective Inspector George Henry Gates' statement quoted in Critchley (ed.), op. cit., p. 106.
4. *People,* 15 September 1946. The paper also added that the interest of the international press 'pales into insignificance before the morbid curiosity of women'.
5. *Daily Express,* 27 September 1945.
6. *News Chronicle,* 10 July 1945, p. 2.
7. In his Victory broadcast on 13 May 1945, Churchill thanked all the services for the part they had played in securing victory. There was, however, no mention of Bomber Command. Bomber Harris campaigned for the rest of his life

to have their achievements and sacrifices recognized. Harris commented that 'the bomber drops things on people and people don't like things being dropped on them, and the fighter shoots at the bomber who drops things. Therefore he is popular whereas the bomber is unpopular. It's as easy as that' (Bishop, *Fighter Boys,* p. xxxii). Only after years of campaigning has a monument to Bomber Command been unveiled in London in 2012, but the controversy continues.

8. Martin, *The Flyer,* p. 152.
9. *Holiday Camp* (1947) directed by Ken Annakin, produced by Sydney Box.
10. The *New Statesman and Nation* expressed little surprise at the increase in violent crimes perpetrated by ex-servicemen: 'They've been trained in lawlessness, ordered to behave like thugs and decorated for doing it . . . what do you expect?', 12 January 1946.
11. Byrne, *Borstal Boy.*
12. Brock, *The Life and Death of Neville Heath.*
13. Letter from James Hodge to Sir Theobald Mathew, Director of Public Prosecutions, 18 May 1951, TNA DPP 2/1522.
14. Taylor, *A Wreath of Roses,* 1949.
15. Early in *The West Pier,* the young psychopath Ralph Gorse ties a schoolgirl to a garden roller on a cricket pitch with a skipping rope, a reference perhaps to the incident reported in the press that Heath had beaten a girl so violently with a ruler that she had to be sent home. Gorse's malevolent adventures continue in *Mr Stimpson and Mr Gorse.* The last book, *Unknown Assailant,* ends with Gorse terrorizing a young woman and tying her up: 'He liked to tie women up in order to get the impression that they were at his mercy, and he also liked to be tied up by women and to feel that he was at theirs' (*Unknown Assailant,* Chapter 15, p. 130).
16. Morland, op. cit., p. 17.
17. Aulier, *Hitchcock's Secret Notebooks,* p. 544.

18. Spoto, *The Dark Side of Genius: The Life of Alfred Hitchcock*, p. 496. In Hitchcock's version Heath would be gay, obsessed with muscle magazines and, at one point, caught masturbating in bed by his mother – a classic Hitchcock anti-hero cut from the same cloth as Norman Bates.

19. According to Fast, Hitchcock said, 'I've just seen Antonioni's *Blow Up!* These Italian directors are a century ahead of me in terms of technique! What have I been doing all this time?' (Spoto, op. cit., p. 496).

20. The 1971 *Frenzy* was based on Arthur La Bern's *Goodbye Piccadilly, Farewell Leicester Square*. The novel is suffused with references to Heath. Though set in the 1960s, it focuses on a penniless, divorced and disillusioned pilot, Dick Blamey DSO, DFC and Bar, falsely accused of murder in an alien London – cleaner but duller than its heyday in the war years. 'This, he thought, is not the heart of London. It's the anus' (p. 27). Hitchcock goes even further in emphasizing the references to Heath in the script. At one point Hetty Porter (Billie Whitelaw) directly quotes a line that Heath had mentioned to Yvonne Symonds: 'He must have been a sexual maniac.'

21. UK Homicide Act (1957) Chapter 2, Part 1 (section 2: 'Persons Suffering from Diminished Responsibility'). Quoted in Hollis, *The Homicide Act*.

22. Orwell, 'Decline of the English Murder' in *Collected Essays Volume IV: In Front of Your Nose 1945–50*, p. 100, originally printed in *Tribune*, 15 February 1946.

23. Later, *The Sunday Mirror*.

24. Orwell, 'Raffles and Miss Blandish', *Collected Essays*, p. 247.

25. *Daily Mail*, 28 September 1946.

26. The National Archives of the UK (TNA): Detective Superintendent H. Lovell Dorset Constabulary, 18 July 1946, MEPO 3/2728.

27. Byrne, op. cit., p. 144.

28. Bixley, *The Guilty and the Innocent*, p. 112.

Prologue

1. The outline of the events at the Strand Palace Hotel is taken from three witness statements opened to the public for the first time in 2011 in a file held at the National Archives (TNA), DPP 2/1522. These are the statements of William Luff (22 June 1946), Thomas Paul (24 June 1946) and Pauline Miriam Brees (27 July 1946). Significantly, Pauline Brees' statement was taken a month after that of the two members of staff of the Strand Palace. Pauline was the widow of Squadron Leader Alec Brees, DFC, who had been killed in a flying accident on 23 August 1945.

2. Benton, Benton and Wood (eds.), *Art Deco 1910–1939*, pp. 217, 239. Bernard had a huge influence on the 'look' of inter-war London in terms of interior design. Having originally worked as a stage designer in Britain and the United States, as well as designing the interiors for the Strand Palace Hotel, he also designed the Cumberland Hotel, the Regent Palace Hotel and the Lyons Corner Houses throughout the 1920s and thirties.

3. Ibid., p. 238.

4. See Allport, *Demobbed*.

5. Thomas Paul says Armstrong was wearing underpants; Luff remembered him as being 'completely nude'. In his subsequent attacks on women, Heath also seems to have been naked. Paul claimed that Pauline was tied with 'a pair of braces or a tie' and Luff remembered a belt. Pauline herself recalls a handkerchief being used to bind her, which is more consistent with Heath's later behaviour.

6. Many newspapers and books further embellished this moment, claiming that Heath was unable to stop beating Pauline when Luff and Paul entered the room. The *News of the World*, 29 September 1946, stated: 'Heath stood over her in maniacal

frenzy and had to be forcibly restrained while [she] was set free.' In *Crime, Punishment and Cure*, Giles Playfair and Derrick Sington suggest that 'the hotel detectives . . . had to restrain Heath forcibly' (p. 78). There is no evidence for this manic behaviour in Luff, Paul or Brees' statements.

7. In his statement on 19 July 1946, TNA HO 144/22871, having interviewed her personally, Spooner wrote that Miss Brees 'appeared of the prostitute class' but later revised his opinion in his overview of the case on 2 October referring to her as 'a respectable young woman'.

8. Pauline Brees, 27 July 1946, TNA DPP 2/1522.

9. No professional production was playing at the theatre at the time as it played host to performances by students from RADA.

10. Dialogue quoted from Pauline Brees, 27 July 1946, TNA DPP 2/1522.

11. Critchley (ed.), *The Trial of Neville George Clevely Heath*, p. 169.

Chapter 1

1. From Clement Attlee's election victory speech 26 July 1945, quoted in Kynaston, *Austerity Britain 1945–51*, p. 76.

2. Entry for Thursday 26 July 1945, Coward, *The Noël Coward Diaries*, p. 36.

3. Kynaston, op. cit., p. 116.

4. *Evening Standard,* 7 June 1946.

5. Ibid.

6. All quotes *News of the World*, 9 June 1946.

7. Imperial War Museum Film Archive, MGH 214, V Day, 8 June 1946.

8. Mass Observation reports quoted in Kynaston, op. cit.,p. 115.

9. *Bournemouth Daily Echo*, 19 June 1946.

10. For details of the progress and challenges of rationing, see

Calder, *The People's War*, pp. 276–79 and 404–408, and Longmate, *How We Lived Then*, pp. 140–55.

11. Quoted in Allport, *Demobbed*, p. 119.
12. Frank Luff, Imperial War Museum Archive: No. 27267.
13. Kynaston, op. cit., p. 118.
14. *Daily Mail*, 1 June 1946.
15. *Daily Express*, 24 June 1946.

Chapter 2

1. *Daily Mirror*, 25 September 1946.
2. Nicholson, *Millions Like Us*, p. 144. Years later Christian Lamb called her memoirs *I Only Joined for the Hat* (Bene Factum Publishing, 2007).
3. Drummond, *Blue for a Girl*, p. 57.
4. Though 'jewellery, handbags, umbrellas and coloured fingernails are not uniform. Make-up, if worn, must not be obvious.' Drummond, op. cit., p. 57.
5. Drummond, op. cit., p. 151.
6. Bigland, *The Story of the WRNS*, p. 183.
7. Yvonne Symonds' evidence at the trial is available in Critchley (ed.), *The Trial of Neville George Clevely Heath*. A handwritten document taken from her statement at Worthing Police Station on 24 June 1946 and her testimony at the Police Court on 20 July 1946 are held in TNA CRIM 1/1806.
8. Wyndham, *Love Is Blue*, p. 10.
9. Crisp, *The Naked Civil Servant*, p. 96. Crisp remembered discussing the attractions of men in uniform with Margery Gardner in the window seat of a cafe in the Kings Road and commented waspishly, 'I should have guessed that she was a born murderee. She used to wear a leopardette coat.'
10. See Francis, *The Flyer*, p. 21.
11. Simpson, *I Burned My Fingers*, pp. 115–116.

12. 'Character of Witnesses', 24 July 1946, TNA MEPO 3/2728.

13. Re. Panama Club, including club rules and layout, see Solomon Joseph, 28 June 1946, TNA DPP 2/1522. Heath had become a member under the name of Armstrong on 20 February 1946 and claimed to be living at the RAF Club in Piccadilly.

14. Edward Louis Barton, 1 July 1946, TNA DPP 2/1522.

15. *News of the World*, 29 September 1946.

16. Nicholson, op. cit., p. 104.

17. Wyndham, op. cit., p. 103.

18. Elizabeth Wyatt, 29 June 1946, TNA DPP 2/1522.

19. Barbara Osborne, 21 June 1946, TNA DPP 2/1522.

20. Ward Lock Red Guide, *Worthing*, p. 22.

21. Ibid., p. 4.

22. *Worthing Herald*, 5 July 1946.

23. Heath himself had little time for the pictures. 'The cinema is mainly a place to go when you want to sit down.' Dr Young's handwritten report, 6 December 1946, TNA PCOM 9/700.

24. *Daily Telegraph*, 21 June 1946.

25. George Girdwood, 25 June 1946, TNA DPP 2/1522.

26. The building – complete with nautical frontage – remains and is now a Cornish pasty shop.

27. Angus Bruce, undated, TNA MEPO 3/2728.

28. John Charters Symonds, 24 June 1946, TNA DPP 2/1522.

29. There is no further trace of Yvonne Symonds in UK archives after 1947. When Major Symonds died in 1977, Yvonne's two children were living in Belgium, so she may have moved abroad to join her mother's family after Heath's trial.

30. The site of the Blue Peter Club still exists on the beach at Angmering, now occupied by an Italian restaurant.

31. This dialogue is taken from Yvonne Symonds' statement at Worthing Police Station, the evidence she gave at West

London Police Court and her testimony at the Old Bailey, TNA CRIM 1/1806.

32. Barratt was actually a superintendent.
33. *People*, 23 June 1946.
34. George Girdwood, 25 June 1946, TNA DPP 2/1522.
35. Yvonne Symonds, 24 June 1946, TNA CRIM 1/1806.
36. Percy Alexander Eagle, Worthing, TNA MEPO 3/2728.

Chapter 3

1. Margery's boyfriend at the time was Peter Tilley Bailey.
2. Typescript of both letters, TNA MEPO 3/2728.
3. Quoted in Adamson, *The Great Detective*, p. 162.
4. Reginald Spooner's report, 18 July 1946, TNA HO 144/22871.
5. 'Character of Witnesses', 24 July 1946, TNA MEPO 3/2728.
6. '"Borrowed" Car Chased Round Hyde Park', *Evening Standard*, 27 September 1945.
7. Ibid.
8. Ibid.
9. Elizabeth Helen Wheat, 22 June 1946, TNA MEPO 3/2728.
10. Wheat, *The Wheats of Sheffield*, p. 249.
11. Ibid.
12. Ibid., p. 250.
13. Letter from Margery Wheat to her parents, 15 March 1936, collection of Melody Gardner.
14. Elizabeth Helen Wheat, 22 June 1946, TNA MEPO 3/2728.
15. Letter from Margery Gardner to Mrs Wheat, undated (probably 1940), collection of Melody Gardner.
16. Lofthouse, *Then and Now, passim*.
17. Mathews, *Chelsea Old Church 1941–1950*, pp. 7–9.
18. 'Grantham Hotel Theft', *Grantham Journal*, 16 January 1942.
19. Ibid.
20. Elizabeth Helen Wheat, 22 June 1946, TNA MEPO 3/2728.

21. Author interview with Melody Gardner, 4 October 2011.
22. Marley (ed.), *The Daily Telegraph Story of the War*, p. 84.
23. The name V1 is an abbreviation of *Vergeltungswaffe Eins* or 'Revenge Weapon Number One'.
24. Gardiner, *Wartime*, p. 549.
25. Calder, *The People's War*, pp. 559 60.
26. Faviell, *A Chelsea Concerto*, p. 135.
27. 'Robot Plane Hits Nurse's Home: Children are Trapped', *Evening Standard*, 17 June 1946.
28. Letter from Margery Gardner to Mrs Wheat, 27 July 1945, collection of Melody Gardner.
29. Kynaston, *Austerity Britain*, p. 197.
30. Ralph Macro Wilson, 24 June 1946, MEPO 3/2728.
31. Letter from Margery Gardner to Mrs Wheat, 27 July 1945.
32. Daniel Hamilton Shields, undated, TNA MEPO 3/2728.
33. Ruth Wright and Mrs Hambrook, 25 June 1946, TNA MEPO 3/2728.
34. Wheat, *The Wheats of Sheffield*, p. 251.
35. Elizabeth Helen Wheat, TNA MEPO 3/2728.
36. Peter Tilley Bailey, 25 June 1946, TNA DPP 2/1522.
37. Further statement of Iris Humphrey, TNA DPP 2/1522.
38. Joyce Frost, 22 June 1946, TNA DPP 2/1522.
39. *A Streetcar Named Desire* premiered in New York in December 1947.

Chapter 4

1. Peter Alan Gardner, 22 June 1946, TNA DPP 2/1522.
2. Further statement of Joyce Frost, 30 June 1946, TNA DPP 2/1522.
3. Ibid.
4. Ibid.
5. Ibid.

6. Peter Tilley Bailey, 22 June 1946 and 25 June 1946, TNA DPP 2/1522. Tilley Bailey said he couldn't remember if this was Tuesday or Wednesday.

7. List of Exhibits Sheet 5, taken from 24 Bramham Gardens SW5 21 June 1946, TNA DPP 2/1522.

8. Joyce Frost's two statements, TNA DPP 2/1522.

9. List of Exhibits Appendix 2, found on armchair in Room 4, Pembridge Court Hotel, 21 June 1946. Property of Margery Gardner. TNA DPP 2/1522.

10. Gynomin advertisement – 'an approved method of family planning', *British Medical Journal*, 27 October 1951.

11. Eva Eileen Cole, 1 July 1946, TNA DPP 2/1522.

12. Mary Catherine Hardie, 26 June 1946, TNA DPP 2/1522. Catherine also stated that she had never met or heard of Margery before, so may not have been aware of the status of her relationship with Peter Tilley Bailey. As Margery perhaps suspected, Tilley Bailey would spend the night with Catherine Hardie at his flat in Coliseum Terrace.

13. Ronald Anthony Edward Birch, 25 June 1946, TNA DPP 2/1522.

14. Iris Humphrey, 22 June 1946, TNA DPP 2/1522.

15. Further statement of Iris Humphrey, TNA DPP 2/1522.

16. Phyllis Mary Brown, 28 June 1946, TNA DPP 2/1522.

17. Harold Harter, 22 June 1946 and further statement of Harold Harter, 27 June 1946, DPP 2/1522.

18. Some newspapers in the UK and abroad (e.g. *Cape Times*, 1 July 1946) reported that Margery left in Harter's taxi singing, 'I've got a date with my sweetie.' There is no evidence of this from any of the many witnesses who were present at the entrance to the club.

19. *Daily Express*, 25 June 1946.

Chapter 5

1. Adamson, *The Great Detective*, p. 161.
2. Ibid., p. 45.
3. Ibid., p. 57.
4. One of Spooner's superior officers, quoted in Adamson, op. cit., p. 274, claimed that Spooner 'was ridiculous with money . . . it flowed through his fingers when he was in a public house. His one fault was that he drank too much.'
5. Adamson, op. cit., p. 116.
6. Ibid., p. 120.
7. '[Spooner] did not appreciate wildness and profusion even in his garden (his flowers were planted in rows, each tied to a stick whether it was necessary or not), and one day, after examining the luxuriant but straggly growth of a peony that Myra's sister Kathleen had given them, and which he had cut and trimmed without effect, he came into the kitchen and told Myra, 'You know, that kind of bush is an embarrassment in my garden.' Adamson, op. cit., p. 275.
8. Ibid, p. 124.
9. See Farndale, *Haw-Haw*.
10. Adamson, op. cit., p. 129.
11. Ibid., p. 159.
12. Quoted in Adamson, op. cit., p. 282.

Chapter 6

1. Rhoda Spooner, 25 June 1946, TNA DPP 2/1522.
2. Further statement of Barbara Osborne, 24 June 1946, TNA DPP 2/1522.
3. Further statement of Elizabeth Wyatt, 16 July 1946, TNA DPP 2/1522.
4. Alice Wyatt, 24 June 1946, TNA DPP 2/1522.
5. Frederick Averill, 2 July 1946, TNA HO 144/22871.

6. Reginald Spooner, 18 July 1946, TNA HO 144/22871.

7. Simpson, *Forty Years of Murder*, p. 126. Simpson's assistant, Jean Scott-Dunn, who was later to become his wife, was 'located under a hairdryer in Knightsbridge' when she was called by the police to attend at the Pembridge Court Hotel.

8. Finger and palm prints are available of Margery Gardner and the hotel staff, as well as photographs of fingerprints on the sink and door handle, TNA MEPO 3/2664.

9. Reginald Spooner's report, 18 July 1946, TNA HO 144/22871, and his review of the case on 2 October 1946, HO 144/22782.

10. Elizabeth Wyatt, TNA DPP 2/1522.

11. Barbara Osborne, TNA DPP 2/1522.

12. Further statement of Alice Wyatt, 18 June 1946, TNA DPP 2/1522.

13. Elsie Mary Ellen Thomas, 23 June 1946, TNA MEPO 3/2728.

14. Procter, *The Street of Disillusion*, p. 111.

15. According to Spooner's overview of the case on 2 October 1946, Heath told his parents that his wife had left him for another man thus 'breaking up' his life, TNA HO 144/22872.

16. Reginald Spooner, 22 June 1946, TNA DPP 2/1522.

17. Reginald Spooner, 1 July 1946, TNA MEPO 3/2728. The list of names, addresses and telephone numbers from Heath's address book are also held in MEPO 3/2728.

18. Reginald Spooner's report, 18 July 1946, TNA HO 144/22871.

19. Dr Keith Simpson, TNA DPP2/1522. Simpson was also to claim in *Forty Years of Murder* that Margery was a masochist: 'she liked being bound and gagged' (p. 127). Despite there being little evidence for this, Simpson quotes Casswell's erroneous assumption in his own autobiography of 1961 that 'a month before her death [Margery] had been in another hotel bedroom and had only been saved from possible murder

by the extremely timely intervention of an hotel detective. She had been heavily thrashed, and Heath was standing over her in an almost fiendish fashion.' This is fully discussed in Chapter 22.

20. Simpson, *Forty Years of Murder*, p. 124.
21. 'Confidential Memo to all News Editors', TNA MEPO 3/2728.

Chapter 7

1. 'Offensive Started in Belgium', *Evening Standard*, 7 June 1917.
2. Lloyd George, *War Memoirs*, Volume IV, p. 2110.
3. 'Great Battle Over Thames', *Evening Standard*, 6 June 1917
4. Parents' report to the court, 8 July 1938, TNA P COM 9/700.
5. Letter from William Heath to Neville Heath, 5 October 1946, TNA HO 144/22871.
6. Letter from Bessie Heath to Isaac Near, 6 October 1946, TNA HO 144/22872.
7. Letter from William Heath to Neville Heath, 5 October 1946, TNA HO 144/22872.
8. Gerald Byrne suggests that the Heaths were descended from James Heath (1757–1834), the celebrated engraver to the court of George III. This is not correct, as the Heaths are actually descended from James Heath (1787–1868) of Rumbolds Whyke in Sussex, a much more humble ancestor.
9. See Gunby, *A Potted History of Ilford*, pp. 88–9.
10. Title of a 1924 book about the case by E. M. Delafield.
11. For further details of this case, see Weis, *Criminal Justice*.
12. See Percy Clevely's testimony in Young (ed.), *The Trial of Frederick Bywaters and Edith Thompson*, p. 18.
13. Weis, op. cit., p. xxix.

14. *People*, 29 October 1946.
15. From handwritten notes by Dr Young, senior medical officer at Wormwood Scrubs, following a 55-minute interview with Heath on 6 September 1946, TNA P COM 9/700.
16. Letter from Bessie Heath to Isaac Near, 6 October 1946, TNA HO 144/22872.
17. Report of Dr Young, senior medical officer at Wormwood Scrubs, 17 September 1946, TNA HO 144/22871.
18. See electoral registers for Merton 1932–1946, Merton Public Library.
19. Rutlish School Prospectus, 1933, Rutlish School Archives, Surrey History Centre.
20. Other than Heath, Rutlish's most famous old boy is former prime minister, John Major (1954–9). Foreword, Brock, *Rutlish School*.
21. 'A Tribute to E. A. A. Varnish' by A. J. Doig (1970), reprinted in Brock, op. cit.
22. Conference notes between inspectors from the Board of Education and the School Governors, 10 March 1933, Rutlish School Archives.
23. Brock, op. cit., p. 15.
24. 'The First Rutlish School Song' (1916), words: John Oxenham, music: James Edward Jones, quoted in Brock, op. cit.
25. See Brock, op. cit., p. 124.
26. Rutlish School Prospectus, 1933, p. 14.
27. Gibson, *The English Vice*, p. 38.
28. *Chums Annual*, Vol. 50, 1927–8, p. 94.
29. 'Boys' Weeklies' in Orwell, *Inside the Whale and Other Essays*, p. 91.
30. Ibid., p. 95.
31. Ibid., p. 100.
32. Arthur Jones quoted in Brock, op. cit., p. 85.
33. Rutlish Archive.

34. Brock, op. cit., p. 86. See also Cave, *Practical Exercises in Spoken English*, p. 3: 'The final aim of all speech-training must be to open the eyes of students to their own deficiencies, and to encourage them to speak clearly, accurately and attractively.'

35. Conference notes between inspectors from the Board of Education and the school governors, 10 March 1933, Rutlish School Archives, p. 2.

36. In his report to the court on Heath, 5 July 1938, Varnish wrote: 'No special aptitude. Good athletics . . . always a bit unsteady, easily influenced and exerted an upsetting influence on others. Boisterous. Lacked steady concentration on particular work for any length of time. Inclined to exaggerate to the point of lying but believing in himself.' TNA P COM 9/700.

37. Casswell, *A Lance for Liberty*, p. 242.

38. 'The Son I Knew', Bessie Heath, *People*, 29 October 1946. The full text of this interview is given in Chapter 23.

39. Byrne, *Borstal Boy*, p. 14.

40. Byrne, op. cit., p. 16.

41. Playfair and Sington, *The Offenders*, pp. 42–4.

42. Byrne does not identify 'Jeanette's' father, but later mentions that Heath was advised by Evelyn Walkden (1893–1970), the trade unionist and later MP for Doncaster. Playfair and Sington claim that their source was a 'former Conservative MP', but Walkden was Labour. Given that it's unlikely for Heath to have known more than one MP who lived locally and that Walkden had a daughter (Vera) the same age as Heath, it's possible that 'Jeanette' was Vera Walkden. She was questioned by the police at the time of the murders but stated that she had not seen Heath for years.

43. Heath came closest to discussing sexual matters with Dr Young in their meeting on 10 September 1946. Young recorded that Heath 'denies any homosexual experience. Denies masturbation or attempts by others to masturbate

him. Says that he had no knowledge of sex until the age of eighteen – when pressed if he did not have some insight into it at puberty he denies it and says he does not think so – a frequent reply to many questions put to him.' TNA P COM 9/700.

44. 'Antecedents of Neville George Clevely Heath alias James Robert Cadogan Armstrong' compiled by Spooner, 20 August 1946. TNA MEPO 3/2728.

45. Pawson & Leaf's report to the court, 4 July 1938, TNA P COM 9/700.

46. *News of the World*, 29 September 1946.

47. 'I Cannot Believe I Did It', *Sunday Pictorial*, 29 September 1946.

48. Ibid.

49. Bishop, *Fighter Boys*, p. 45.

50. Ibid., p. 45.

51. Ibid., p. 46.

52. Ibid., p. 51.

53. *Biggles: The Camels Are Coming* by W. E. Johns, quoted in Bishop, op. cit. p. 52.

54. Beaton, *Winged Squadrons*, p. 45.

55. David, *My Autobiography*, p. 12.

56. Bishop, *Fighter Boys*, p. 59.

57. Ibid., p. 61.

58. Ibid.

59. Ibid., p. 60.

60. Ibid., p. 60: 'Flying fighters required a particular softness of touch. Horsemen, yachtsmen and pianists, the prevailing wisdom held, made the best fighter pilots.'

61. Ibid., p. 62.

62. Quoted in Byrne, op. cit., p. 18, though no source is given.

63. Capt. Allen MacNeil Dyson-Perrins, 16 July 1946, TNA MEPO 3/2728.

64. Letter re. Pilot Officer N. G. C. Heath No. 79 (Fighter)

Squadron, 3 August 1937, TNA AIR 43/10 RAF Courts Martial Book.

65. 'RAF Officer Not Guilty of Desertion', *Evening Standard*, 20 August 1937.
66. Ibid.
67. Minterne, *The History of 73 Squadron*, p. 23.
68. Kent, *One of the Few*, p. 45.
69. *Evening Standard*, 20 August 1937.
70. Ibid.
71. Ibid.
72. *Daily Mirror*, 21 August 1937.
73. Arlene Blakely, 27 April 1938, MEPO 3/2728.
74. *Daily Mirror*, 12 November 1937.
75. Ibid.
76. Heath's father then started a new job, managing Faulkner's, a hairdressing shop on the station concourse at Waterloo. This was one of a chain of hairdressing shops situated at various London railway stations which also sold locks, clothes and hosiery – last-minute purchases before taking the train.
77. *Daily Mirror*, 12 November 1937.
78. Probation officer's report, 6 July 1938, TNA P COM 9/700: 'Average intelligence and ability. Good general conduct apart from boyish pranks.'
79. Ibid.
80. Mrs Archdall, 24 March 1938, TNA MEPO 3/2728.
81. Letter from Leicestershire Constabulary to New Scotland Yard, 1 April 1938, TNA MEPO 3/2728.
82. Heath's parents' report to the Court. 8 July 1938, TNA P COM 9/700.
83. Metropolitan Police letter, 9 April 1938, MEPO 3/2728.
84. Brock, *The Life and Death of Neville Heath*, p. 110–11.
85. Handwritten note by Heath, 8 April 1938, TNA MEPO 3/2728.

86. Bulman was the name of an instructor who had taught Heath to fly at Leicester in 1935.

87. From a report of lady visitor I. W. Davies, 16 June 1938, TNA P COM 9/700.

88. Chaplain's remarks (Arthur Casey), 15 June 1938, TNA P COM 9/700.

89. Letter from Heath to the editor of the *Daily Mirror*, 15 June 1938, TNA P COM 9/700.

90. *Evening Standard*, 12 July 1938.

Chapter 8

1. Letter from Heath to C. A. Joyce, 8 October 1946, TNA HO 144/22872.

2. *Guardian*, 18 October 2002.

3. Byrne, *Borstal Boy*, p. 25.

4. Behan, *Borstal Boy*, p. 206.

5. Behan, op. cit., p. 211.

6. Letter from Heath to C. A. Joyce, 8 October 1946, TNA HO 144/22872.

7. Byrne, op. cit., pp. 25–7.

8. Heath's physical statistics at Hollesley Bay are in his borstal record, TNA P COM 9/700.

9. Byrne, op. cit., p. 25.

10. From the printed statement that Neville Chamberlain waved as he stepped off the plane on 30 September 1938.

11. Housemaster's report, 20 April 1939, TNA P COM 9/700.

12. Behan, op. cit., p. 219.

13. Ibid.

14. Anderson shelters were mass-produced, costing the government £5 each. They were issued to 1.5 million families in 1939 and to over 2 million by April 1940 when steel shortages brought an end to production. See Inwood, *A History of London*, p. 777.

15. 27 April 1939.

16. Housemaster's report, 19 July 1939, TNA P COM 9/700.

17. Confidential report by Mr Scott, Director of the Borstal Association, 23 August 1946, P COM 9/700.

18. Letter from Neville Heath to Mr Scott, 15 September 1946, TNA P COM 9/700.

19. Peggy Dixon, 9 July 1946, TNA MEPO 3/2728.

20. Confidential report by Mr Scott, Director of the Borstal Association, 23 August 1946, P COM 9/700.

21. Ibid., re. a letter from Heath, 17 July 1940.

22. *Sunday Pictorial*, 29 September 1946.

23. Norbert Thomas Gaffrey, undated, MEPO 3/2728.

24. This story of Heath's part in the raid on Fort Rutbah was told in the *Sunday Pictorial*, 29 September 1946: 'Every officer of the RASC who tried to take part in the war at this stage was classified as unsuitable – but they'd never let one leave the organisation.'

25. Hill, *Portrait of a Sadist*.

26. Coward, *Middle East Diary*, entry for 15 August 1943, p. 49.

27. Cooper, *Cairo in the War, 1939–1945*.

28. Robert Lees, 'Venereal Diseases in the Armed Forces Overseas (2)', *British Journal of Venereal Diseases 22* (1946), p. 163.

29. Imperial War Musuem Documents 286, private papers of G. C. Tylee.

30. Hill, op, cit., p. 78.

31. Ibid., p. 85.

32. Ibid., p. 18.

33. The rand was introduced in 1961.

34. Morton, *In Search of South Africa*, p. 209.

35. Wells, *South Africa*, p. 251.

36. One of the great and lasting images of South Africa during the war was the middle-aged soprano Perla Siedle Gibson, Durban's 'Lady in White'. Mrs Gibson stood at the docks,

singing rousing and patriotic songs to troop ships as they left Durban Harbour. She sang throughout the war – popular songs, anthems and sentimental ballads. For many troops, she was an iconic maternal figure who represented the warm welcome and emotional farewell they received from the people of South Africa. (See Gibson, *Durban's Lady in White*.)

37.   Walker, *A History of Southern Africa*, p. 251.

Chapter 9

1.   Smuts' influence within the Allies was so strong that a plan was mooted in 1940 – and supported by George VI – that if Churchill were to die unexpectedly, Smuts would take his place.

2.   Reader's Digest, *Illustrated History of South Africa*, p. 347.

3.   Ibid., p. 352.

4.   Bryant, *As We Were*, p. 82.

5.   Ibid., p. 83.

6.   Documentation Centre of the South African National Defence Force and Service Record World War 2, Pretoria, DSCO 5892.

7.   DSCO 5906.

8.   Morton, *In Search of South* Africa, p. 239.

9.   Ibid., p. 300.

10. Elizabeth was a member of the Hardcastle Rivers family and not the Pitt Rivers family as was incorrectly reported in the British press at the time of the murders.

11. 'Heath's Ex-wife Tells of Runaway Romance', *News of the World*, 29 September 1946.

12. Peggy Dixon, 9 July 1946, TNA MEPO 3/2828.

13. Mr Scott's report, based on a letter from Heath, 5 March 1943, TNA P COM 9/700.

14. *Sunday Pictorial*, 29 September 1946.

15. Harold Vincent Guthrie, undated, TNA MEPO 3/2728.

16. Ibid.

17. Lister, *The Very Merry Moira*, pp. 82–3.

18. Letter from Heath to Elizabeth Armstrong, 14 September 1946, TNA HO 144/22872.

19. DSCO 5941-2.

20. Letter from Heath's commanding officer to the director of Air Personnel, 8 December 1943, DSCO 5952.

21. Handwritten letter from Heath to the director of Air Personnel and Org. Pretoria, 18 March 1943, DSCO 5944.

22. Letter from C. J. Jooste, adjutant general, 19 April 1943, and another on 21 December 1943, confirming retention of Heath's services, DSCO 5951.

23. Letter from Heath to Elizabeth Armstrong, 14 September 1946, TNA HO 144/22872.

24. The fact that Heath had a different name and date of birth on his official documents will have helped this subterfuge.

25. Heath was seconded from the SAAF on 23 May 1944 and originally attached to No. 3 AFU South Cerney near Cirencester and the satellite station of Bibury until 15 August 1944. He was then posted to No. 13 OTU at Finmere until 29 September. On 4 October he joined 180 Squadron and was posted to Belgium, TNA MEPO 3/2728.

26. Quoted in Bishop, *Bomber Boys*, p. xl.

27. Ibid., p. xxxviii.

28. Wilson, *Men of Air*, preface.

29. Quoted in Bishop, op. cit., p. 61.

30. Fielding Johnson's statement was taken by Heath's solicitors some time before the trial but is undated, HO 144/22872.

31. Air Ministry, *Psychological Disorders in Flying Personnel of the Royal Air Force, Investigated During the War, 1939–45*, compiled by Group Captain CP Symonds and Squadron Leader Dennis Williams, London HMSO, 1947.

32. Beaton, *Winged Squadrons*, p. 39.

33. No category was allowed for psychopathic personality. This omission is highlighted in the report. Possibly in the light of

Heath's trial, it was considered that such statistics might be misinterpreted – presumably by the press – and that the psychopathic state would probably develop symptoms under one of the other headings anyway.

34. Air Ministry, *Psychological Disorders in Flying Personnel*: 'Even the most seasoned pilot may show that loss of confidence which, unless immediately treated, will end in a frank anxiety state. Suddenly, for some reason not obvious to the outsider, some minor accident, private worries, or even the awakening of a too lively imagination, may liberate a series of repressions.'

35. Wyndham, *Love Is Blue*, p. 188. Seventy-two million Benzedrine tablets were officially issued to the British military during the Second World War. See *On Speed: The many lives of amphetamines*, Nicolas Rasmussen, New York University Press, 2008, p. 71.

36. Quoted in Wells, *Courage and Air Warfare*, p. 200.

37. Nichol and Rennell, *Tail End Charlies*, p. 158.

38. Ibid., p. 158.

39. Bishop, op. cit., p. 160.

40. Ibid., p. 161.

41. Kershaw, *Never Surrender*, p. 277.

42. Beaton, op. cit., p. 31.

43. Bishop, op. cit., p. 163.

44. Kershaw, op. cit., p. 281.

45. Peter Godfrey in 'How I Met Neville Heath', quoted in *Master Detective* magazine, September 1990.

46. William Spurrett Fielding-Johnson, TNA HO 144/ 22872.

Chapter 10

1. 'Antecedent History of Neville George Clevely Heath alias James Robert Cadogan Armstrong' compiled by Spooner, 21 August 1946, TNA MEPO 3/2728.

2. Confidential report by Mr Scott, director of the Borstal Association, 23 August 1946, P COM 9/700.

3. Handwritten life story by Heath, TNA P COM 9/700.

4. From Heath's defence at Durban Magistrates' Court, 19 July 1945, TNA DSCO 5972.

5. *Sunday Pictorial*, 5 October 1946.

6. Elizabeth Armstrong in 'How I Met Neville Heath' by Peter Godfrey, quoted in *Master Detective* magazine, September 1990.

7. Desertion is quoted in the Armstrongs' divorce petition, 7 September 1945, National Archives Repository, Pretoria, 8044.

8. *Sunday Pictorial*, 29 September 1946.

9. See DSCO 5969, Magistrates' Court Documents.

10. *Sunday Pictorial*, 5 October 1946.

11. The relationship is also confirmed in a letter on 19 April 1945 from Mr Williams' solicitors in Nottingham, Browne, Jacobson & Hallam, to Captain Steele, the administration officer at South Africa House in Trafalgar Square, DSCO 5955.

12. Zita Williams, 6 July 1946, TNA MEPO 3/2728.

13. Letter from Browne, Jacobson & Hallam to Hayman, Godfrey & Sanderson, solicitors, 30 August 1945, Johannesburg, DSCO 6015.

14. 'Owing to the circumstances in which our client is placed, it is imperative that she should know the full position . . .' DSCO 5955.

15. In a letter from E. V. H Mickdal to the South African Commissioner of Police, Witwatersrand Division, it was claimed that 'Armstrong was engaged or was about to become

engaged to a young lady in Durban, but on her hearing that he was a married man the engagement fell through. It is believed that the young lady concerned is a daughter of one of the Natal sugar magnates.' 27 July 1944 in TNA MEPO 3/2728.

16. Sir Edward Cecil George Cadogan (1880–1962) had been knighted in 1939 and had served in the RAF in the war.

17. Zita Williams, 6 July 1946, TNA MEPO 3/2728.

18. Mr Scott's report, quoting his own entry into the Borstal Association Official Record on 20 August 1945, p. 4. He ends: 'I can only suggest that there may be reasons for investigating the possibility of Heath being a schizophrenic type.' 23 August 1946, P COM 9/700.

19. Letter from Heath to Elizabeth Armstrong, 27 July 1945, National Archives Repository, Pretoria, 8029.

20. 31 July 1945, DSCO 5962/3.

21. Letter from L. Botha, director of the Queen's Hotel to Neville Heath, 11 August 1945, DSCO 5967.

22. Letter from Heath at the SAAF base in Roberts Heights, Pretoria, to Messrs Hayman, Godfrey & Sanderson in Johannesburg, 9 August 1945, National Archives Repository (NAR), Pretoria, 8035.

23. Letter from Heath to Messrs Hayman, Godfrey & Sanderson, 1 September 1945: 'Dear Sir, I am advising you that I have forwarded, signed, to Mrs Rivers, the document which hitherto I have declined to sign. This should enable my wife to obtain what she wants without difficulty . . . Could you obtain consent from Mrs Rivers to renew the bail should the case be remanded for a further period . . .' NAR, 8038.

24. On 30 August 1945 in the Supreme Court, Heath officially gave up his rights to his son: 'I furthermore declare that I consent to and have no objection to and Order being made by the above named Honourable Court depriving me of all such rights of guardianship in respect of such minor child,

and granting such rights to my wife . . .' NAR 8041.

25. Flight Lt. Chapman, DSCO 6005-6.

26. Major Donnelly, DSCO 6003-4.

27. Neville Heath, DSCO 5972.

28. Telex to intercept Heath's letters, 31 August 1945, DSCO 5974.

29. Heath's defence quoted in Chaplin's statement, DSCO 5976.

30. Flying Officer James Bainbridge Chaplin RAF, 7 September 1945, DSCO 5975.

31. In his letter of 15 November 1945 to the adjutant general, H. B. Wakefield, the Rivers' family solicitor Mr Friedman had also looked over the recent charges against Heath and concluded that 'quite frankly, he was extremely fortunate not to be found guilty, and it seems that he was given the benefit of the doubt in this case', DSCO 6012.

32. Charles Friedman, 27 July 1946, TNA MEPO 3/2728.

33. The court martial took place on 4 December, DSCO 6023

34. Document issuing court martial, 13 December 1945, DSCO 6020.

35. See letter from E. E. Crowe at the Office of the High Commissioner for the United Kingdom, Cape Town, 16 February 1946, TNA MEPO 3/2728.

36. *New Statesman and Nation*, 27 October 1945, pp. 277–8.

Chapter 11

1. Kent (ed.), *An Encyclopaedia of London*, p. 42.

2. For a detailed inventory of the damaged buildings of London, see Kent, op. cit.

3. Beaton and Pope-Hennessy, *History Under Fire*, p. 45.

4. See Kent, *The Lost Treasures of London*, and Richards, *The Bombed Buildings of Britain*.

5. Chapman, *Madame Tussaud's Chamber of Horrors*, p. 215.

6. *The Times*, quoted in Kent, *The Lost Treasures of London*, p. 33.

7. See *The London County Council Bomb Damage Maps 1939–1945* edited by Ann Saunders with an introduction by Robin Woolven, London Topographical Society and London Metropolitan Archives, 2005.

8. R. S. R. Fitter, *London's Natural History* (1945), quoted in Inwood, *A History of London*, p. 810.

9. Kent, *The Lost Treasures of London*, p. 120.

10. See Prologue, p. 1–7.

11. Letter from South African Commission for the United Kingdom to Inspector Riggs, Wimbledon CID, 27 February 1946, MEPO 3/2728.

12. Metropolitan Police Enquiry Officers' Records, Royal Air Force, Bush House, Kingsway, 25 March 1946, TNA MEPO 3/2728.

13. After his arrest, Spooner had Heath's two log books examined under an ultraviolet lamp at Scotland Yard. This revealed numerous alterations in the records, claiming many more missions than Heath had, in fact, accomplished. These alterations had been done extremely skilfully, but the fingerprint bureau photographed the alteration on the first page of one of the log books, and this clearly showed the name J. R. C. Armstrong beneath that of N. G. C. Heath. These changes had all been effected by the use of chemicals. The most plausible explanation for the alteration of the log books is that during April and May, he was negotiating with various air-transport firms for employment as a pilot. Clearly his references would need to be in his own name if he was to avoid any enquiry into his SAAF connections, which had resulted in his being deported. See 'Antecedent History' compiled by Spooner, MEPO 3/2728. Photocopies of doctored log book entries are in TNA HO 144/22871.

14. Ralph Fisher, 26 June 1946, TNA MEPO 3/2728.

15. Muriel Frances Silvester, 5 August 1946, TNA MEPO 3/2728.

16. Jill Rosemary Harris, 23 June 1946, TNA MEPO 3/2728.

17. DS Cains' interview with the manageress of the Red Lion Hotel and various individuals at the Luton Flying Club, Luton Borough Police, 23 June 1946, TNA MEPO 3/2728.

18. Until 2028.

19. See 'Antecedents of Neville George Clevely Heath alias James Robert Cadogan Armstrong', compiled by Spooner, TNA MEPO 3/2728.

20. Lister, *The Very Merry Moira*, pp. 82–3. Lister claimed to have dated Heath between the murders of Margery Gardner and Doreen Marshall: 'The only thing that may have saved me is that I am blonde and both girls were brunettes.' This was repeated in many of Lister's obituaries when she died in 2007. Though she may well have dated him, it cannot have occurred as she suggests (i.e. in the days between the two murders), as Heath was on the run along the south coast after the murder of Margery Gardner.

21. Ibid.

22. Quoted in Byrne, *Borstal Boy*, p. 48.

23. Harry Ashbrook, 23 June 1946, TNA DPP 2/1522.

24. Heath had actually been discussing the purchase of some planes with an Arthur Coombes from Reading. Coombes had been convicted of nine air-traffic offences as well as charges for false pretences in 1939. He and Heath had discussed buying planes that cost between £695 and £5,500, even the cheapest of which was well beyond Heath's means, TNA MEPO 3/2728.

25. Reginald Spooner, 22 June 1946, TNA DPP 2/1522.

26. *People*, 29 October 1946.

27. *Sunday Pictorial*, 29 September 1946.

28. This was later quashed on appeal.

29. Leslie Terry, 25 June 1946, TNA DPP 2/1522.

30. 'Character of Witnesses', TNA MEPO 3/2728. Terry was

known to be identical with Leslie Turkington, CRO No.
4888/25.
31. 'I Found Blood on My Hands', *Sunday Pictorial*, 13 October
1946.
32. Ibid.
33. *Sunday Pictorial*, 23 October 1946.

Chapter 12

1. Letter to R. Morgan at the Home Office requesting to intercept the post, 3 July 1946, TNA MEPO 3/2728.
2. Chief Inspector G. Carmill, 24 June 1946, TNA MEPO
3/2728.
3. Mr Macro Wilson also identified Margery from the contact
sheet of photos that had appeared in the *Daily Express* on 24
June 1946, TNA MEPO 3/2728 60B.
4. Peter Alan Gardner, 22 June 1946, TNA DPP 2/1522.
5. 'Character of Witnesses', 24 July 1946, TNA MEPO 3/2728.
6. See e.g. Ronald Anthony Birch, 22 June 1946, TNA DPP
2/1522: 'I regarded her as a particularly quiet girl and have
never seen her the worse for drink.'
7. Ralph Macro Wilson, 26 June 1946, TNA MEPO 3/2728.
8. Percy Alexander Eagle, 1 July 1946, TNA MEPO 3/2728.
9. Reginald Spooner, 25 June 1946, TNA MEPO 3/2728.
10. Lawrence Kelly, 15 July 1946, TNA DPP 2/1522.
11. Statement of DI Percy Alexander Eagle, items recovered from
the Ocean Hotel Annex: '3 nails found under the sheet on the
right hand side of the bed. 1 bed sheet covering the mattress on
the bed, the sheet bearing marks of excrement on the right
hand side and what appeared to be bloodstains on the left hand
side' (DPP 2/1522). On 4 July, perhaps due to the evidence of
blood and the presence of the nails, Spooner noted that
'although up to now [Miss Symonds] has not admitted that any
incident took place, I feel certain that it did' (MEPO 3/2728).

12. List of property taken by Detective Inspector Eagle from the Ocean Hotel Annex, Worthing, and Miss Yvonne Symonds, on Monday 26 June 1946, and handed to Sergeant Kelly, Notting Hill Police Station, the same day, TNA MEPO 3/2728.

13. *Daily Mirror*, 29 June 1946.

14. The letter was posted on 22 June 1946 and received at Scotland Yard on 24 June 1946, TNA DPP 2/1522.

15. *Evening News*, 3 July 1946.

16. *News Chronicle*, 26 June 1946.

17. Anonymous typed letter to the superintendent, Criminal Investigation Department, New Scotland Yard, 1 July 1946. The letter began: 'Why does not Scotland Yard publish a good photograph of the man ("Lt-Col") HEATH in the daily newspapers? If the public knew what he looked like it might save you chasing up false clues. On the other hand it might help to trace him' (TNA MEPO 3/2728).

18. Percy Alexander Eagle, 1 July 1946, TNA MEPO 3/2728.

19. *Daily Mirror*, 27 June 1946.

20. Trevethan Frampton, 22 June 1946, TNA DPP 2/1522.

21. Reginald Spooner's report, 19 July 1946 TNA HO 144 22872.

22. Re. the police petrol coupons, DS Frampton, 8 July 1946, TNA MEPO 3/2728.

Chapter 13

1. Closing speech for the prosecution in Critchley (ed.), *The Trial of Neville George Clevely Heath*, p. 210.

2. Ward Lock Red Guide, *Bournemouth*, p. 34.

3. Ibid.

4. Hardy, *Tess of the D'Urbervilles*, p. 491.

5. Ibid., p. 498.

6. Ward Lock Red Guide, *Bournemouth*, p. 41.

7. See Edington, *Bournemouth and the Second World War*, p. 105

8. Ibid.

9. The Americans dubbed Bournemouth without (apparently) irony, 'the Miami of Britain'.
10. *Bournemouth Echo*, 29 March 1944.
11. *Bournemouth Echo*, 10 June 1946.
12. *Bournemouth Times*, 8 December 1944.
13. *Sphere*, 7 September 1948.
14. Tollard Royal advertisement in *Bournemouth, Britain's All Season Resort: The Official Guide*, published by Bournemouth Corporation, 1946.
15. Violet Ruth Lay, 14 July 1946, MEPO 3/2728.
16. Jones, *Rupert Brooke*, pp. 110, 304.

Chapter 14

1. Ivor Arthur Relf, 23 July 1946, TNA MEPO 3/2728.
2. Ivor Arthur Relf, 10 July 1946, TNA DPP 2/1524.
3. Arthur James White, 10 July 1946, TNA DPP 2/1524.
4. Frederick Charles Wilkinson, 10 July 1946, TNA DPP 2/1524.
5. Charles Peter Rylatt, 15 July 1946, TNA DPP 2/1524.
6. Bernard Harold Tutt, 12 July 1946, TNA DPP 2/1524.
7. In her autobiography, *Stepping into the Spotlight: The ITMA Years* (Arrow, 1976), the Scots actress Molly Weir claimed that Heath tried to pick her up one afternoon in the restaurant at Bobby's Department Store in Bournemouth. 'The most noticeable thing about him were his eyes – blue and shining and full of a curious excitement' (p. 70). He asked her not to return to London that night but to stay with him in Bournemouth. Weir claims that this meeting took place just after 5 p.m. on Wednesday 3 July and that she, therefore, had had a narrow escape. If this is true (though it may be that Weir met Heath on another day) Heath must have met her between having tea with Doreen Marshall at the Tollard Royal and having dinner with her there.

8. The two statements from Peggy (Margaret Clare) Waring are held in TNA MEPO 3/2728.
9. Peggy Waring's first statement, 7 July 1946, TNA MEPO 3/2728.
10. Ibid.
11. Ivor Arthur Relf, 23 July 1946, TNA DPP 2/1522.
12. Though Frederick Wilkinson the night porter had noted that Brook 'did not appear to have a lot of money. The only thing he paid for in cash was for after dinner drinks in the lounge. The rest of his expenses would be embodied in his bill.' Frederick Charles Wilkinson, 10 July 1946, TNA DPP 2 /1524.
13. Bernard Harold Tutt, 12 July 1946, TNA DPP2/1524.
14. The events of Saturday are all from Peggy Waring's second statement, 13 July 1946, TNA MEPO 3/2728.
15. Ibid.
16 Ibid.

Chapter 15

1. Alexander John Brough, 11 July 1946, TNA DPP 2/1524. Brough suggests that tickets No. 1012 and 1013 were purchased together by the same person, implying that at this point Joan was going to accompany her sister to Bournemouth.
2. *Daily Mirror*, 27 September 1946.
3. Email to the author from Julia Young concerning her maternal grandfather, Charles Marshall, 11 March 2012.
4. Bigland, *The Story of the WRNS*, p. 20.
5. Drummond, *Blue for a Girl*, p. 45. As Doreen had learned, even office routine and correspondence was different from civil practice. 'W.R.N.S officers must know that "Dear Sir" is not the mode of address in the Navy, neither is the personal pronoun permissible. Instead, "It is requested that . . ."' Scott, *British Women in War*, p. 23.

6. See *The People's War* BBC website, www.bbc.co.uk/history/ ww2peopleswar/stories/48/a1153748.shtml

7. Charles Marshall, 13 August 1946, TNA DPP 2/1524.

8. Joan Cruickshanks, 10 July 1946, TNA DPP 2/1524.

9. Charles Marshall, 13 August 1946, TNA DPP 2/1524.

10. Elsie Isobel Jones, 10 July 1946, TNA DPP 2/1524.

11. George Wisecarver, 13 July 1946, TNA MEPO 3/2728.

12. Charles Marshall, 9 July 1946, TNA DPP 2/1524.

13. *Bournemouth Echo*, 3 July 1946.

14. Heath's statement, 2.45 a.m., 7 July 1946, witnessed by Detective Inspector George Gates. This statement was commenced at 11.50 p.m. on 6 July 1946, MEPO 3/2728.

15. Ibid.

16. Heinz Abisch, 13 July 1946, TNA DPP 2/1524.

17. James William Newland, 7 July 1946, TNA DPP 2/1524.

18. Sydney Walter Bush, 7 July 1946, TNA DPP 2/1524.

19. She actually arrived by taxi.

20. Heath's statement, exhibit 14, TNA DPP 2/1524.

21. Ivor Arthur Relf , 10 July 1946, TNA DPP 2/1524.

22. Heinz Abisch, 13 July 1946, TNA DPP 2/1524.

23. Detective Superintendent Lovell's report to the chief constable of Dorset, Major L. W. Peel Yates, 18 July 1946, TNA DPP 2/1524.

24. Arthur Charles Marsh, 12 July 1946, TNA DPP 2/1524.

25. Winifred Marjorie Parfitt, 11 July 1946, TNA DPP 2/1524.

26. *Radio Times* Vol. 91, No. 1187, 28 June 1946.

27. Gladys Davy Phillips, 13 August 1946, TNA DPP 2/1524.

28. Arthur White, 6 August 1946, TNA DPP 2/1524.

29. Frederick Charles Wilkinson, 10 July 1946, TNA DPP 2/1524.

30. Ibid.

Chapter 16

1. Frederick Charles Wilkinson, 6 August 1946, DPP 2/1524.
2. Frederick Charles Wilkinson, 10 July 1946, DPP 2/1524.
3. Alice Hemmingway, 10 July 1946, DPP 2/1524.
4. Frederick Charles Wilkinson, 6 August 1946, DPP 2/1524.
5. Karl John Hambitzer, 12 July 1946, TNA DPP 2/1524.
6. Alice Hemmingway, 10 July 1946, TNA DPP 2/1524.
7. Harry Taylor, 11 July 1946, TNA DPP 2/1524.
8. Ellen Janie Bayliss, 10 July 1946, TNA DPP 2/1524.
9. Alfred Jesse Phillips, 12 July 1946, TNA DPP 2/1524.
10. Heinz Abisch, 13 July 1946, TNA DPP 2/1524.
11. Robert Donald Cook, 10 July 1946, TNA MEPO 3/2728.
12. Arthur White, 10 July 1946, TNA DPP 2/1524.
13. Ibid.
14. The address of Heath's former fiancée, Peggy Dixon.
15. Henry Walter Burles, 6 August 1946, TNA DPP 2/1524.
16. Gladys Davy Phillips, 13 August 1946, TNA DPP 2/1524.
17. Ivor Arthur Relf, 6 August 1946, TNA DPP 2/1524.
18. Stanley Lionel Pack, 13 July 1946, TNA DPP 2/1524.
19. Ibid.
20. Harry Berkoff, 6 Aug 1946, TNA DPP 2/1524.
21. Clive Eugene Miles, TNA CRIM 1/1806.

Chapter 17

1. George Robert Suter, 13 July 1946, TNA DPP 2/1524.
2. Email to the author from Michael Suter, 30 May 2012.
3. George Robert Suter, 3 July 1946, TNA MEPO 3/2728.
4. *Bournemouth Echo*, 5 November 1980.
5. This conversation is taken from Suter's witness statement.
6. Heath later said he was mistaken and that they had met in the morning.
7. *Daily Express*, 9 July 1946.

8. Ibid.

9. Leslie Ewart Johnson, undated, TNA DPP 2/1522, DPP 2/1524.

10. Leslie Ewart Johnson, undated, TNA MEPO 3/2728.

11. Initially he spoke to DI Wilfred Daws.

12. Email to the author from Michael Suter, 30 May 2012.

13. Leslie Ewart Johnson, TNA DPP 2/1524.

14. George Henry Gates, TNA MEPO 3/2728.

15. List of Exhibits Sheet 9 On Person – Heath. Removed by Bournemouth Police on 6 July 1946, TNA DPP 2/1522.

16. List of Exhibits Sheet 10, in jacket found hanging on clothes peg in Lounge, Tollard Royal Hotel, Bournemouth. Taken possession of by Divisional Detective Inspector Spooner on 7 July 1946, TNA DPP 2/1522.

17. Leslie Ewart Johnson, TNA DPP 2/1524.

18. George Henry Gates, TNA DPP 2/1524.

19. TNA DPP 2/1522.

20. The forensic laboratory in Hendon later confirmed that hairs on the scarf were from Margery Gardner's head and that this scarf had been used to gag her, possibly contributing to her suffocation.

21. Particulars of handkerchiefs traced to Heath's possession, 31 August 1946, TNA HO 144/22781.

22. Metropolitan Police Laboratory, Hendon, 11 July 1946, TNA MEPO 3/2728.

23. See Reginald Spooner's statement, 17 July 1946, TNA MEPO 3/2728.

24. Further statement of Harold Harter, 8 July 1946, TNA DPP 2/1522.

25. Reginald Spooner, 29 July 1946, TNA DPP 2/1522.

26. *Daily Mail*, 9 July 1946.

27. Adamson, *The Great Detective*, p. 177.

28. Newsprint clipping translated from Swedish: 'Record Bloodhound at Fault in Hunt for Lust Murderer', MEPO 3/2728.

Chapter 18

1. Kathleen Evans, 9 July 1946, TNA DPP 2/1524.
2. Francis George Bishop, 13 August 1946, TNA DPP 2/1524.
3. *News Chronicle*, 10 July 1946.
4. *Daily Mail*, 12 July 1946.
5. The description of the crime scene is in Detective Sergeant Bishop's and Crichton McGaffey's statements. McGaffey also includes his post-mortem report, TNA CRIM 1/1806. He first examined the body at the scene at 11 a.m. and the post-mortem was conducted at Poole at 2.30 p.m.
6. This seems unlikely as she would have been self-conscious of the sanitary towel she was wearing in anticipation of her period.
7. Bishop found this handkerchief that had probably been used to gag Doreen 15 feet to the west of the body. Bishop's statement, TNA P COM 9/700.
8. Clive Eugene Miles' statement, TNA CRIM 1/1806.
9. *Sunday Pictorial*, 13 October 1946.
10. Critchley (ed.), *The Trial of Neville George Clevely Heath*, p. 132.
11. 'Theory of Second Murder – A Defence for the First', *Daily Mirror*, 27 September 1946.

Chapter 19

1. Letter from Heath to Bessie Heath, 9 July 1946, TNA MEPO 3/2728.
2. Archives of the Solicitors' Regulation Centre, Disciplinary Hearing, 18 May 1951.
3. See Reginald Spooner's letter to Home Office, 18 July 1946, MEPO 3/2728.
4. Letter from Home Office to New Scotland Yard, 16 July 1946, MEPO 3/2728. See also correspondence re. the letter in HO 144/22872.

5. Letter from Heath to Leslie Terry, 11 July 1946, quoted in Byrne, *Borstal Boy*, p. 80.

6. 'Character of Witnesses', TNA MEPO 3/2728. Spooner further states that 'he is unscrupulous and may even yet endeavour to turn his association with Heath on the day of the murder against us, if given the opportunity'.

7. Heath's handwritten life story, TNA P COM 9/700.

8. Handwritten by the governor of Brixton Prison, 23 July 1946, TNA HO 144/22871.

9. Terry negotiated the deal with Hugh Cudlipp, the editor of the *Sunday Pictorial*. As the government had recently lifted the controls on newspaper rationing, Cudlipp felt that the story 'could be expected to sell unlimited quantities of papers'. Byrne, *Borstal Boy*, p. 78.

10. As well as friends and family, several women he didn't know sent him letters in prison and also corresponded with his mother.

11. *Sunday Pictorial*, 11 August 1946.

12. Letter from Heath to Isaac Near, 8 October 1946, TNA HO 144/22872: 'I definitely feel that the letter from Pinner requires no answer, unless there is a repetition. Then go for it!'

13. In 'Character of Witnesses', TNA MEPO 3/2728, Spooner says '[Terry] has been a frequent visitor to Heath in HM Prison, Brixton'.

14. Letter from Heath to Leslie Terry, 19 July 1946, quoted in *Sunday Pictorial*, 29 September 1946.

15. Brock suggests that Doreen's mother had the pen engraved for her, DPP 2/1254. Brock, *The Life and Death of Neville Heath*, pp. 110–111.

16. *Daily Mirror*, 7 August 1946.

17. Critchley (ed.), *The Trial of Neville George Clevely Heath*, p. 32.

18. *Daily Herald*, 25 September 1946.

19. See Casswell, *A Lance for Liberty*, pp. 197–222.

20. Casswell, op. cit., p. 242.

21. Ibid., p. 248.
22. Dr Young, 17 September 1946, TNA HO 144/22872.
23. Ibid.
24. Dr Grierson's assessment, 16 September 1946, TNA HO 144/22872.
25. See 'Antecedents of Neville George Clevely Heath alias James Robert Cadogan Armstrong', compiled by Spooner, TNA MEPO 3/2728.
26. Letter from Heath to Leslie Terry, 15 July 1946, quoted in Byrne, *Borstal Boy*, p. 84.
27. *News of the World*, 6 October 1946.
28. Ibid.
29. *Daily Express*, *Daily Mail*, 10 September 1946.

Chapter 20

1. Letter from Heath to Elizabeth Armstrong, 14 September 1946, TNA HO 144/22872.

Chapter 21

1. *Daily Mail*, 24 September 1946.
2. *Daily Herald*, 25 September 1946.
3. Ibid.
4. *Sunday Dispatch*, 22 September 1946.
5. 'Welsh Judge to Try Heath', *Western Mail*, 21 August 1946.
6. *Daily Mail*, 25 September 1946.
7. Ibid.
8. Ibid.
9. Ibid.
10. *News Chronicle*, 25 September 1946.
11. *Daily Mirror*, 25 September 1946.
12. Critchley (ed.), *The Trial of Neville George Clevely Heath*, p. 128.
13. Critchley, op. cit., p. 132.

14. Pronounced 'McNaughten'.
15. *Psychological Treatment of Criminals*, HMSO, 1938.
16. Critchley, op. cit., pp. 147–8.
17. Ibid.
18. Casswell, op. cit., p. 249.
19. Critchley, op. cit., p. 155.
20. Ibid., p. 150.
21. Questions to the jury, handwritten in pencil, 29 September 1946, TNA CRIM 1/1806.
22. Letter from Isaac Near to the Home Office, 7 October 1946, TNA HO 144/22872: 'Unfortunately, very shortly before the said trial, the witness in question sustained so severe a heart attack that he had to be removed to a hospital.'
23. Critchley, op. cit., pp. 187–8.
24. Ibid., p. 213.
25. Ibid., p. 218.
26. *Daily Graphic*, 27 September 1946.
27. Casswell, op. cit., p. 255.
28. *Daily Herald*, 27 September 1946.
29. *News Chronicle*, 27 September 1946.
30. *Daily Herald*, 27 September 1946.
31. Ibid.
32. Ibid.
33. Quoted in Garfield, *Our Hidden Lives*, pp. 284–5.

Chapter 22

1. TNA HO 144/22872.
2. *Sunday Express*, 20 September 1946.
3. Letter from Heath to Isaac Near, 2 October 1946, TNA P COM 9/700.
4. Casswell, *A Lance for Liberty*, p. 249.
5. Letter from Heath to Bessie Heath, 29 September 1946, TNA HO 144/22872.

6. Ibid.
7. For the investigation into the murder of Vera Page, see TNA MEPO 3/1671.
8. Florrie Porter is discussed in TNA MEPO 3/2728.
9. In a recent discussion of the case, Neil Root claims that 'the police files on Neville Heath . . . have never been de-classified'. In actuality most of the Heath archives have been available for public study for some years. This author success-fully had the majority of the material in DPP 1/1522 and DPP 1/1524 released in 2011. Root also claims that the files were withheld because of 'an unconnected murder that remains unsolved'. The National Archives have restricted some information in the files but this is only in relation to the privacy of third parties. Contrary to Root's suggestion, there is no evidence that Heath was responsible (or even suspected) of any other murders than those of Margery Gardner and Doreen Marshall.
10. Reginald Spooner's report, 19 July 1946, TNA HO 144 22872.
11. Peter Tilley Bailey, 25 June 1946, TNA DPP 2/1522.
12. Further statement of Leonard William Luff, 26 June 1946, TNA DPP 2/1522: 'I have been shewn [sic] six photographs by Detective Sergeant Swarbrick. The woman in the large photograph and the woman on the seat with the child [i.e. the photograph of Margery Gardner and her daughter Melody] certainly appear to me to be identical with the woman I saw in Room 506 as described in my earlier state-ment [i.e. Pauline Brees].'
13. 'Hotel Detective Says – Margery Gardner Had One Escape', *News of the World*, 29 September 1946.
14. Casswell, op. cit., p. 239: 'It is almost certain that a month before her death [Margery] had been with Heath to another hotel bedroom and had only been saved then from possible murder by the timely intervention of an hotel detective.' As

has been outlined in the text and notes, this was definitely Pauline Brees and not Margery Gardner.

15. As recently as 2011, Neil Root suggests that Margery had dated Heath previously and that she 'probably knows it is going to be another wild night out, followed by extreme sex, which both of them enjoy'. There is no evidence for these assumptions (indeed, the contrary if Margery's friends, lovers and her husband are to be believed). Root is solely reliant on secondary sources with no original research and repeats many of the errors and questionable assumptions which have accumulated around the case over the preceding sixty-five years.

16. Pauline Brees, 27 July 1946, TNA DPP 2/1522.

17. Peggy Waring's second statement, 13 July 1946, TNA MEPO 3/2728.

18. Confidential report by Mr Scott, Director of the Borstal Association, 23 August 1946, P COM 9/700

19. Though he may have attempted to use the three nails on her – or himself.

20. This may be unlikely, as she knew she was expecting her period, as confirmed by her sister.

21. Reginald Spooner's report, 2 October 1946, TNA HO 144 22872.

22. Letter from Heath to Near, 2 October 1945, TNA P COM 9/700.

23. *Daily Mirror*, 27 September 1946.

24. *Daily Express*, 27 September 1946.

25. G. F. Nash of St John's Crescent SW9 wrote to the Home Secretary on 30 July 1946, asking 'If a description of this man and his mental condition had been widely and emphatically publicised in all probability the second murder would not have been committed. Why was it not? Because you think you know what's good for us?' TNA MEPO 3/2728.

26. *Daily Mirror*, 27 September 1946.

27. Ibid.

28. Quoted from Hansard, TNA HO 144/22872.

29. 'Heath Appeal Move Likely This Week', *Sunday Dispatch*, 29 September 1946.

30. Like Heath, True was educated at a grammar school and in the First World War had joined the Royal Flying Corps. In 1922 he murdered a prostitute, Olive Young. He then pawned her jewellery. At his trial, the prosecution relied on the M'Naghten Rules to prove that True was not insane in the eyes of the law. He was sentenced to death. The case was rejected on appeal, but the Home Secretary intervened and True was re-examined by three psychiatrists who all declared that he was insane. (See Carswell, Donald, *The Trial of Ronald True*, William Hodge, 1925.)

31. Letter from Heath to Bessie Heath, 30 September 1946, TNA HO 144/22872.

32. Letter from Heath to Isaac Near, 9 October 1946, TNA HO 144 22871.

33. Letter from Drs Norwood East and Hopwood to HM Prison Pentonville, 11 October 1946, TNA HO 144/22872.

34. Letter from Rosemary Tyndale-Biscoe to James Chuter Ede, 9 October 1946, TNA HO 144/22872.

35. 11 October 1946, TNA HO 144/22872.

36. Letter from Rosemary Tyndale-Biscoe to James Chuter Ede, 14 October 1946, TNA HO 144/22872.

37. *Sunday Despatch*, 13 October 1946.

38. *News of the World*, 6 October 1946.

39. Handwritten note by Mrs Van der Elst and message taken by a secretary at the Home Office after Mrs Van der Elst's visit, 15 October 1946, TNA HO 144/22872.

40. *Daily Telegraph*, 15 October 1946.

41. *Daily Mirror*, 15 October 1946.

42. Letter from Heath to Isaac Near, 14 October 1946, TNA HO 144/22872.

43. Pierrepoint, *Executioner: Pierrepoint*, p. 127.

44. *Bournemouth Echo*, 16 October 1946.

45. See 'Mrs Van Der Elst Fined', *Star*, 16 October 1946, and 'Heath Hanged: Crowd Mob Mrs Van Der Elst', *Evening News*, 16 October 1946.

46. Pentonville Prison directive from the governor, 2 October 1946, TNA P COM 9/700.

47. As well as Heath, Pierrepoint used this special strap on Haigh and Josef Kramer, the 'Beast of Belsen'.

48. Pierrepoint, op. cit., p. 129.

49. Chapman, *Madame Tussaud's Chamber of Horrors*, p. 222.

50. On the day of Heath's execution, Madame Tussaud's opened at 9.20 a.m. in order for the public to view the newest addition to the Chamber of Horrors. Though having had several changes of clothes in the interim, in 2013, the wax figure of Heath is still on display at Madame Tussaud's in London, standing beside George Joseph Smith and Dr Crippen.

51. Prison Medical Report, TNA P COM 9/700.

52. Pierrepoint, op. cit., pp. 129–30. Pierrepoint's description here is not specifically relating to Heath, but to an anonymous prisoner, but in recording it, Pierrepoint was attempting to describe a 'typical' execution as processed by him.

53. Prison Medical Report, TNA P COM 9/700.

54. Declaration of the Sheriff and Heath's death certificate signed by Dr Liddell, TNA HO 144/22872.

55. Adamson, *The Great Detective*, p. 179.

56. The fact that Heath had a double whisky just before he died is confirmed in the prison hospital records. There are several variants of Heath's last words including, '*Under the circumstances*, you might make that a double', TNA P COM 9/700.

Chapter 23

1. Between his arrest and execution, Heath's parents received hundreds of letters of sympathy from strangers. These prompted Bessie Heath to give this interview with Barry Halton, a reporter for the *People*. Mrs Heath did not accept payment for the interview: 'I could not make money out of my boy,' she told Gerald Byrne (Byrne, *Borstal Boy*, p. 79). At her request, a donation was made to the Royal Air Force Benevolent Fund.

Afterword

1. Beevor, *The Second World War*, p. 1.
2. Peter's widow, Kathleen, went on to commit suicide on 26 August 1961, taking an overdose of sleeping tablets.
3. Fabian, *London After Dark*, p. 59.
4. Author interview with Melody Gardner, 24 October 2011.
5. Author interview with Julia Young, 19 October 2011.
6. Adamson, *The Great Detective*, p. 280.
7. Ibid., p. 282.
8. Ibid., p. 179.
9. *News of the World*, 29 September 1946.
10. Ibid.

Appendix

1. All in TNA PCOM 9/700.

Sean O'Connor is a writer, director and producer and has worked in theatre, radio, television and film. In 2011, he produced the feature film version of Terence Rattigan's *The Deep Blue Sea*, directed by Terence Davies. He is the editor of the BBC's long-running radio drama, *The Archers*. His Shakespeare adaptation, *Juliet and her Romeo*, played to great acclaim at Bristol Old Vic in 2010. He lives in London.